A MARVEL COMICS EVENT

CIVIL WAR

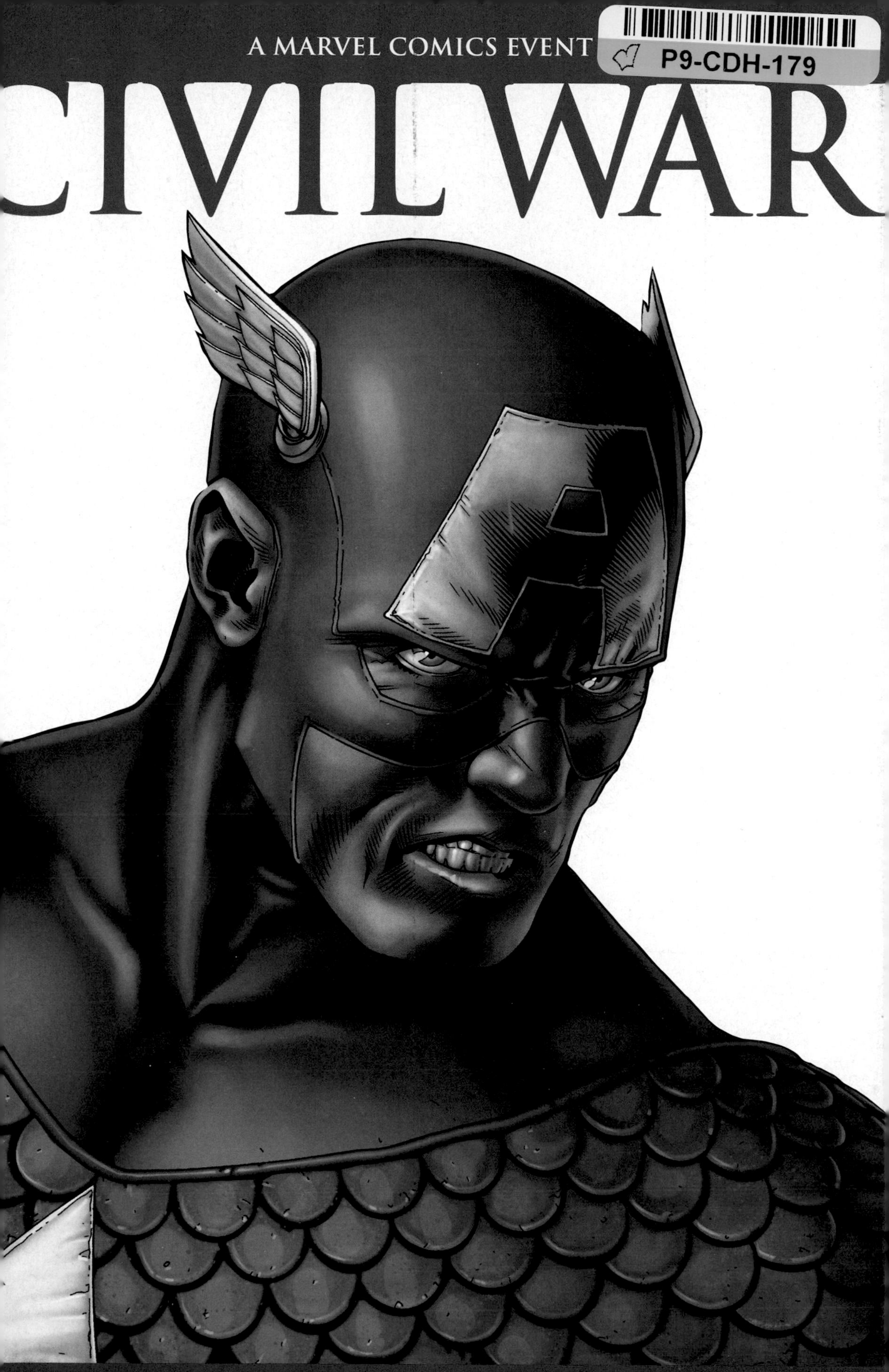

A

MARVEL COMICS

PRESENTATION

CIVIL

CIVIL WAR. Contains material originally published in magazine form as CIVIL WAR #1-7. Fifteenth printing 2018. ISBN 978-0-7851-2179-4. Published by MARVEL WORLDWIDE, INC., a subsidiary of MARVEL ENTERTAINMENT, LLC. OFFICE OF PUBLICATION: 135 West 50th Street, New York, NY 10020. Copyright © 2007 MARVEL No similarity between any of the names, characters, persons, and/or institutions in this magazine with those of any living or dead person or institution is intended, and any such similarity which may exist is purely coincidental. **Printed in Canada.** DAN BUCKLEY, President, Marvel Entertainment; JOHN NEE, Publisher; JOE QUESADA, Chief Creative Officer; TOM BREVOORT, SVP of Publishing; DAVID BOGART, SVP of Business Affairs & Operations, Publishing & Partnership; DAVID GABRIEL, SVP of Sales & Marketing, Publishing; JEFF YOUNGQUIST, VP of Production & Special Projects; DAN CARR, Executive Director of Publishing Technology; ALEX MORALES, Director of Publishing Operations; DAN EDINGTON, Managing Editor; SUSAN CRESPI, Production Manager; STAN LEE, Chairman Emeritus. For information regarding advertising in Marvel Comics or on Marvel.com, please contact Vit DeBellis, Custom Solutions & Integrated Advertising Manager, at vdebellis@marvel.com. For Marvel subscription inquiries, please call 888-511-5480. **Manufactured between 6/20/2018 and 7/10/2018 by SOLISCO PRINTERS, SCOTT, QC, CANADA.**

20 19 18 17 16 15

WRITER
MARK MILLAR

PENCILER
STEVE MCNIVEN

INKERS
DEXTER VINES WITH
MARK MORALES, STEVE MCNIVEN,
JOHN DELL & TIM TOWNSEND

COLORIST
MORRY HOLLOWELL

LETTERER
VC'S CHRIS ELIOPOULOS

ASSISTANT EDITORS
MOLLY LAZER &
AUBREY SITTERSON

ASSOCIATE EDITOR
ANDY SCHMIDT

EDITOR
TOM BREVOORT

SPECIAL THANKS TO
LAURA MARTIN, DAVE MCCAIG
PAUL MOUNTS, WIL QUINTANA &
ANDREW CROSSLEY

WAR

COLLECTION EDITOR
JENNIFER GRÜNWALD

ASSISTANT EDITOR
CAITLIN O'CONNELL

ASSOCIATE MANAGING EDITOR
KATERI WOODY

EDITOR, SPECIAL PROJECTS
MARK D. BEAZLEY

VP PRODUCTION & SPECIAL PROJECTS
JEFF YOUNGQUIST

SVP PRINT, SALES & MARKETING
DAVID GABRIEL

BOOK DESIGNER
DAYLE CHESLER

EDITOR IN CHIEF
C.B. CEBULSKI

CHIEF CREATIVE OFFICER
JOE QUESADA

PRESIDENT
DAN BUCKLEY

EXECUTIVE PRODUCER
ALAN FINE

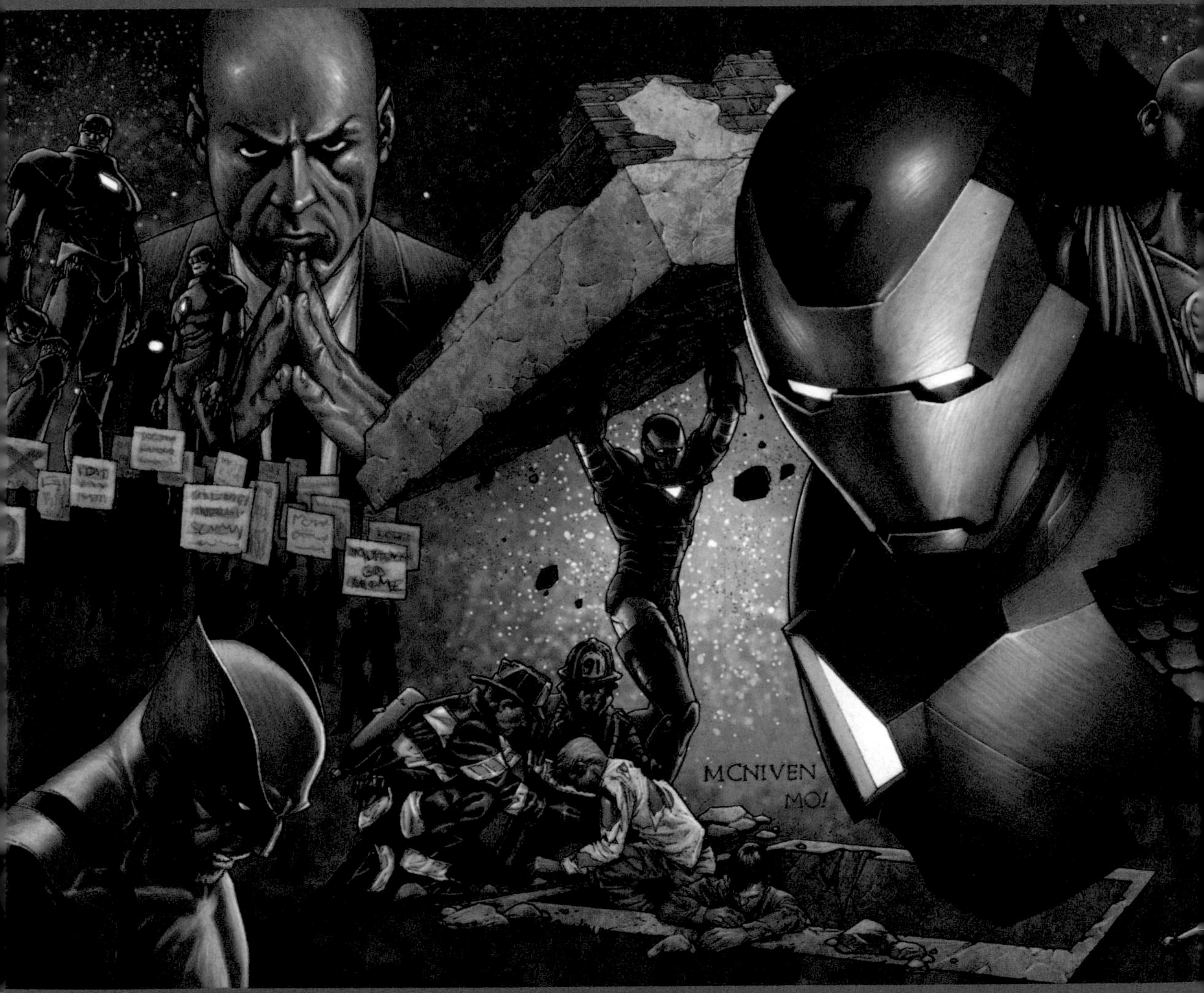
MCNIVEN
MO!

CIVIL WAR #1

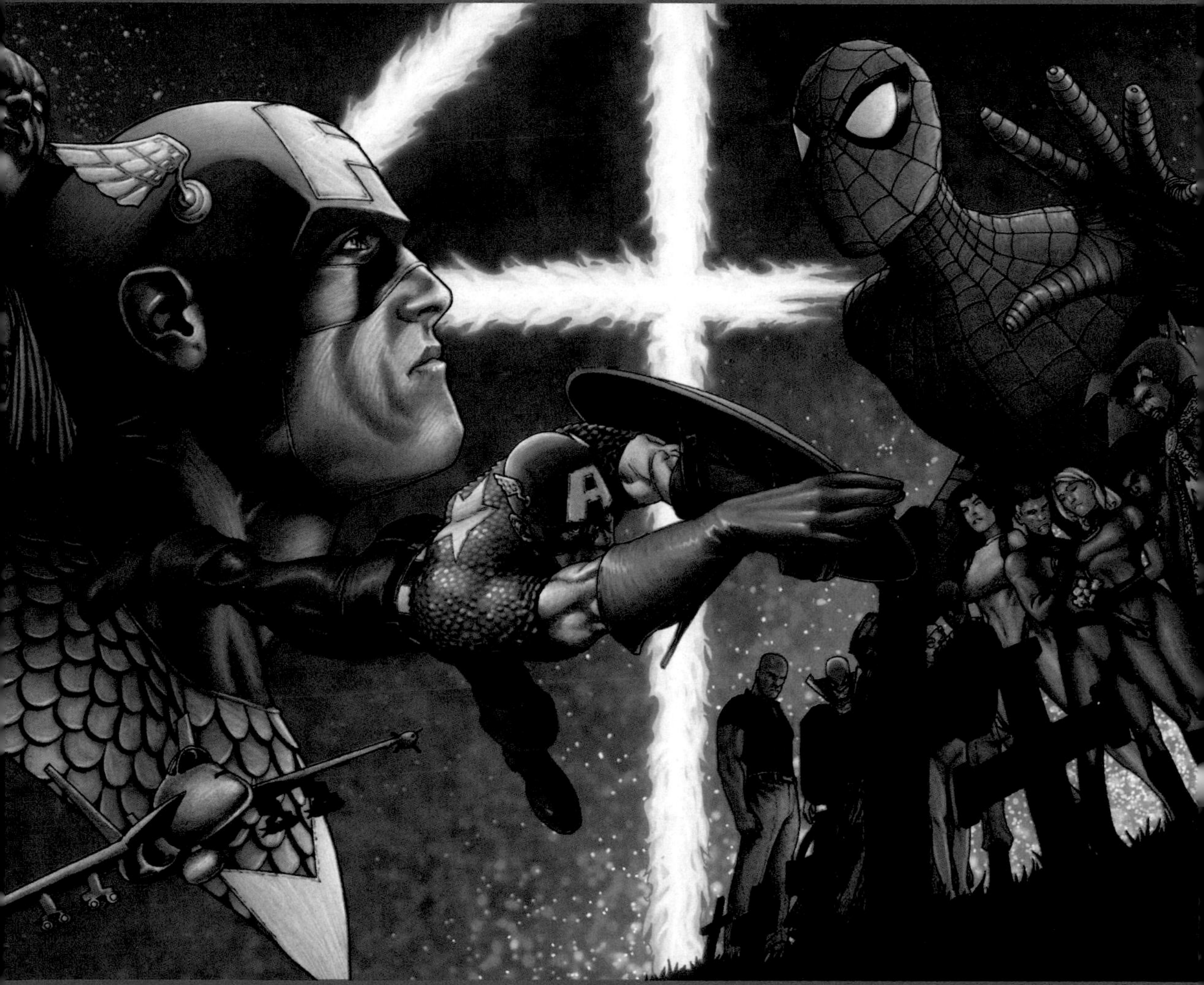

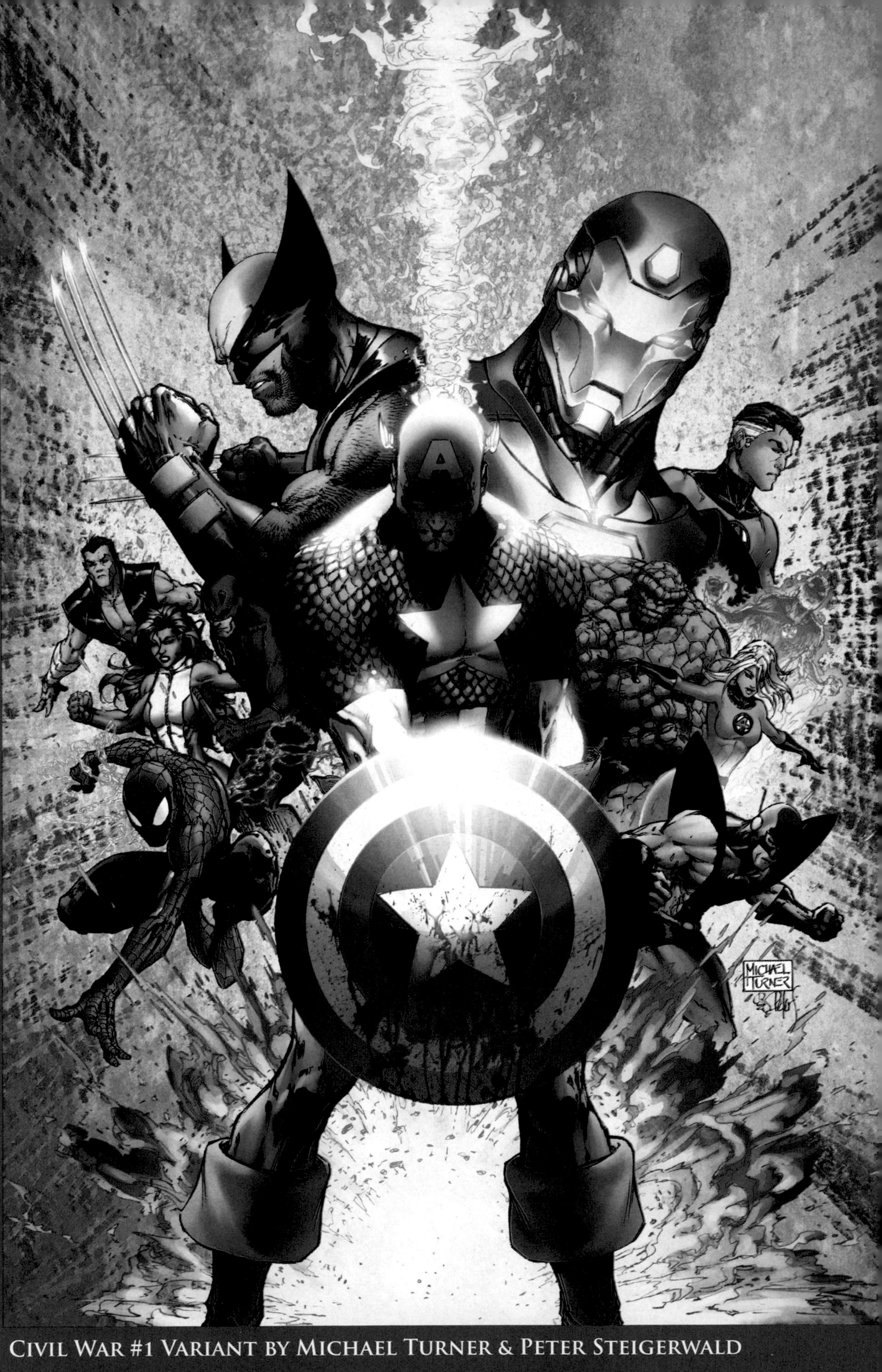
MICHAEL TURNER

Civil War #1 Variant by Michael Turner & Peter Steigerwald

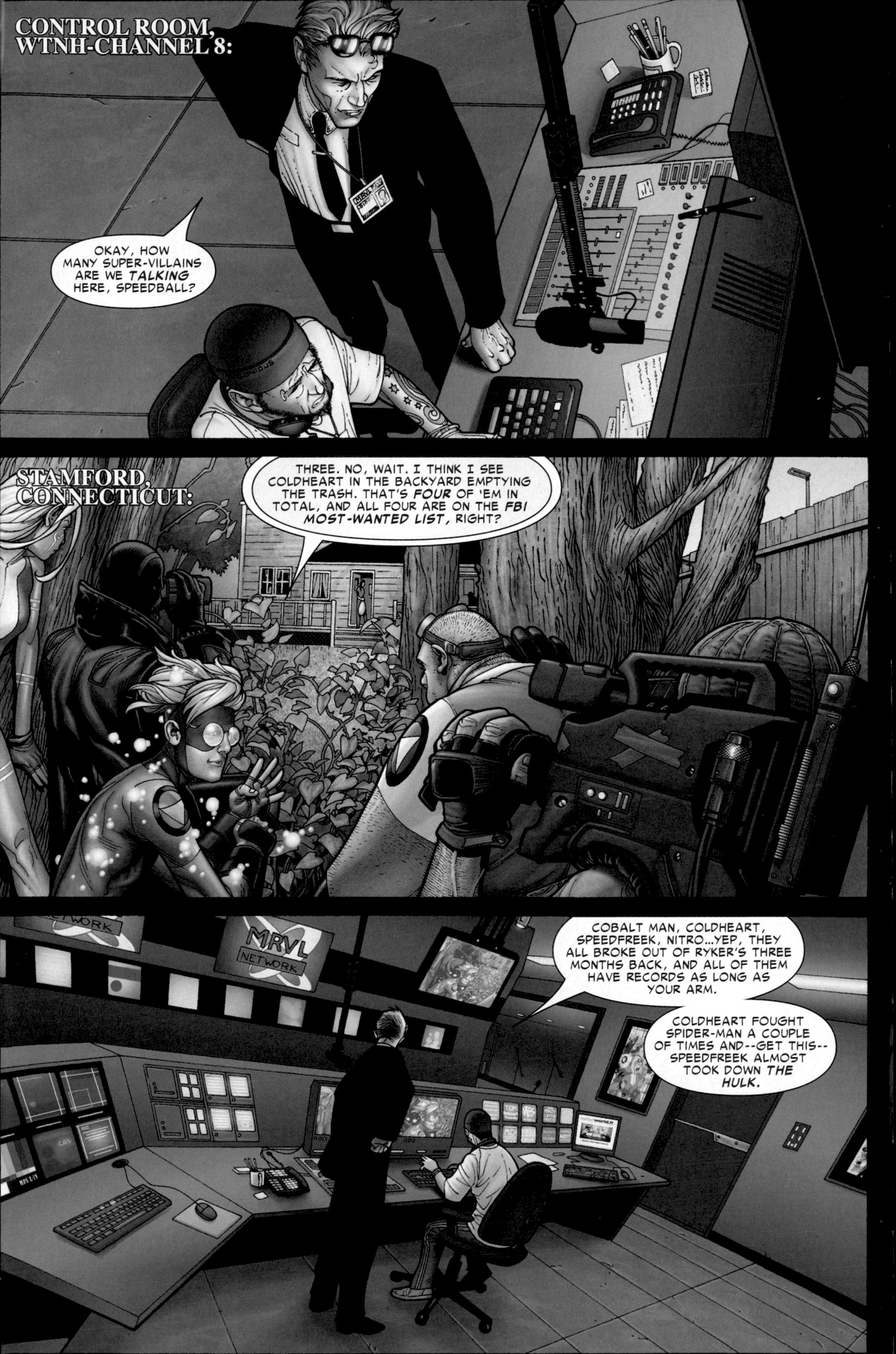
CONTROL ROOM, WTNH-CHANNEL 8:
OKAY, HOW MANY SUPER-VILLAINS ARE WE *TALKING* HERE, SPEEDBALL?
STAMFORD, CONNECTICUT:
THREE. NO, WAIT. I THINK I SEE COLDHEART IN THE BACKYARD EMPTYING THE TRASH. THAT'S *FOUR* OF 'EM IN TOTAL, AND ALL FOUR ARE ON THE *FBI MOST-WANTED LIST*, RIGHT?
MRVL NETWORK
COBALT MAN, COLDHEART, SPEEDFREEK, NITRO...YEP, THEY ALL BROKE OUT OF RYKER'S THREE MONTHS BACK, AND ALL OF THEM HAVE RECORDS AS LONG AS YOUR ARM.
COLDHEART FOUGHT SPIDER-MAN A COUPLE OF TIMES AND--GET THIS--SPEEDFREEK ALMOST TOOK DOWN *THE HULK.*

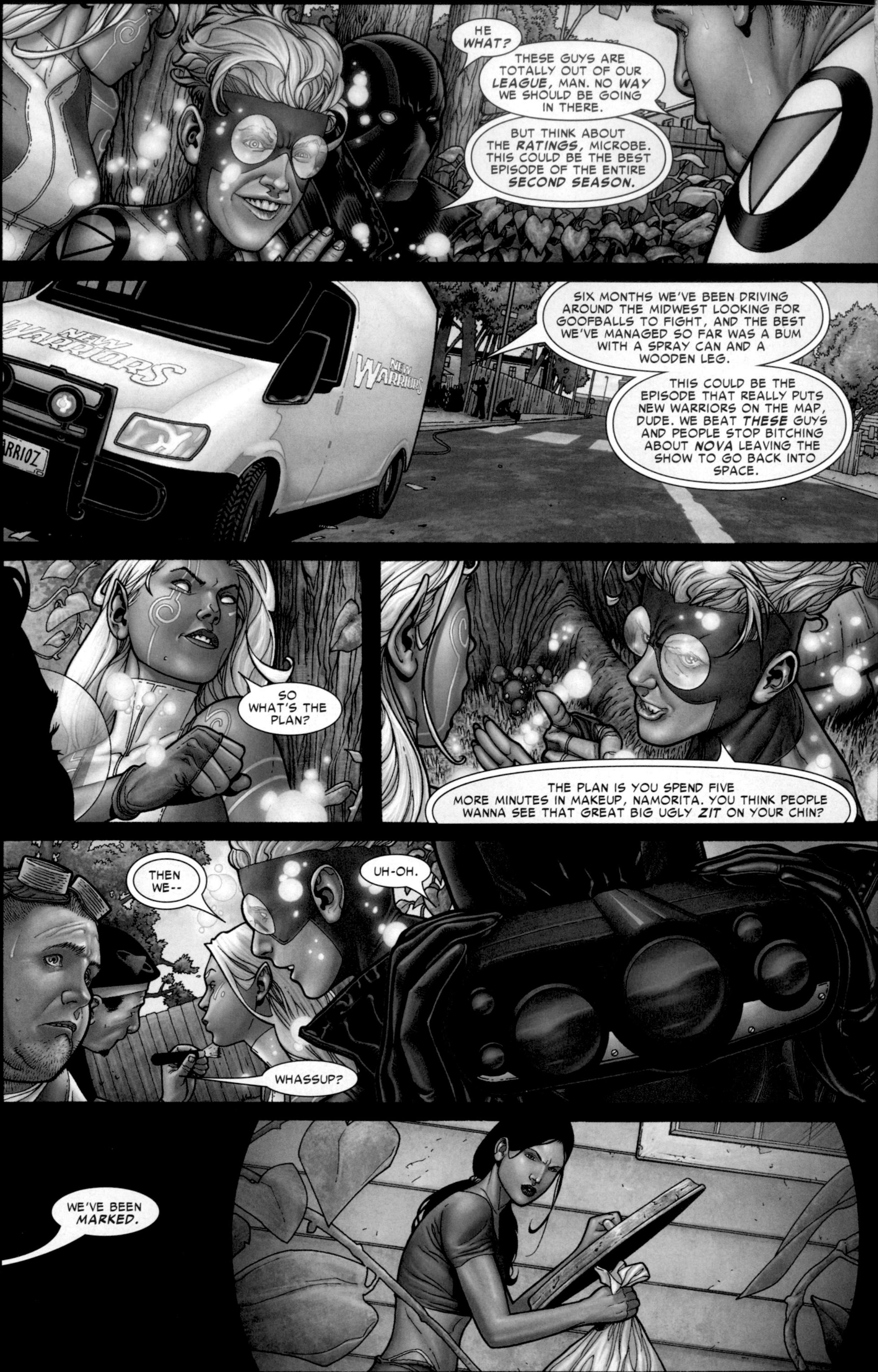

HE *WHAT?*
THESE GUYS ARE TOTALLY OUT OF OUR *LEAGUE*, MAN. NO *WAY* WE SHOULD BE GOING IN THERE.
BUT THINK ABOUT THE ***RATINGS***, MICROBE. THIS COULD BE THE BEST EPISODE OF THE ENTIRE ***SECOND SEASON.***
NEW WARRIORS
WARRIOZ
SIX MONTHS WE'VE BEEN DRIVING AROUND THE MIDWEST LOOKING FOR GOOFBALLS TO FIGHT, AND THE BEST WE'VE MANAGED SO FAR WAS A BUM WITH A SPRAY CAN AND A WOODEN LEG.
THIS COULD BE THE EPISODE THAT REALLY PUTS NEW WARRIORS ON THE MAP, DUDE. WE BEAT ***THESE*** GUYS AND PEOPLE STOP BITCHING ABOUT ***NOVA*** LEAVING THE SHOW TO GO BACK INTO SPACE.
SO WHAT'S THE PLAN?
THE PLAN IS YOU SPEND FIVE MORE MINUTES IN MAKEUP, NAMORITA. YOU THINK PEOPLE WANNA SEE THAT GREAT BIG UGLY ***ZIT*** ON YOUR CHIN?
THEN WE--
UH-OH.
WHASSUP?
WE'VE BEEN ***MARKED.***

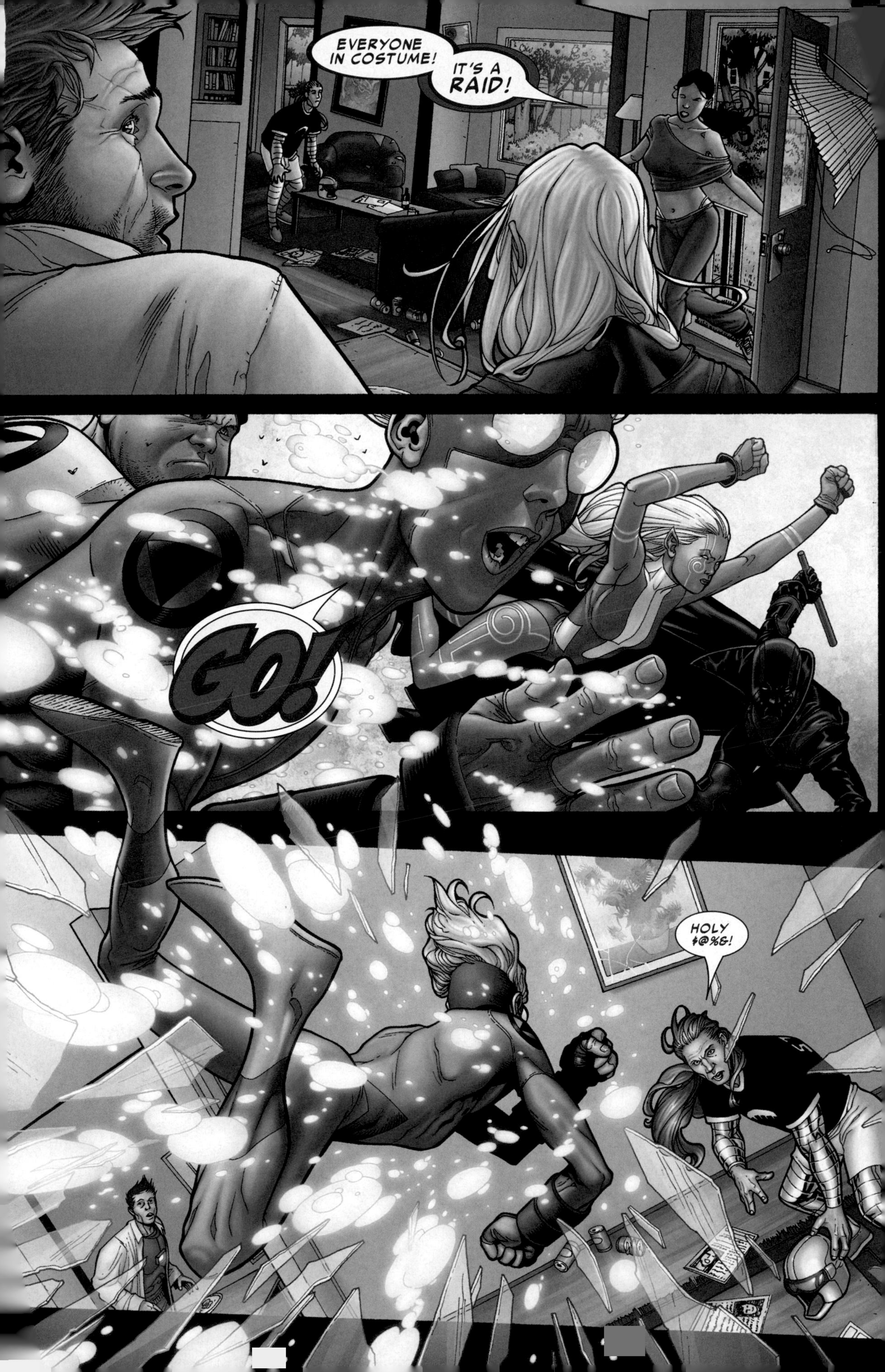
EVERYONE IN COSTUME!
IT'S A RAID!
GO!
HOLY $@%&!

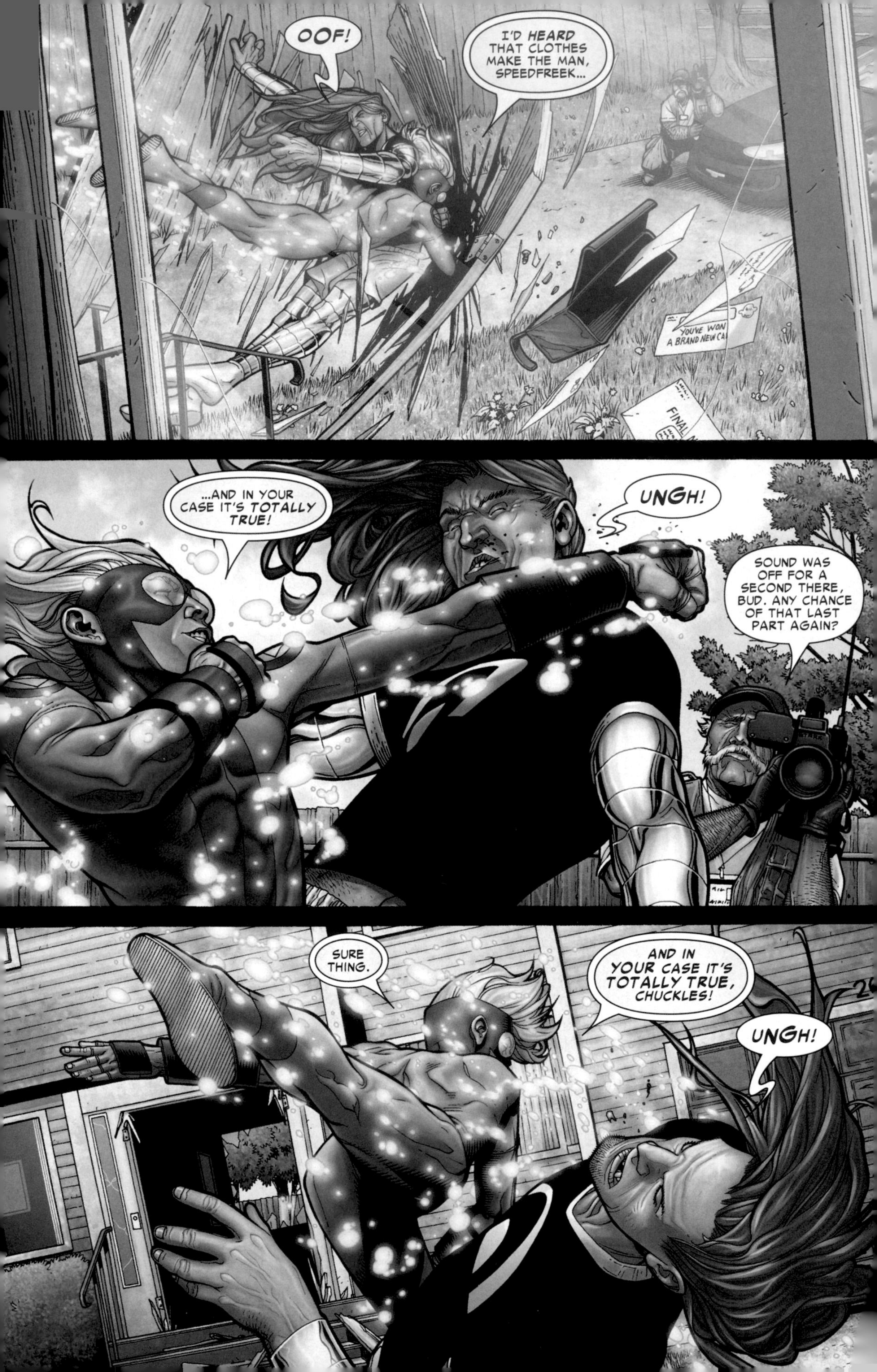
OOF!
I'D HEARD THAT CLOTHES MAKE THE MAN, SPEEDFREEK...
YOU'VE WON A BRAND NEW CA
FINAL
...AND IN YOUR CASE IT'S TOTALLY TRUE!
UNGH!
SOUND WAS OFF FOR A SECOND THERE, BUD. ANY CHANCE OF THAT LAST PART AGAIN?
SURE THING.
AND IN YOUR CASE IT'S TOTALLY TRUE, CHUCKLES!
UNGH!

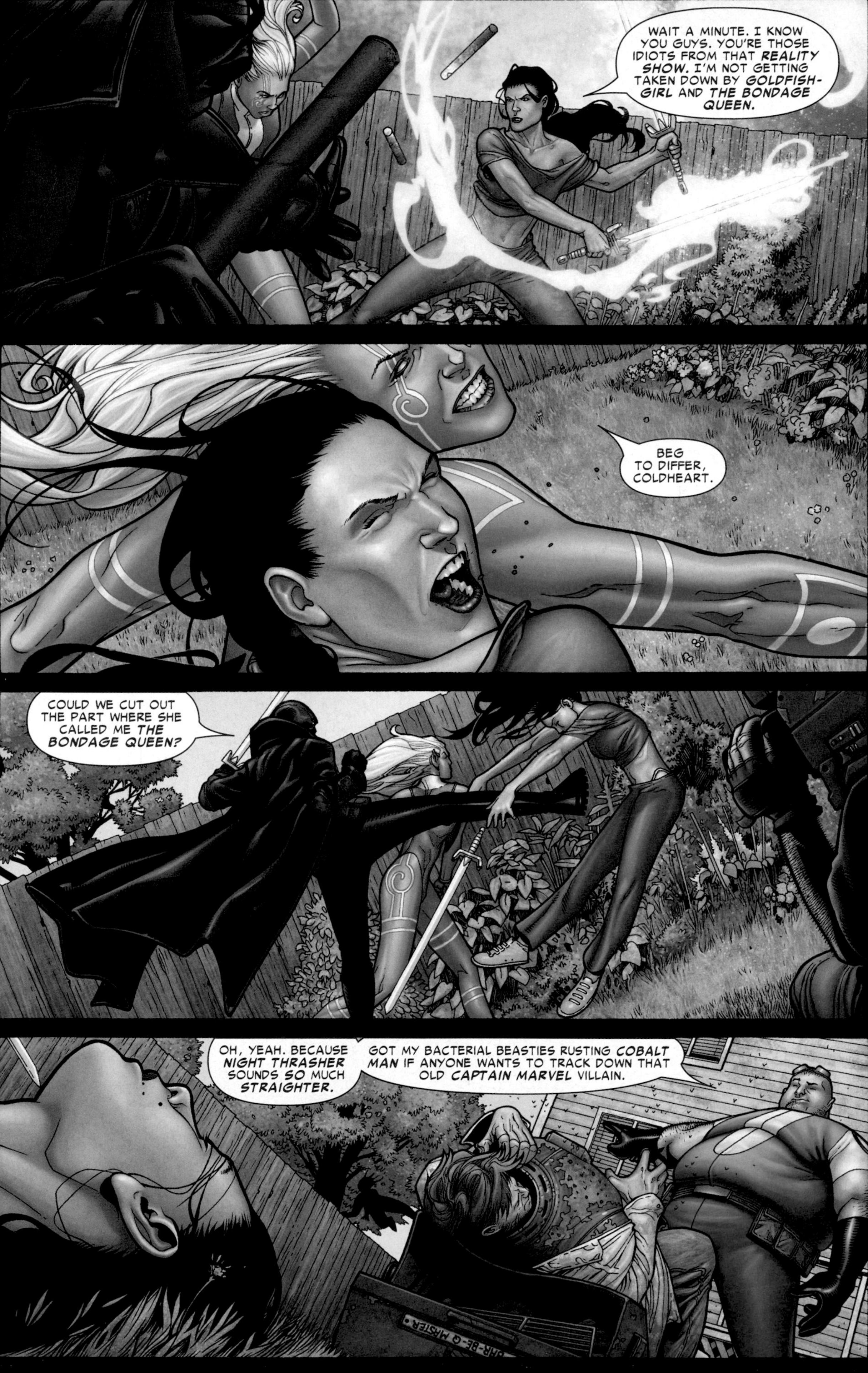
WAIT A MINUTE. I KNOW YOU GUYS. YOU'RE THOSE IDIOTS FROM THAT *REALITY SHOW*. I'M NOT GETTING TAKEN DOWN BY *GOLDFISH-GIRL* AND *THE BONDAGE QUEEN*.
BEG TO DIFFER, COLDHEART.
COULD WE CUT OUT THE PART WHERE SHE CALLED ME *THE BONDAGE QUEEN?*
OH, YEAH. BECAUSE *NIGHT THRASHER* SOUNDS *SO* MUCH *STRAIGHTER*.
GOT MY BACTERIAL BEASTIES RUSTING *COBALT MAN* IF ANYONE WANTS TO TRACK DOWN THAT OLD *CAPTAIN MARVEL* VILLAIN.
BAR-BE-Q MASTER

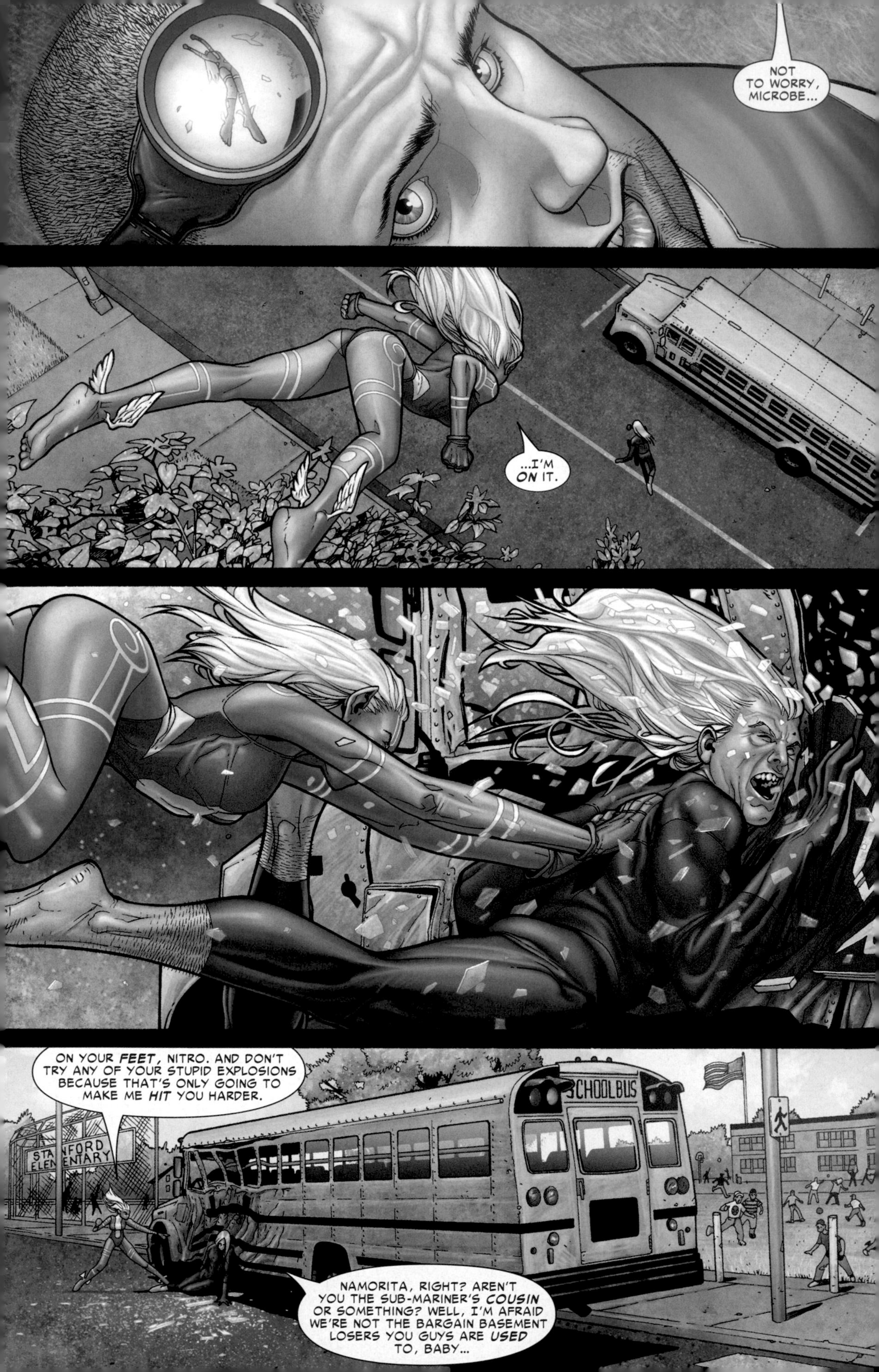
NOT TO WORRY, MICROBE...
...I'M ON IT.
ON YOUR FEET, NITRO. AND DON'T TRY ANY OF YOUR STUPID EXPLOSIONS BECAUSE THAT'S ONLY GOING TO MAKE ME HIT YOU HARDER.
SCHOOLBUS
STANFORD ELEMENTARY
NAMORITA, RIGHT? AREN'T YOU THE SUB-MARINER'S COUSIN OR SOMETHING? WELL, I'M AFRAID WE'RE NOT THE BARGAIN BASEMENT LOSERS YOU GUYS ARE USED TO, BABY...

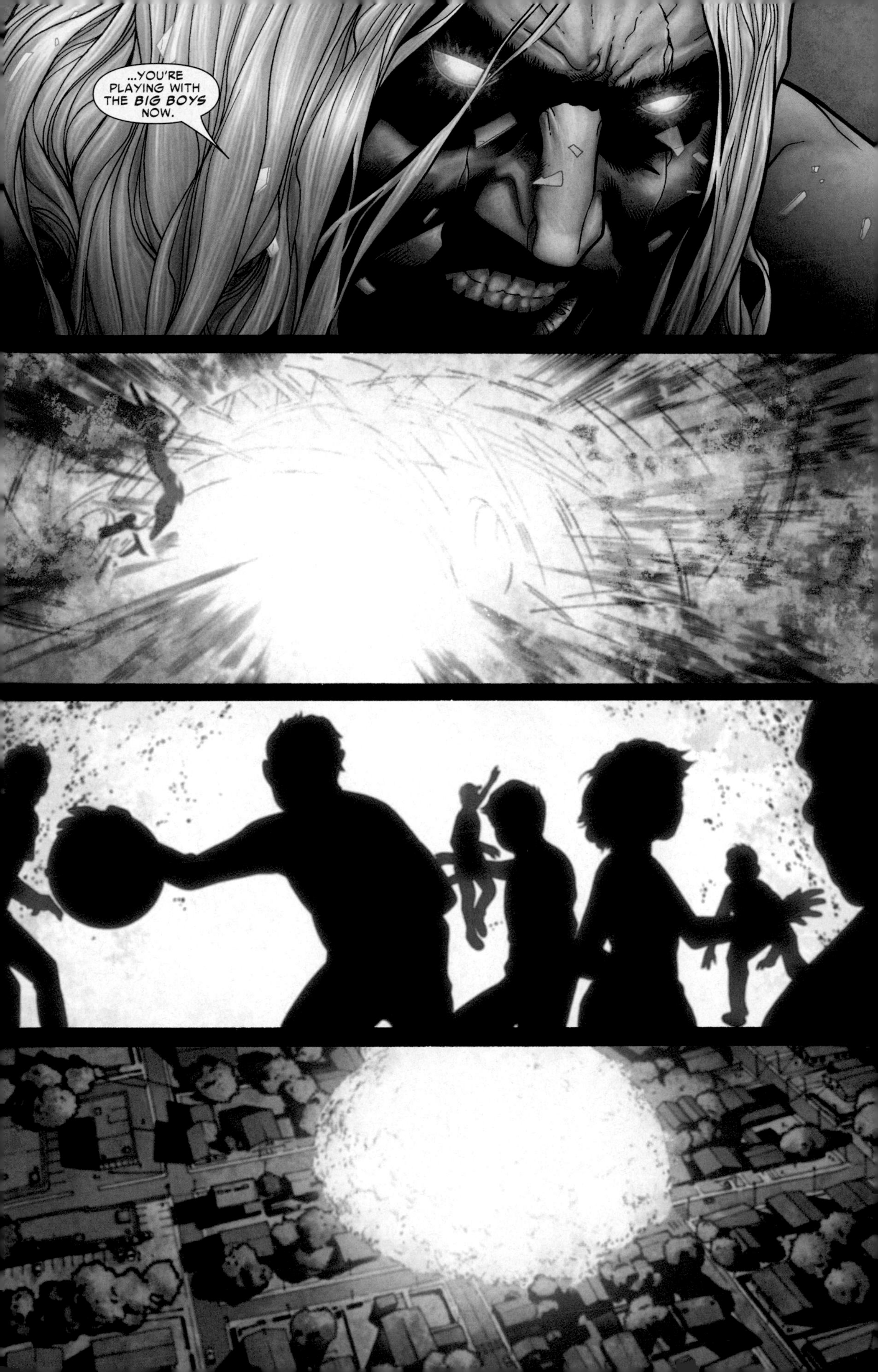
...YOU'RE PLAYING WITH THE BIG BOYS NOW.

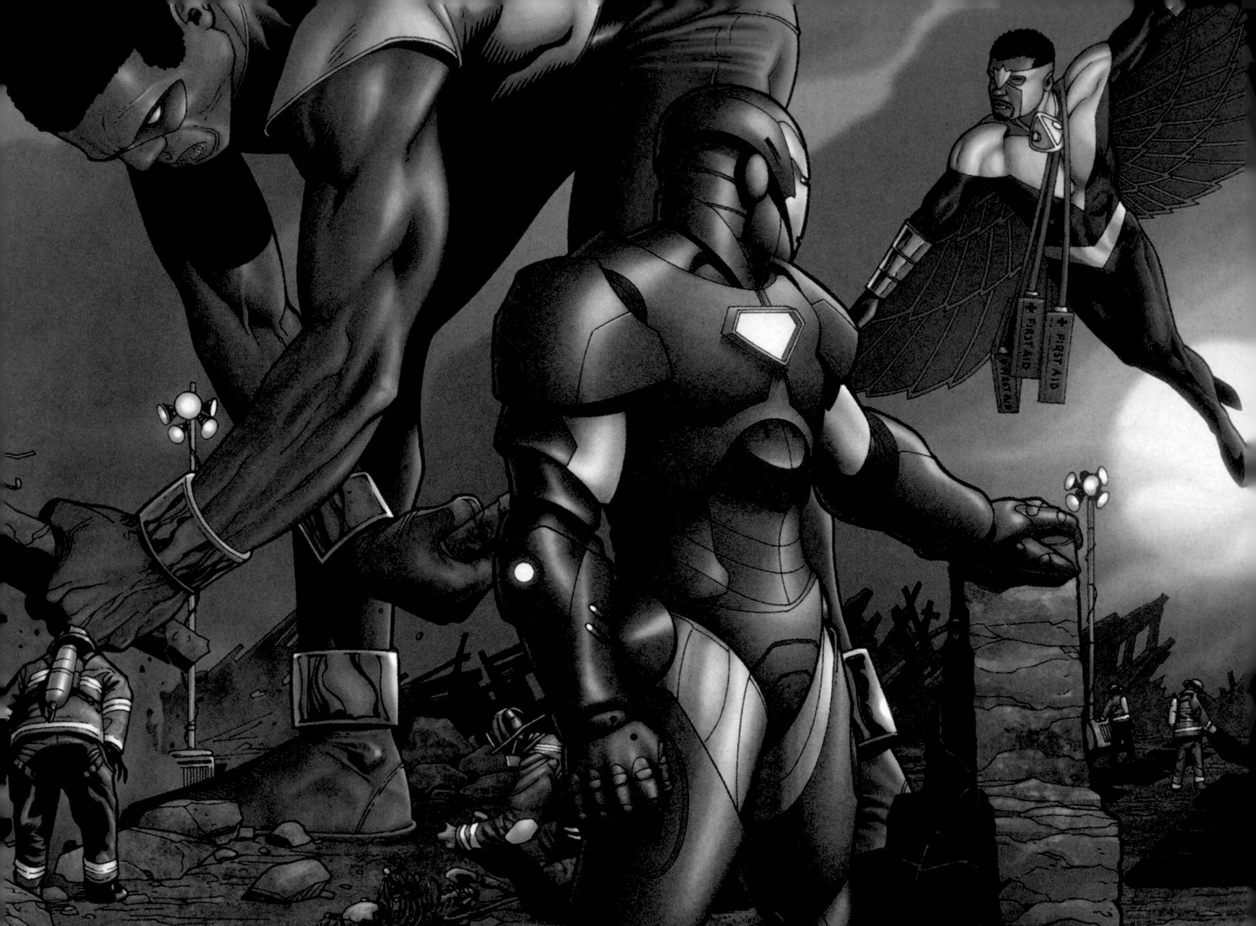
FIRST AID
FIRST AID

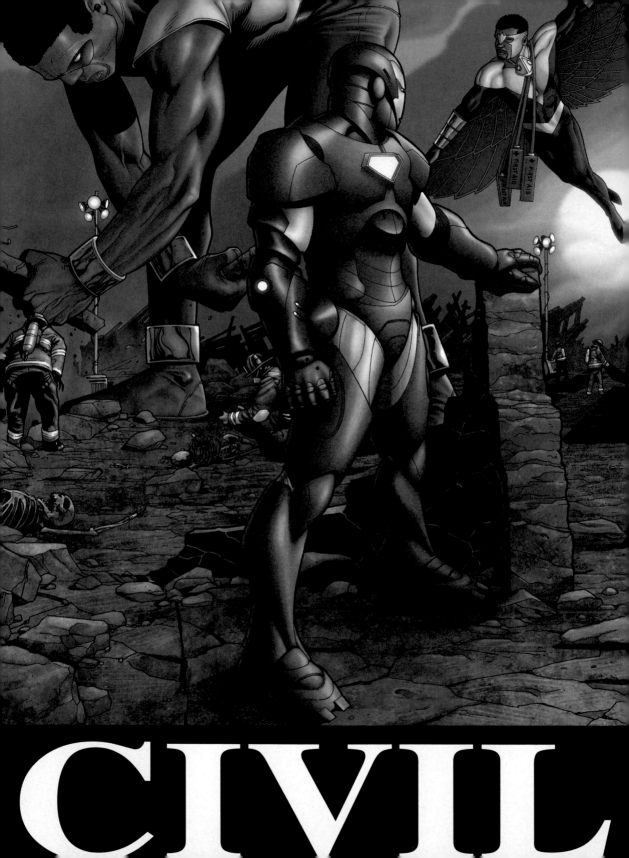

CIVIL

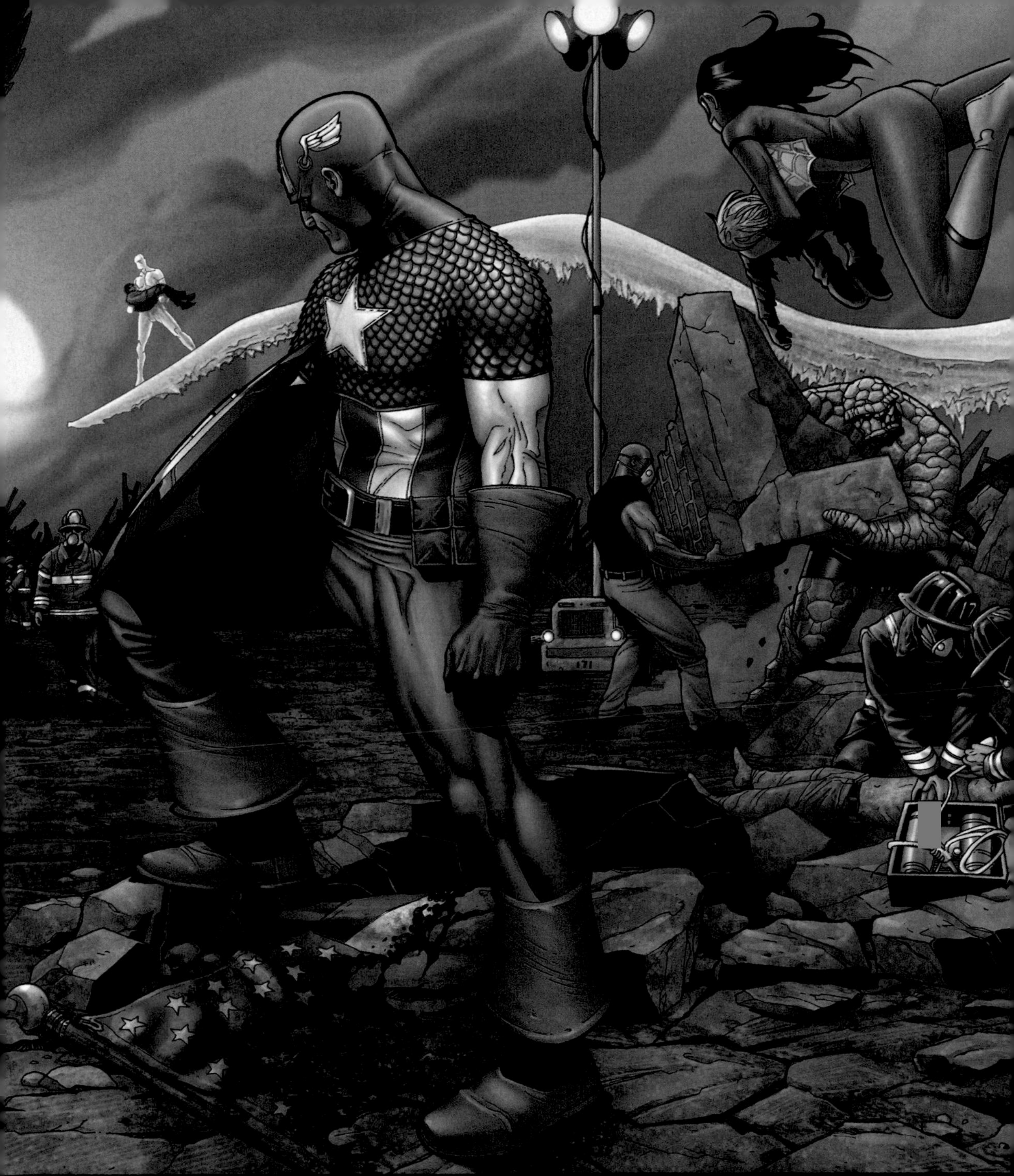

WAR

PART ONE OF SEVEN

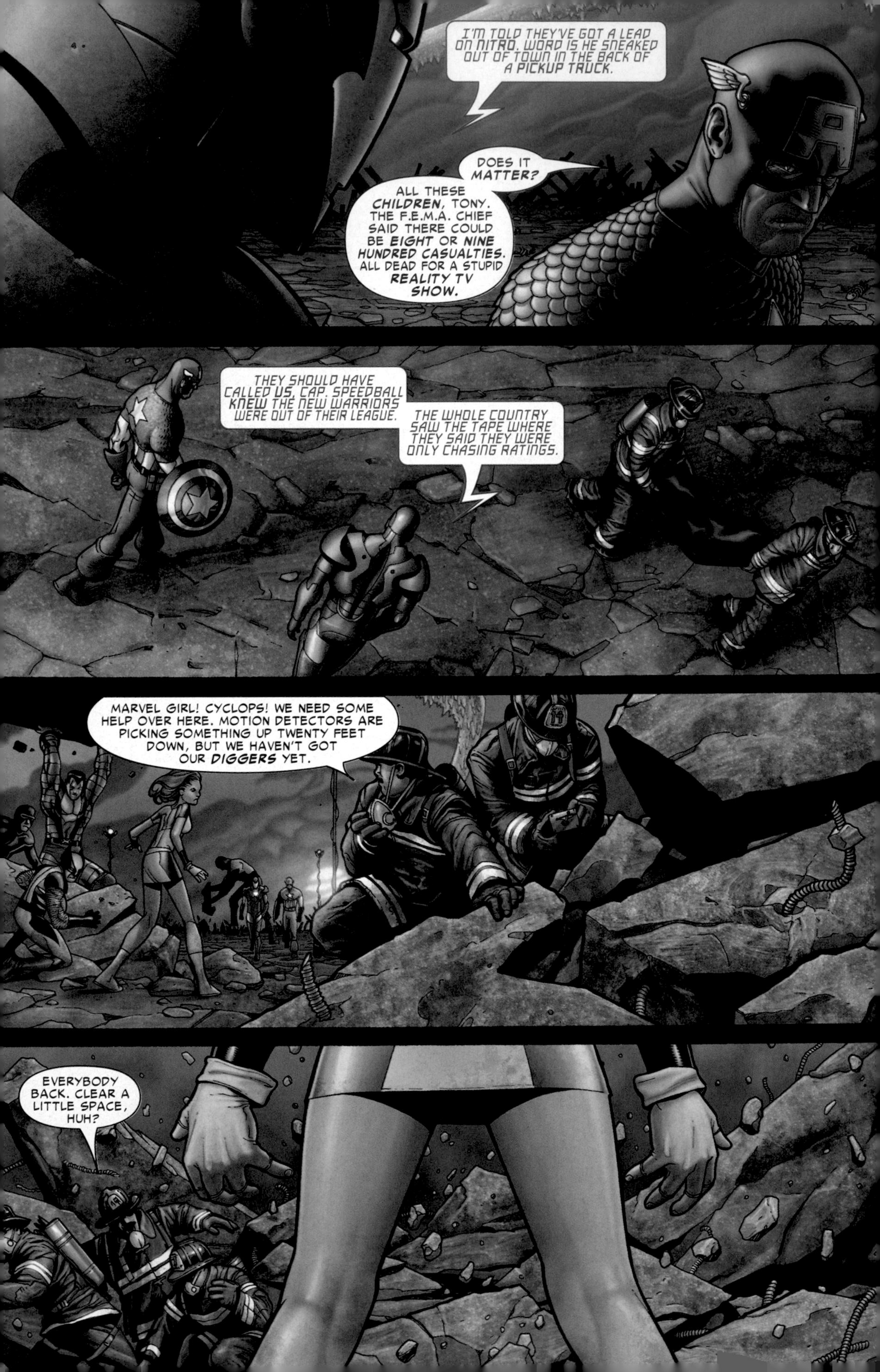
I'M TOLD THEY'VE GOT A LEAD ON NITRO. WORD IS HE SNEAKED OUT OF TOWN IN THE BACK OF A PICKUP TRUCK.
DOES IT MATTER?
ALL THESE CHILDREN, TONY. THE F.E.M.A. CHIEF SAID THERE COULD BE EIGHT OR NINE HUNDRED CASUALTIES. ALL DEAD FOR A STUPID REALITY TV SHOW.
THEY SHOULD HAVE CALLED US, CAP. SPEEDBALL KNEW THE NEW WARRIORS WERE OUT OF THEIR LEAGUE.
THE WHOLE COUNTRY SAW THE TAPE WHERE THEY SAID THEY WERE ONLY CHASING RATINGS.
MARVEL GIRL! CYCLOPS! WE NEED SOME HELP OVER HERE. MOTION DETECTORS ARE PICKING SOMETHING UP TWENTY FEET DOWN, BUT WE HAVEN'T GOT OUR DIGGERS YET.
EVERYBODY BACK. CLEAR A LITTLE SPACE, HUH?

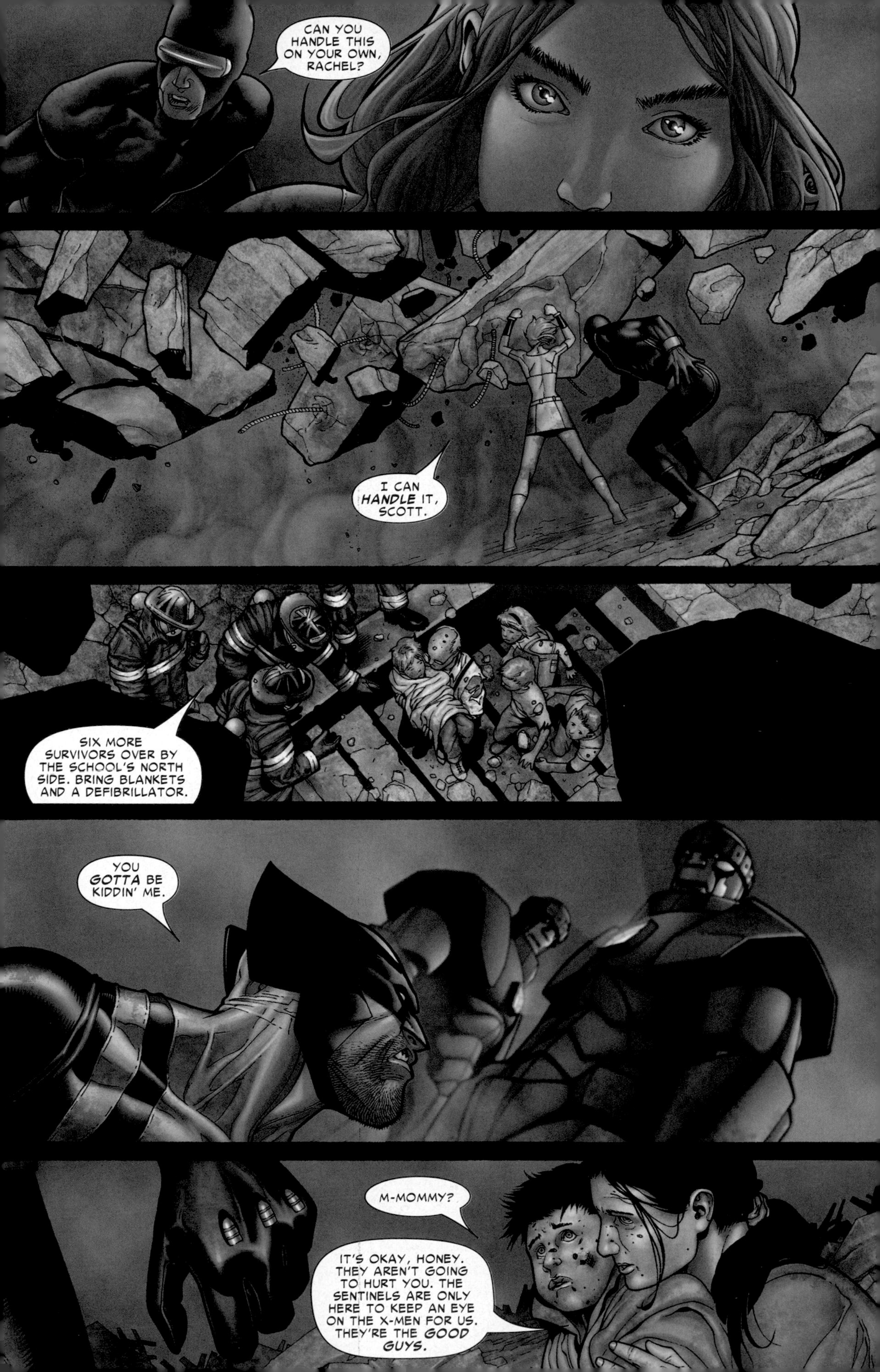
CAN YOU HANDLE THIS ON YOUR OWN, RACHEL?
I CAN HANDLE IT, SCOTT.
SIX MORE SURVIVORS OVER BY THE SCHOOL'S NORTH SIDE. BRING BLANKETS AND A DEFIBRILLATOR.
YOU GOTTA BE KIDDIN' ME.
M-MOMMY?
IT'S OKAY, HONEY. THEY AREN'T GOING TO HURT YOU. THE SENTINELS ARE ONLY HERE TO KEEP AN EYE ON THE X-MEN FOR US. THEY'RE THE GOOD GUYS.

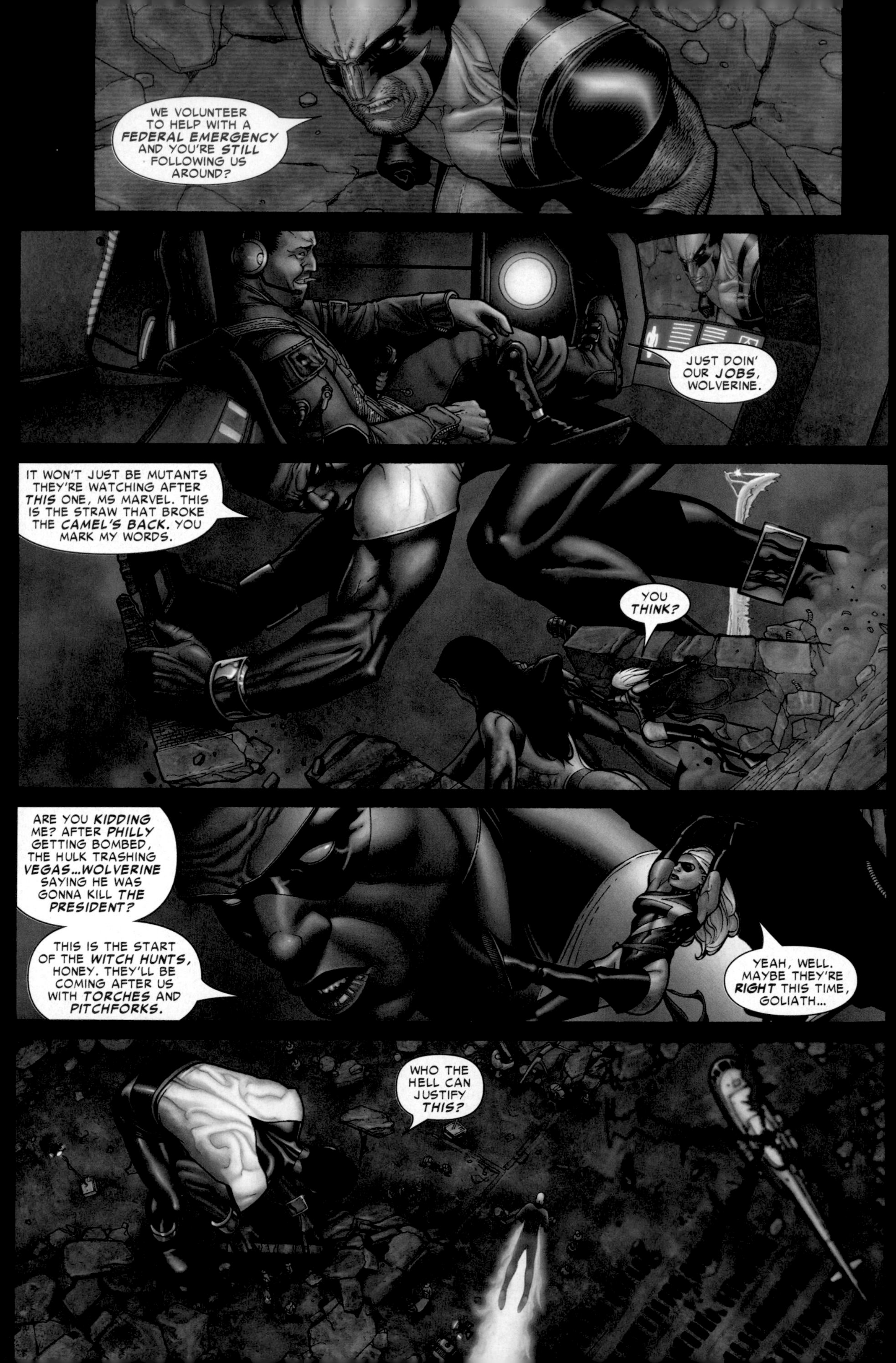
WE VOLUNTEER TO HELP WITH A FEDERAL EMERGENCY AND YOU'RE STILL FOLLOWING US AROUND?
JUST DOIN' OUR JOBS, WOLVERINE.
IT WON'T JUST BE MUTANTS THEY'RE WATCHING AFTER THIS ONE, MS MARVEL. THIS IS THE STRAW THAT BROKE THE CAMEL'S BACK. YOU MARK MY WORDS.
YOU THINK?
ARE YOU KIDDING ME? AFTER PHILLY GETTING BOMBED, THE HULK TRASHING VEGAS...WOLVERINE SAYING HE WAS GONNA KILL THE PRESIDENT?
THIS IS THE START OF THE WITCH HUNTS, HONEY. THEY'LL BE COMING AFTER US WITH TORCHES AND PITCHFORKS.
YEAH, WELL. MAYBE THEY'RE RIGHT THIS TIME, GOLIATH...
WHO THE HELL CAN JUSTIFY THIS?

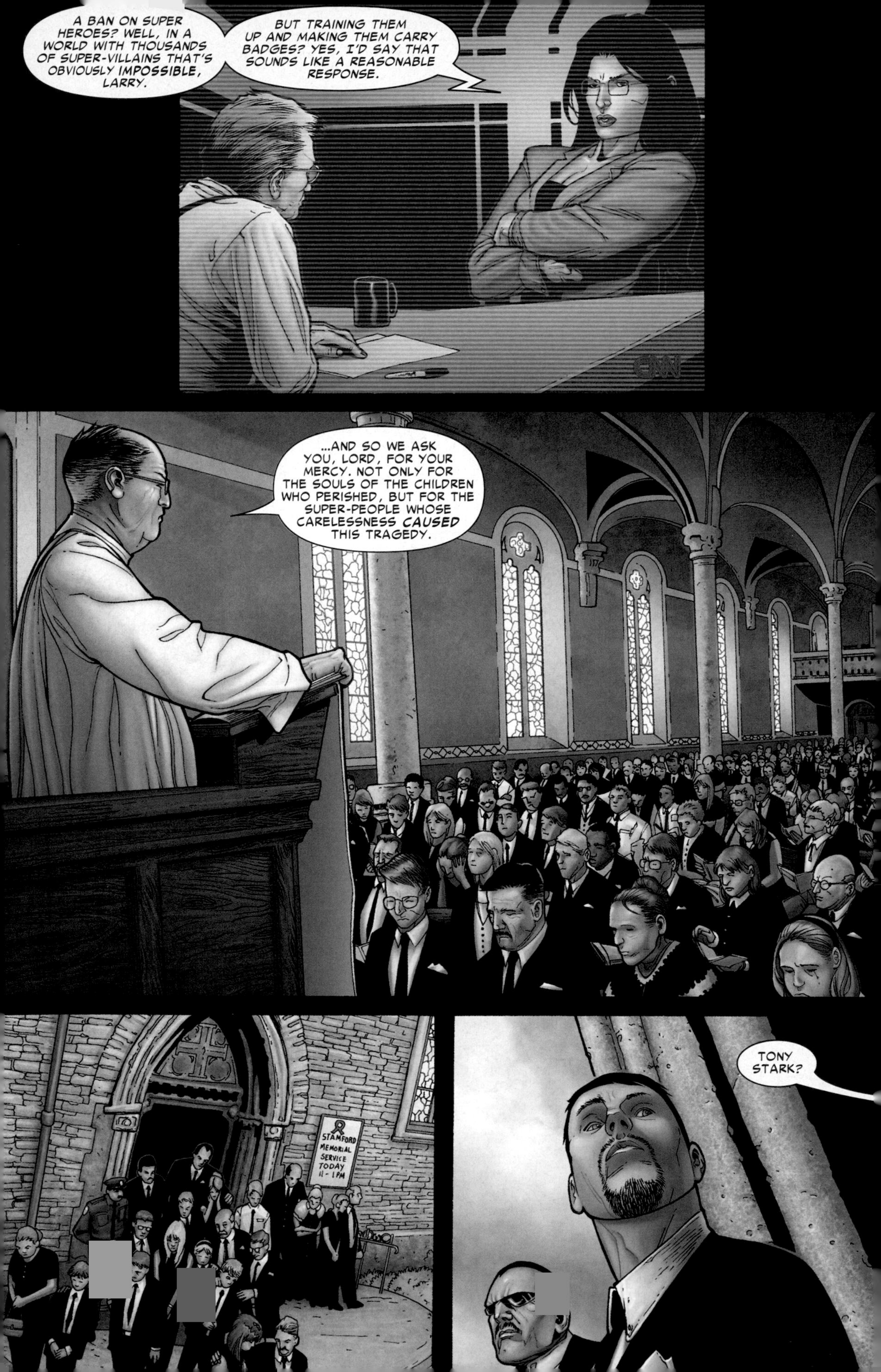
A BAN ON SUPER HEROES? WELL, IN A WORLD WITH THOUSANDS OF SUPER-VILLAINS THAT'S OBVIOUSLY IMPOSSIBLE, LARRY.
BUT TRAINING THEM UP AND MAKING THEM CARRY BADGES? YES, I'D SAY THAT SOUNDS LIKE A REASONABLE RESPONSE.
...AND SO WE ASK YOU, LORD, FOR YOUR MERCY. NOT ONLY FOR THE SOULS OF THE CHILDREN WHO PERISHED, BUT FOR THE SUPER-PEOPLE WHOSE CARELESSNESS CAUSED THIS TRAGEDY.
STAMFORD MEMORIAL SERVICE TODAY 11 - 1PM
TONY STARK?

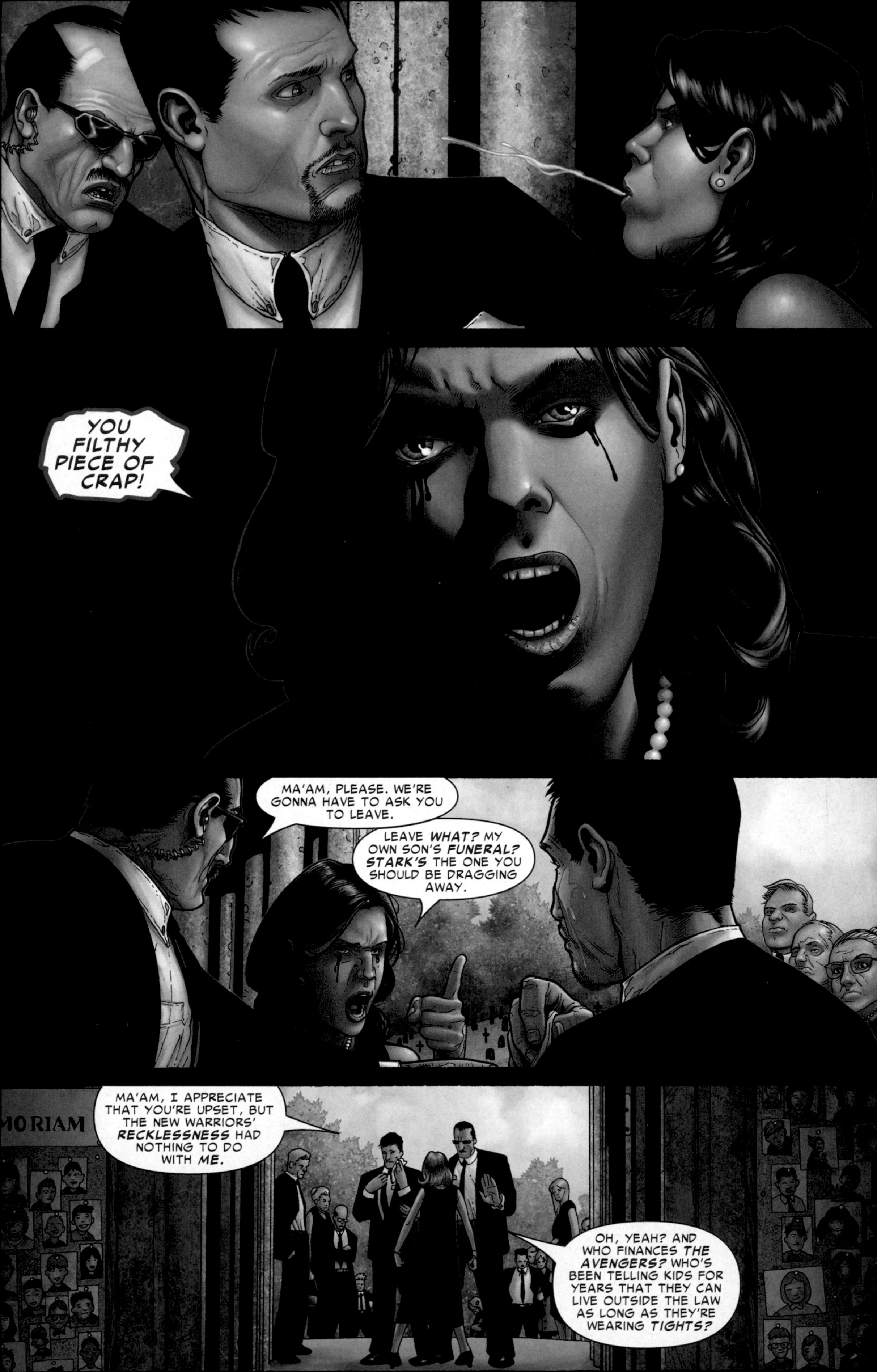
YOU FILTHY PIECE OF CRAP!
MA'AM, PLEASE. WE'RE GONNA HAVE TO ASK YOU TO LEAVE.
LEAVE *WHAT?* MY OWN SON'S *FUNERAL? STARK'S* THE ONE YOU SHOULD BE DRAGGING AWAY.
MA'AM, I APPRECIATE THAT YOU'RE UPSET, BUT THE NEW WARRIORS' *RECKLESSNESS* HAD NOTHING TO DO WITH *ME.*
OH, YEAH? AND WHO FINANCES *THE AVENGERS?* WHO'S BEEN TELLING KIDS FOR YEARS THAT THEY CAN LIVE OUTSIDE THE LAW AS LONG AS THEY'RE WEARING *TIGHTS?*

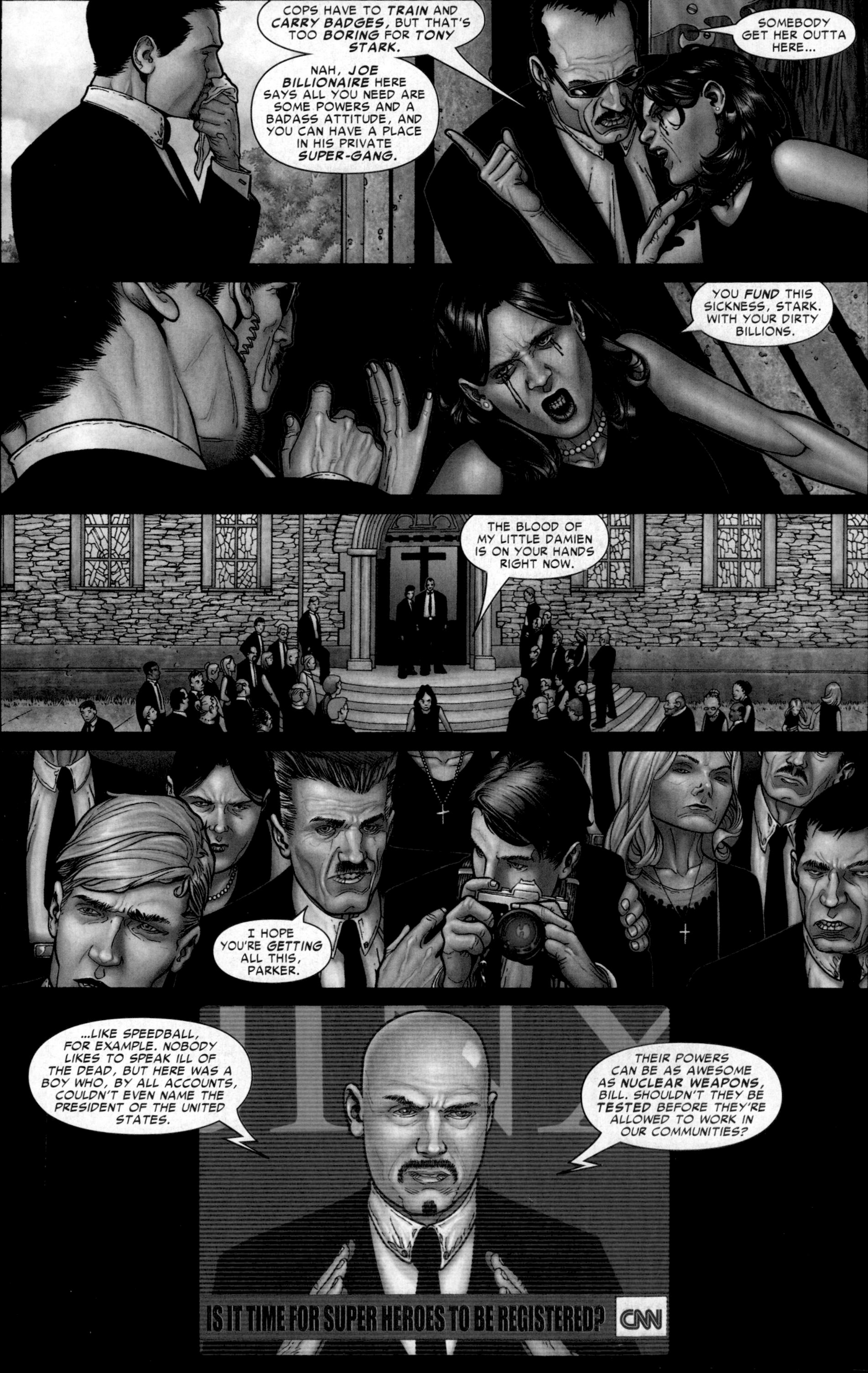

COPS HAVE TO TRAIN AND CARRY BADGES, BUT THAT'S TOO BORING FOR TONY STARK.
NAH, JOE BILLIONAIRE HERE SAYS ALL YOU NEED ARE SOME POWERS AND A BADASS ATTITUDE, AND YOU CAN HAVE A PLACE IN HIS PRIVATE SUPER-GANG.
SOMEBODY GET HER OUTTA HERE...
YOU FUND THIS SICKNESS, STARK. WITH YOUR DIRTY BILLIONS.
THE BLOOD OF MY LITTLE DAMIEN IS ON YOUR HANDS RIGHT NOW.
I HOPE YOU'RE GETTING ALL THIS, PARKER.
...LIKE SPEEDBALL, FOR EXAMPLE. NOBODY LIKES TO SPEAK ILL OF THE DEAD, BUT HERE WAS A BOY WHO, BY ALL ACCOUNTS, COULDN'T EVEN NAME THE PRESIDENT OF THE UNITED STATES.
THEIR POWERS CAN BE AS AWESOME AS NUCLEAR WEAPONS, BILL. SHOULDN'T THEY BE TESTED BEFORE THEY'RE ALLOWED TO WORK IN OUR COMMUNITIES?
IS IT TIME FOR SUPER HEROES TO BE REGISTERED?
CNN

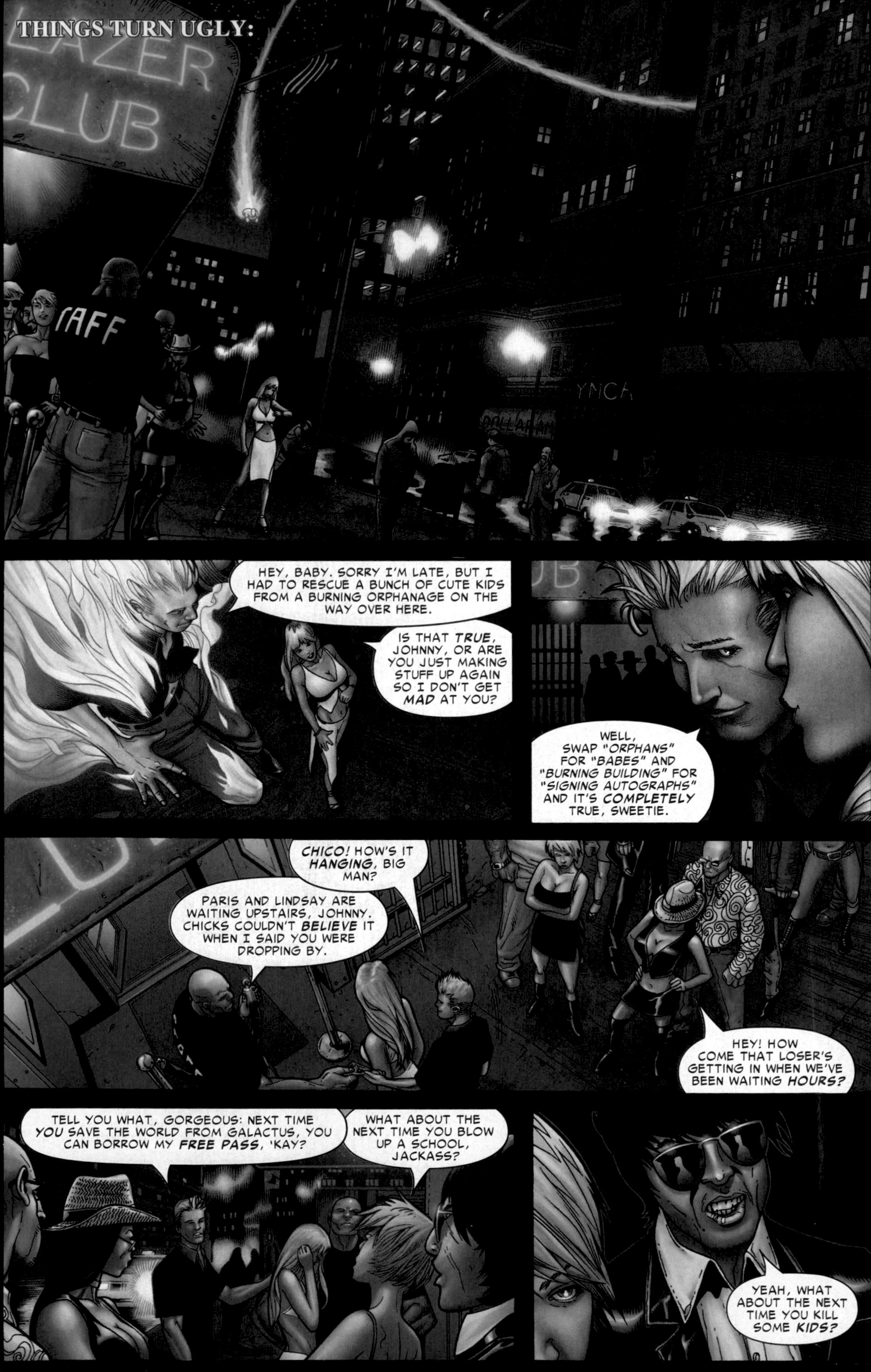
THINGS TURN UGLY:
LAZER CLUB
HEY, BABY. SORRY I'M LATE, BUT I HAD TO RESCUE A BUNCH OF CUTE KIDS FROM A BURNING ORPHANAGE ON THE WAY OVER HERE.
IS THAT TRUE, JOHNNY, OR ARE YOU JUST MAKING STUFF UP AGAIN SO I DON'T GET MAD AT YOU?
WELL, SWAP "ORPHANS" FOR "BABES" AND "BURNING BUILDING" FOR "SIGNING AUTOGRAPHS" AND IT'S COMPLETELY TRUE, SWEETIE.
CHICO! HOW'S IT HANGING, BIG MAN?
PARIS AND LINDSAY ARE WAITING UPSTAIRS, JOHNNY. CHICKS COULDN'T BELIEVE IT WHEN I SAID YOU WERE DROPPING BY.
HEY! HOW COME THAT LOSER'S GETTING IN WHEN WE'VE BEEN WAITING HOURS?
TELL YOU WHAT, GORGEOUS: NEXT TIME YOU SAVE THE WORLD FROM GALACTUS, YOU CAN BORROW MY FREE PASS, 'KAY?
WHAT ABOUT THE NEXT TIME YOU BLOW UP A SCHOOL, JACKASS?
YEAH, WHAT ABOUT THE NEXT TIME YOU KILL SOME KIDS?

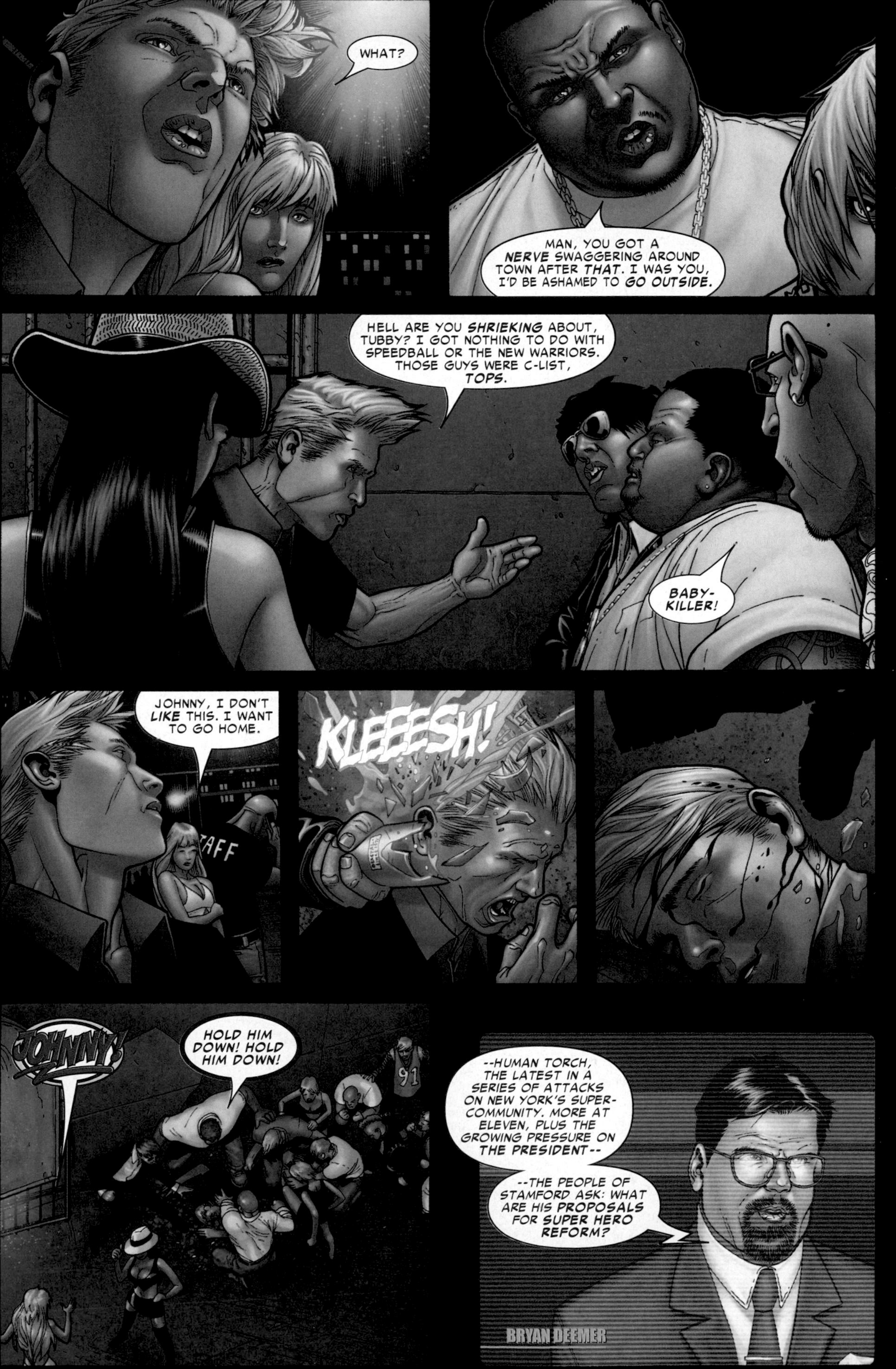
WHAT?
MAN, YOU GOT A NERVE SWAGGERING AROUND TOWN AFTER THAT. I WAS YOU, I'D BE ASHAMED TO GO OUTSIDE.
HELL ARE YOU SHRIEKING ABOUT, TUBBY? I GOT NOTHING TO DO WITH SPEEDBALL OR THE NEW WARRIORS. THOSE GUYS WERE C-LIST, TOPS.
BABY-KILLER!
JOHNNY, I DON'T LIKE THIS. I WANT TO GO HOME.
KLEEESH!
JOHNNY!
HOLD HIM DOWN! HOLD HIM DOWN!
--HUMAN TORCH, THE LATEST IN A SERIES OF ATTACKS ON NEW YORK'S SUPER-COMMUNITY. MORE AT ELEVEN, PLUS THE GROWING PRESSURE ON THE PRESIDENT--
--THE PEOPLE OF STAMFORD ASK: WHAT ARE HIS PROPOSALS FOR SUPER HERO REFORM?
BRYAN DEEMER

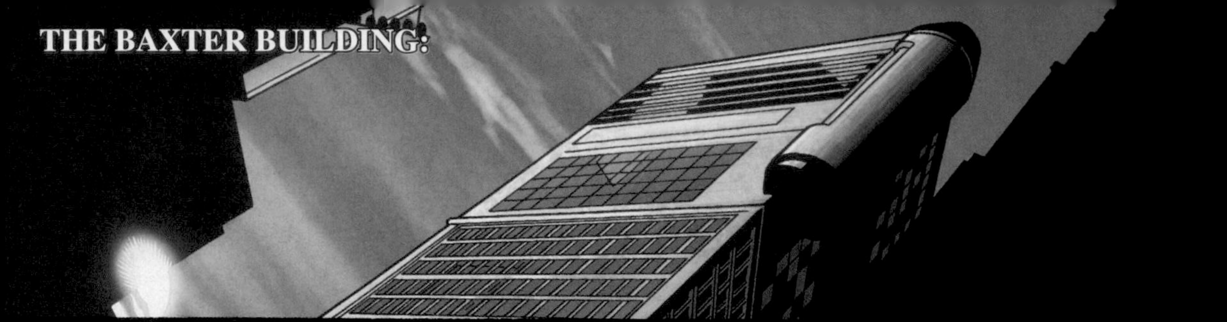
THE BAXTER BUILDING:

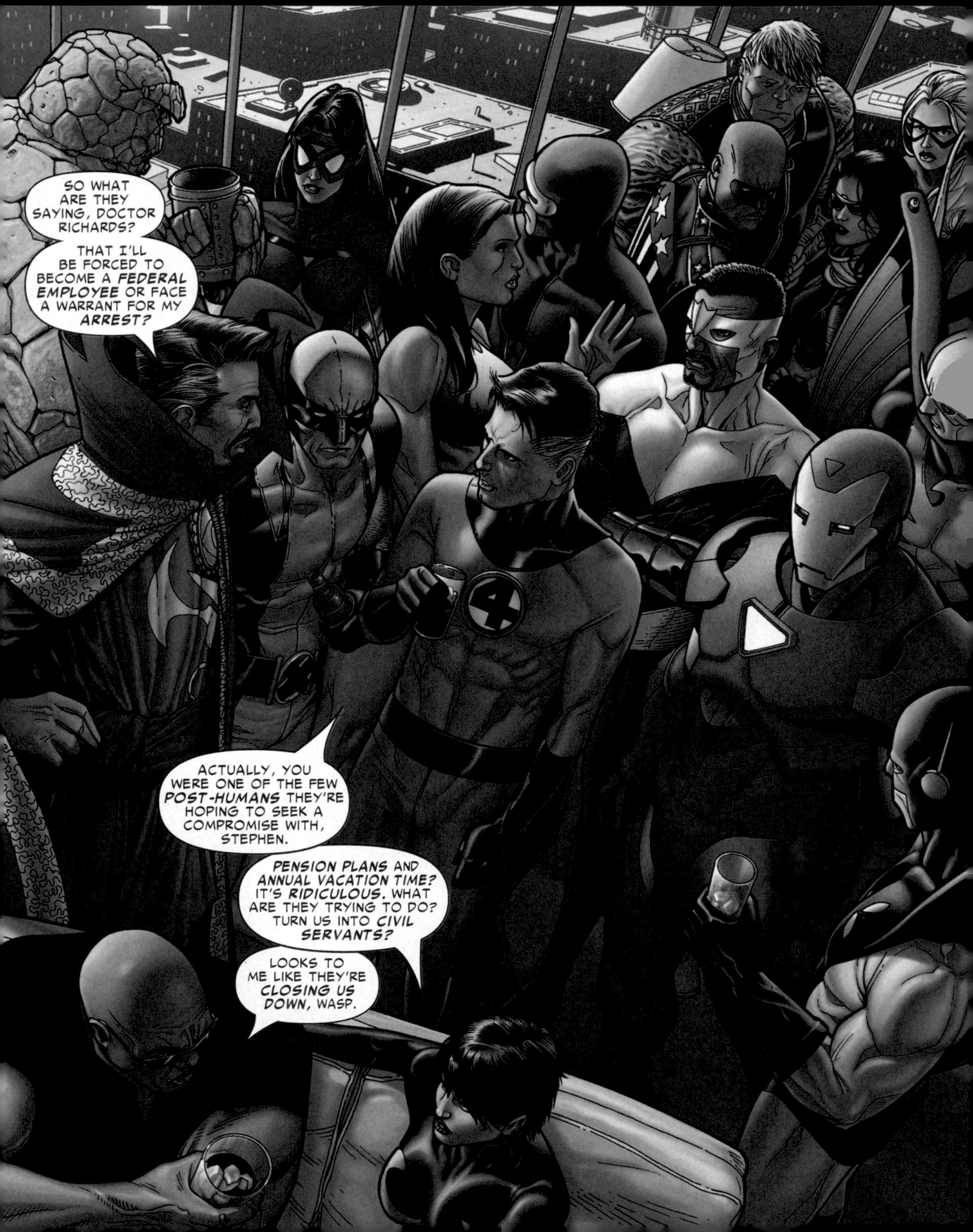
SO WHAT ARE THEY SAYING, DOCTOR RICHARDS?
THAT I'LL BE FORCED TO BECOME A *FEDERAL EMPLOYEE* OR FACE A WARRANT FOR MY *ARREST?*
ACTUALLY, YOU WERE ONE OF THE FEW *POST-HUMANS* THEY'RE HOPING TO SEEK A COMPROMISE WITH, STEPHEN.
PENSION PLANS AND *ANNUAL VACATION TIME?* IT'S *RIDICULOUS.* WHAT ARE THEY TRYING TO DO? TURN US INTO *CIVIL SERVANTS?*
LOOKS TO ME LIKE THEY'RE *CLOSING US DOWN,* WASP.

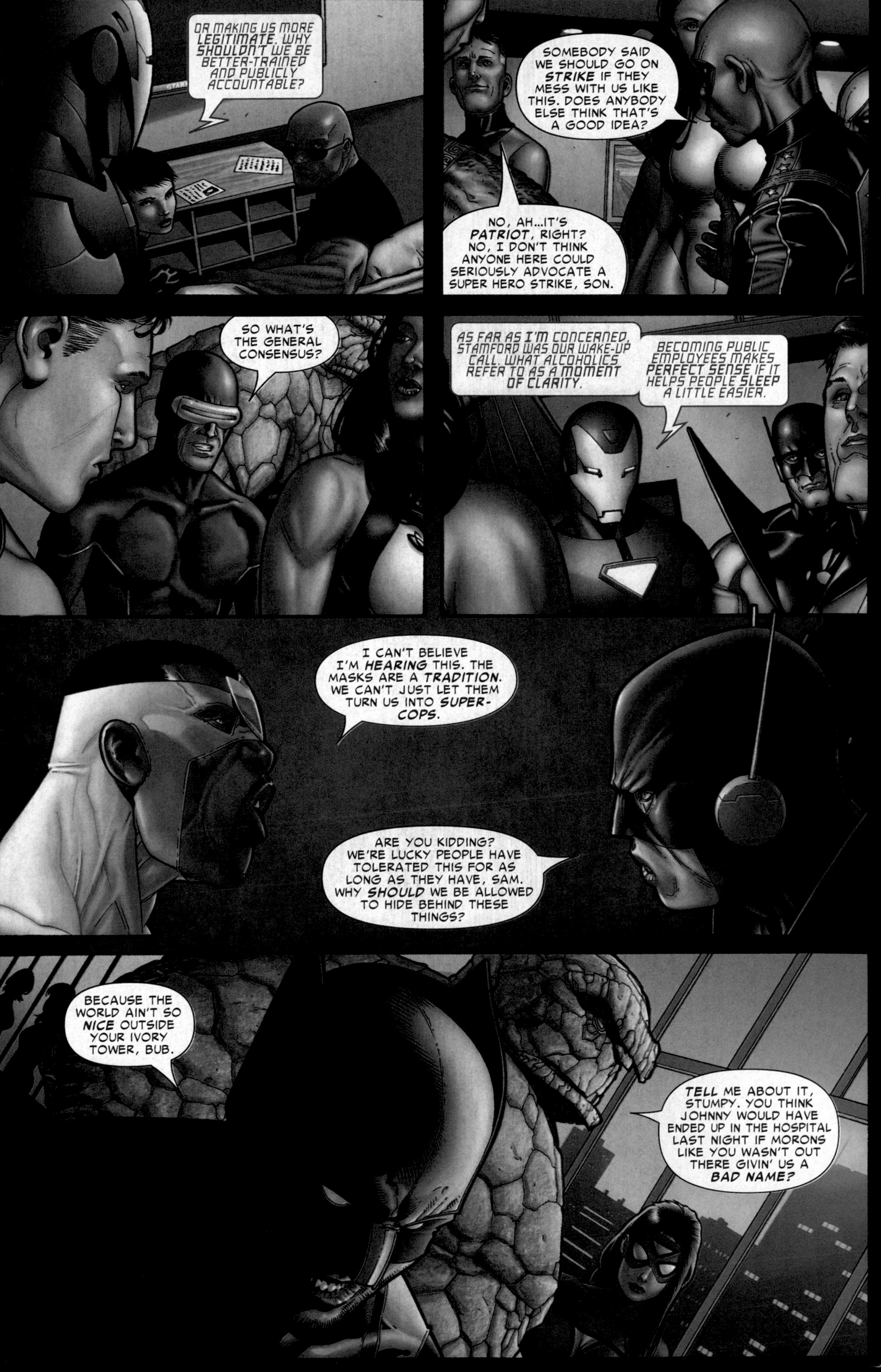

OR MAKING US MORE LEGITIMATE. WHY SHOULDN'T WE BE BETTER-TRAINED AND PUBLICLY ACCOUNTABLE?
SOMEBODY SAID WE SHOULD GO ON STRIKE IF THEY MESS WITH US LIKE THIS. DOES ANYBODY ELSE THINK THAT'S A GOOD IDEA?
NO, AH...IT'S PATRIOT, RIGHT? NO, I DON'T THINK ANYONE HERE COULD SERIOUSLY ADVOCATE A SUPER HERO STRIKE, SON.
SO WHAT'S THE GENERAL CONSENSUS?
AS FAR AS I'M CONCERNED, STAMFORD WAS OUR WAKE-UP CALL. WHAT ALCOHOLICS REFER TO AS A MOMENT OF CLARITY.
BECOMING PUBLIC EMPLOYEES MAKES PERFECT SENSE IF IT HELPS PEOPLE SLEEP A LITTLE EASIER.
I CAN'T BELIEVE I'M HEARING THIS. THE MASKS ARE A TRADITION. WE CAN'T JUST LET THEM TURN US INTO SUPER-COPS.
ARE YOU KIDDING? WE'RE LUCKY PEOPLE HAVE TOLERATED THIS FOR AS LONG AS THEY HAVE, SAM. WHY SHOULD WE BE ALLOWED TO HIDE BEHIND THESE THINGS?
BECAUSE THE WORLD AIN'T SO NICE OUTSIDE YOUR IVORY TOWER, BUB.
TELL ME ABOUT IT, STUMPY. YOU THINK JOHNNY WOULD HAVE ENDED UP IN THE HOSPITAL LAST NIGHT IF MORONS LIKE YOU WASN'T OUT THERE GIVIN' US A BAD NAME?

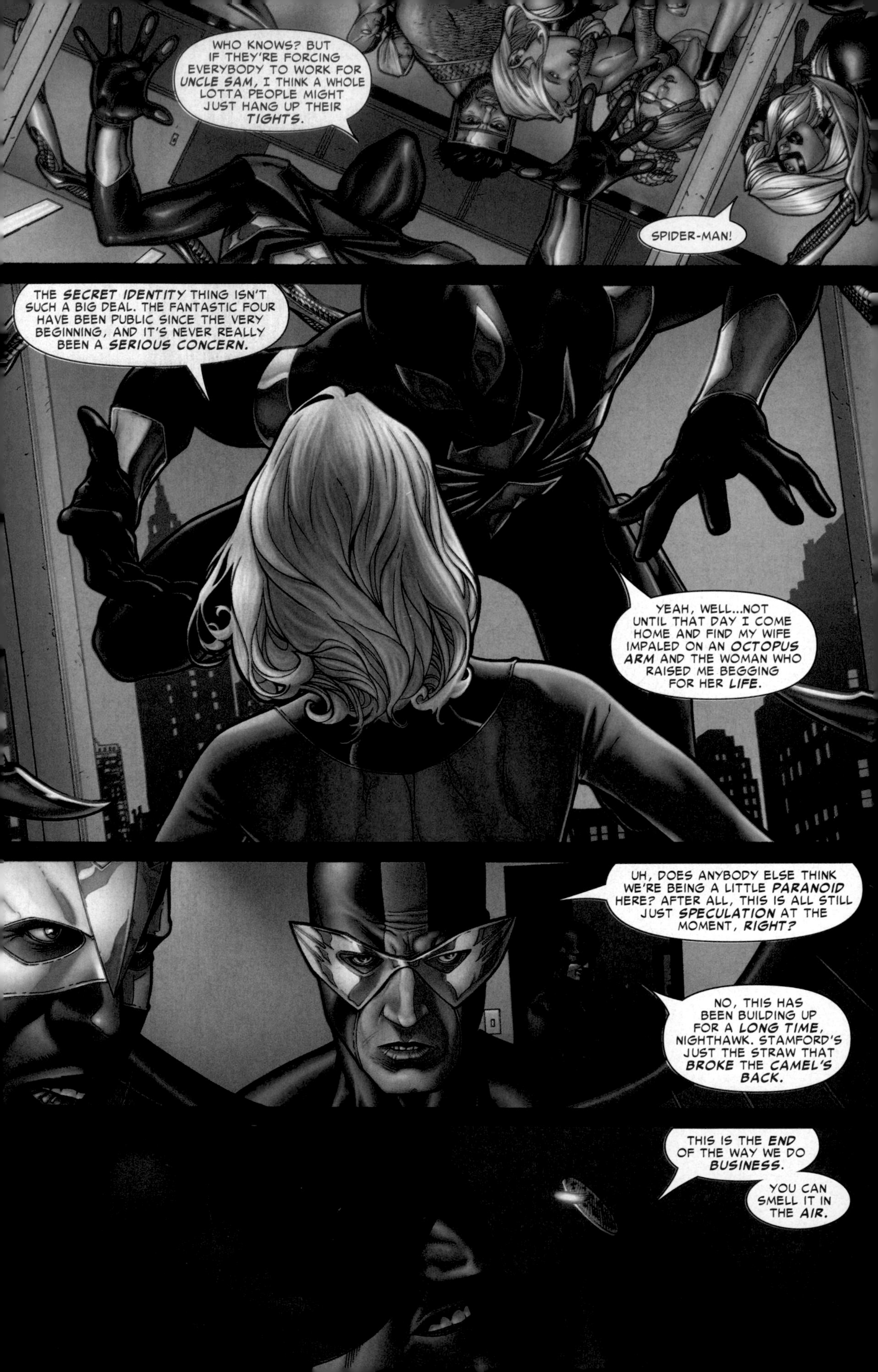
WHO KNOWS? BUT IF THEY'RE FORCING EVERYBODY TO WORK FOR UNCLE SAM, I THINK A WHOLE LOTTA PEOPLE MIGHT JUST HANG UP THEIR TIGHTS.
SPIDER-MAN!
THE SECRET IDENTITY THING ISN'T SUCH A BIG DEAL. THE FANTASTIC FOUR HAVE BEEN PUBLIC SINCE THE VERY BEGINNING, AND IT'S NEVER REALLY BEEN A SERIOUS CONCERN.
YEAH, WELL...NOT UNTIL THAT DAY I COME HOME AND FIND MY WIFE IMPALED ON AN OCTOPUS ARM AND THE WOMAN WHO RAISED ME BEGGING FOR HER LIFE.
UH, DOES ANYBODY ELSE THINK WE'RE BEING A LITTLE PARANOID HERE? AFTER ALL, THIS IS ALL STILL JUST SPECULATION AT THE MOMENT, RIGHT?
NO, THIS HAS BEEN BUILDING UP FOR A LONG TIME, NIGHTHAWK. STAMFORD'S JUST THE STRAW THAT BROKE THE CAMEL'S BACK.
THIS IS THE END OF THE WAY WE DO BUSINESS.
YOU CAN SMELL IT IN THE AIR.

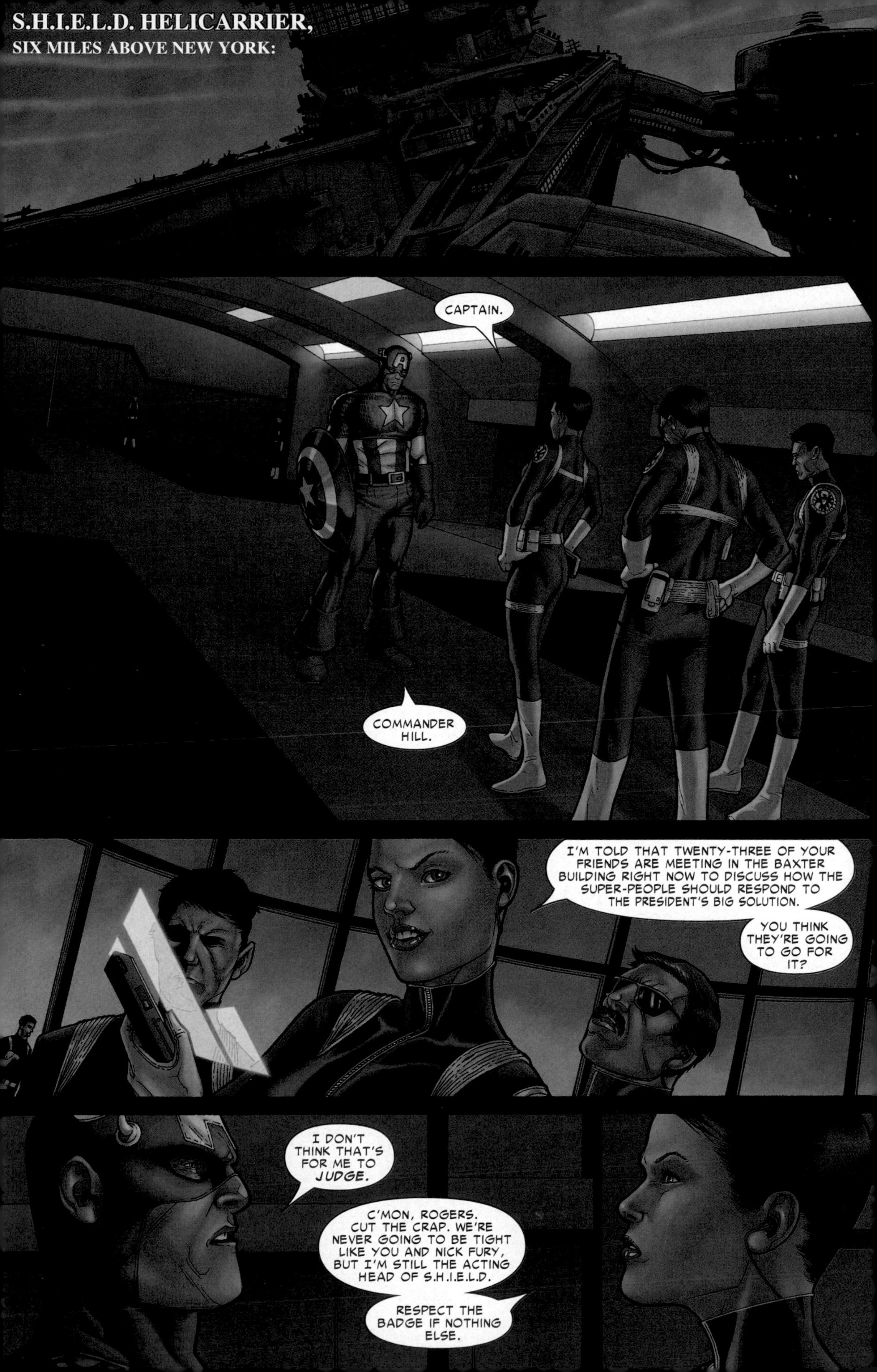
S.H.I.E.L.D. HELICARRIER,
SIX MILES ABOVE NEW YORK:
CAPTAIN.
COMMANDER HILL.
I'M TOLD THAT TWENTY-THREE OF YOUR FRIENDS ARE MEETING IN THE BAXTER BUILDING RIGHT NOW TO DISCUSS HOW THE SUPER-PEOPLE SHOULD RESPOND TO THE PRESIDENT'S BIG SOLUTION.
YOU THINK THEY'RE GOING TO GO FOR IT?
I DON'T THINK THAT'S FOR ME TO JUDGE.
C'MON, ROGERS. CUT THE CRAP. WE'RE NEVER GOING TO BE TIGHT LIKE YOU AND NICK FURY, BUT I'M STILL THE ACTING HEAD OF S.H.I.E.L.D.
RESPECT THE BADGE IF NOTHING ELSE.

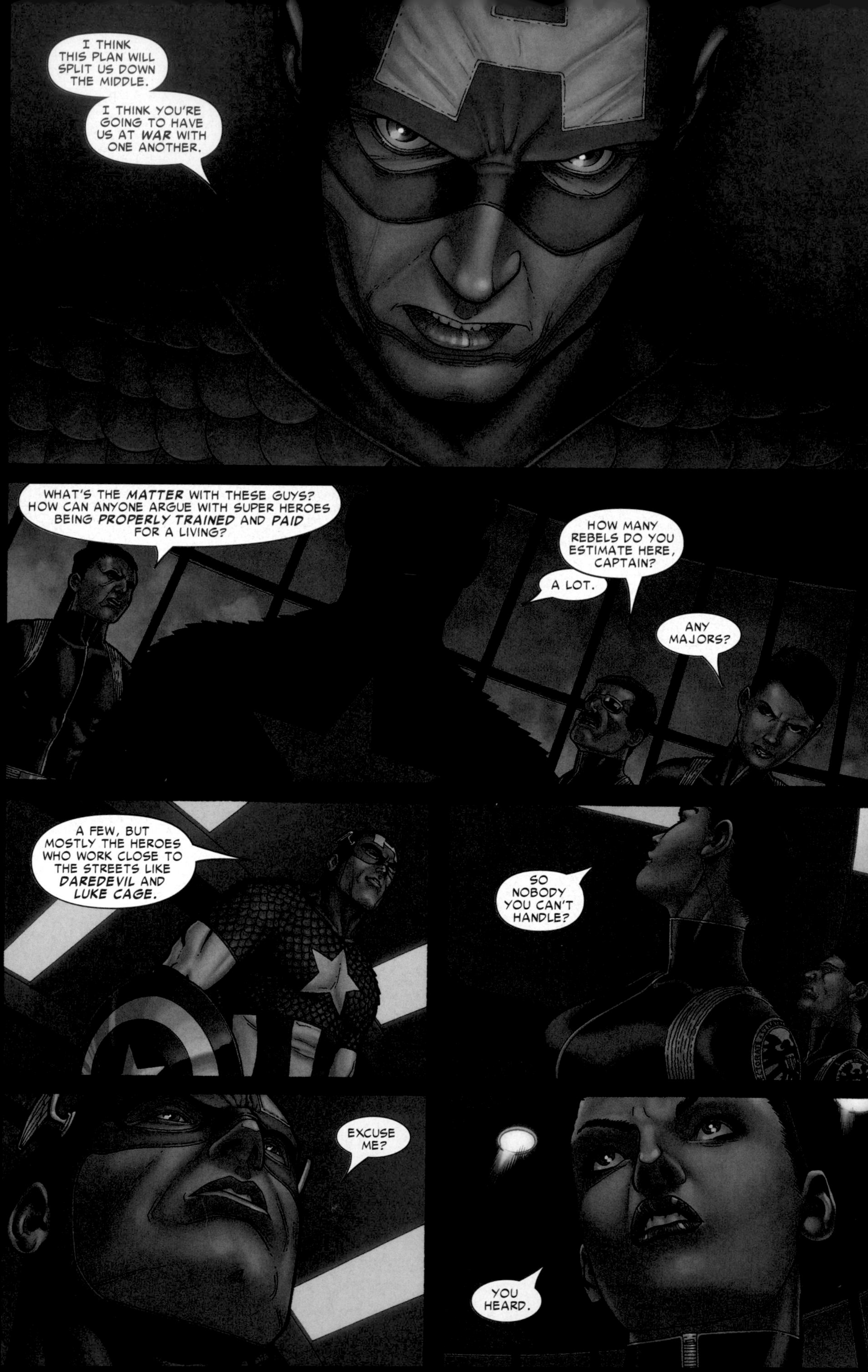
I THINK THIS PLAN WILL SPLIT US DOWN THE MIDDLE.
I THINK YOU'RE GOING TO HAVE US AT WAR WITH ONE ANOTHER.
WHAT'S THE MATTER WITH THESE GUYS? HOW CAN ANYONE ARGUE WITH SUPER HEROES BEING PROPERLY TRAINED AND PAID FOR A LIVING?
HOW MANY REBELS DO YOU ESTIMATE HERE, CAPTAIN?
A LOT.
ANY MAJORS?
A FEW, BUT MOSTLY THE HEROES WHO WORK CLOSE TO THE STREETS LIKE DAREDEVIL AND LUKE CAGE.
SO NOBODY YOU CAN'T HANDLE?
EXCUSE ME?
YOU HEARD.

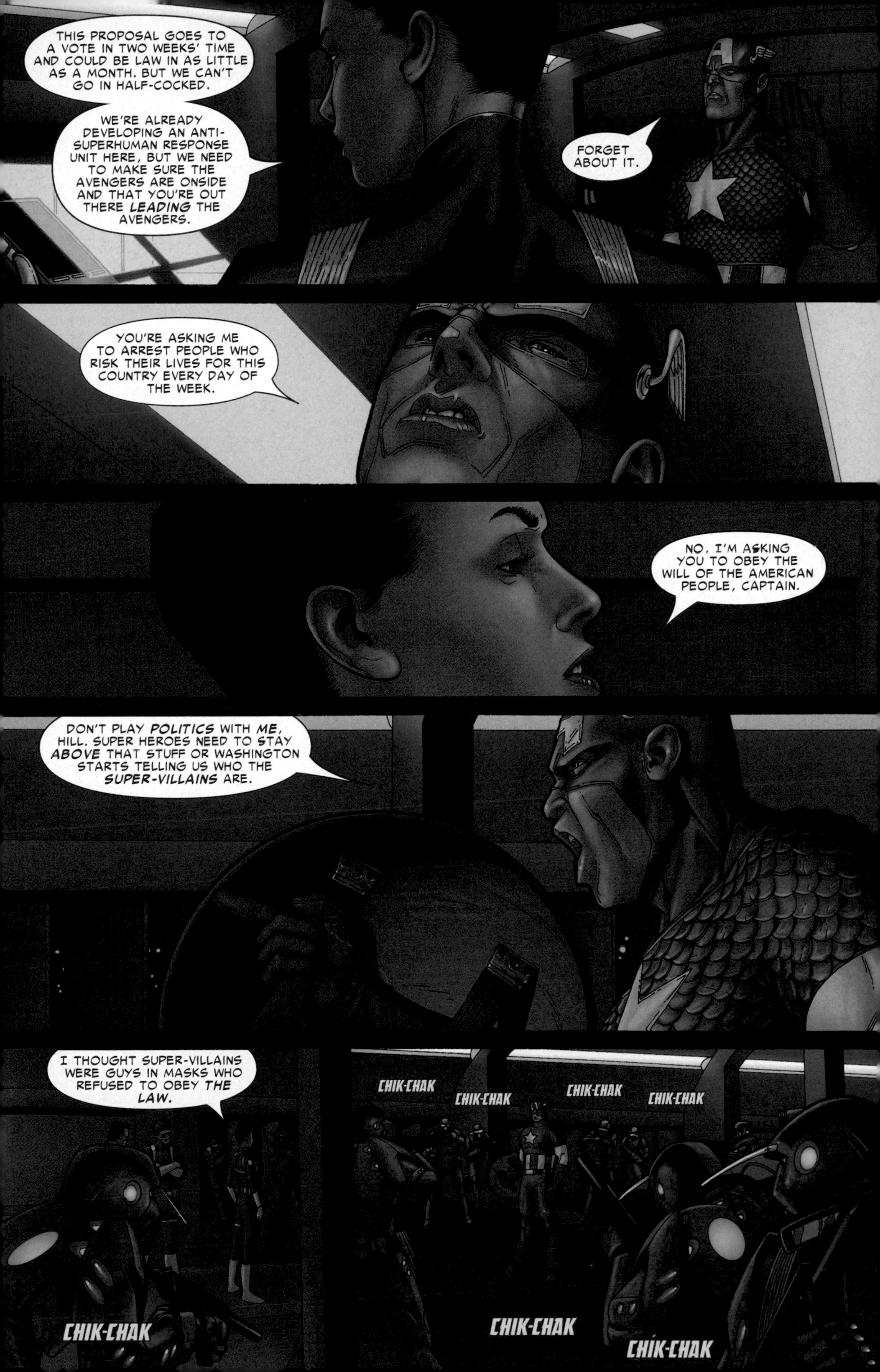
THIS PROPOSAL GOES TO A VOTE IN TWO WEEKS' TIME AND COULD BE LAW IN AS LITTLE AS A MONTH. BUT WE CAN'T GO IN HALF-COCKED.
WE'RE ALREADY DEVELOPING AN ANTI-SUPERHUMAN RESPONSE UNIT HERE, BUT WE NEED TO MAKE SURE THE AVENGERS ARE ONSIDE AND THAT YOU'RE OUT THERE *LEADING* THE AVENGERS.
FORGET ABOUT IT.
YOU'RE ASKING ME TO ARREST PEOPLE WHO RISK THEIR LIVES FOR THIS COUNTRY EVERY DAY OF THE WEEK.
NO, I'M ASKING YOU TO OBEY THE WILL OF THE AMERICAN PEOPLE, CAPTAIN.
DON'T PLAY *POLITICS* WITH *ME*, HILL. SUPER HEROES NEED TO STAY *ABOVE* THAT STUFF OR WASHINGTON STARTS TELLING US WHO THE *SUPER-VILLAINS* ARE.
I THOUGHT SUPER-VILLAINS WERE GUYS IN MASKS WHO REFUSED TO OBEY *THE LAW*.
CHIK-CHAK
CHIK-CHAK
CHIK-CHAK
CHIK-CHAK
CHIK-CHAK
CHIK-CHAK
CHIK-CHAK

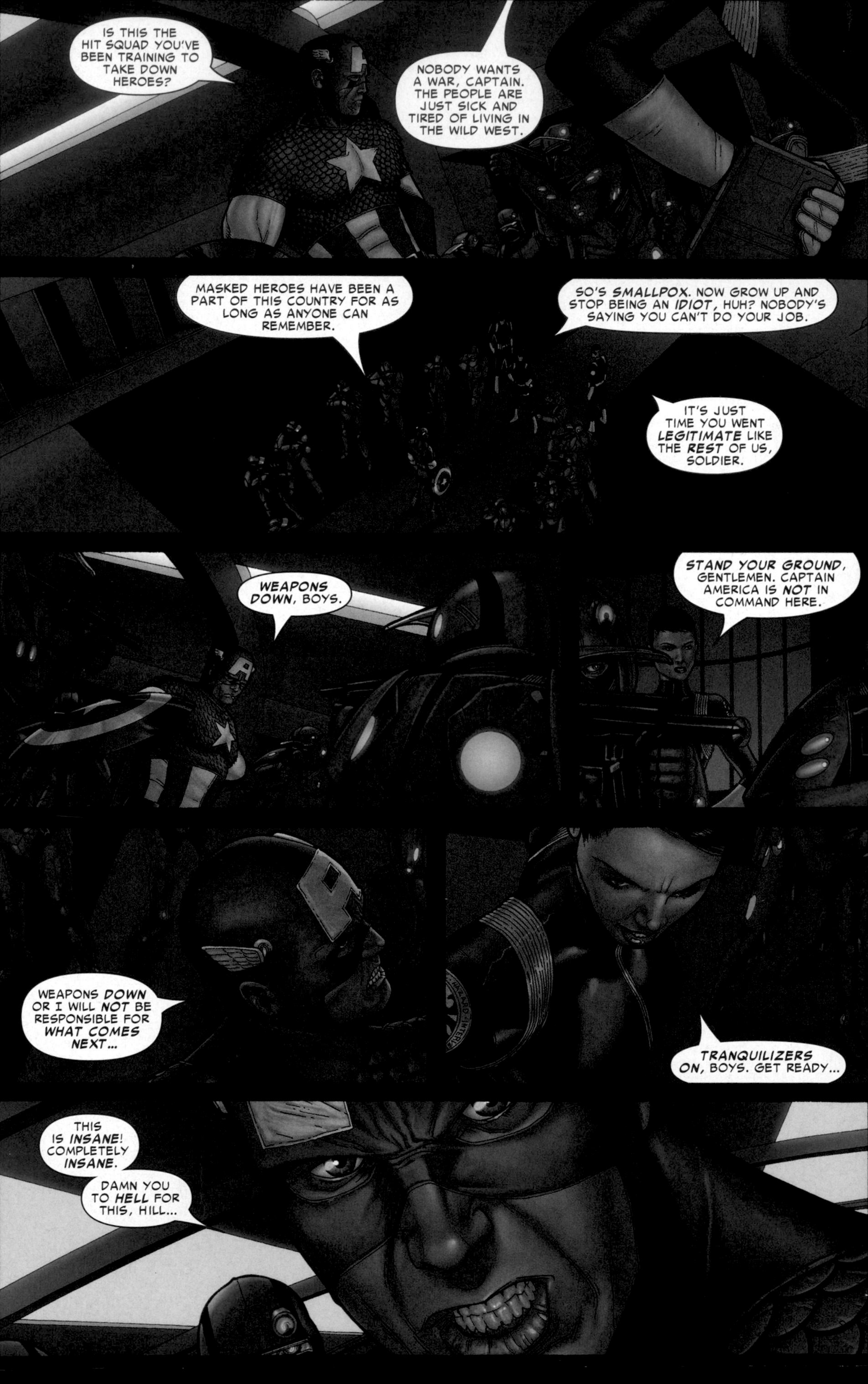
IS THIS THE HIT SQUAD YOU'VE BEEN TRAINING TO TAKE DOWN HEROES?
NOBODY WANTS A WAR, CAPTAIN. THE PEOPLE ARE JUST SICK AND TIRED OF LIVING IN THE WILD WEST.
MASKED HEROES HAVE BEEN A PART OF THIS COUNTRY FOR AS LONG AS ANYONE CAN REMEMBER.
SO'S SMALLPOX. NOW GROW UP AND STOP BEING AN IDIOT, HUH? NOBODY'S SAYING YOU CAN'T DO YOUR JOB.
IT'S JUST TIME YOU WENT LEGITIMATE LIKE THE REST OF US, SOLDIER.
WEAPONS DOWN, BOYS.
STAND YOUR GROUND, GENTLEMEN. CAPTAIN AMERICA IS NOT IN COMMAND HERE.
WEAPONS DOWN OR I WILL NOT BE RESPONSIBLE FOR WHAT COMES NEXT...
TRANQUILIZERS ON, BOYS. GET READY...
THIS IS INSANE! COMPLETELY INSANE.
DAMN YOU TO HELL FOR THIS, HILL...

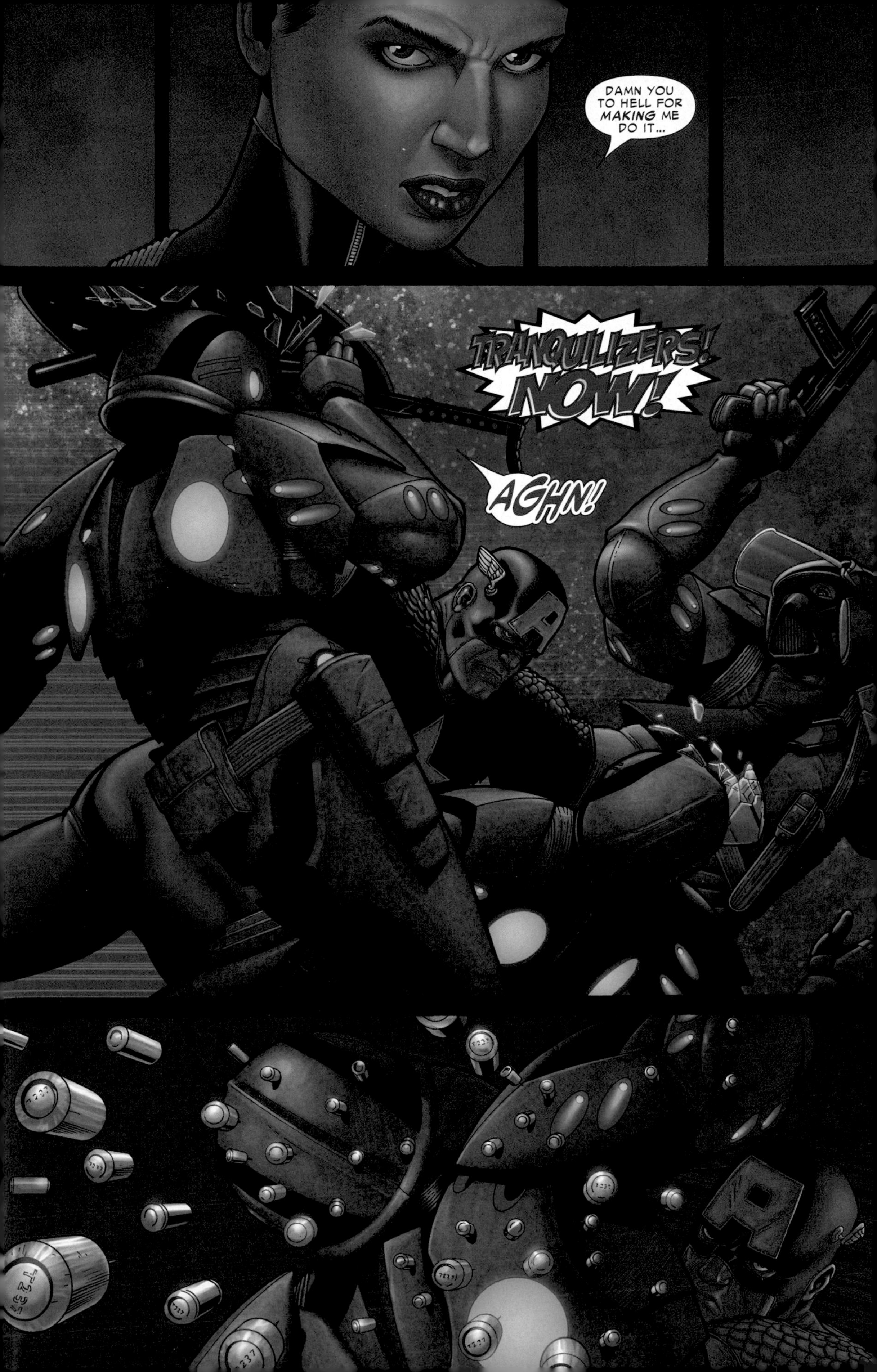
DAMN YOU TO HELL FOR MAKING ME DO IT...
TRANQUILIZERS! NOW!
AGHN!

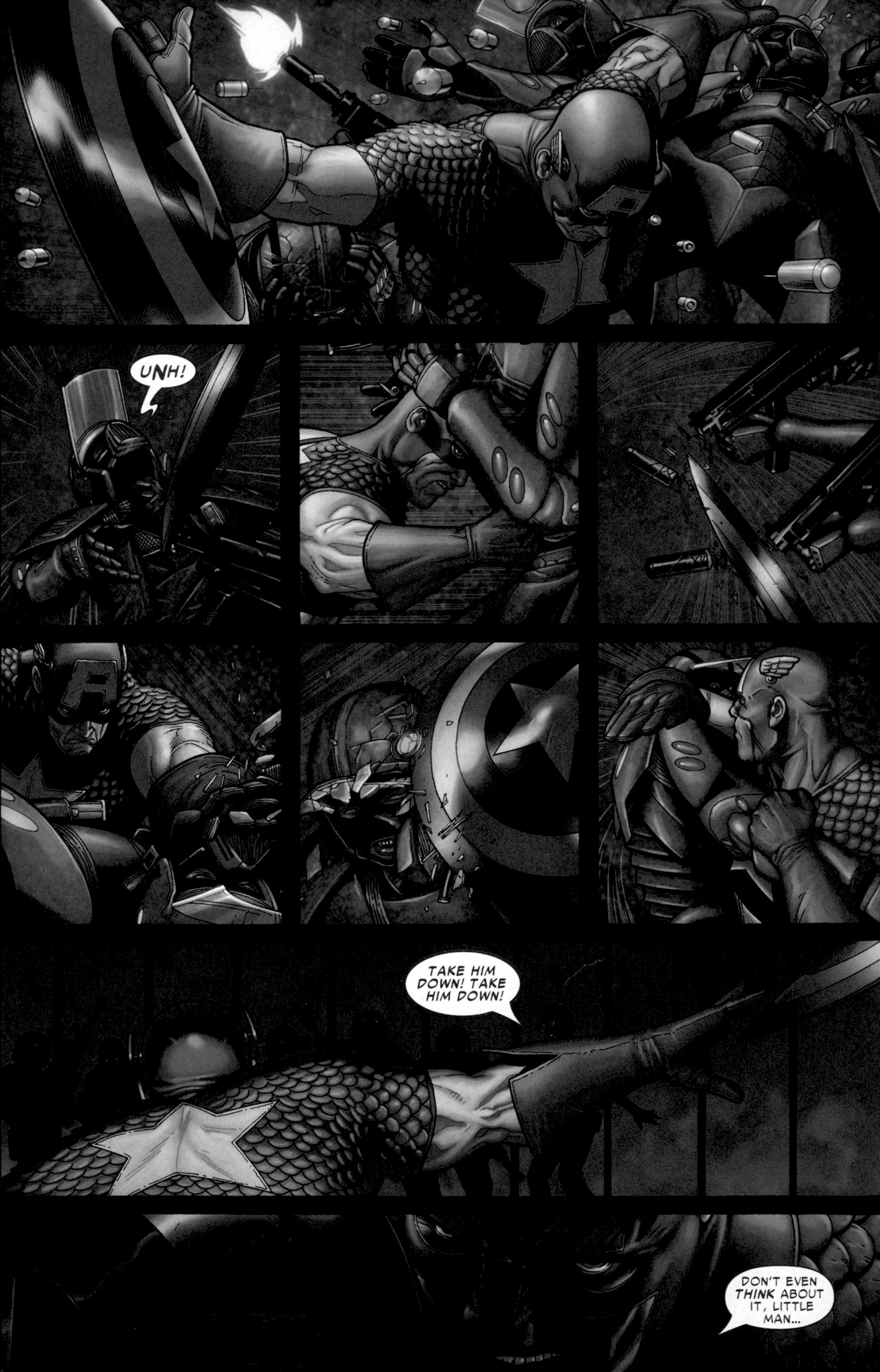
UNH!
TAKE HIM DOWN! TAKE HIM DOWN!
DON'T EVEN THINK ABOUT IT, LITTLE MAN...

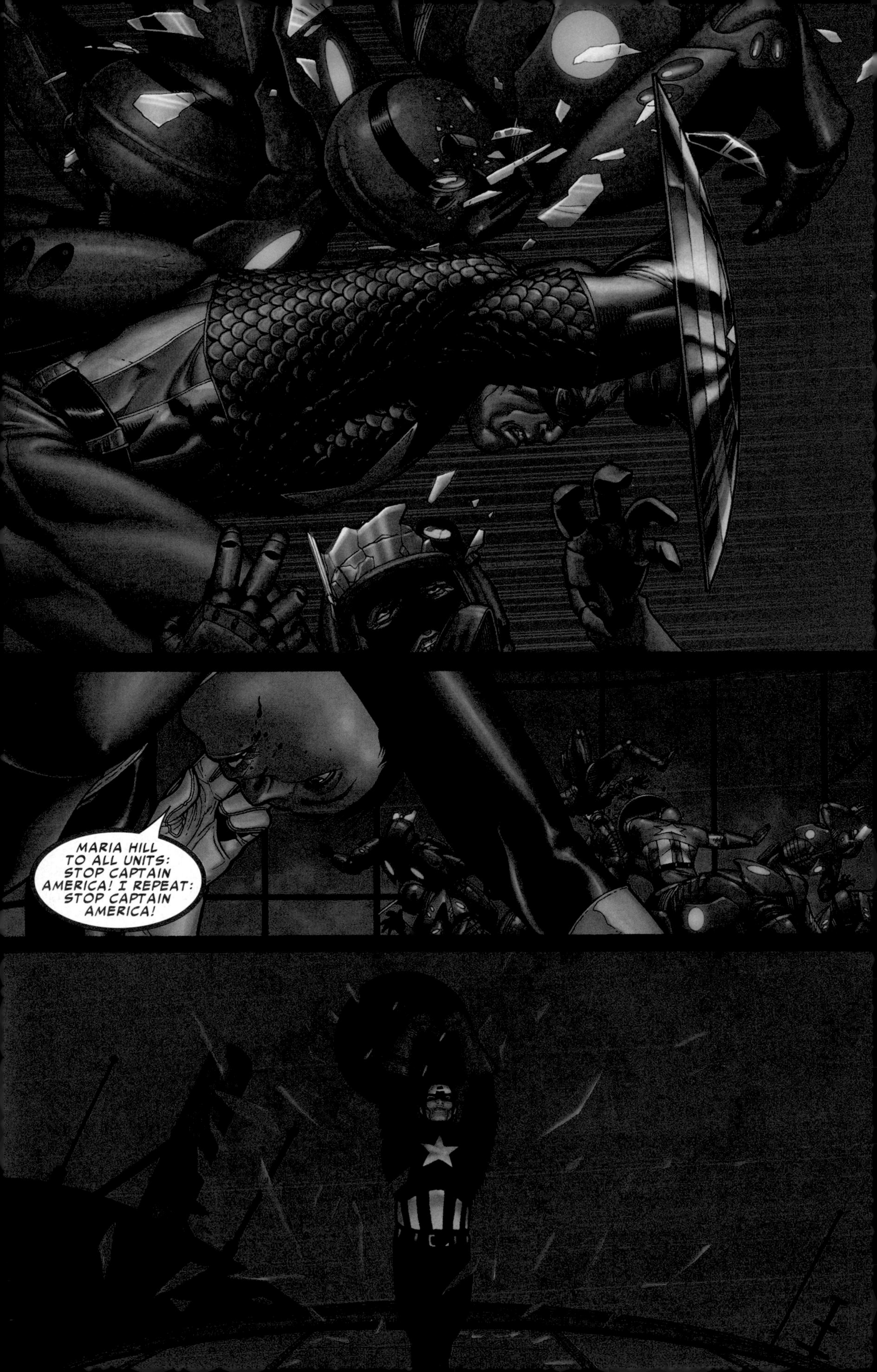
MARIA HILL TO ALL UNITS: STOP CAPTAIN AMERICA! I REPEAT: STOP CAPTAIN AMERICA!

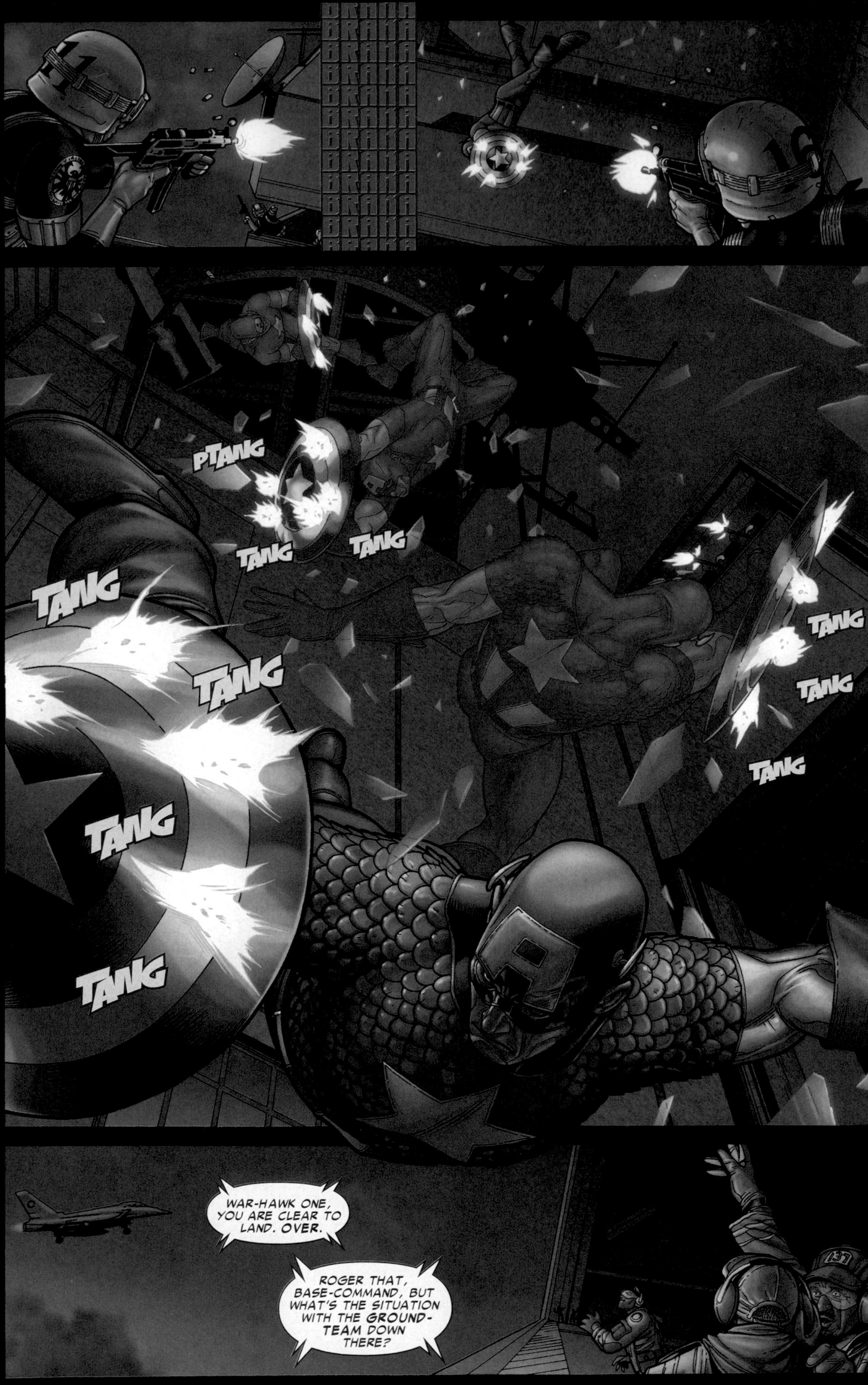
BRAKA BRAKA BRAKA BRAKA BRAKA BRAKA BRAKA BRAKA BRAKA BRAKA BRAKA
PTANG
TANG
TANG
TANG
TANG
TANG
TANG
TANG
TANG
TANG
WAR-HAWK ONE, YOU ARE CLEAR TO LAND. OVER.
ROGER THAT, BASE-COMMAND, BUT WHAT'S THE SITUATION WITH THE GROUND-TEAM DOWN THERE?

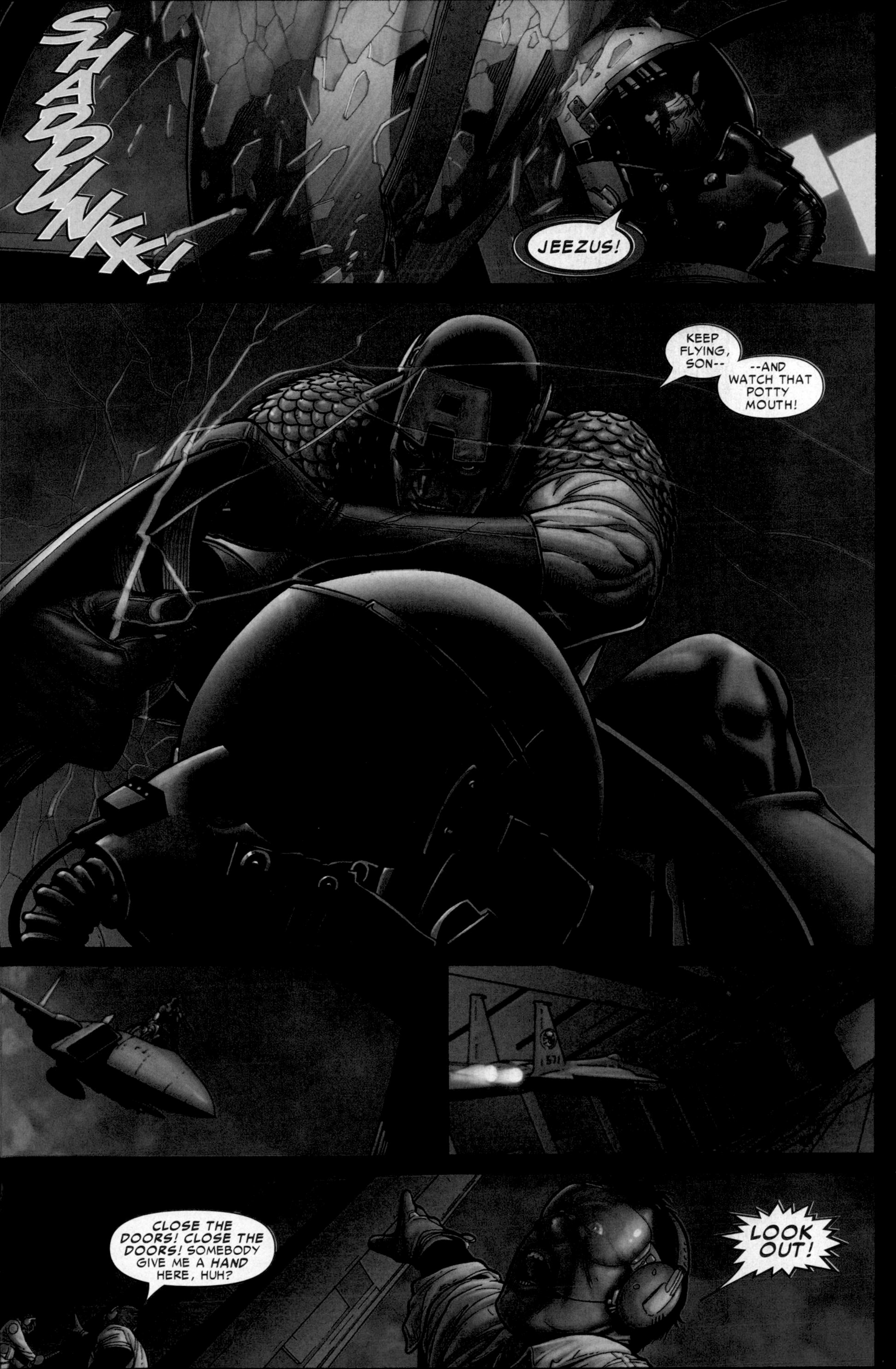
SHADUNKK!
JEEZUS!
KEEP FLYING, SON--
--AND WATCH THAT POTTY MOUTH!
CLOSE THE DOORS! CLOSE THE DOORS! SOMEBODY GIVE ME A HAND HERE, HUH?
LOOK OUT!

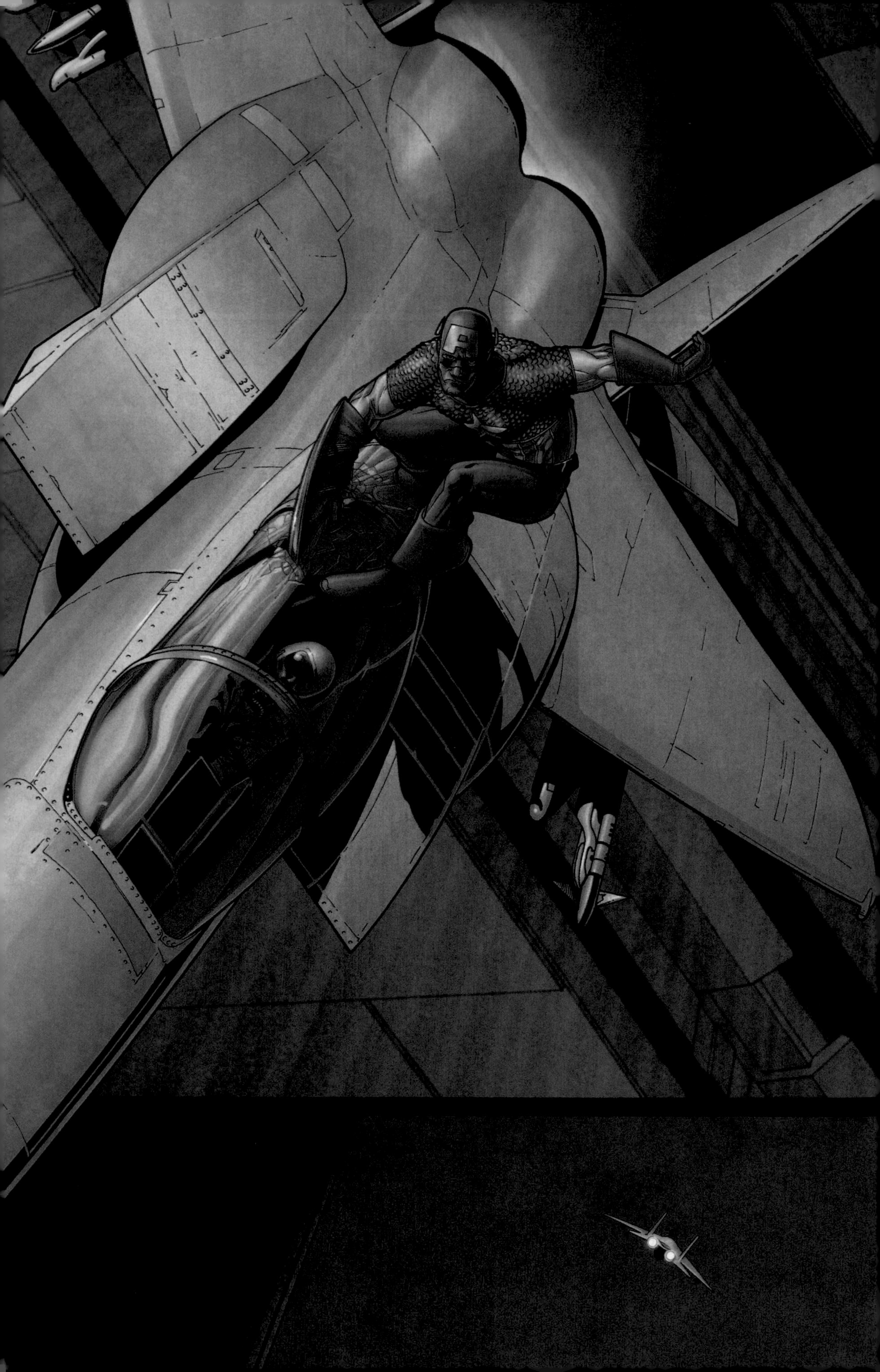

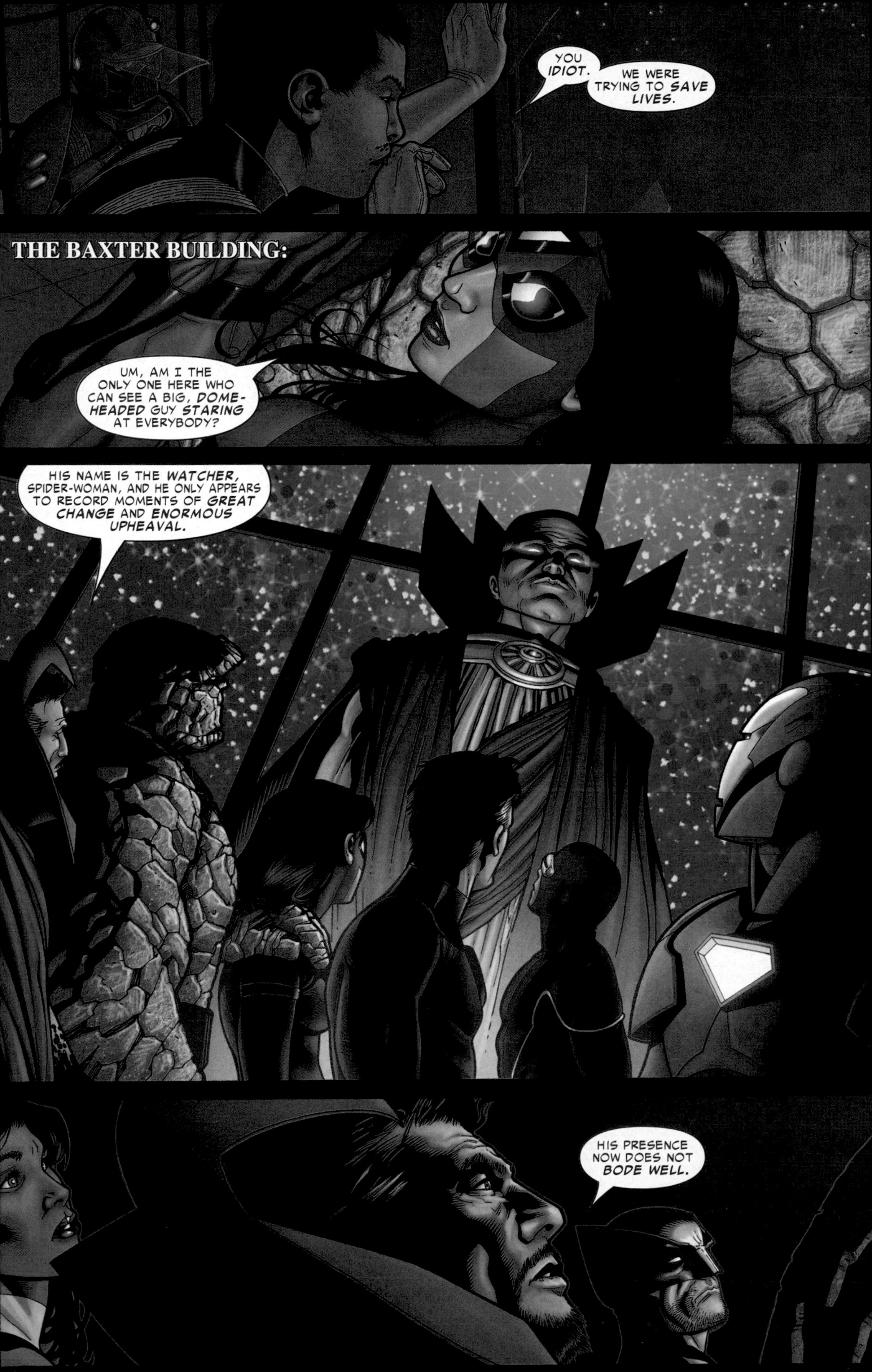
YOU IDIOT.
WE WERE TRYING TO SAVE LIVES.
THE BAXTER BUILDING:
UM, AM I THE ONLY ONE HERE WHO CAN SEE A BIG, DOME-HEADED GUY STARING AT EVERYBODY?
HIS NAME IS THE WATCHER, SPIDER-WOMAN, AND HE ONLY APPEARS TO RECORD MOMENTS OF GREAT CHANGE AND ENORMOUS UPHEAVAL.
HIS PRESENCE NOW DOES NOT BODE WELL.

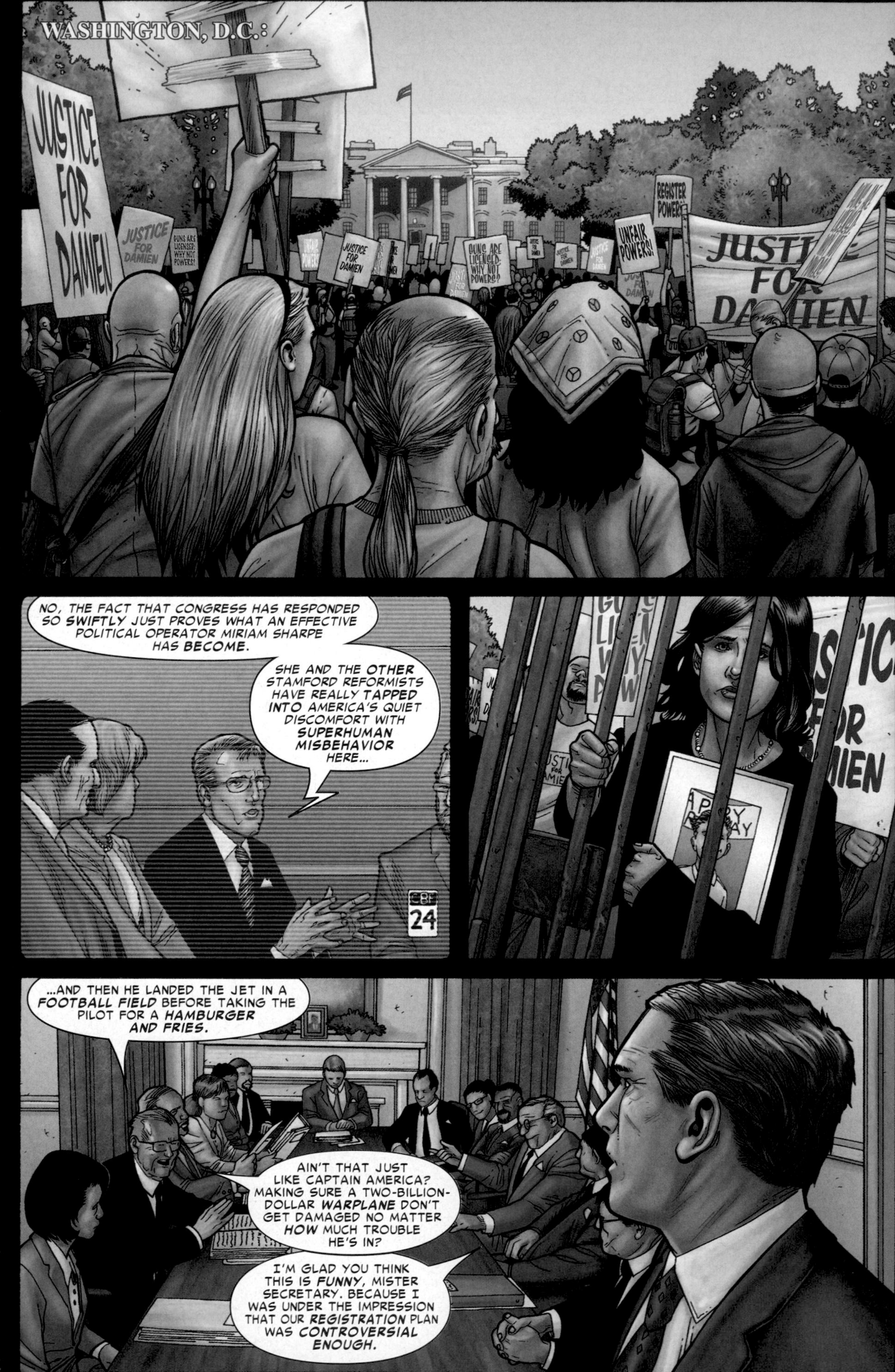
WASHINGTON, D.C.:
JUSTICE FOR DAMIEN
JUSTICE FOR DAMIEN
GUNS ARE LICENSED: WHY NOT POWERS?
UNFAIR POWERS
JUSTICE FOR DAMIEN
GUNS ARE LICENSED: WHY NOT POWERS?
REGISTER POWERS
UNFAIR POWERS!
JUSTICE FOR DAMIEN
NO, THE FACT THAT CONGRESS HAS RESPONDED SO SWIFTLY JUST PROVES WHAT AN EFFECTIVE POLITICAL OPERATOR MIRIAM SHARPE HAS BECOME.
SHE AND THE OTHER STAMFORD REFORMISTS HAVE REALLY TAPPED INTO AMERICA'S QUIET DISCOMFORT WITH SUPERHUMAN MISBEHAVIOR HERE...
CBF 24
...AND THEN HE LANDED THE JET IN A FOOTBALL FIELD BEFORE TAKING THE PILOT FOR A HAMBURGER AND FRIES.
AIN'T THAT JUST LIKE CAPTAIN AMERICA? MAKING SURE A TWO-BILLION-DOLLAR WARPLANE DON'T GET DAMAGED NO MATTER HOW MUCH TROUBLE HE'S IN?
I'M GLAD YOU THINK THIS IS FUNNY, MISTER SECRETARY. BECAUSE I WAS UNDER THE IMPRESSION THAT OUR REGISTRATION PLAN WAS CONTROVERSIAL ENOUGH.

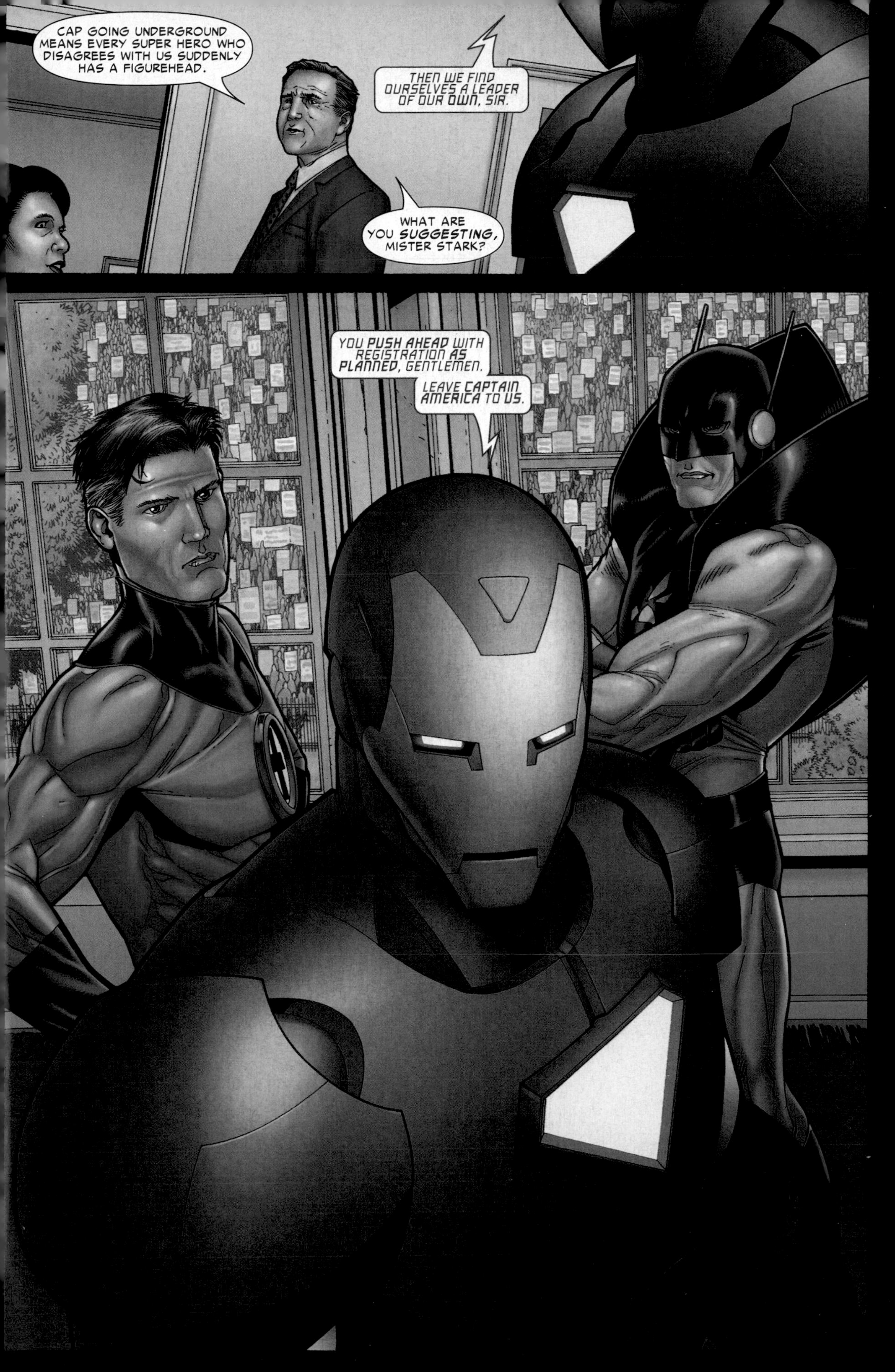
CAP GOING UNDERGROUND MEANS EVERY SUPER HERO WHO DISAGREES WITH US SUDDENLY HAS A FIGUREHEAD.
THEN WE FIND OURSELVES A LEADER OF OUR OWN, SIR.
WHAT ARE YOU SUGGESTING, MISTER STARK?
YOU PUSH AHEAD WITH REGISTRATION AS PLANNED, GENTLEMEN.
LEAVE CAPTAIN AMERICA TO US.

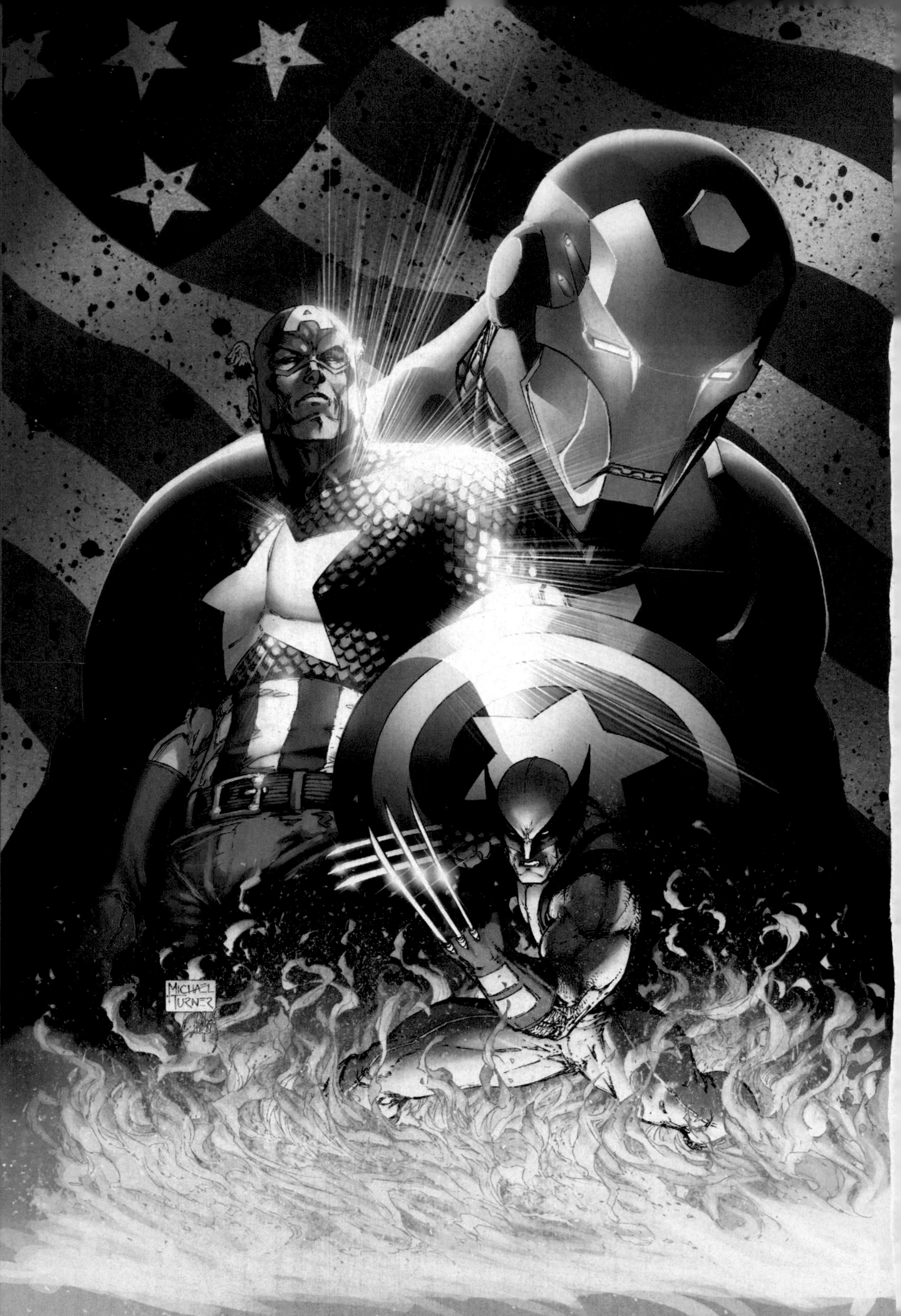
MICHAEL
TURNER

CIVIL WAR #1 ASPEN VARIANT BY MICHAEL TURNER & PETER STEIGERWALD

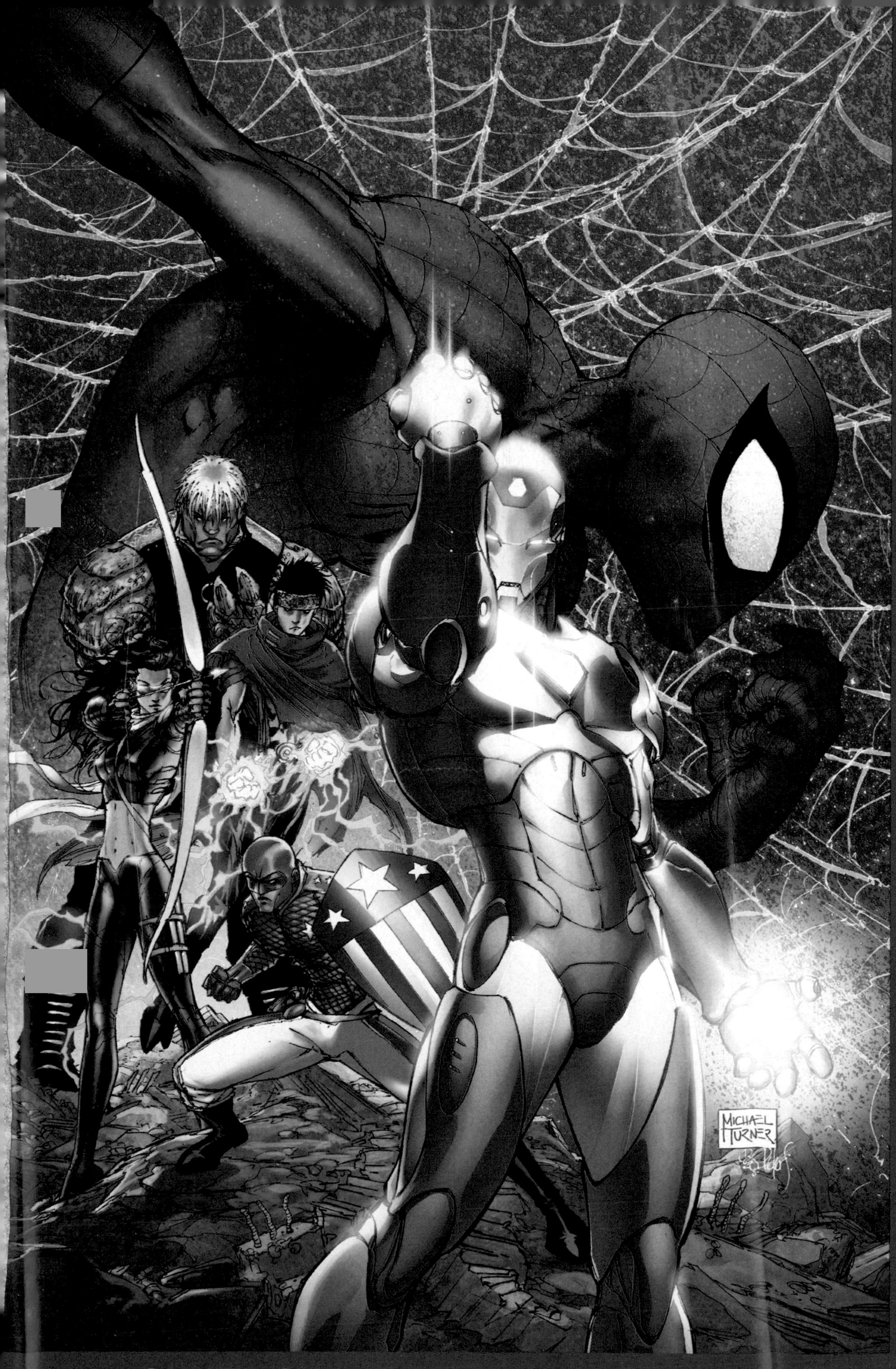
MICHAEL TURNER

CIVIL WAR #2 VARIANT BY MICHAEL TURNER & PETER STEIGERWALD

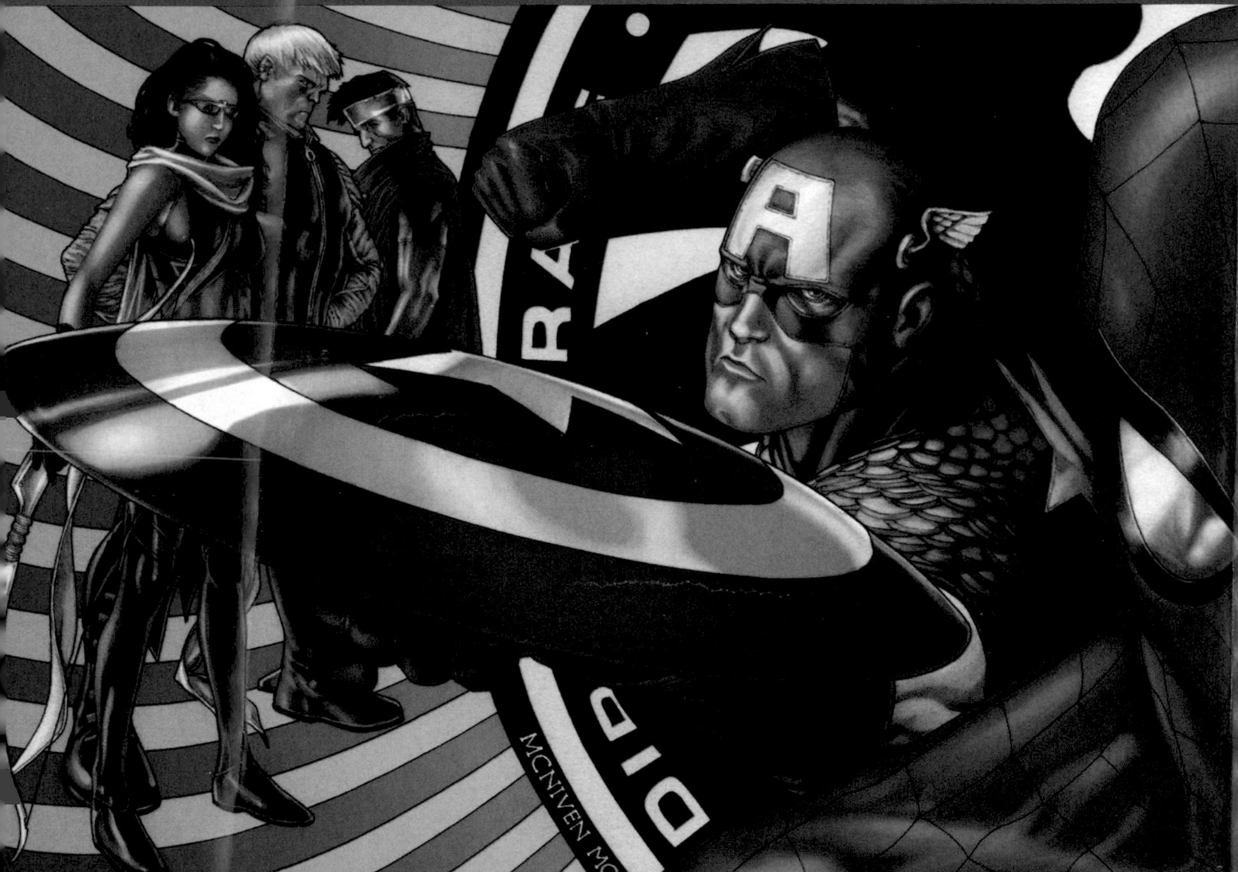
MCNIVEN MO!

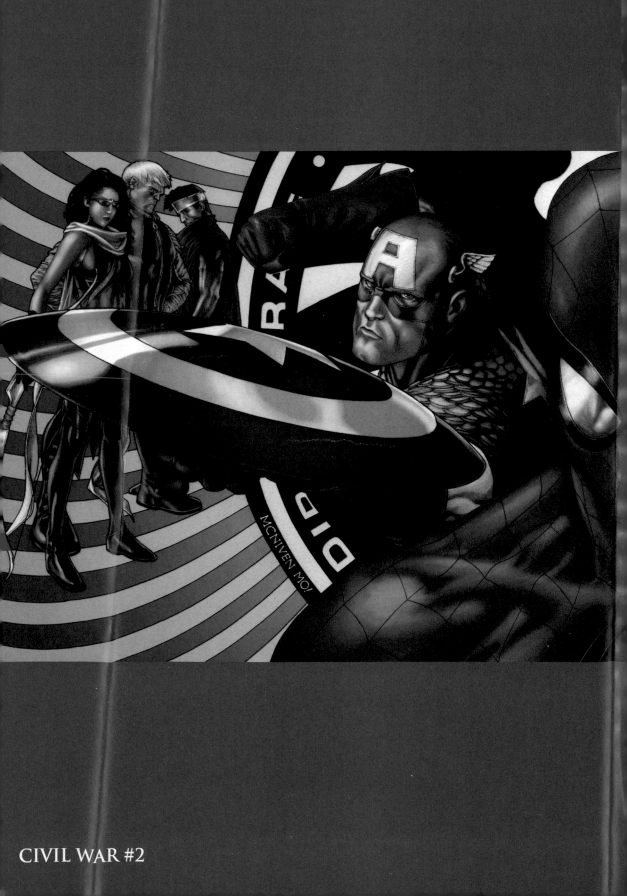

CIVIL WAR #2

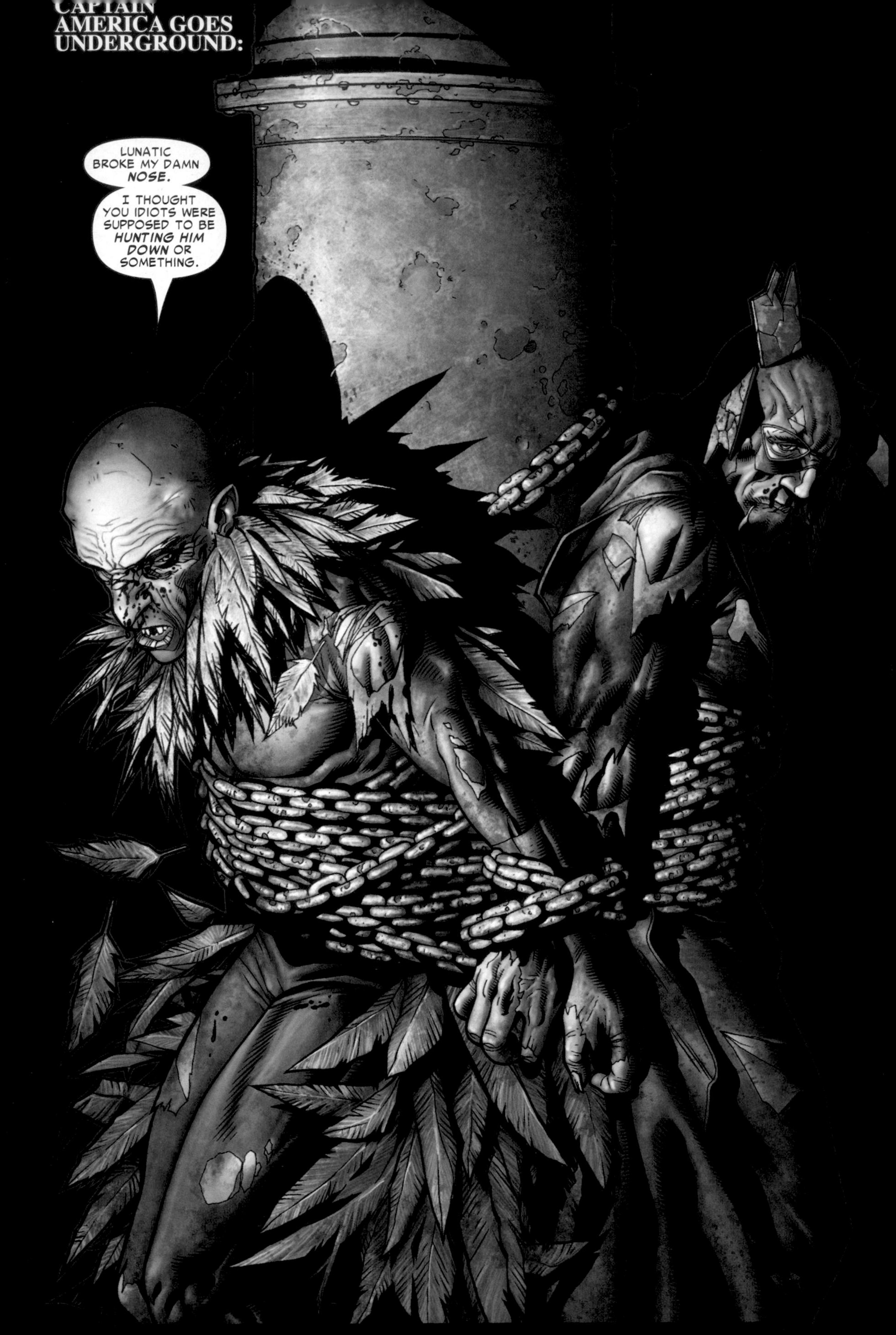
CAPTAIN AMERICA GOES UNDERGROUND:
LUNATIC BROKE MY DAMN NOSE.
I THOUGHT YOU IDIOTS WERE SUPPOSED TO BE HUNTING HIM DOWN OR SOMETHING.

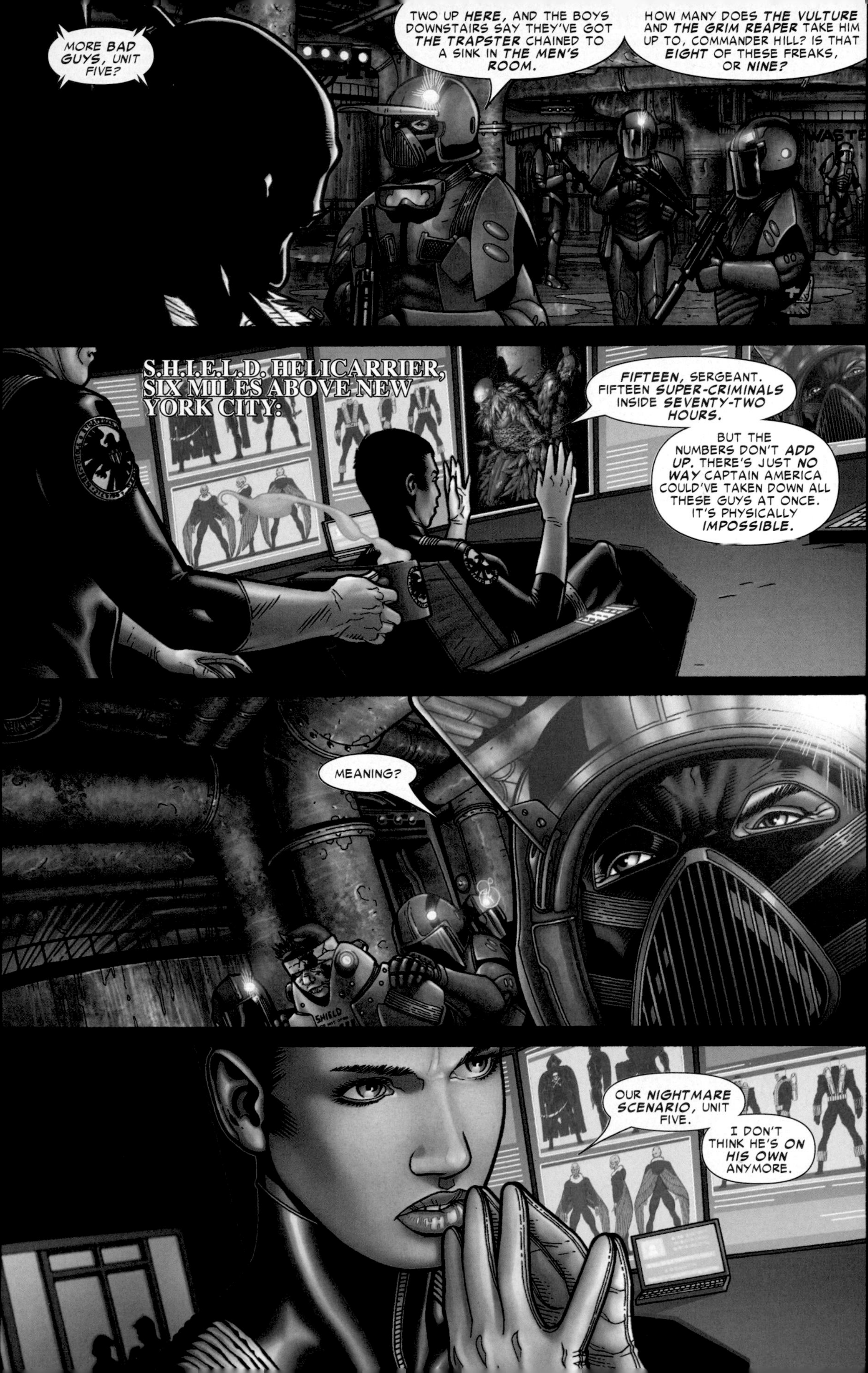
MORE BAD GUYS, UNIT FIVE?
TWO UP HERE, AND THE BOYS DOWNSTAIRS SAY THEY'VE GOT THE TRAPSTER CHAINED TO A SINK IN THE MEN'S ROOM.
HOW MANY DOES THE VULTURE AND THE GRIM REAPER TAKE HIM UP TO, COMMANDER HILL? IS THAT EIGHT OF THESE FREAKS, OR NINE?
WASTE
S.H.I.E.L.D. HELICARRIER, SIX MILES ABOVE NEW YORK CITY:
FIFTEEN, SERGEANT. FIFTEEN SUPER-CRIMINALS INSIDE SEVENTY-TWO HOURS.
BUT THE NUMBERS DON'T ADD UP. THERE'S JUST NO WAY CAPTAIN AMERICA COULD'VE TAKEN DOWN ALL THESE GUYS AT ONCE. IT'S PHYSICALLY IMPOSSIBLE.
MEANING?
SHIELD
OUR NIGHTMARE SCENARIO, UNIT FIVE.
I DON'T THINK HE'S ON HIS OWN ANYMORE.

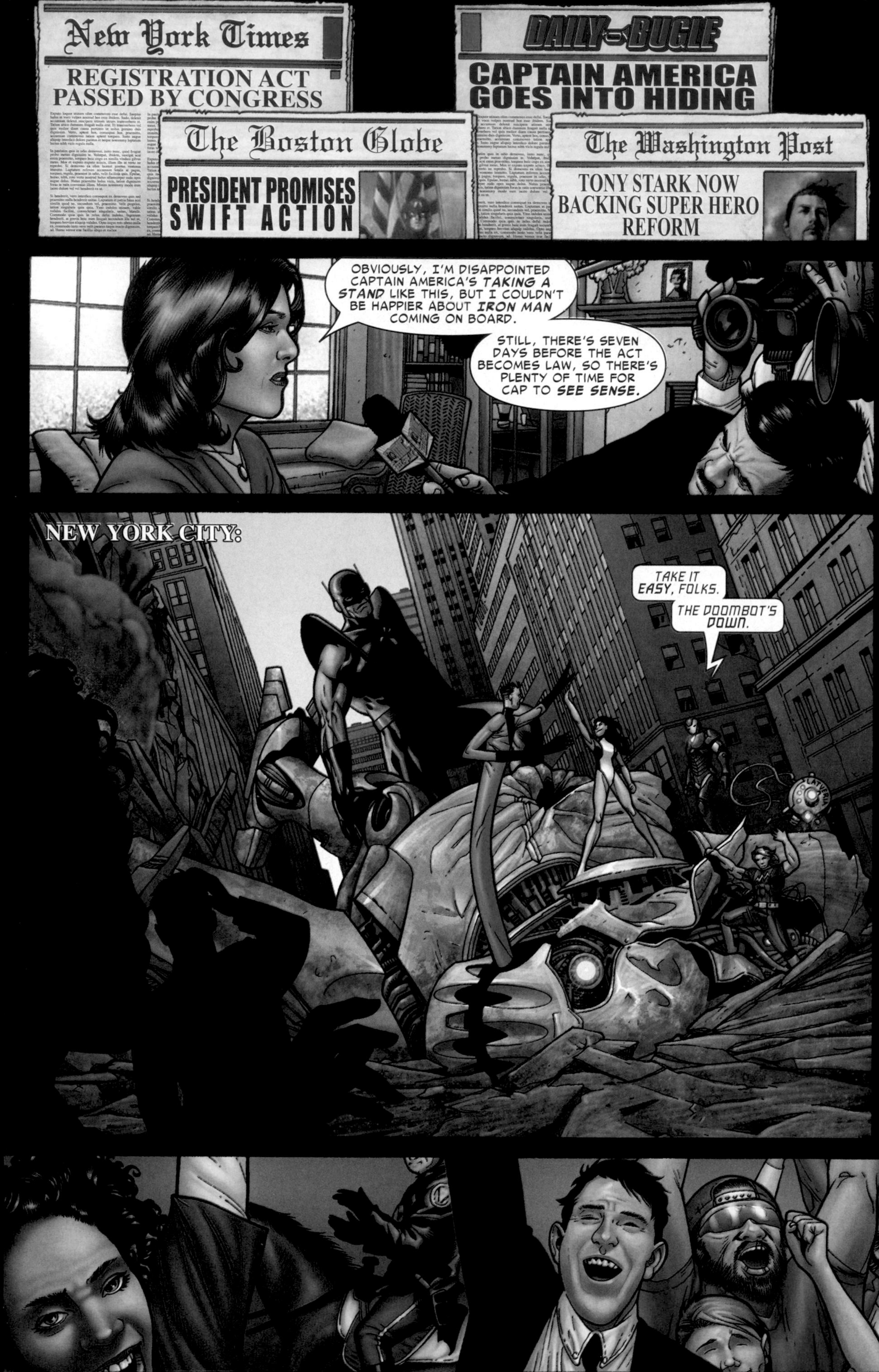
New York Times
REGISTRATION ACT PASSED BY CONGRESS
DAILY BUGLE
CAPTAIN AMERICA GOES INTO HIDING
The Boston Globe
PRESIDENT PROMISES SWIFT ACTION
The Washington Post
TONY STARK NOW BACKING SUPER HERO REFORM
OBVIOUSLY, I'M DISAPPOINTED CAPTAIN AMERICA'S TAKING A STAND LIKE THIS, BUT I COULDN'T BE HAPPIER ABOUT IRON MAN COMING ON BOARD.
STILL, THERE'S SEVEN DAYS BEFORE THE ACT BECOMES LAW, SO THERE'S PLENTY OF TIME FOR CAP TO SEE SENSE.
NEW YORK CITY:
TAKE IT EASY, FOLKS.
THE DOOMBOT'S DOWN.
LATVERIA

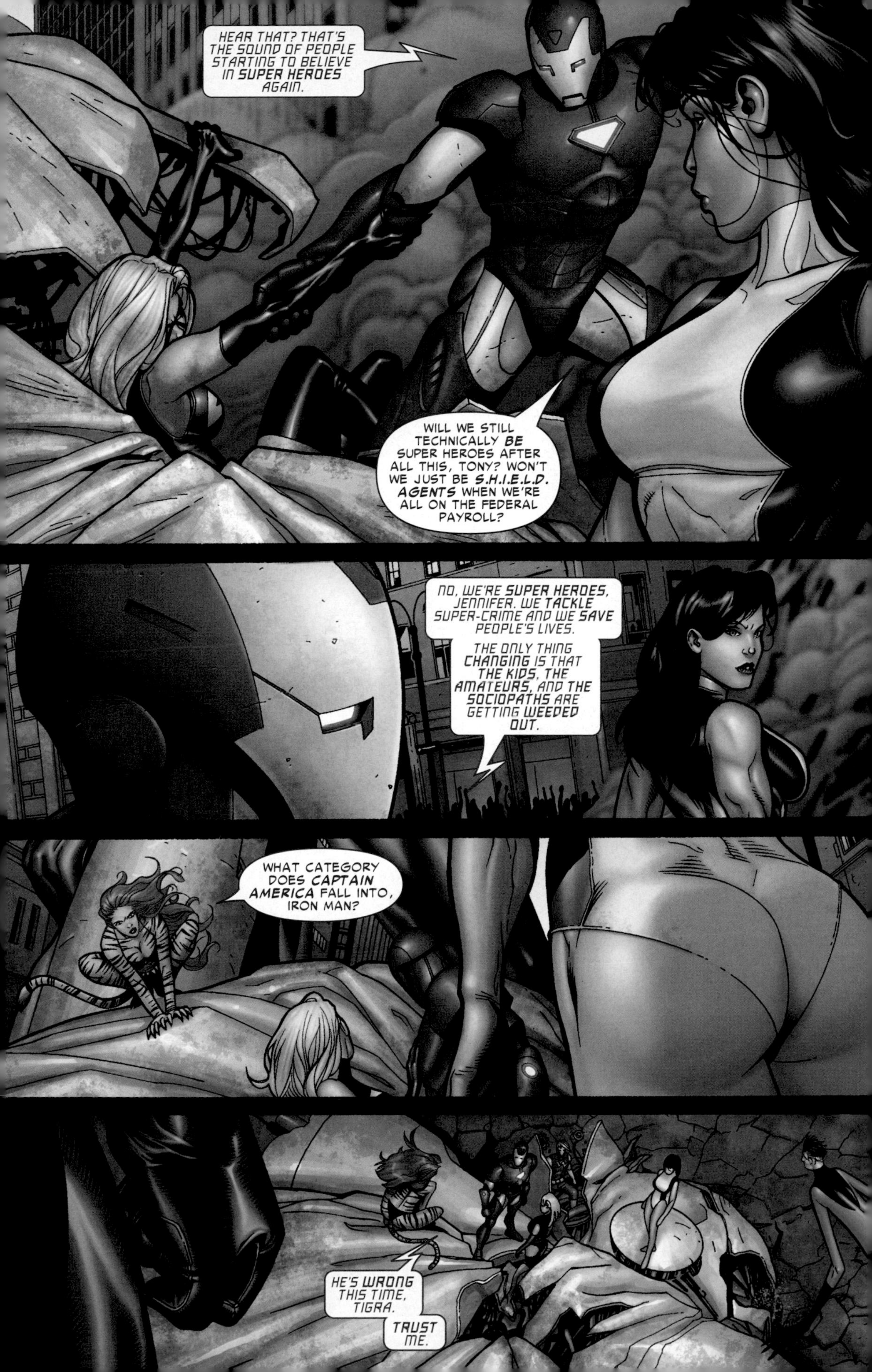
HEAR THAT? THAT'S THE SOUND OF PEOPLE STARTING TO BELIEVE IN SUPER HEROES AGAIN.
WILL WE STILL TECHNICALLY BE SUPER HEROES AFTER ALL THIS, TONY? WON'T WE JUST BE S.H.I.E.L.D. AGENTS WHEN WE'RE ALL ON THE FEDERAL PAYROLL?
NO, WE'RE SUPER HEROES, JENNIFER. WE TACKLE SUPER-CRIME AND WE SAVE PEOPLE'S LIVES.
THE ONLY THING CHANGING IS THAT THE KIDS, THE AMATEURS, AND THE SOCIOPATHS ARE GETTING WEEDED OUT.
WHAT CATEGORY DOES CAPTAIN AMERICA FALL INTO, IRON MAN?
HE'S WRONG THIS TIME, TIGRA.
TRUST ME.

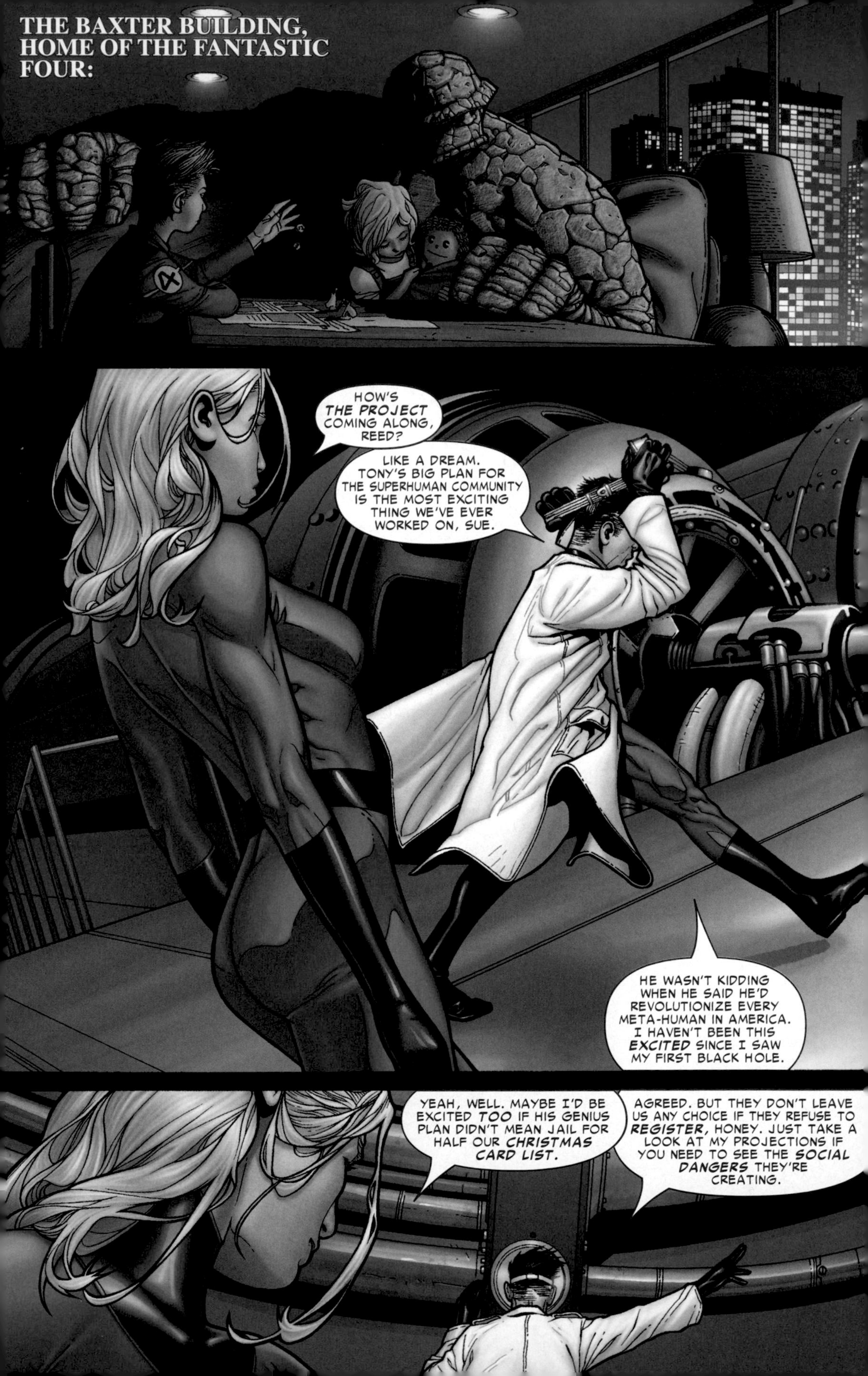
THE BAXTER BUILDING, HOME OF THE FANTASTIC FOUR:
HOW'S THE PROJECT COMING ALONG, REED?
LIKE A DREAM. TONY'S BIG PLAN FOR THE SUPERHUMAN COMMUNITY IS THE MOST EXCITING THING WE'VE EVER WORKED ON, SUE.
HE WASN'T KIDDING WHEN HE SAID HE'D REVOLUTIONIZE EVERY META-HUMAN IN AMERICA. I HAVEN'T BEEN THIS EXCITED SINCE I SAW MY FIRST BLACK HOLE.
YEAH, WELL. MAYBE I'D BE EXCITED TOO IF HIS GENIUS PLAN DIDN'T MEAN JAIL FOR HALF OUR CHRISTMAS CARD LIST.
AGREED. BUT THEY DON'T LEAVE US ANY CHOICE IF THEY REFUSE TO REGISTER, HONEY. JUST TAKE A LOOK AT MY PROJECTIONS IF YOU NEED TO SEE THE SOCIAL DANGERS THEY'RE CREATING.

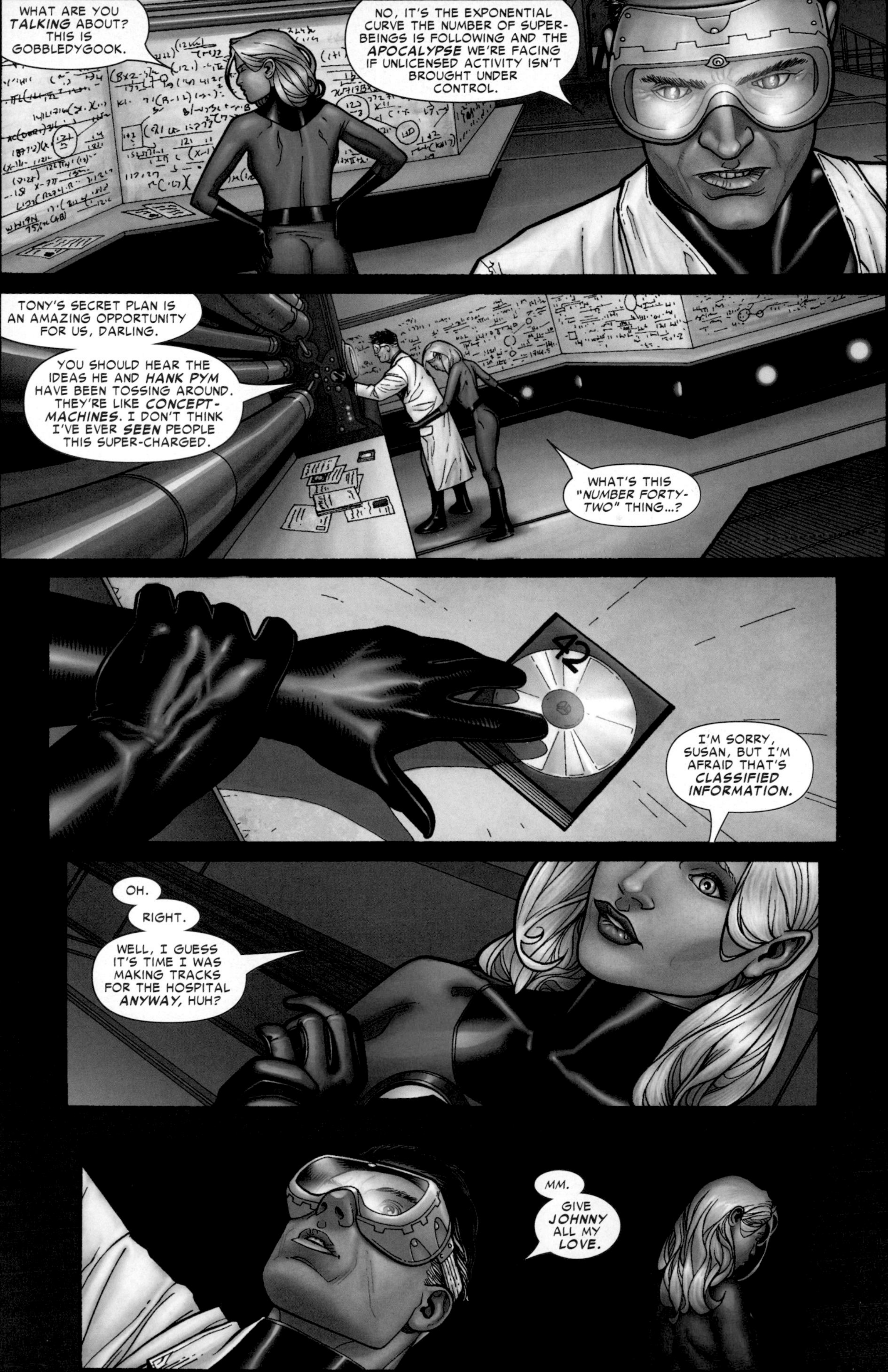
WHAT ARE YOU TALKING ABOUT? THIS IS GOBBLEDYGOOK.
NO, IT'S THE EXPONENTIAL CURVE THE NUMBER OF SUPER-BEINGS IS FOLLOWING AND THE APOCALYPSE WE'RE FACING IF UNLICENSED ACTIVITY ISN'T BROUGHT UNDER CONTROL.
TONY'S SECRET PLAN IS AN AMAZING OPPORTUNITY FOR US, DARLING.
YOU SHOULD HEAR THE IDEAS HE AND HANK PYM HAVE BEEN TOSSING AROUND. THEY'RE LIKE CONCEPT-MACHINES. I DON'T THINK I'VE EVER SEEN PEOPLE THIS SUPER-CHARGED.
WHAT'S THIS "NUMBER FORTY-TWO" THING...?
42
I'M SORRY, SUSAN, BUT I'M AFRAID THAT'S CLASSIFIED INFORMATION.
OH.
RIGHT.
WELL, I GUESS IT'S TIME I WAS MAKING TRACKS FOR THE HOSPITAL ANYWAY, HUH?
MM.
GIVE JOHNNY ALL MY LOVE.

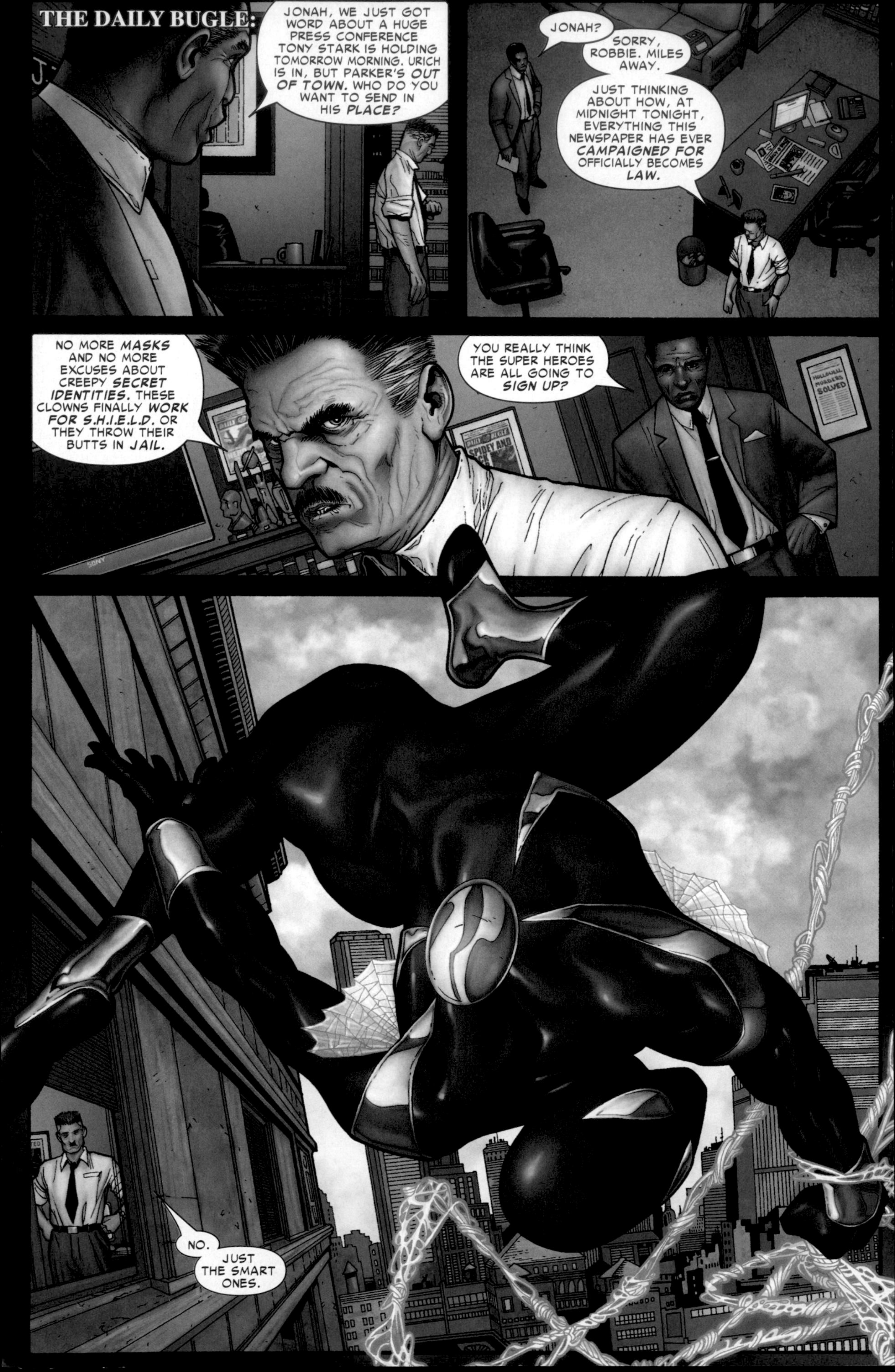
THE DAILY BUGLE:
JONAH, WE JUST GOT WORD ABOUT A HUGE PRESS CONFERENCE TONY STARK IS HOLDING TOMORROW MORNING. URICH IS IN, BUT PARKER'S OUT OF TOWN. WHO DO YOU WANT TO SEND IN HIS PLACE?
JONAH?
SORRY, ROBBIE. MILES AWAY.
JUST THINKING ABOUT HOW, AT MIDNIGHT TONIGHT, EVERYTHING THIS NEWSPAPER HAS EVER CAMPAIGNED FOR OFFICIALLY BECOMES LAW.
NO MORE MASKS AND NO MORE EXCUSES ABOUT CREEPY SECRET IDENTITIES. THESE CLOWNS FINALLY WORK FOR S.H.I.E.L.D. OR THEY THROW THEIR BUTTS IN JAIL.
YOU REALLY THINK THE SUPER HEROES ARE ALL GOING TO SIGN UP?
NO.
JUST THE SMART ONES.

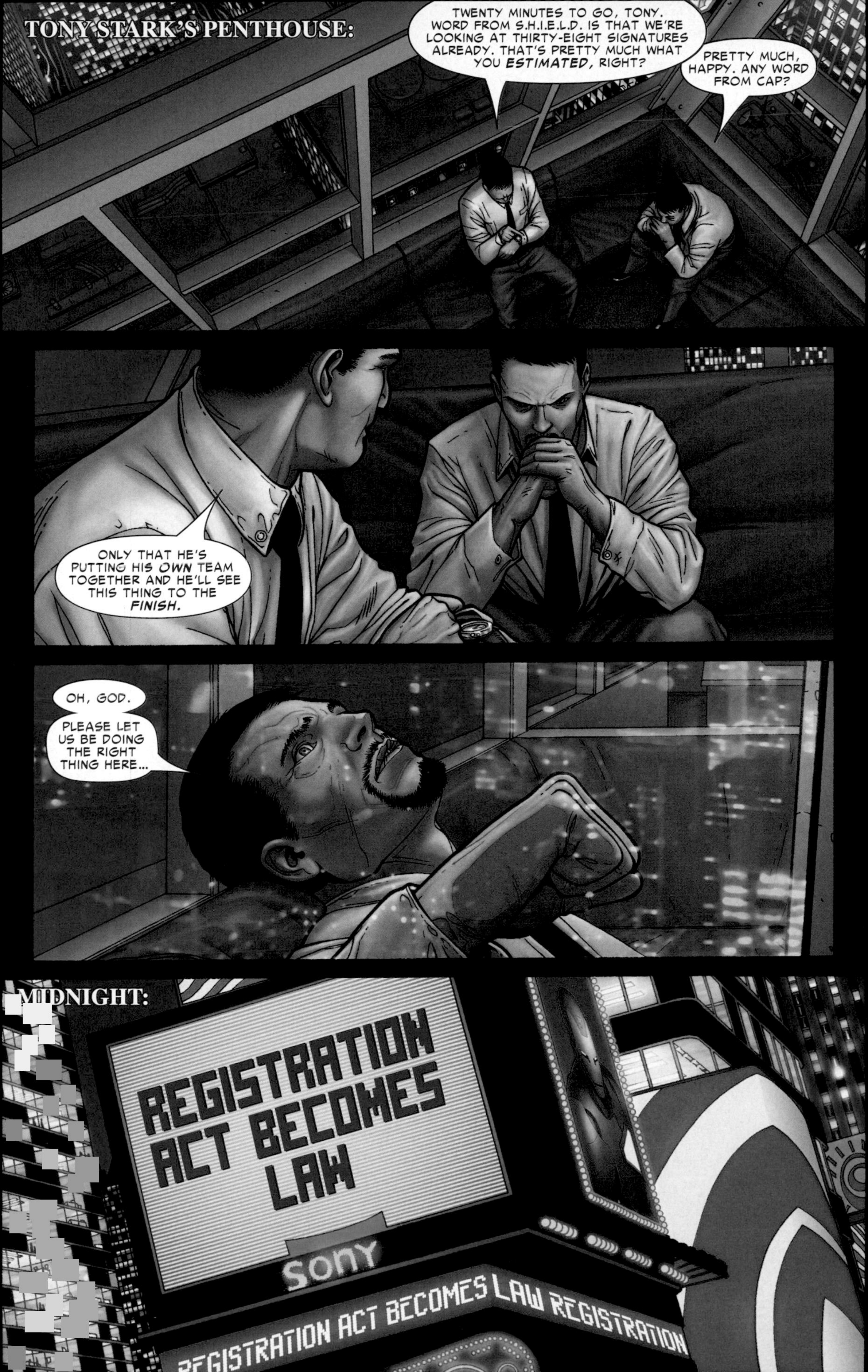
TONY STARK'S PENTHOUSE:
TWENTY MINUTES TO GO, TONY. WORD FROM S.H.I.E.L.D. IS THAT WE'RE LOOKING AT THIRTY-EIGHT SIGNATURES ALREADY. THAT'S PRETTY MUCH WHAT YOU ESTIMATED, RIGHT?
PRETTY MUCH, HAPPY. ANY WORD FROM CAP?
ONLY THAT HE'S PUTTING HIS OWN TEAM TOGETHER AND HE'LL SEE THIS THING TO THE FINISH.
OH, GOD.
PLEASE LET US BE DOING THE RIGHT THING HERE...
MIDNIGHT:
REGISTRATION ACT BECOMES LAW
SONY
REGISTRATION ACT BECOMES LAW REGISTRATION

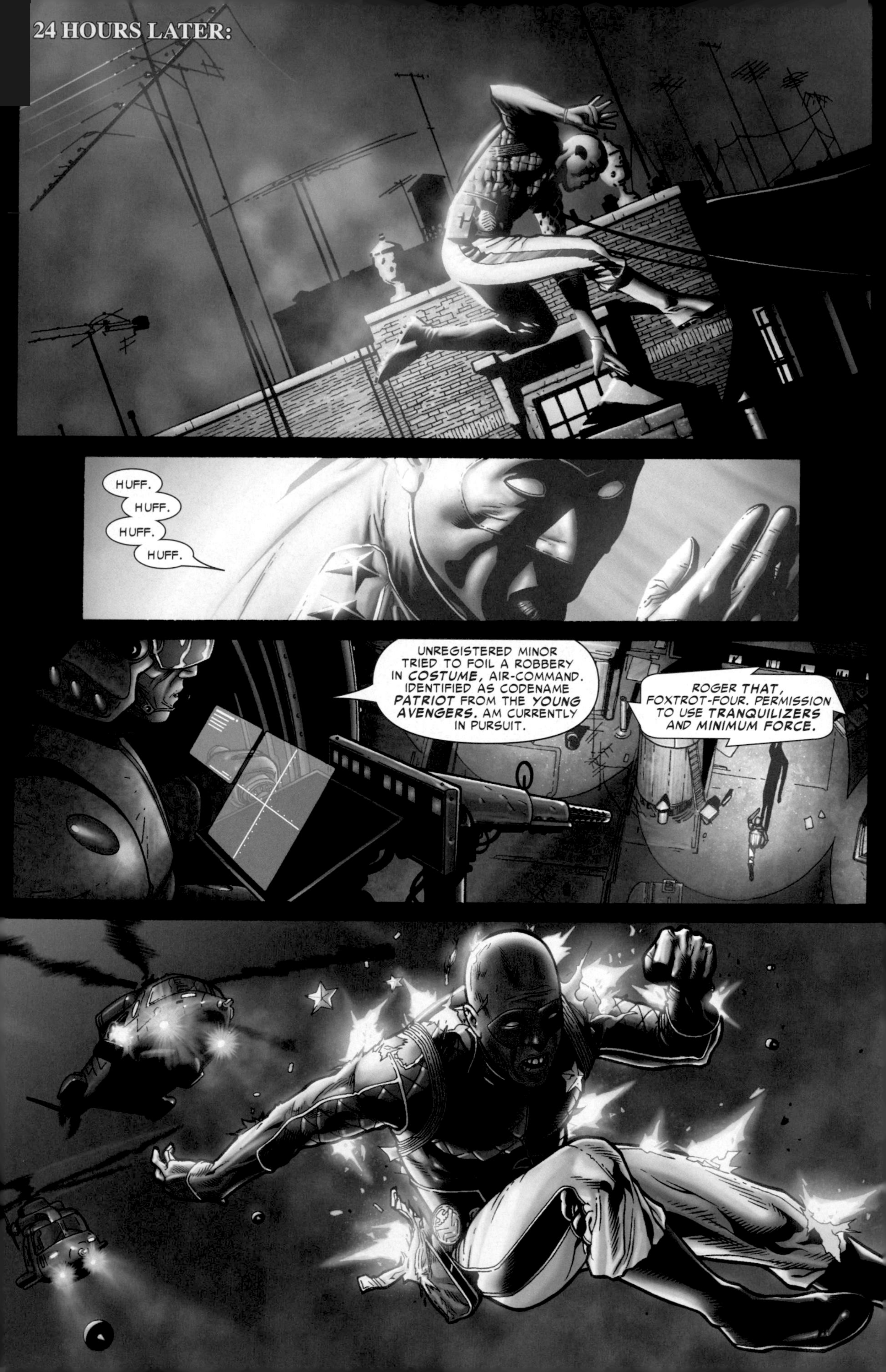
24 HOURS LATER:
HUFF.
HUFF.
HUFF.
HUFF.
UNREGISTERED MINOR TRIED TO FOIL A ROBBERY IN COSTUME, AIR-COMMAND. IDENTIFIED AS CODENAME PATRIOT FROM THE YOUNG AVENGERS. AM CURRENTLY IN PURSUIT.
ROGER THAT, FOXTROT-FOUR. PERMISSION TO USE TRANQUILIZERS AND MINIMUM FORCE.

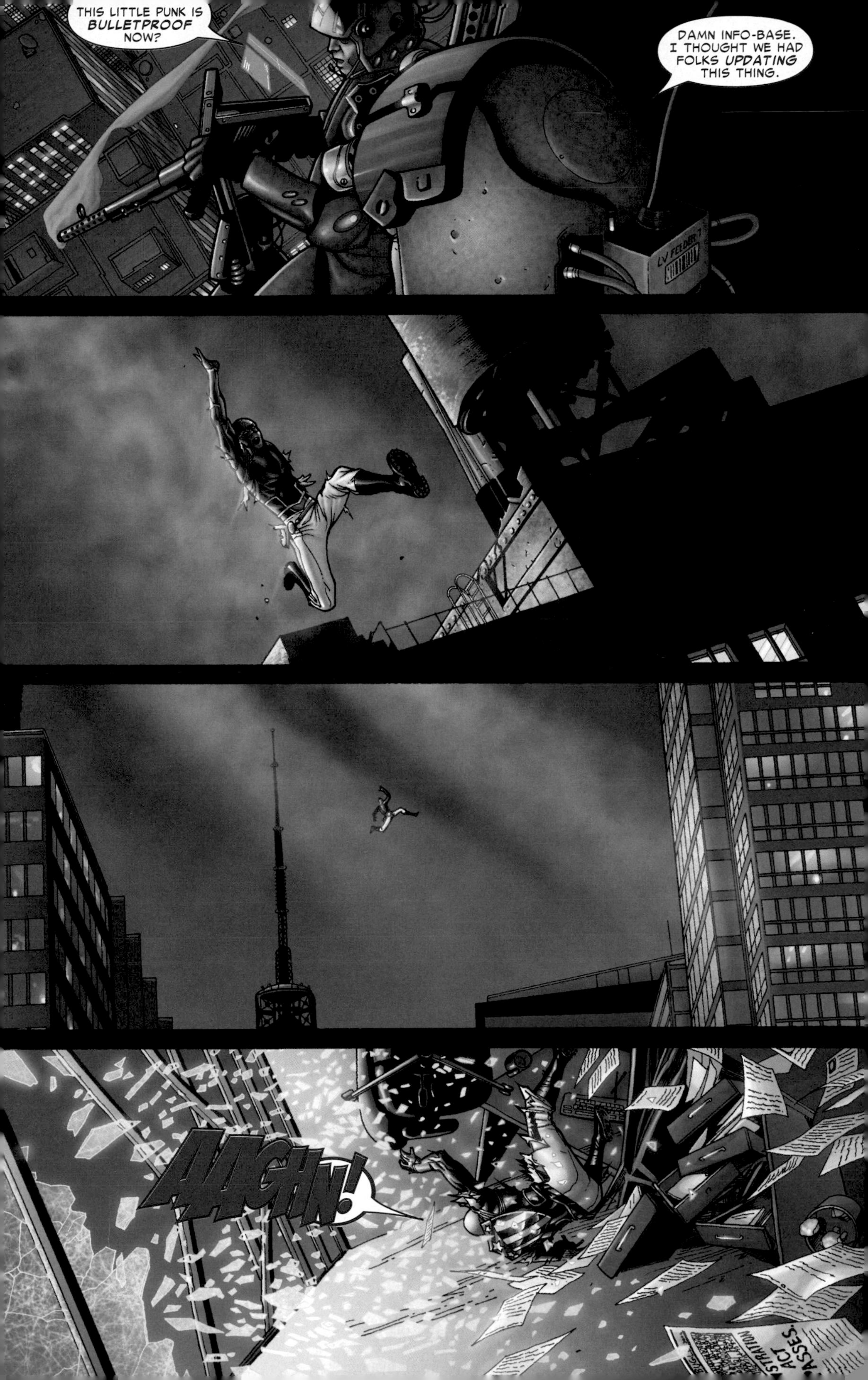
THIS LITTLE PUNK IS BULLETPROOF NOW?
DAMN INFO-BASE. I THOUGHT WE HAD FOLKS UPDATING THIS THING.
AAAGHN!

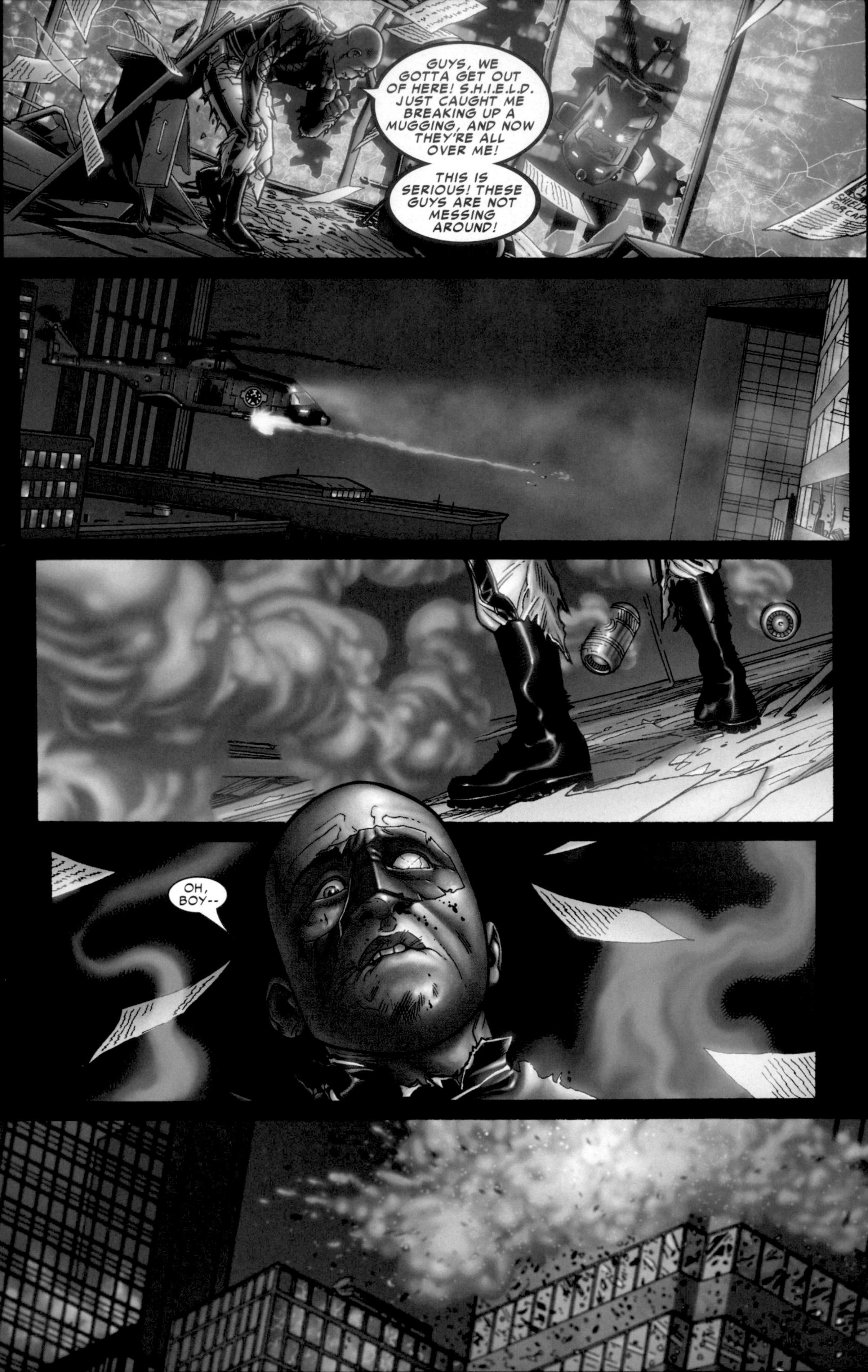
GUYS, WE GOTTA GET OUT OF HERE! S.H.I.E.L.D. JUST CAUGHT ME BREAKING UP A MUGGING, AND NOW THEY'RE ALL OVER ME!
THIS IS SERIOUS! THESE GUYS ARE NOT MESSING AROUND!
OH, BOY--

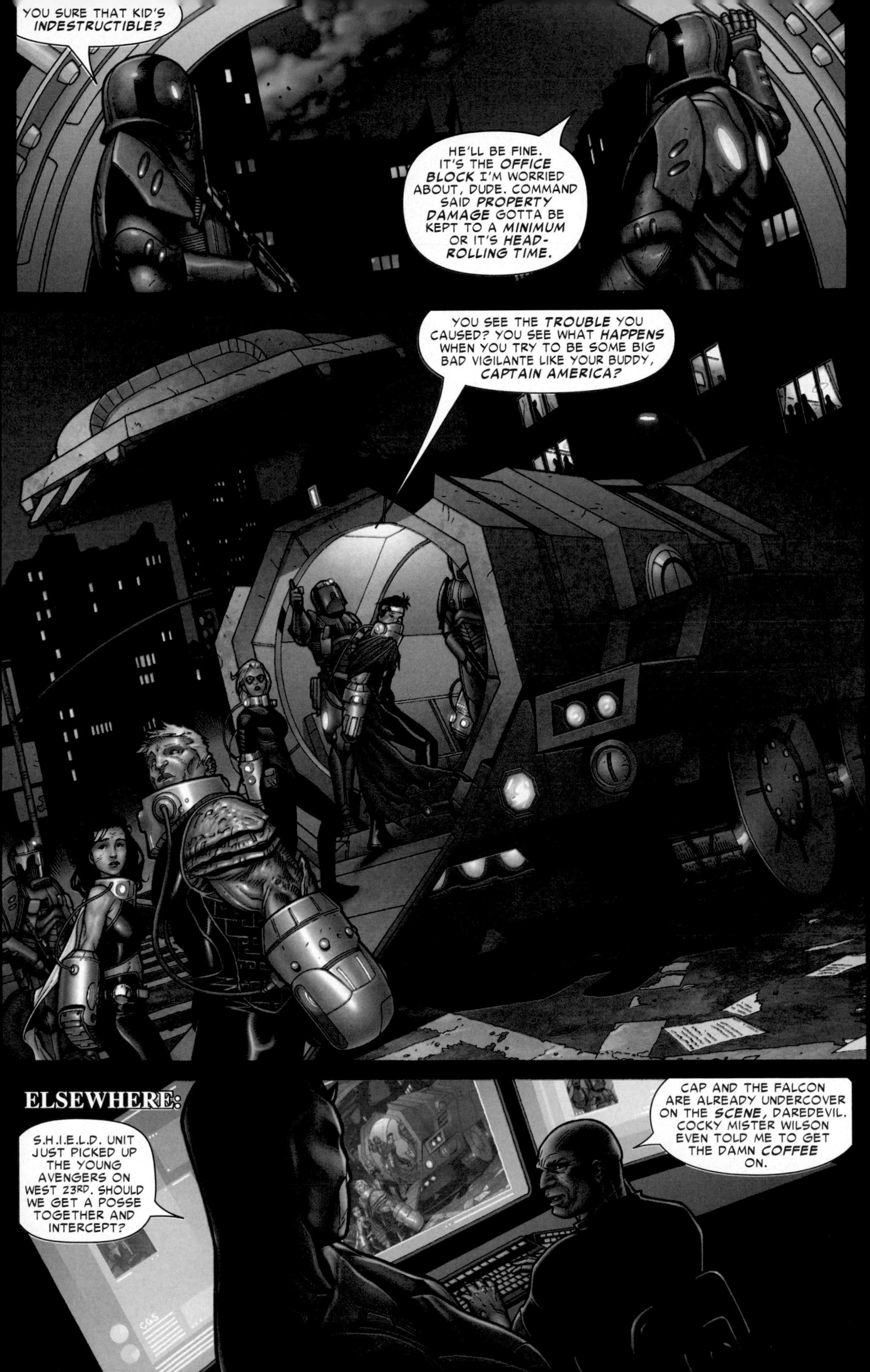

YOU SURE THAT KID'S INDESTRUCTIBLE?
HE'LL BE FINE. IT'S THE OFFICE BLOCK I'M WORRIED ABOUT, DUDE. COMMAND SAID PROPERTY DAMAGE GOTTA BE KEPT TO A MINIMUM OR IT'S HEAD-ROLLING TIME.
YOU SEE THE TROUBLE YOU CAUSED? YOU SEE WHAT HAPPENS WHEN YOU TRY TO BE SOME BIG BAD VIGILANTE LIKE YOUR BUDDY, CAPTAIN AMERICA?
ELSEWHERE:
S.H.I.E.L.D. UNIT JUST PICKED UP THE YOUNG AVENGERS ON WEST 23RD. SHOULD WE GET A POSSE TOGETHER AND INTERCEPT?
CAP AND THE FALCON ARE ALREADY UNDERCOVER ON THE SCENE, DAREDEVIL. COCKY MISTER WILSON EVEN TOLD ME TO GET THE DAMN COFFEE ON.

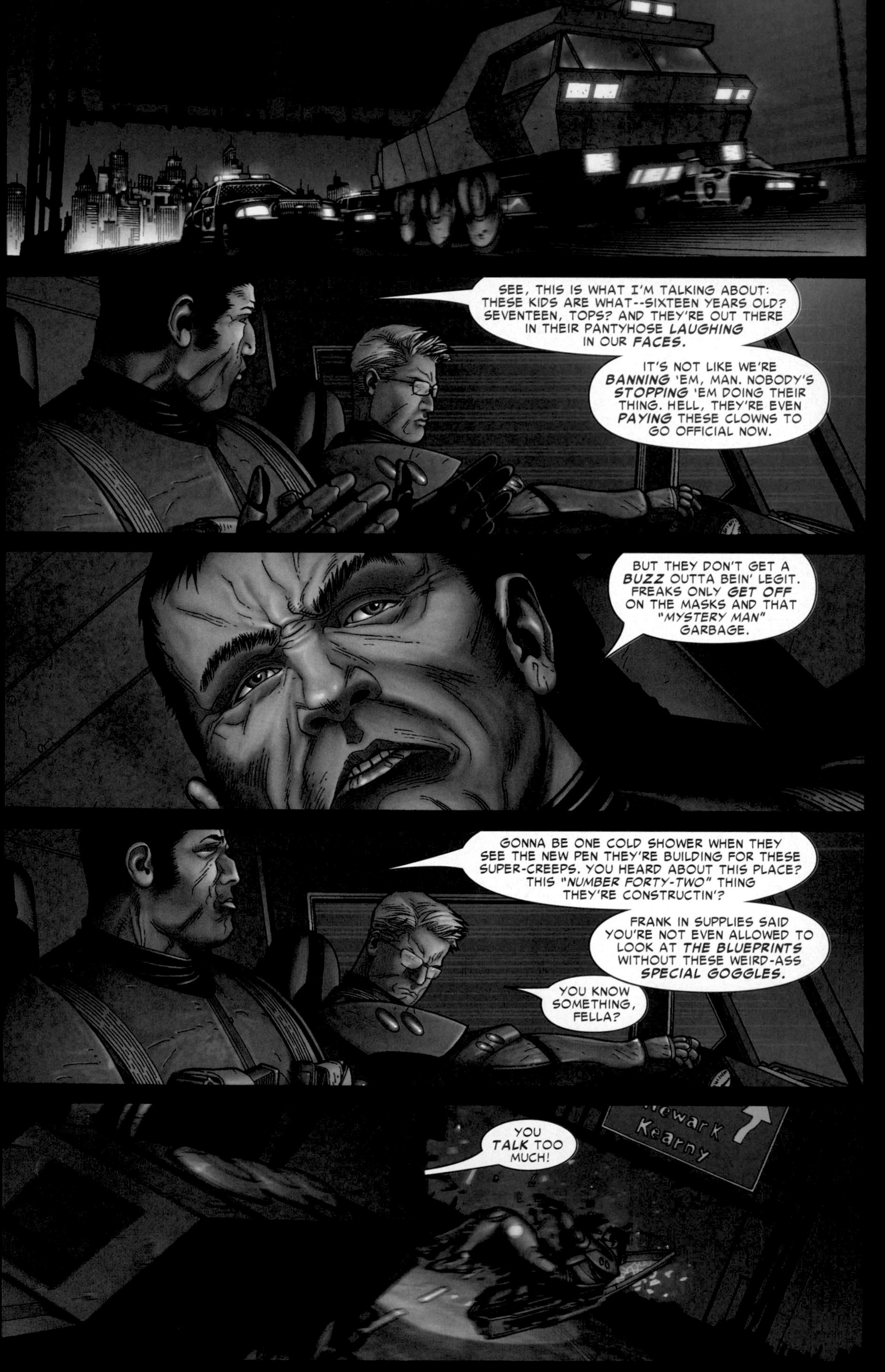

SEE, THIS IS WHAT I'M TALKING ABOUT: THESE KIDS ARE WHAT--SIXTEEN YEARS OLD? SEVENTEEN, TOPS? AND THEY'RE OUT THERE IN THEIR PANTYHOSE *LAUGHING* IN OUR *FACES*.
IT'S NOT LIKE WE'RE *BANNING* 'EM, MAN. NOBODY'S *STOPPING* 'EM DOING THEIR THING. HELL, THEY'RE EVEN *PAYING* THESE CLOWNS TO GO OFFICIAL NOW.
BUT THEY DON'T GET A *BUZZ* OUTTA BEIN' LEGIT. FREAKS ONLY *GET OFF* ON THE MASKS AND THAT "*MYSTERY MAN*" GARBAGE.
GONNA BE ONE COLD SHOWER WHEN THEY SEE THE NEW PEN THEY'RE BUILDING FOR THESE SUPER-CREEPS. YOU HEARD ABOUT THIS PLACE? THIS "*NUMBER FORTY-TWO*" THING THEY'RE CONSTRUCTIN'?
FRANK IN SUPPLIES SAID YOU'RE NOT EVEN ALLOWED TO LOOK AT *THE BLUEPRINTS* WITHOUT THESE WEIRD-ASS *SPECIAL GOGGLES*.
YOU KNOW SOMETHING, FELLA?
YOU *TALK* TOO MUCH!
Kearny

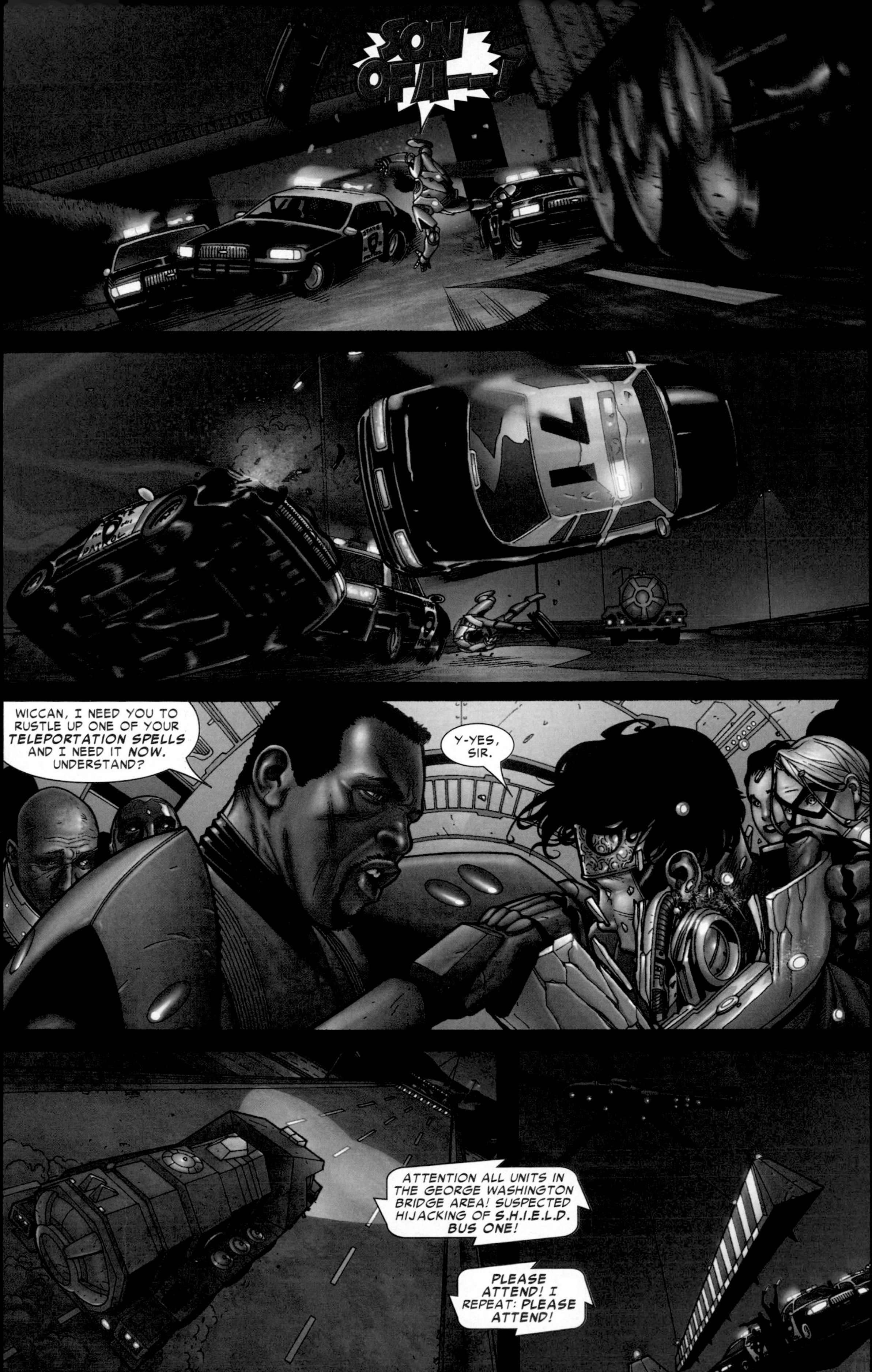
SON OF A--!
WICCAN, I NEED YOU TO RUSTLE UP ONE OF YOUR *TELEPORTATION SPELLS* AND I NEED IT *NOW.* UNDERSTAND?
Y-YES, SIR.
ATTENTION ALL UNITS IN THE GEORGE WASHINGTON BRIDGE AREA! SUSPECTED HIJACKING OF S.H.I.E.L.D. BUS ONE!
PLEASE ATTEND! I REPEAT: PLEASE ATTEND!

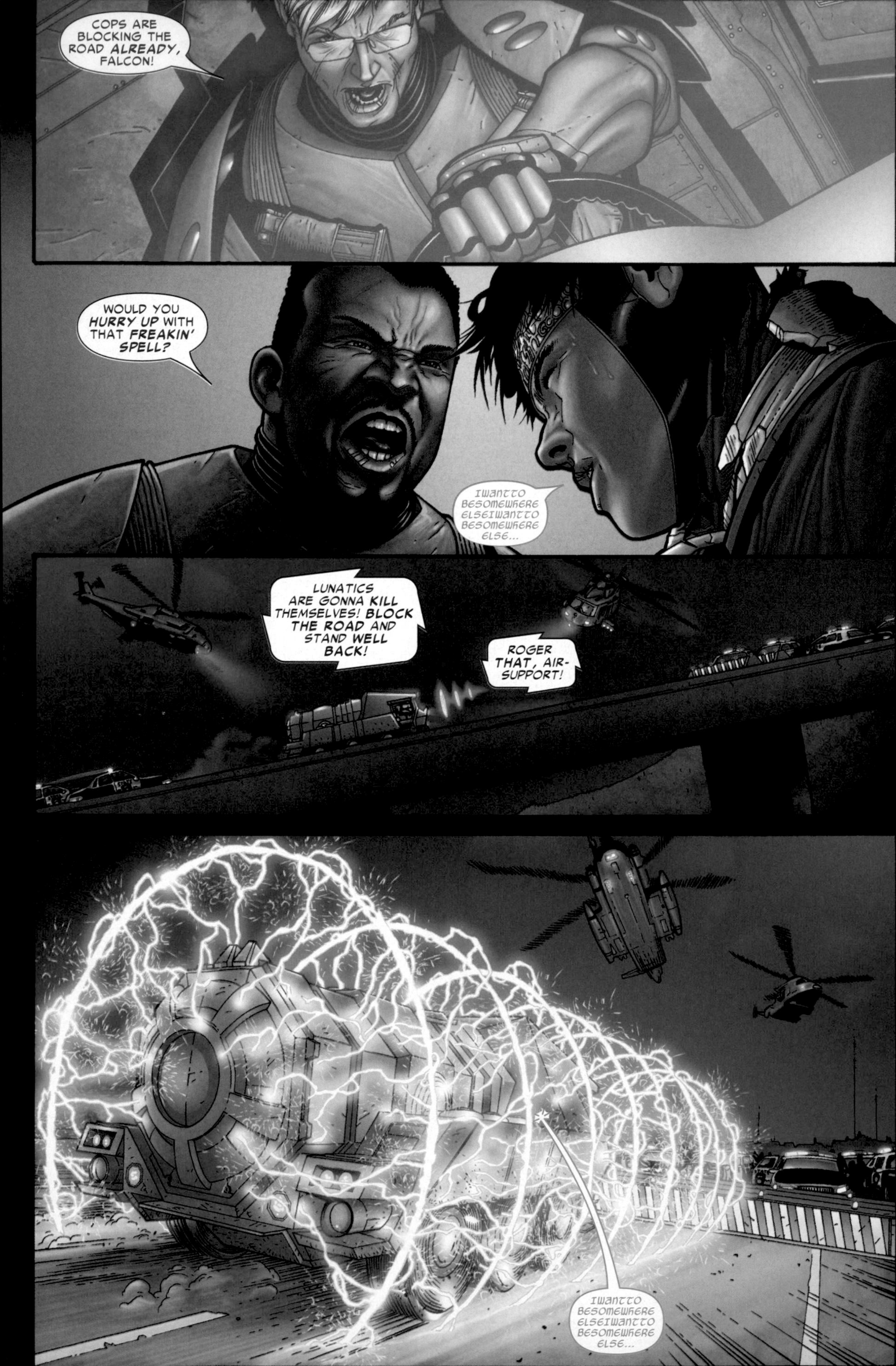

COPS ARE BLOCKING THE ROAD ALREADY, FALCON!
WOULD YOU HURRY UP WITH THAT FREAKIN' SPELL?
IWANTTO BESOMEWHERE ELSEIWANTTO BESOMEWHERE ELSE...
LUNATICS ARE GONNA KILL THEMSELVES! BLOCK THE ROAD AND STAND WELL BACK!
ROGER THAT, AIR-SUPPORT!
IWANTTO BESOMEWHERE ELSEIWANTTO BESOMEWHERE ELSE...

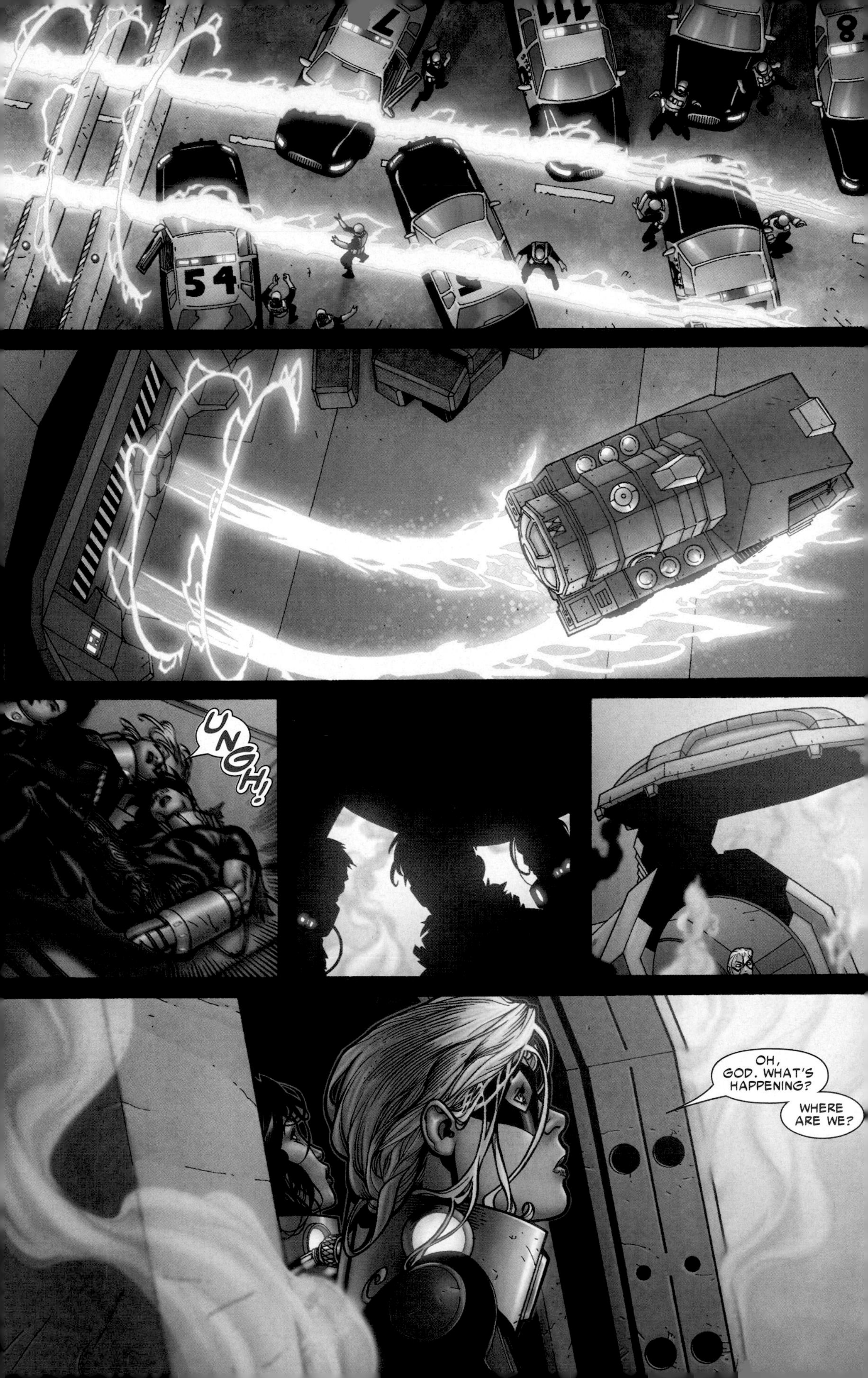
UNGH!
OH, GOD. WHAT'S HAPPENING?
WHERE ARE WE?

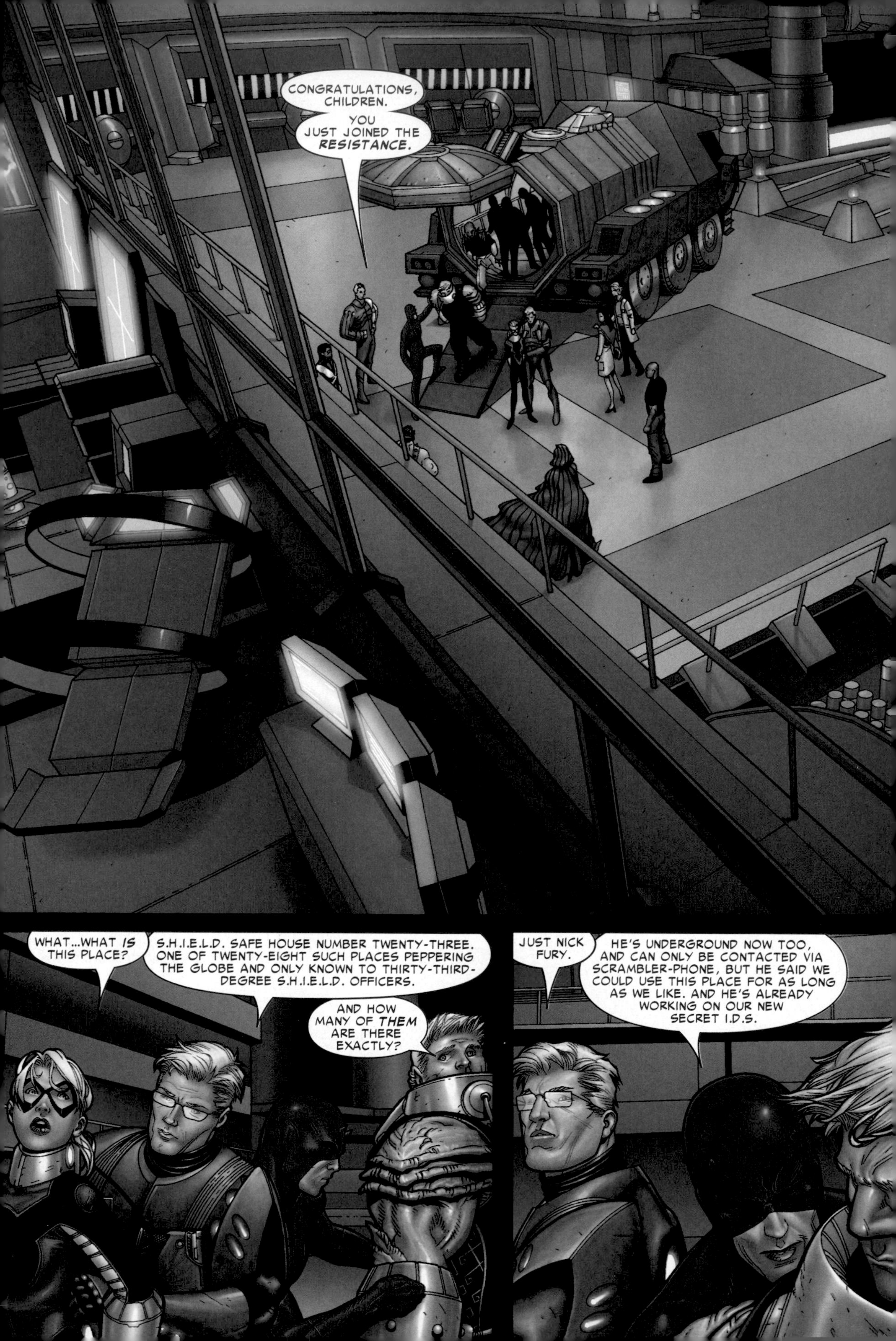
CONGRATULATIONS, CHILDREN.
YOU JUST JOINED THE *RESISTANCE*.
WHAT...WHAT *IS* THIS PLACE?
S.H.I.E.L.D. SAFE HOUSE NUMBER TWENTY-THREE. ONE OF TWENTY-EIGHT SUCH PLACES PEPPERING THE GLOBE AND ONLY KNOWN TO THIRTY-THIRD-DEGREE S.H.I.E.L.D. OFFICERS.
AND HOW MANY OF *THEM* ARE THERE EXACTLY?
JUST NICK FURY.
HE'S UNDERGROUND NOW TOO, AND CAN ONLY BE CONTACTED VIA SCRAMBLER-PHONE, BUT HE SAID WE COULD USE THIS PLACE FOR AS LONG AS WE LIKE. AND HE'S ALREADY WORKING ON OUR NEW SECRET I.D.S.

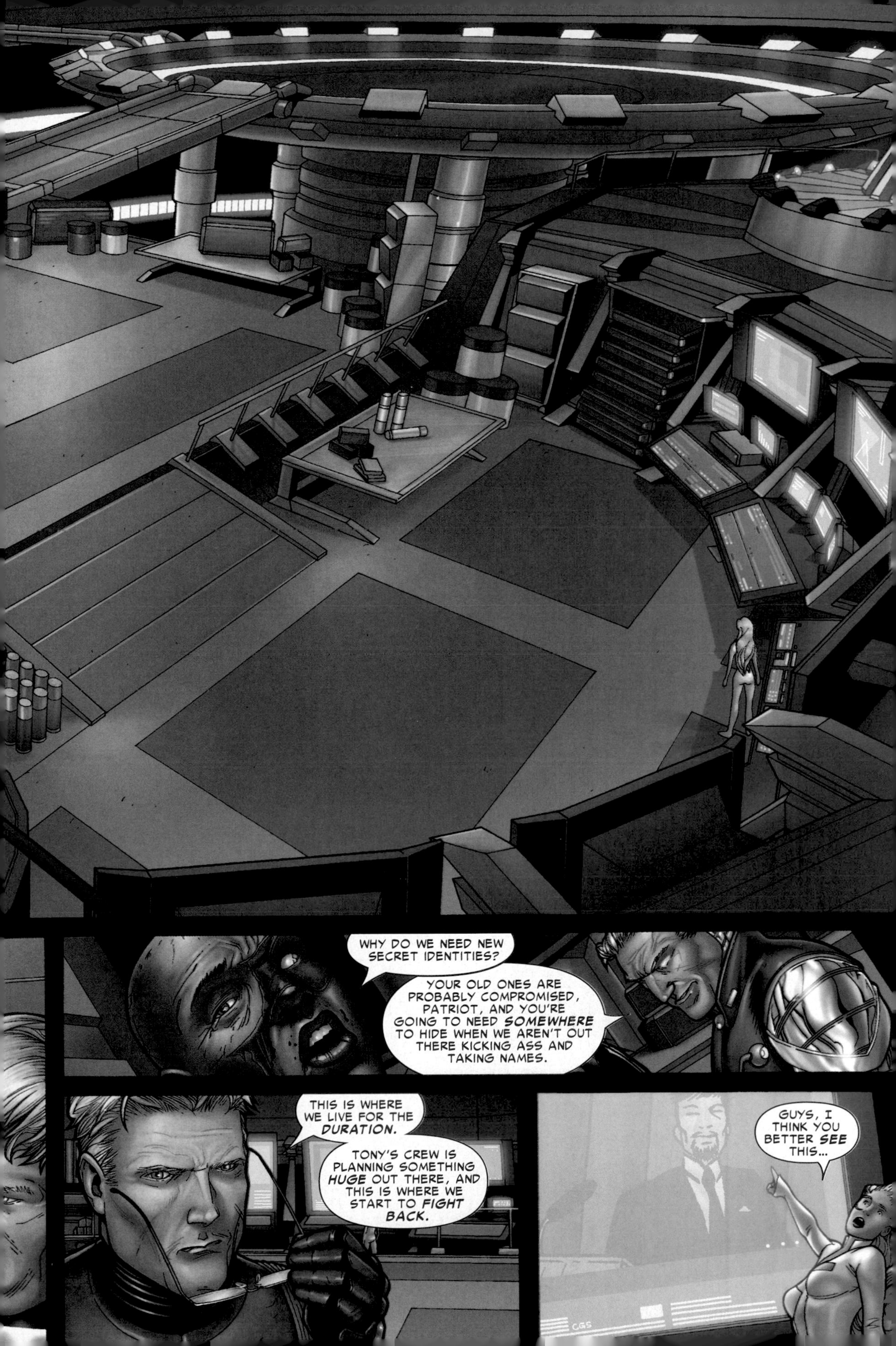
WHY DO WE NEED NEW SECRET IDENTITIES?
YOUR OLD ONES ARE PROBABLY COMPROMISED, PATRIOT, AND YOU'RE GOING TO NEED SOMEWHERE TO HIDE WHEN WE AREN'T OUT THERE KICKING ASS AND TAKING NAMES.
THIS IS WHERE WE LIVE FOR THE DURATION.
TONY'S CREW IS PLANNING SOMETHING HUGE OUT THERE, AND THIS IS WHERE WE START TO FIGHT BACK.
GUYS, I THINK YOU BETTER SEE THIS...

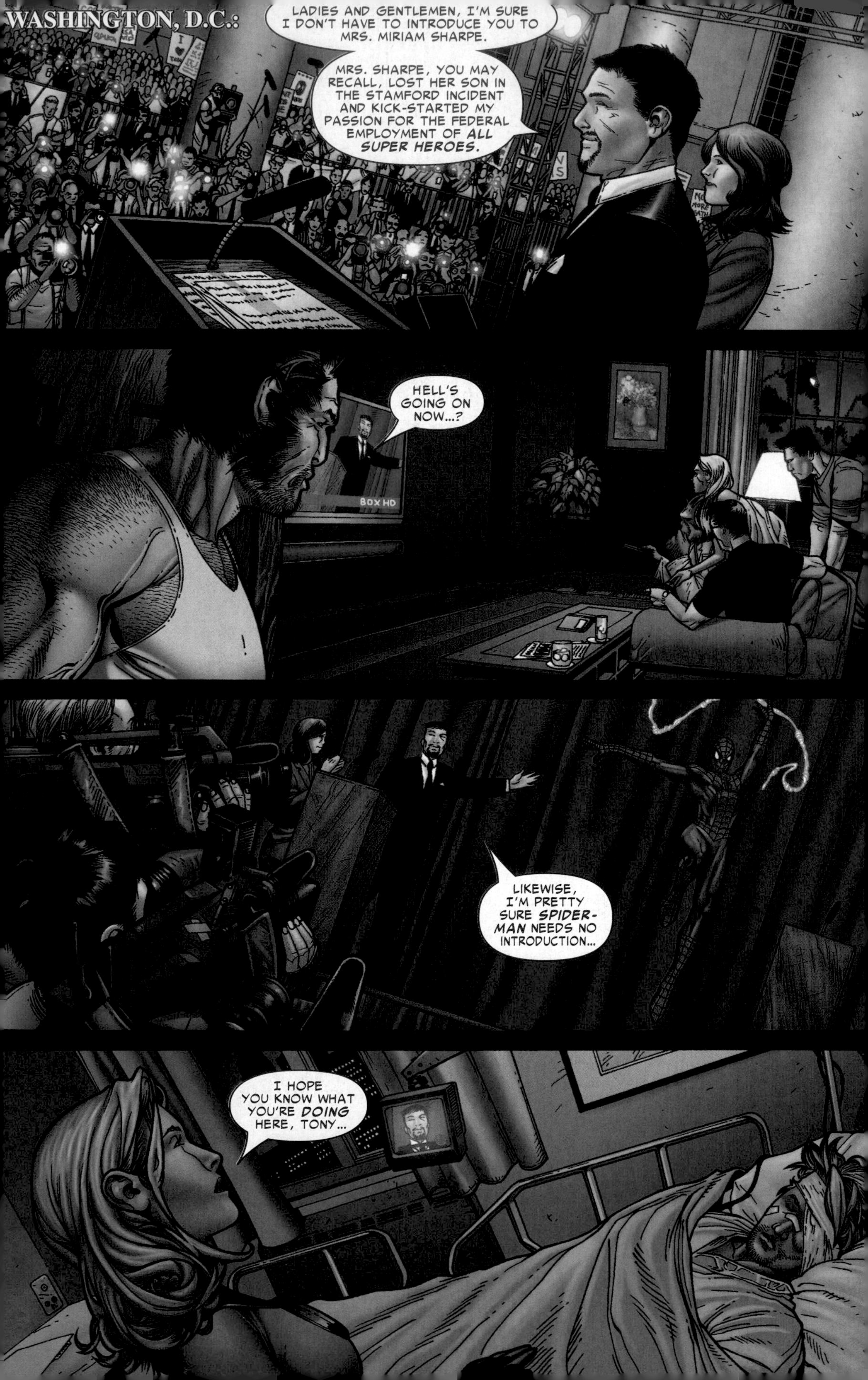
WASHINGTON, D.C.:
LADIES AND GENTLEMEN, I'M SURE I DON'T HAVE TO INTRODUCE YOU TO MRS. MIRIAM SHARPE.
MRS. SHARPE, YOU MAY RECALL, LOST HER SON IN THE STAMFORD INCIDENT AND KICK-STARTED MY PASSION FOR THE FEDERAL EMPLOYMENT OF *ALL SUPER HEROES.*
HELL'S GOING ON NOW...?
BOX HD
LIKEWISE, I'M PRETTY SURE *SPIDER-MAN* NEEDS NO INTRODUCTION...
I HOPE YOU KNOW WHAT YOU'RE *DOING* HERE, TONY...

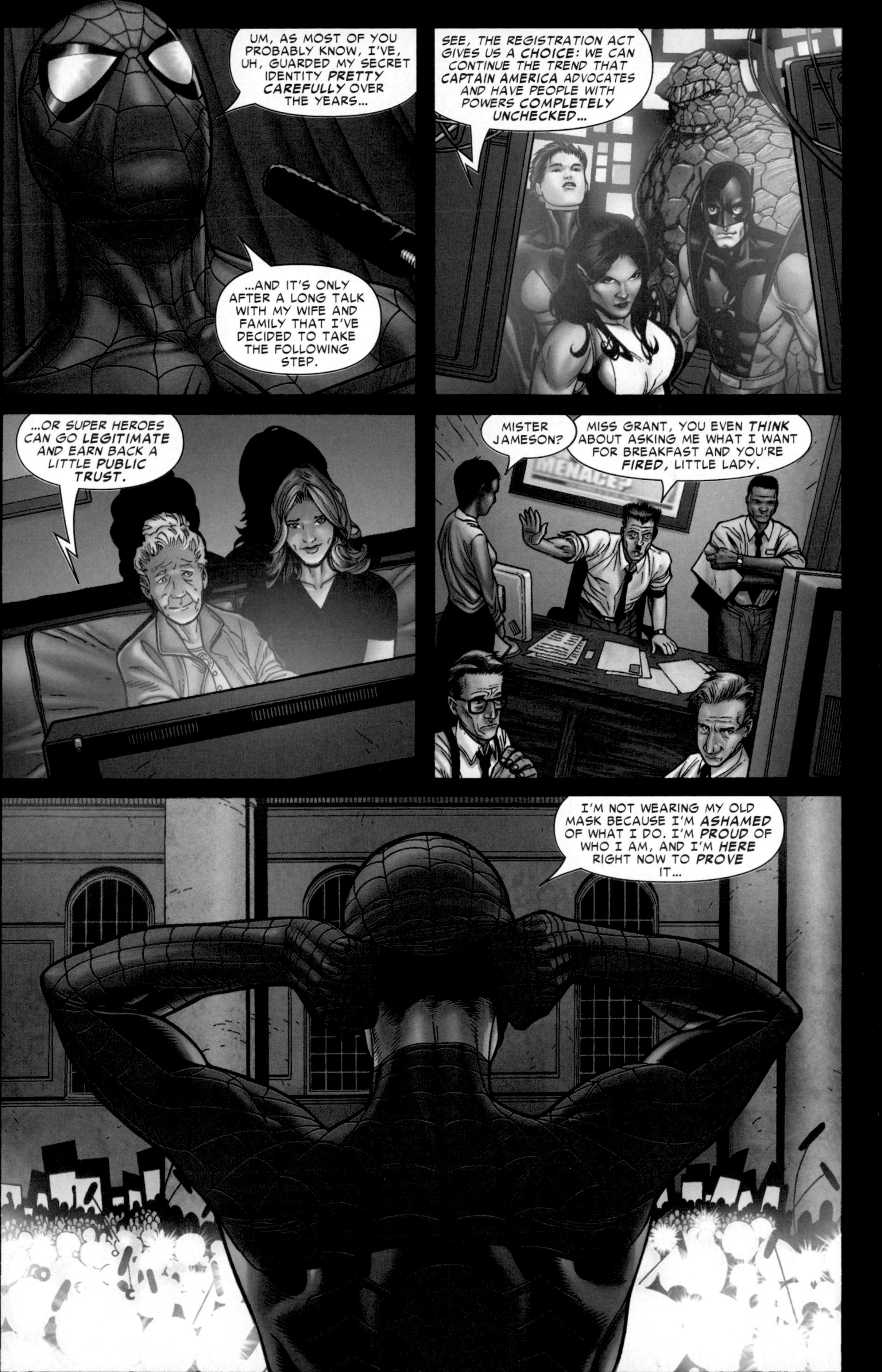
UM, AS MOST OF YOU PROBABLY KNOW, I'VE, UH, GUARDED MY SECRET IDENTITY PRETTY CAREFULLY OVER THE YEARS...
...AND IT'S ONLY AFTER A LONG TALK WITH MY WIFE AND FAMILY THAT I'VE DECIDED TO TAKE THE FOLLOWING STEP.
SEE, THE REGISTRATION ACT GIVES US A CHOICE: WE CAN CONTINUE THE TREND THAT CAPTAIN AMERICA ADVOCATES AND HAVE PEOPLE WITH POWERS COMPLETELY UNCHECKED...
...OR SUPER HEROES CAN GO LEGITIMATE AND EARN BACK A LITTLE PUBLIC TRUST.
MISTER JAMESON?
MISS GRANT, YOU EVEN THINK ABOUT ASKING ME WHAT I WANT FOR BREAKFAST AND YOU'RE FIRED, LITTLE LADY.
I'M NOT WEARING MY OLD MASK BECAUSE I'M ASHAMED OF WHAT I DO. I'M PROUD OF WHO I AM, AND I'M HERE RIGHT NOW TO PROVE IT...

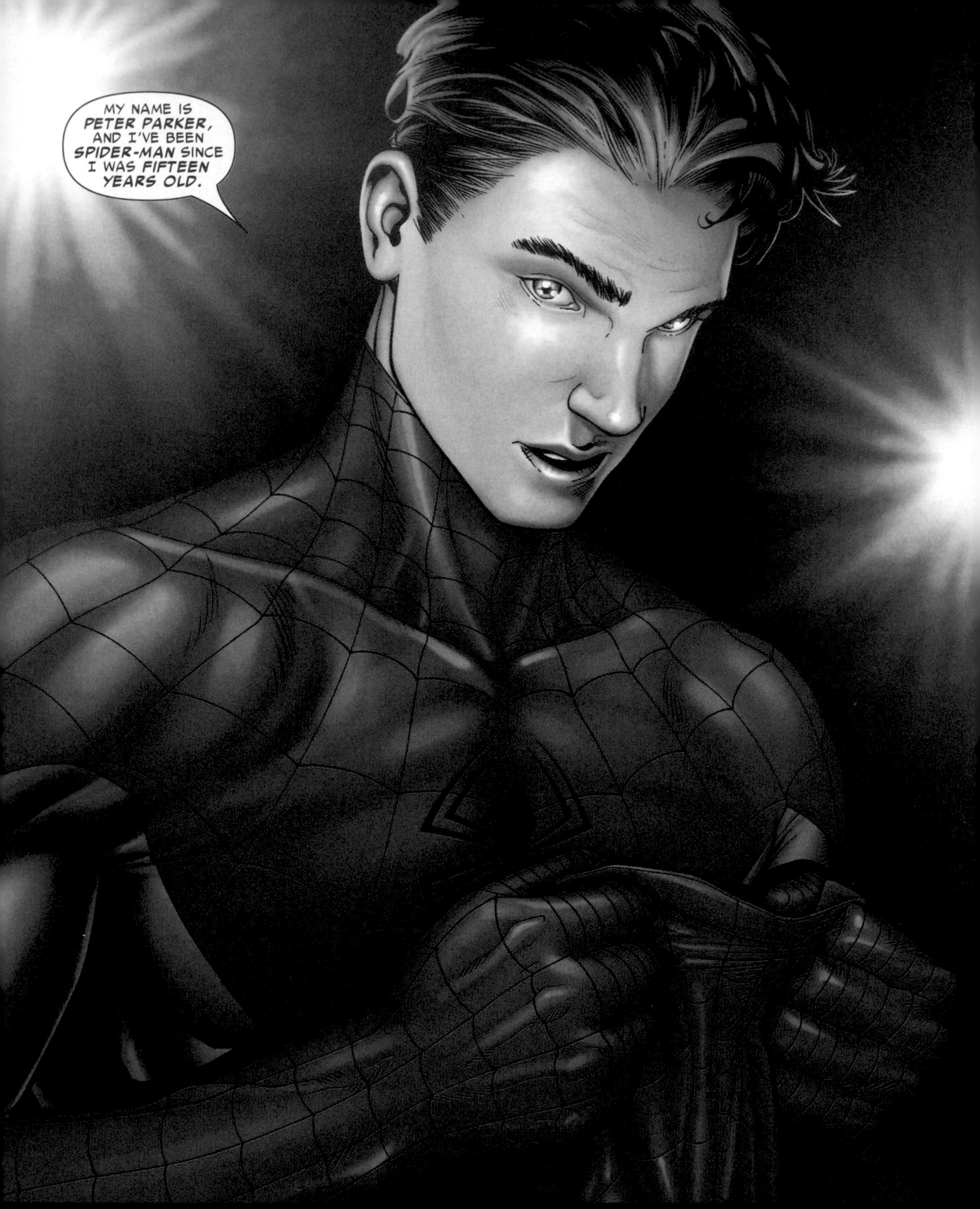
MY NAME IS PETER PARKER, AND I'VE BEEN SPIDER-MAN SINCE I WAS FIFTEEN YEARS OLD.

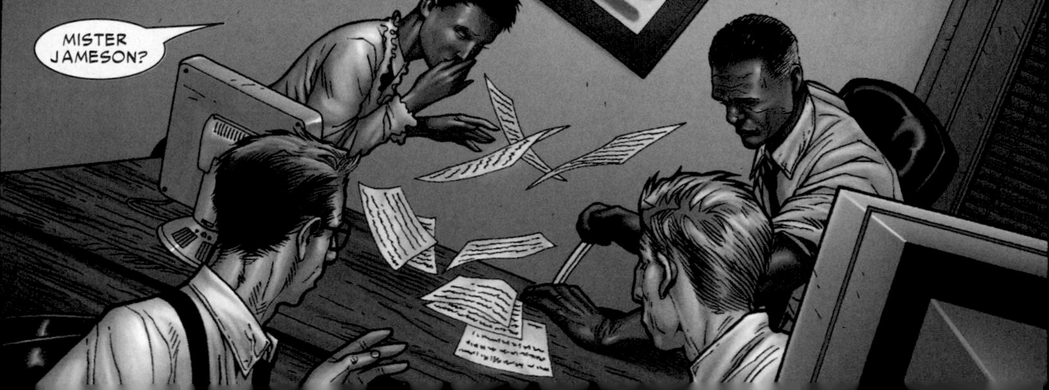
MISTER JAMESON?

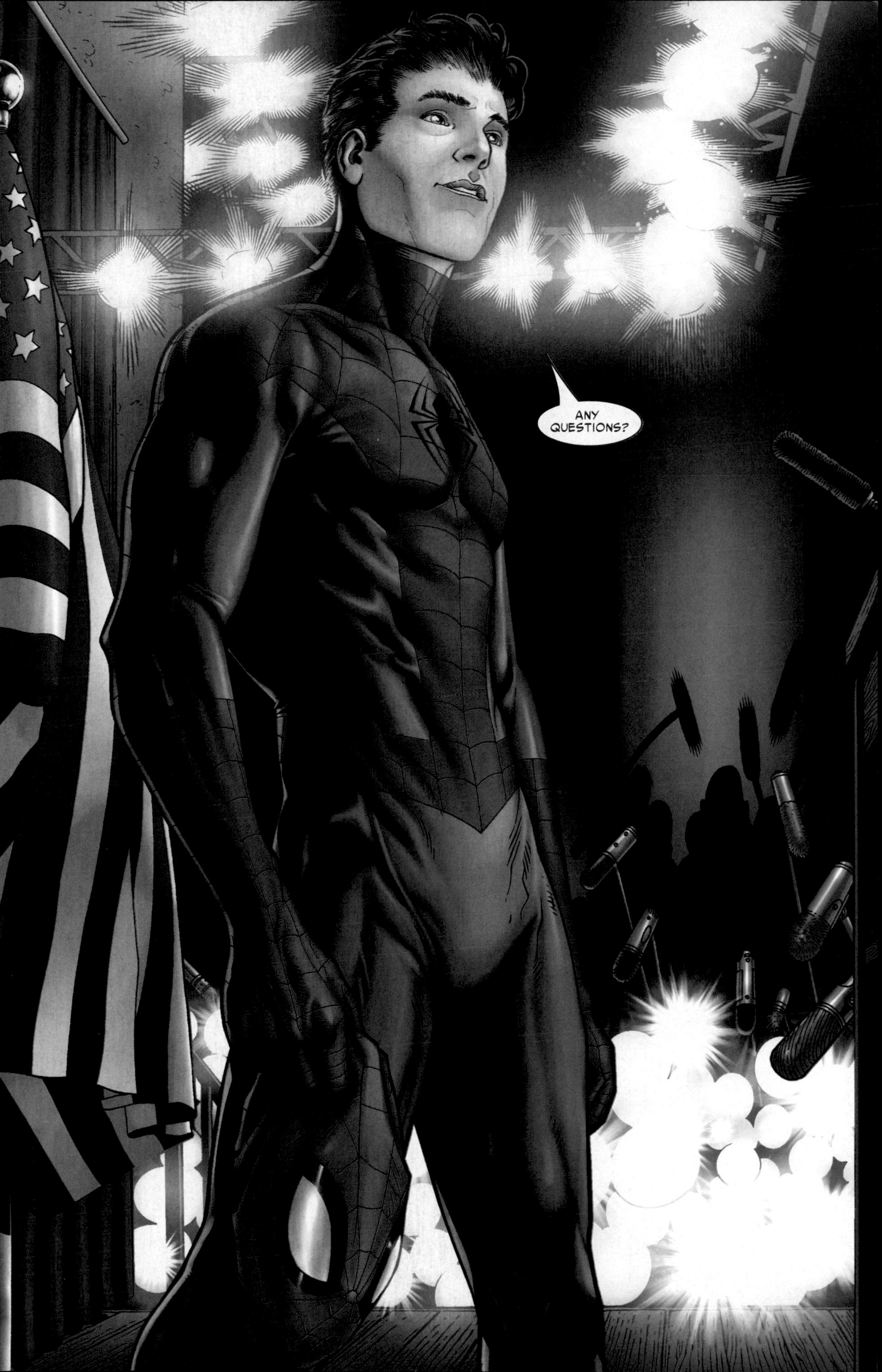
ANY QUESTIONS?

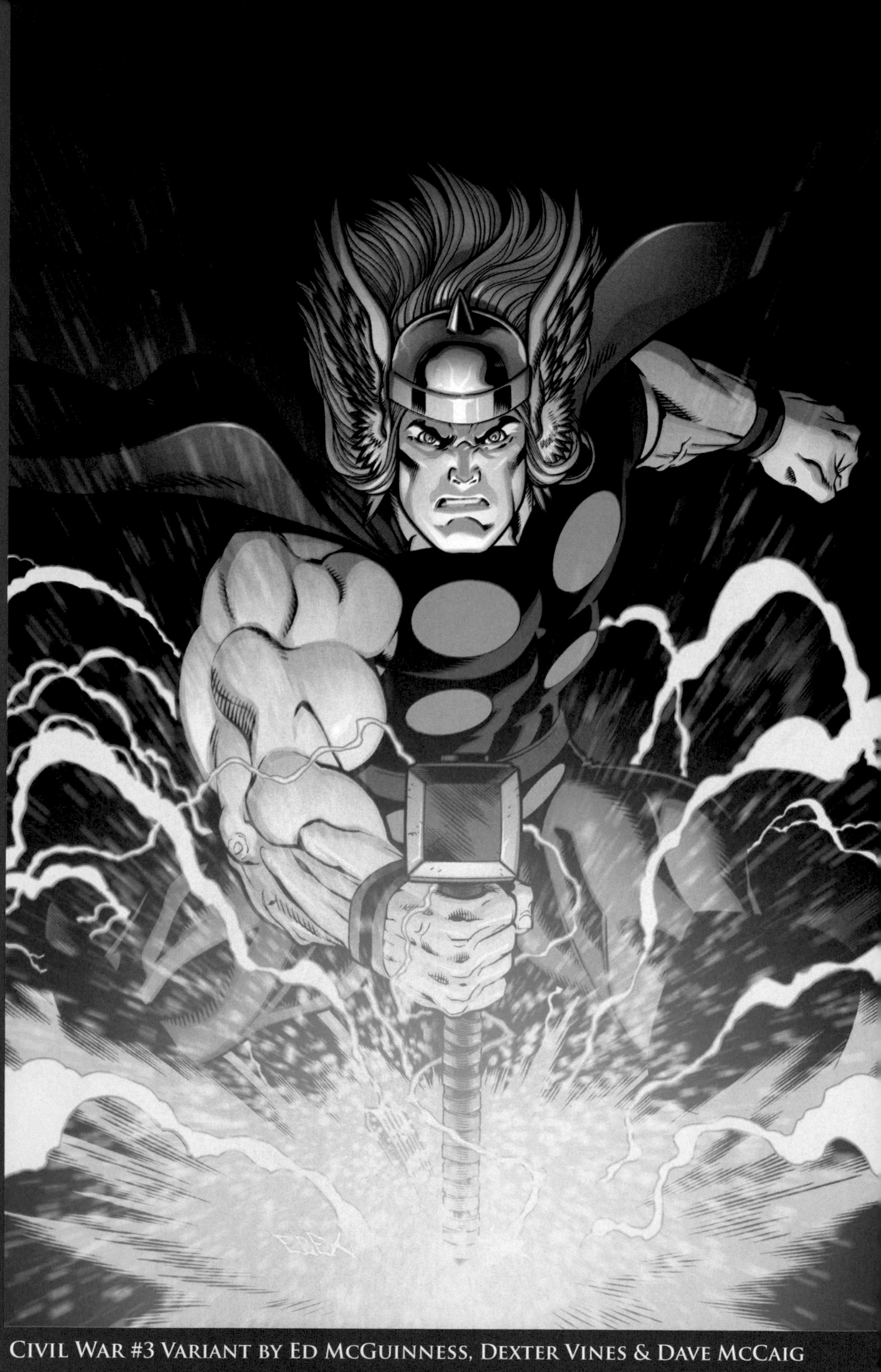

CIVIL WAR #3 VARIANT BY ED MCGUINNESS, DEXTER VINES & DAVE MCCAIG

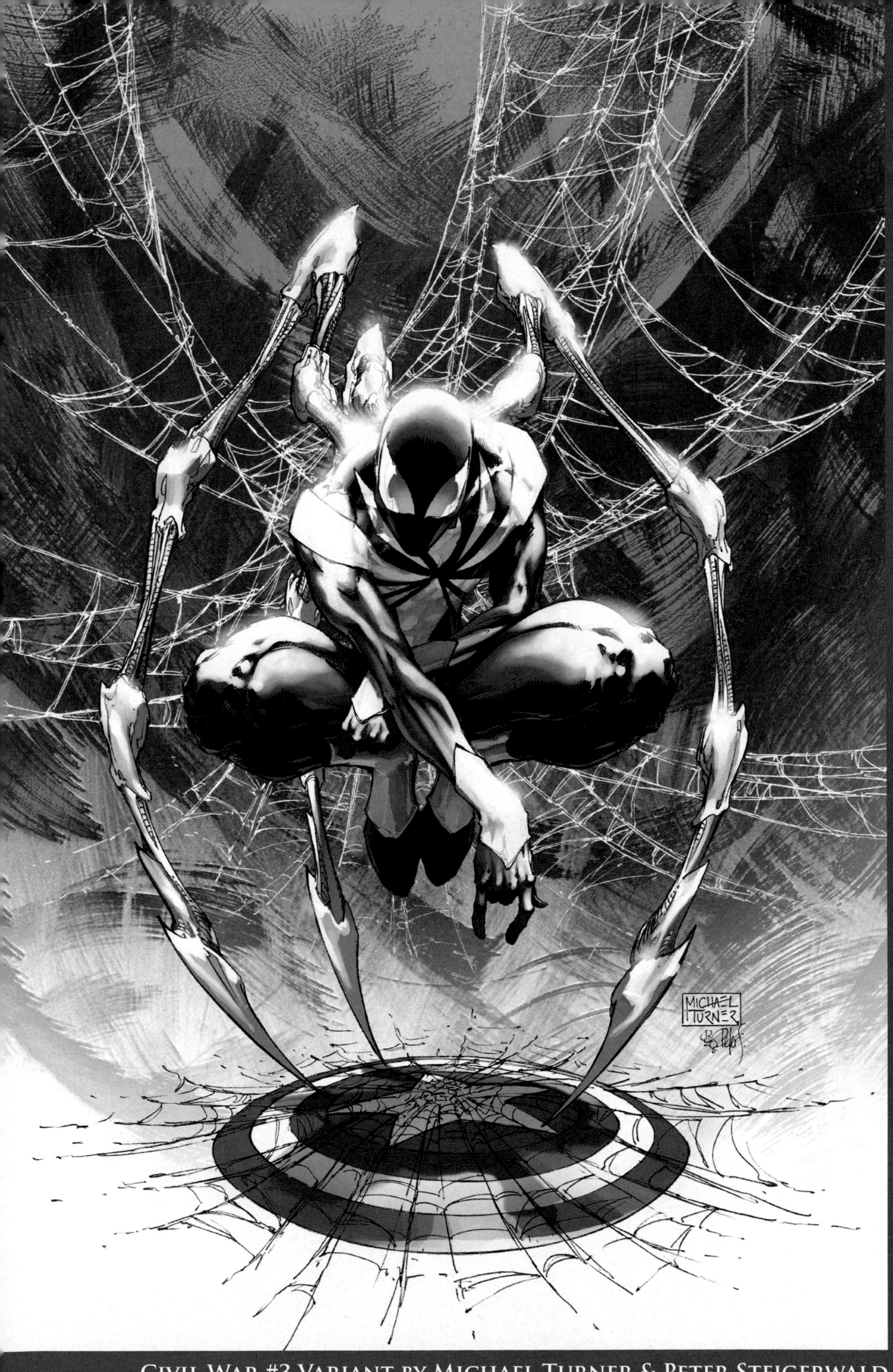
MICHAEL TURNER

Civil War #3 Variant by Michael Turner & Peter Steigerwald

MCNIVEN MO!

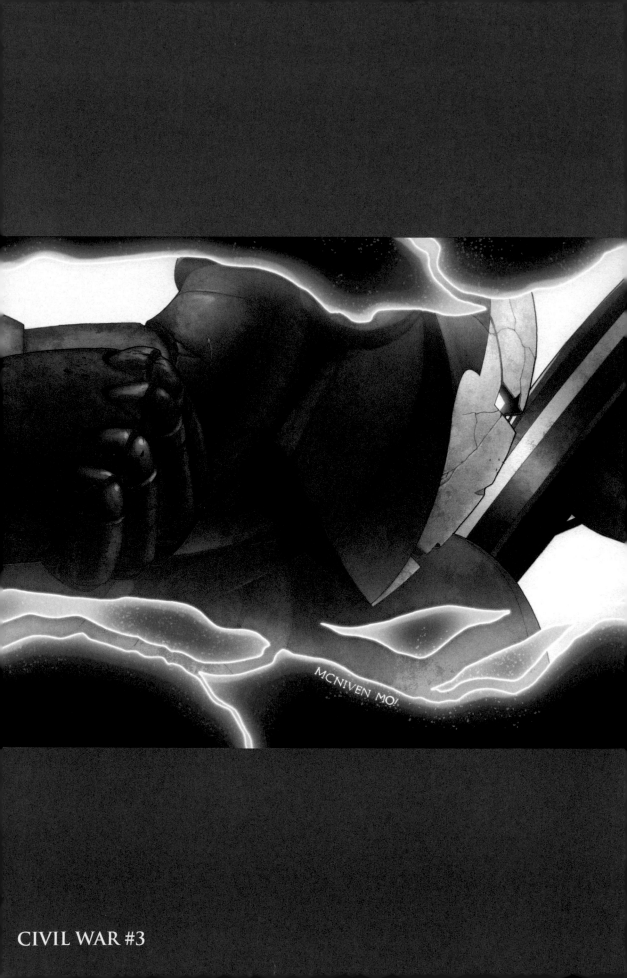

CIVIL WAR #3

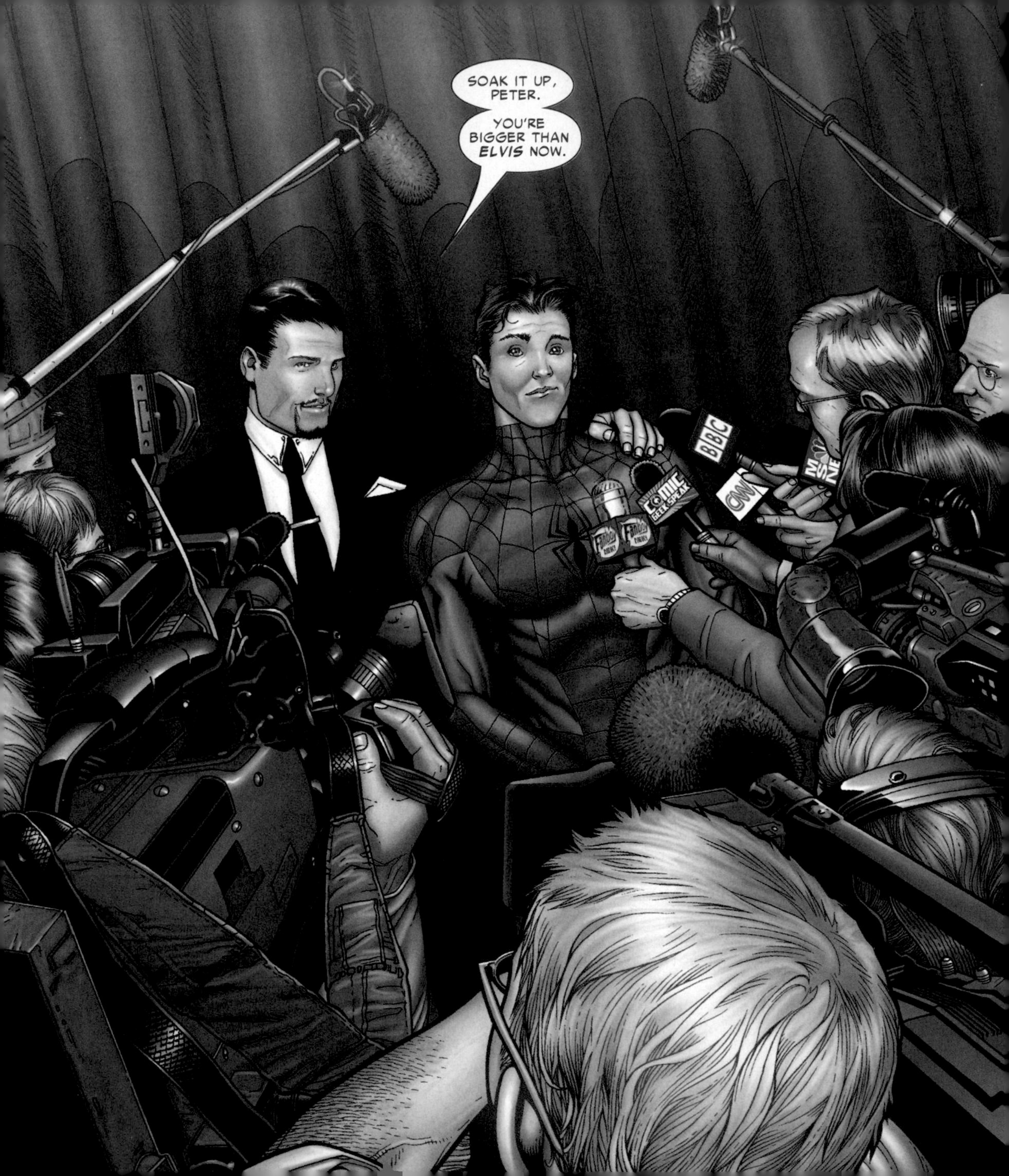
SOAK IT UP, PETER.
YOU'RE BIGGER THAN *ELVIS* NOW.
BBC
COMIC GEEK SPEAK
CNN

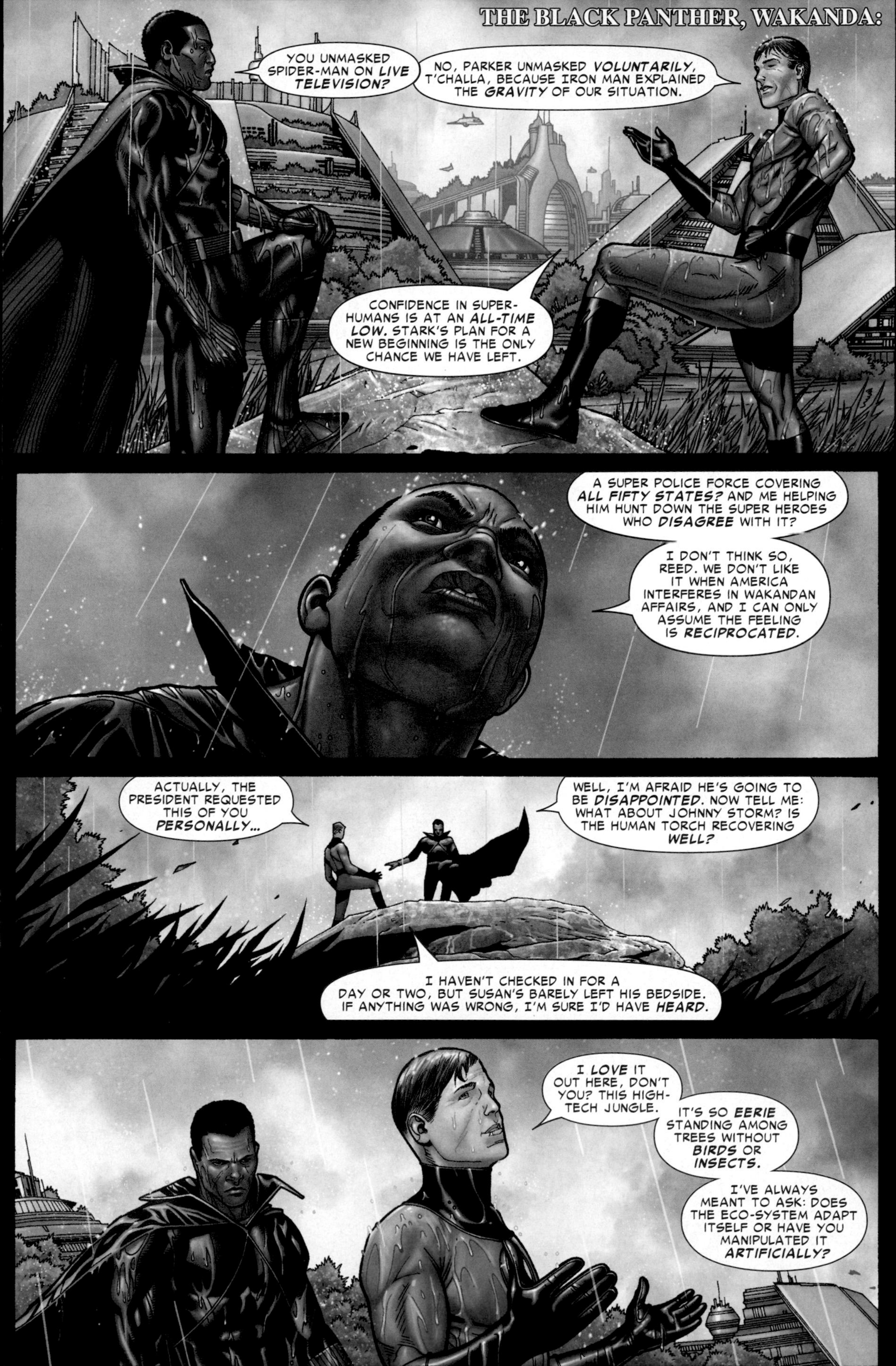
THE BLACK PANTHER, WAKANDA:
YOU UNMASKED SPIDER-MAN ON LIVE TELEVISION?
NO, PARKER UNMASKED VOLUNTARILY, T'CHALLA, BECAUSE IRON MAN EXPLAINED THE GRAVITY OF OUR SITUATION.
CONFIDENCE IN SUPER-HUMANS IS AT AN ALL-TIME LOW. STARK'S PLAN FOR A NEW BEGINNING IS THE ONLY CHANCE WE HAVE LEFT.
A SUPER POLICE FORCE COVERING ALL FIFTY STATES? AND ME HELPING HIM HUNT DOWN THE SUPER HEROES WHO DISAGREE WITH IT?
I DON'T THINK SO, REED. WE DON'T LIKE IT WHEN AMERICA INTERFERES IN WAKANDAN AFFAIRS, AND I CAN ONLY ASSUME THE FEELING IS RECIPROCATED.
ACTUALLY, THE PRESIDENT REQUESTED THIS OF YOU PERSONALLY...
WELL, I'M AFRAID HE'S GOING TO BE DISAPPOINTED. NOW TELL ME: WHAT ABOUT JOHNNY STORM? IS THE HUMAN TORCH RECOVERING WELL?
I HAVEN'T CHECKED IN FOR A DAY OR TWO, BUT SUSAN'S BARELY LEFT HIS BEDSIDE. IF ANYTHING WAS WRONG, I'M SURE I'D HAVE HEARD.
I LOVE IT OUT HERE, DON'T YOU? THIS HIGH-TECH JUNGLE.
IT'S SO EERIE STANDING AMONG TREES WITHOUT BIRDS OR INSECTS.
I'VE ALWAYS MEANT TO ASK: DOES THE ECO-SYSTEM ADAPT ITSELF OR HAVE YOU MANIPULATED IT ARTIFICIALLY?

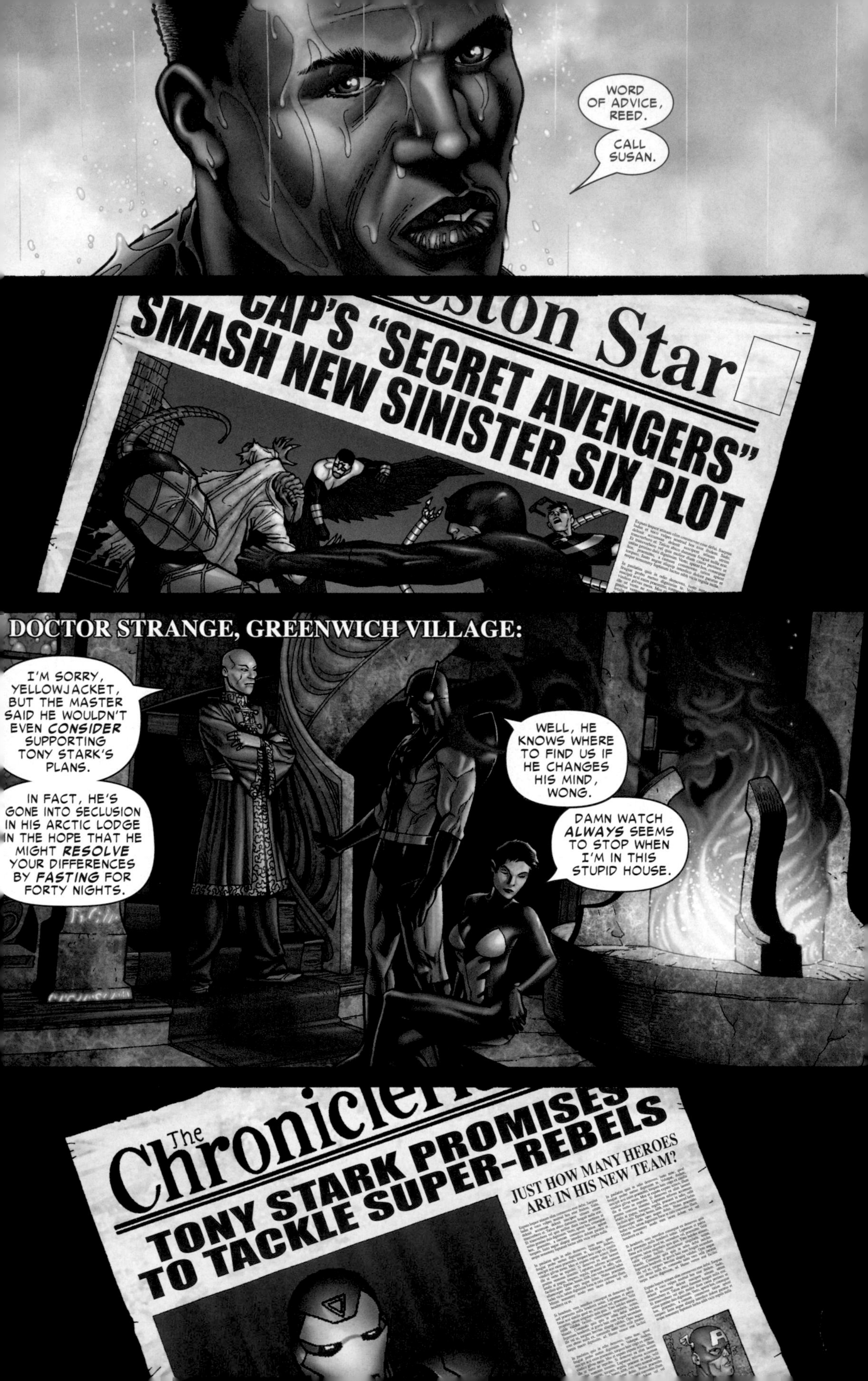
WORD OF ADVICE, REED.
CALL SUSAN.
Boston Star
CAP'S "SECRET AVENGERS" SMASH NEW SINISTER SIX PLOT
DOCTOR STRANGE, GREENWICH VILLAGE:
I'M SORRY, YELLOWJACKET, BUT THE MASTER SAID HE WOULDN'T EVEN CONSIDER SUPPORTING TONY STARK'S PLANS.
IN FACT, HE'S GONE INTO SECLUSION IN HIS ARCTIC LODGE IN THE HOPE THAT HE MIGHT RESOLVE YOUR DIFFERENCES BY FASTING FOR FORTY NIGHTS.
WELL, HE KNOWS WHERE TO FIND US IF HE CHANGES HIS MIND, WONG.
DAMN WATCH ALWAYS SEEMS TO STOP WHEN I'M IN THIS STUPID HOUSE.
The Chronicle
TONY STARK PROMISES TO TACKLE SUPER-REBELS
JUST HOW MANY HEROES ARE IN HIS NEW TEAM?

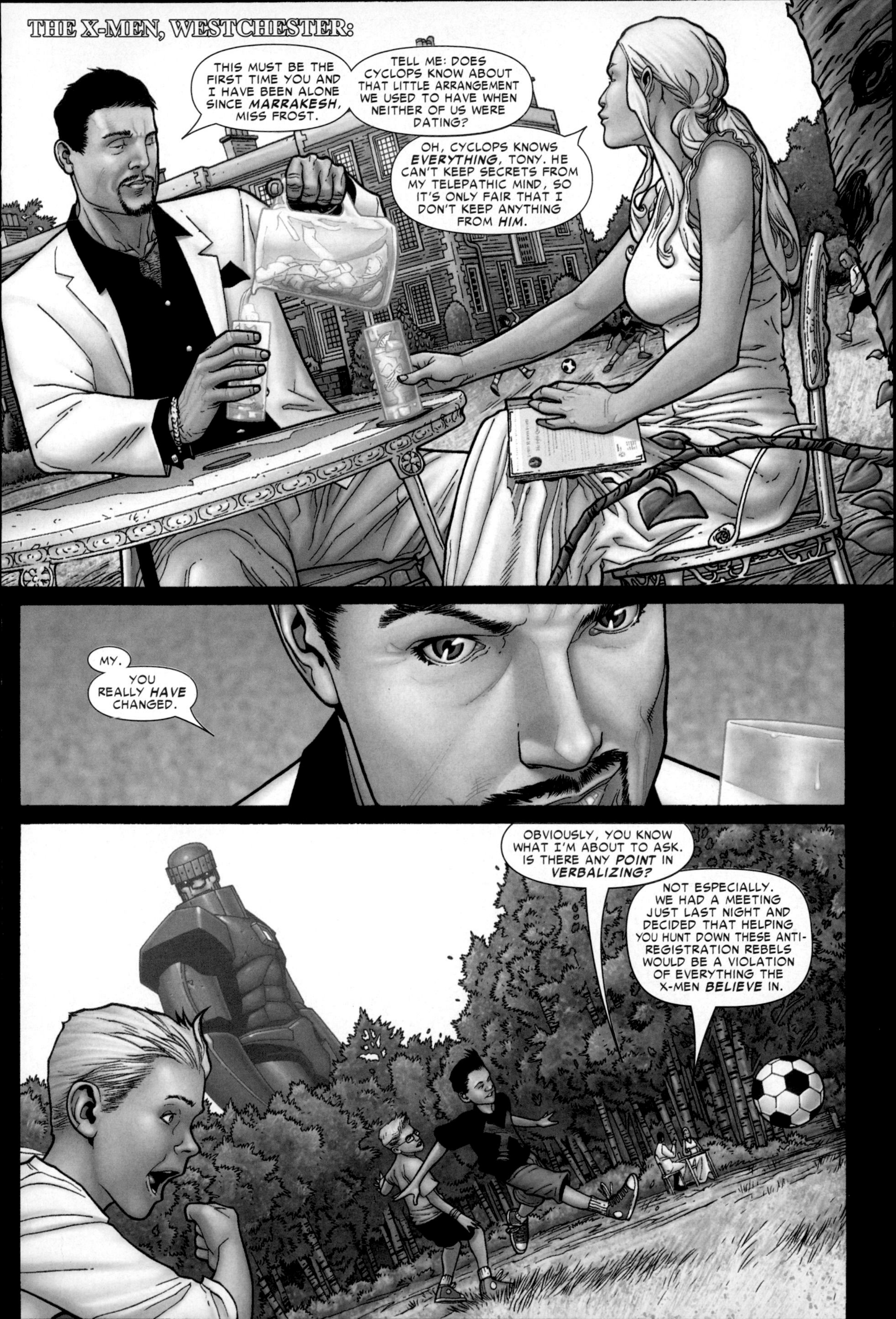
THE X-MEN, WESTCHESTER:
THIS MUST BE THE FIRST TIME YOU AND I HAVE BEEN ALONE SINCE MARRAKESH, MISS FROST.
TELL ME: DOES CYCLOPS KNOW ABOUT THAT LITTLE ARRANGEMENT WE USED TO HAVE WHEN NEITHER OF US WERE DATING?
OH, CYCLOPS KNOWS EVERYTHING, TONY. HE CAN'T KEEP SECRETS FROM MY TELEPATHIC MIND, SO IT'S ONLY FAIR THAT I DON'T KEEP ANYTHING FROM HIM.
MY.
YOU REALLY HAVE CHANGED.
OBVIOUSLY, YOU KNOW WHAT I'M ABOUT TO ASK. IS THERE ANY POINT IN VERBALIZING?
NOT ESPECIALLY. WE HAD A MEETING JUST LAST NIGHT AND DECIDED THAT HELPING YOU HUNT DOWN THESE ANTI-REGISTRATION REBELS WOULD BE A VIOLATION OF EVERYTHING THE X-MEN BELIEVE IN.

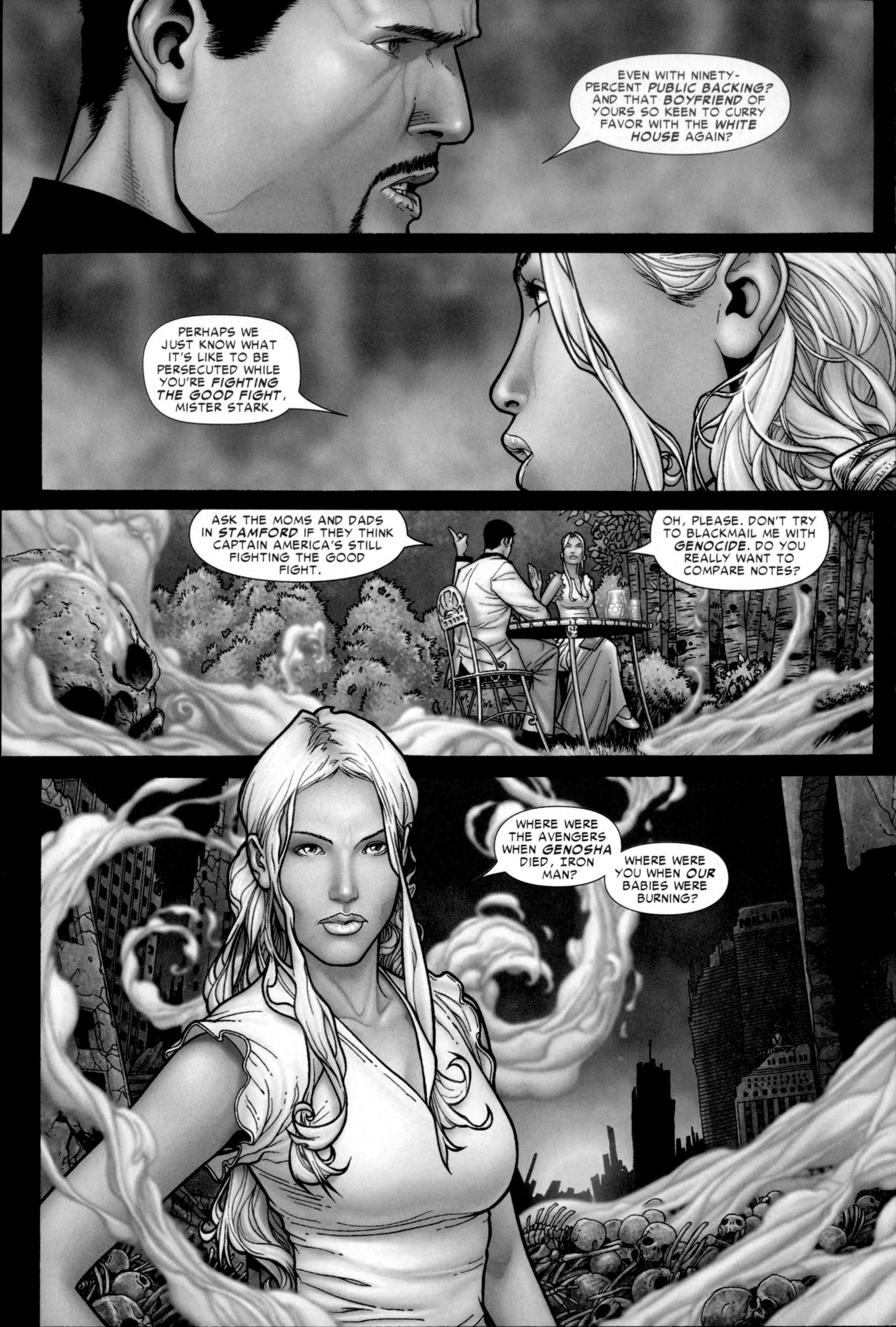
EVEN WITH NINETY-PERCENT PUBLIC BACKING? AND THAT BOYFRIEND OF YOURS SO KEEN TO CURRY FAVOR WITH THE WHITE HOUSE AGAIN?
PERHAPS WE JUST KNOW WHAT IT'S LIKE TO BE PERSECUTED WHILE YOU'RE FIGHTING THE GOOD FIGHT, MISTER STARK.
ASK THE MOMS AND DADS IN STAMFORD IF THEY THINK CAPTAIN AMERICA'S STILL FIGHTING THE GOOD FIGHT.
OH, PLEASE. DON'T TRY TO BLACKMAIL ME WITH GENOCIDE. DO YOU REALLY WANT TO COMPARE NOTES?
WHERE WERE THE AVENGERS WHEN GENOSHA DIED, IRON MAN?
WHERE WERE YOU WHEN OUR BABIES WERE BURNING?

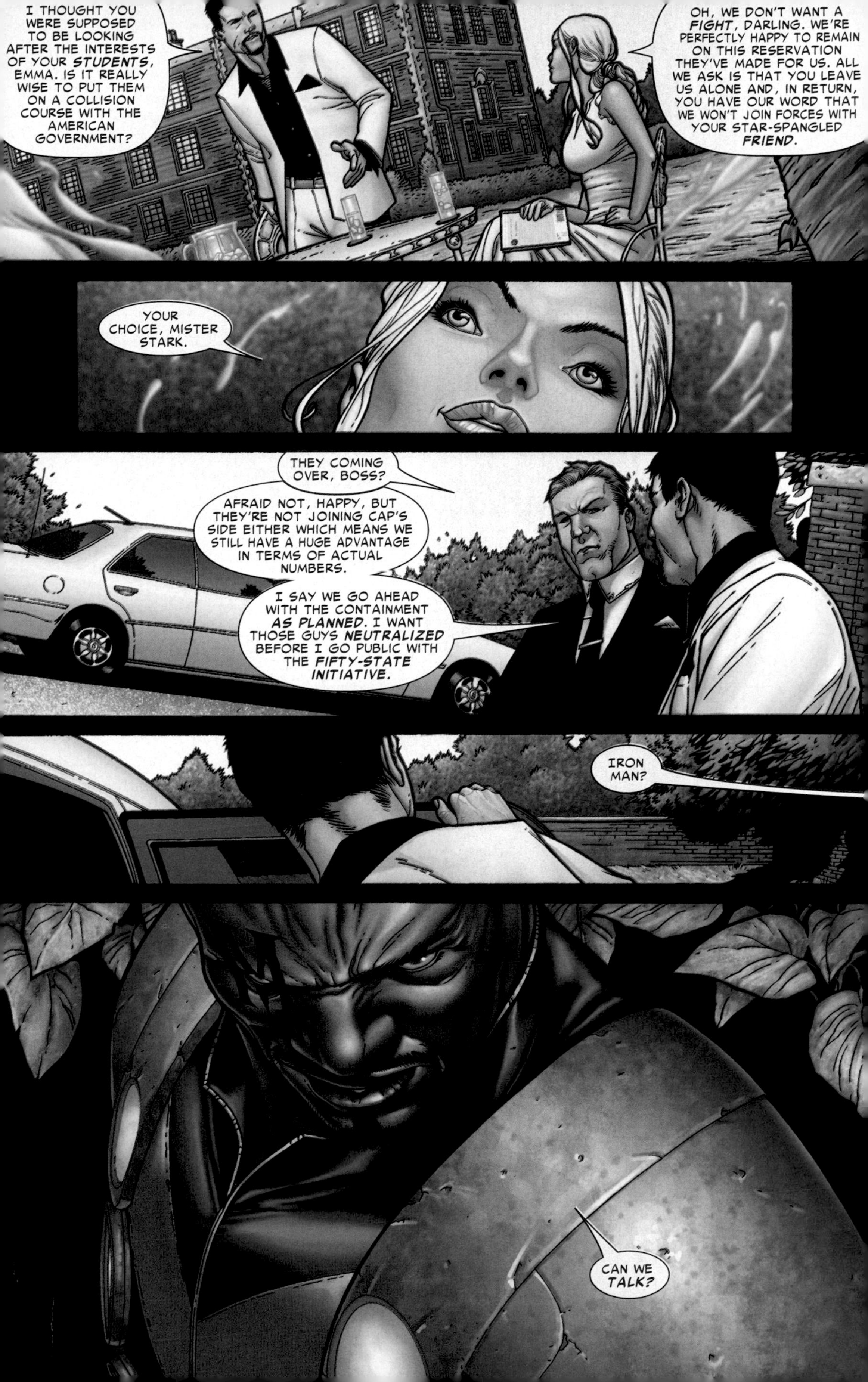
I THOUGHT YOU WERE SUPPOSED TO BE LOOKING AFTER THE INTERESTS OF YOUR STUDENTS, EMMA. IS IT REALLY WISE TO PUT THEM ON A COLLISION COURSE WITH THE AMERICAN GOVERNMENT?
OH, WE DON'T WANT A FIGHT, DARLING. WE'RE PERFECTLY HAPPY TO REMAIN ON THIS RESERVATION THEY'VE MADE FOR US. ALL WE ASK IS THAT YOU LEAVE US ALONE AND, IN RETURN, YOU HAVE OUR WORD THAT WE WON'T JOIN FORCES WITH YOUR STAR-SPANGLED FRIEND.
YOUR CHOICE, MISTER STARK.
THEY COMING OVER, BOSS?
AFRAID NOT, HAPPY, BUT THEY'RE NOT JOINING CAP'S SIDE EITHER WHICH MEANS WE STILL HAVE A HUGE ADVANTAGE IN TERMS OF ACTUAL NUMBERS.
I SAY WE GO AHEAD WITH THE CONTAINMENT AS PLANNED. I WANT THOSE GUYS NEUTRALIZED BEFORE I GO PUBLIC WITH THE FIFTY-STATE INITIATIVE.
IRON MAN?
CAN WE TALK?

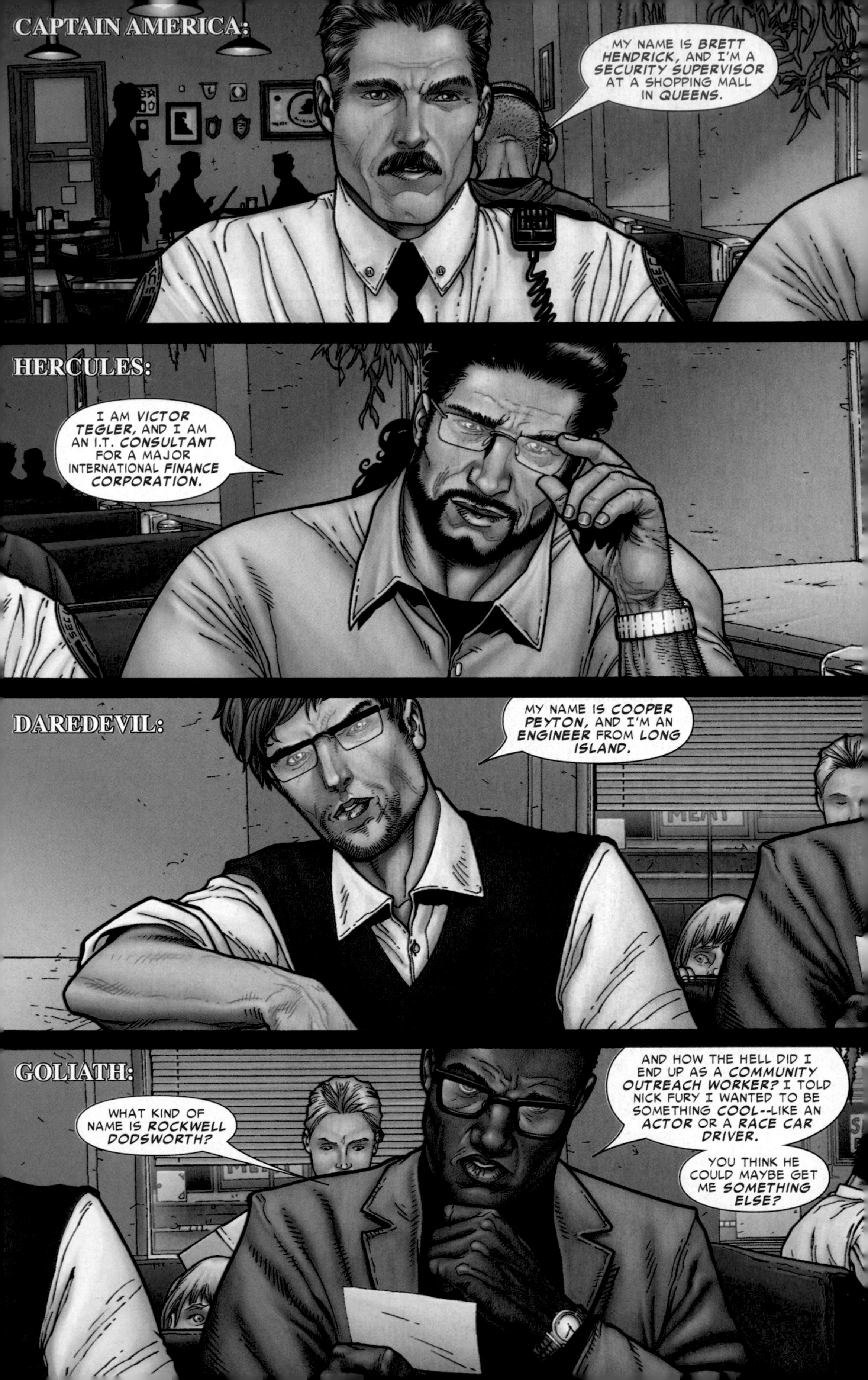
CAPTAIN AMERICA:
MY NAME IS BRETT HENDRICK, AND I'M A SECURITY SUPERVISOR AT A SHOPPING MALL IN QUEENS.
HERCULES:
I AM VICTOR TEGLER, AND I AM AN I.T. CONSULTANT FOR A MAJOR INTERNATIONAL FINANCE CORPORATION.
DAREDEVIL:
MY NAME IS COOPER PEYTON, AND I'M AN ENGINEER FROM LONG ISLAND.
GOLIATH:
WHAT KIND OF NAME IS ROCKWELL DODSWORTH?
AND HOW THE HELL DID I END UP AS A COMMUNITY OUTREACH WORKER? I TOLD NICK FURY I WANTED TO BE SOMETHING COOL--LIKE AN ACTOR OR A RACE CAR DRIVER.
YOU THINK HE COULD MAYBE GET ME SOMETHING ELSE?

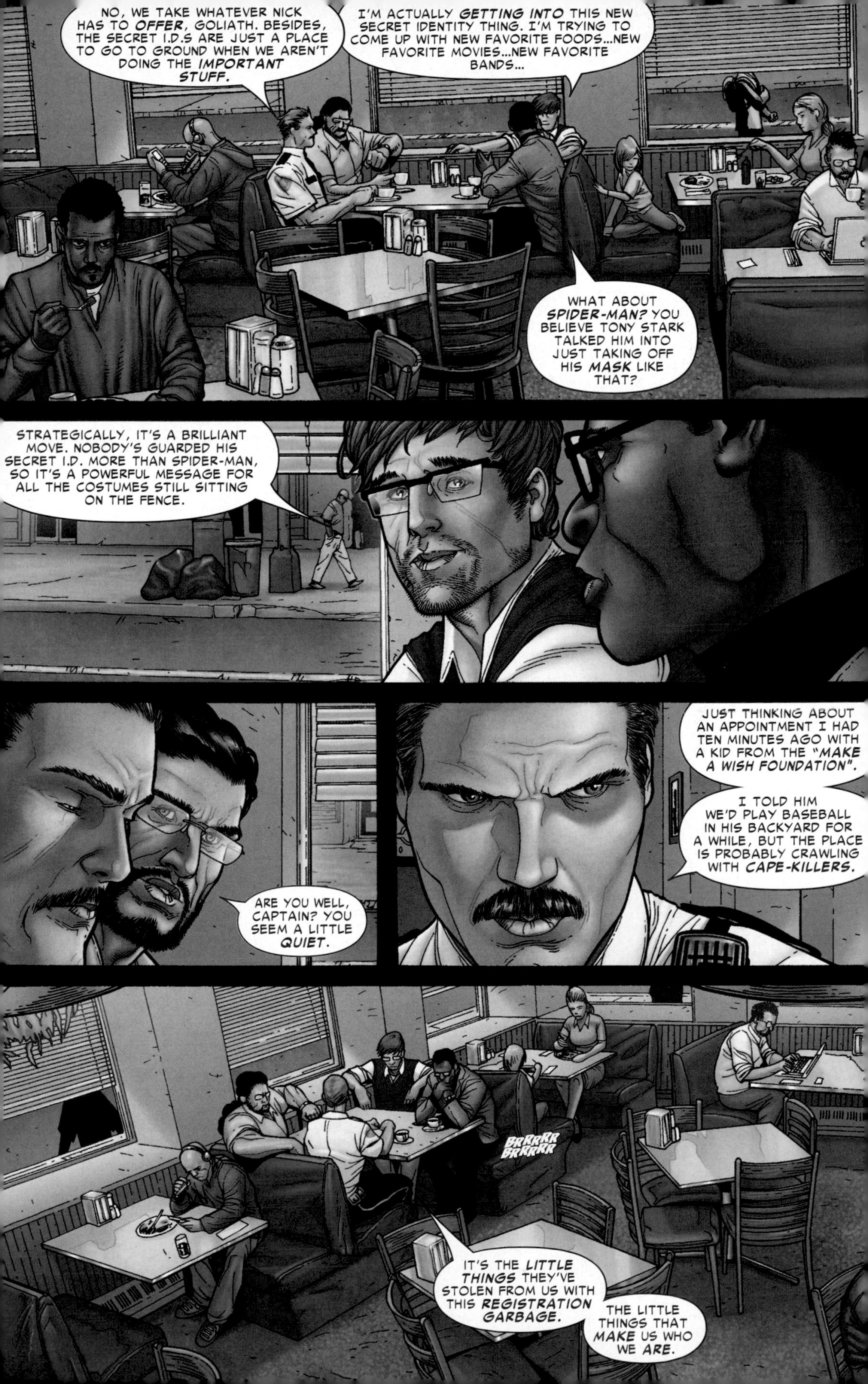
NO, WE TAKE WHATEVER NICK HAS TO OFFER, GOLIATH. BESIDES, THE SECRET I.D.S ARE JUST A PLACE TO GO TO GROUND WHEN WE AREN'T DOING THE IMPORTANT STUFF.
I'M ACTUALLY GETTING INTO THIS NEW SECRET IDENTITY THING. I'M TRYING TO COME UP WITH NEW FAVORITE FOODS...NEW FAVORITE MOVIES...NEW FAVORITE BANDS...
WHAT ABOUT SPIDER-MAN? YOU BELIEVE TONY STARK TALKED HIM INTO JUST TAKING OFF HIS MASK LIKE THAT?
STRATEGICALLY, IT'S A BRILLIANT MOVE. NOBODY'S GUARDED HIS SECRET I.D. MORE THAN SPIDER-MAN, SO IT'S A POWERFUL MESSAGE FOR ALL THE COSTUMES STILL SITTING ON THE FENCE.
ARE YOU WELL, CAPTAIN? YOU SEEM A LITTLE QUIET.
JUST THINKING ABOUT AN APPOINTMENT I HAD TEN MINUTES AGO WITH A KID FROM THE "MAKE A WISH FOUNDATION".
I TOLD HIM WE'D PLAY BASEBALL IN HIS BACKYARD FOR A WHILE, BUT THE PLACE IS PROBABLY CRAWLING WITH CAPE-KILLERS.
BRRRRR BRRRRR
IT'S THE LITTLE THINGS THEY'VE STOLEN FROM US WITH THIS REGISTRATION GARBAGE.
THE LITTLE THINGS THAT MAKE US WHO WE ARE.

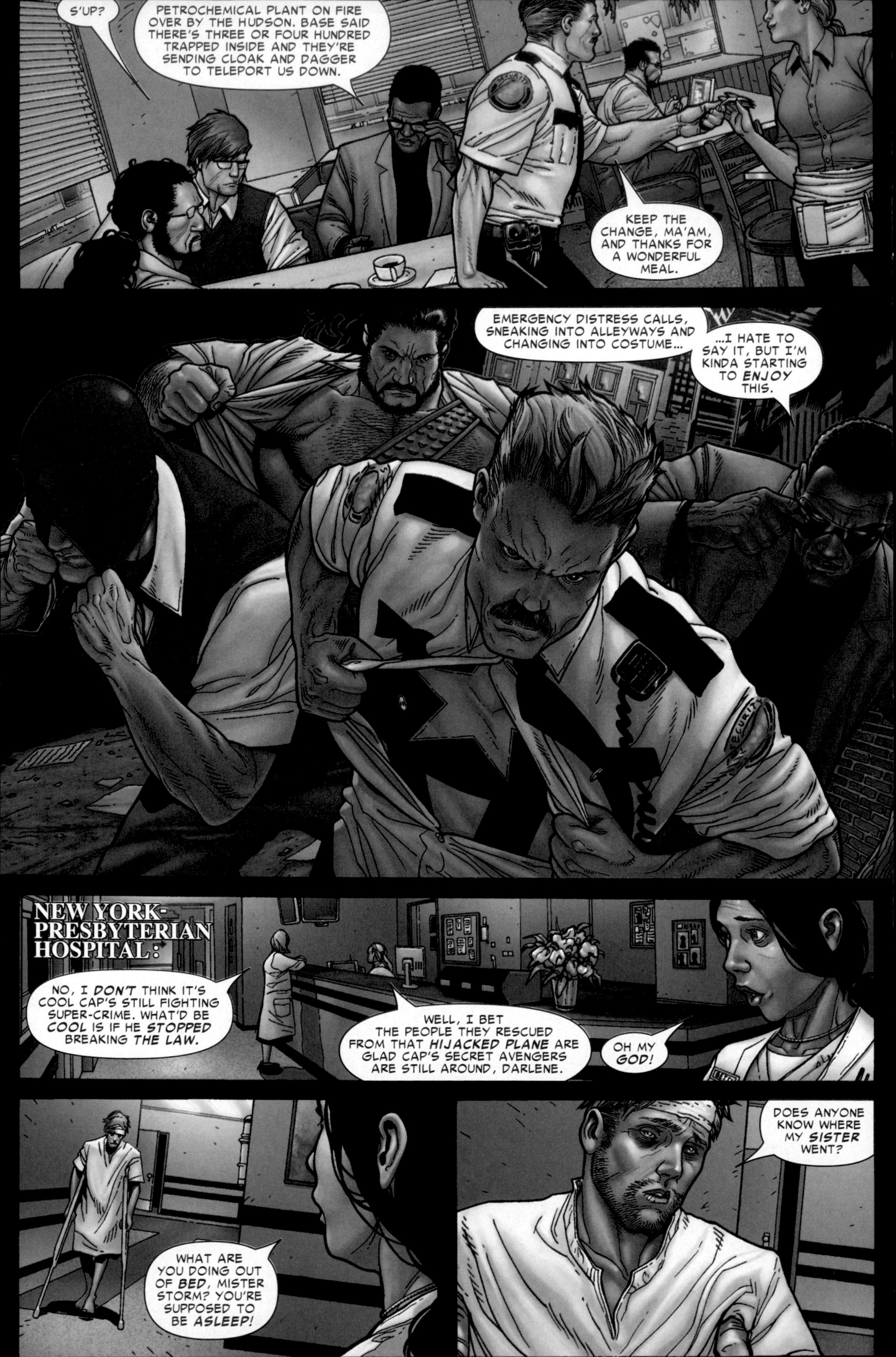
S'UP?
PETROCHEMICAL PLANT ON FIRE OVER BY THE HUDSON. BASE SAID THERE'S THREE OR FOUR HUNDRED TRAPPED INSIDE AND THEY'RE SENDING CLOAK AND DAGGER TO TELEPORT US DOWN.
KEEP THE CHANGE, MA'AM, AND THANKS FOR A WONDERFUL MEAL.
EMERGENCY DISTRESS CALLS, SNEAKING INTO ALLEYWAYS AND CHANGING INTO COSTUME...
...I HATE TO SAY IT, BUT I'M KINDA STARTING TO ENJOY THIS.
NEW YORK-PRESBYTERIAN HOSPITAL:
NO, I DON'T THINK IT'S COOL CAP'S STILL FIGHTING SUPER-CRIME. WHAT'D BE COOL IS IF HE STOPPED BREAKING THE LAW.
WELL, I BET THE PEOPLE THEY RESCUED FROM THAT HIJACKED PLANE ARE GLAD CAP'S SECRET AVENGERS ARE STILL AROUND, DARLENE.
OH MY GOD!
WHAT ARE YOU DOING OUT OF BED, MISTER STORM? YOU'RE SUPPOSED TO BE ASLEEP!
DOES ANYONE KNOW WHERE MY SISTER WENT?

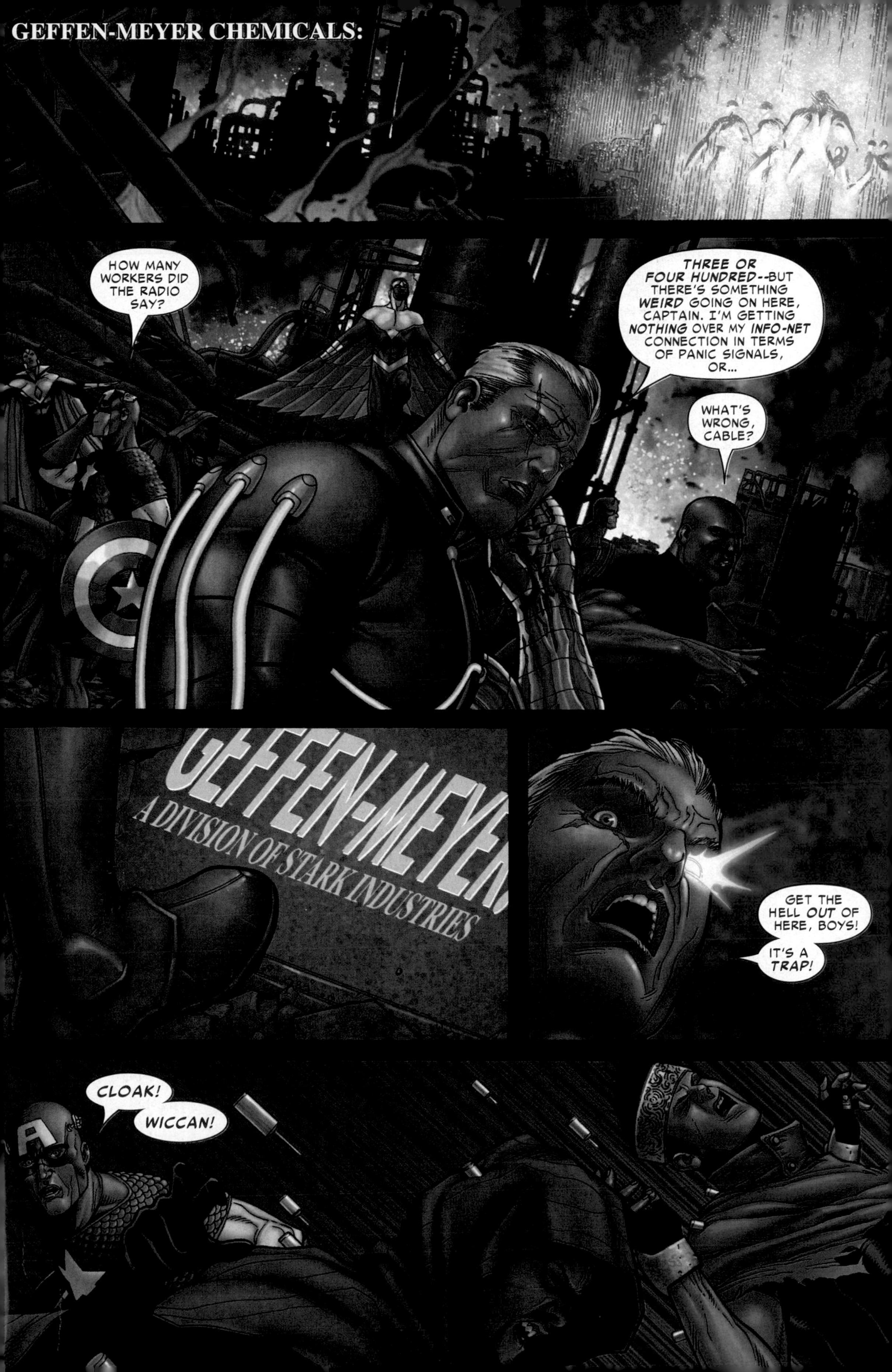
GEFFEN-MEYER CHEMICALS:
HOW MANY WORKERS DID THE RADIO SAY?
THREE OR FOUR HUNDRED--BUT THERE'S SOMETHING WEIRD GOING ON HERE, CAPTAIN. I'M GETTING NOTHING OVER MY INFO-NET CONNECTION IN TERMS OF PANIC SIGNALS, OR...
WHAT'S WRONG, CABLE?
GEFFEN-MEYER
A DIVISION OF STARK INDUSTRIES
GET THE HELL OUT OF HERE, BOYS!
IT'S A TRAP!
CLOAK!
WICCAN!

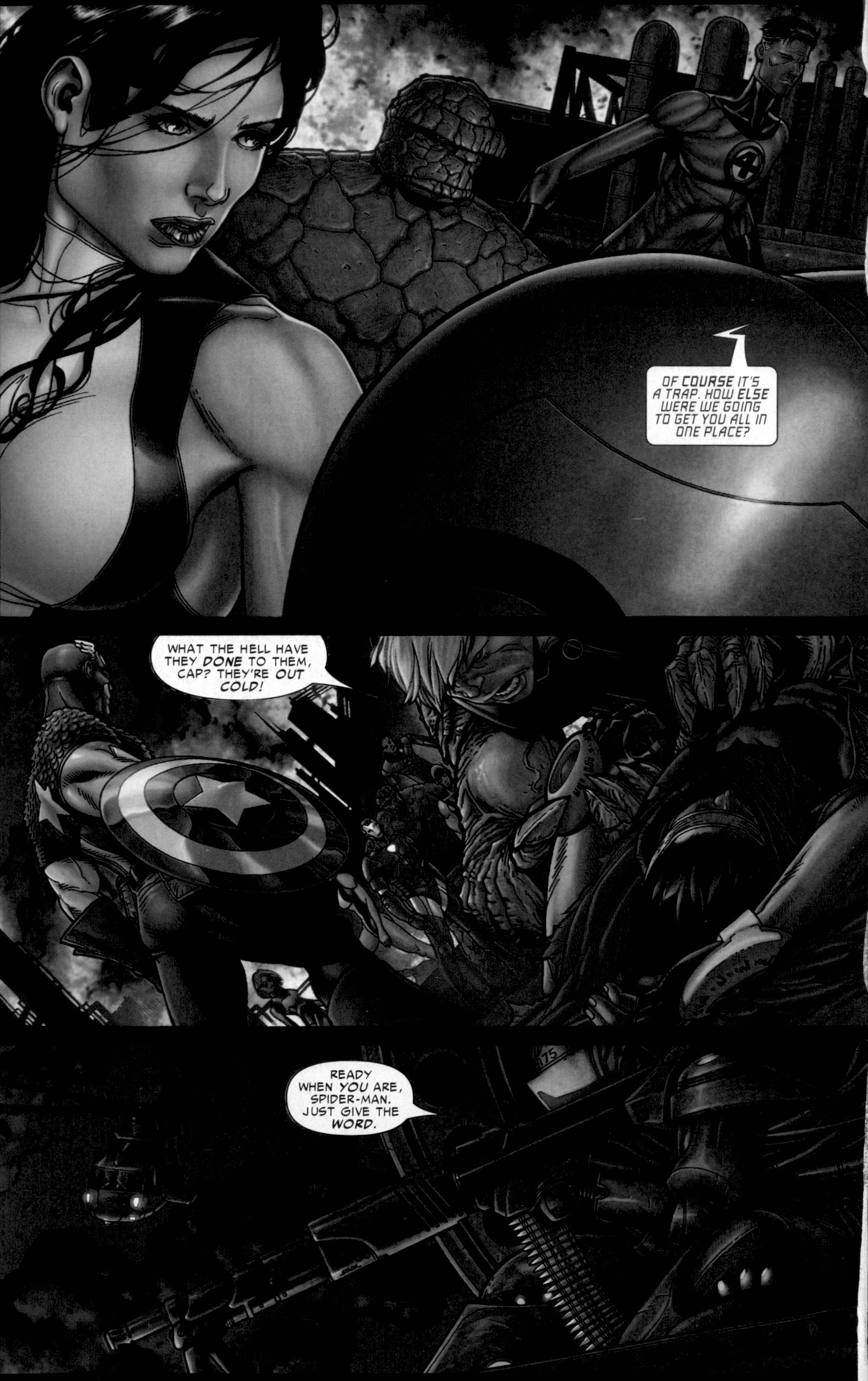
OF COURSE IT'S A TRAP. HOW ELSE WERE WE GOING TO GET YOU ALL IN ONE PLACE?
WHAT THE HELL HAVE THEY DONE TO THEM, CAP? THEY'RE OUT COLD!
READY WHEN YOU ARE, SPIDER-MAN. JUST GIVE THE WORD.

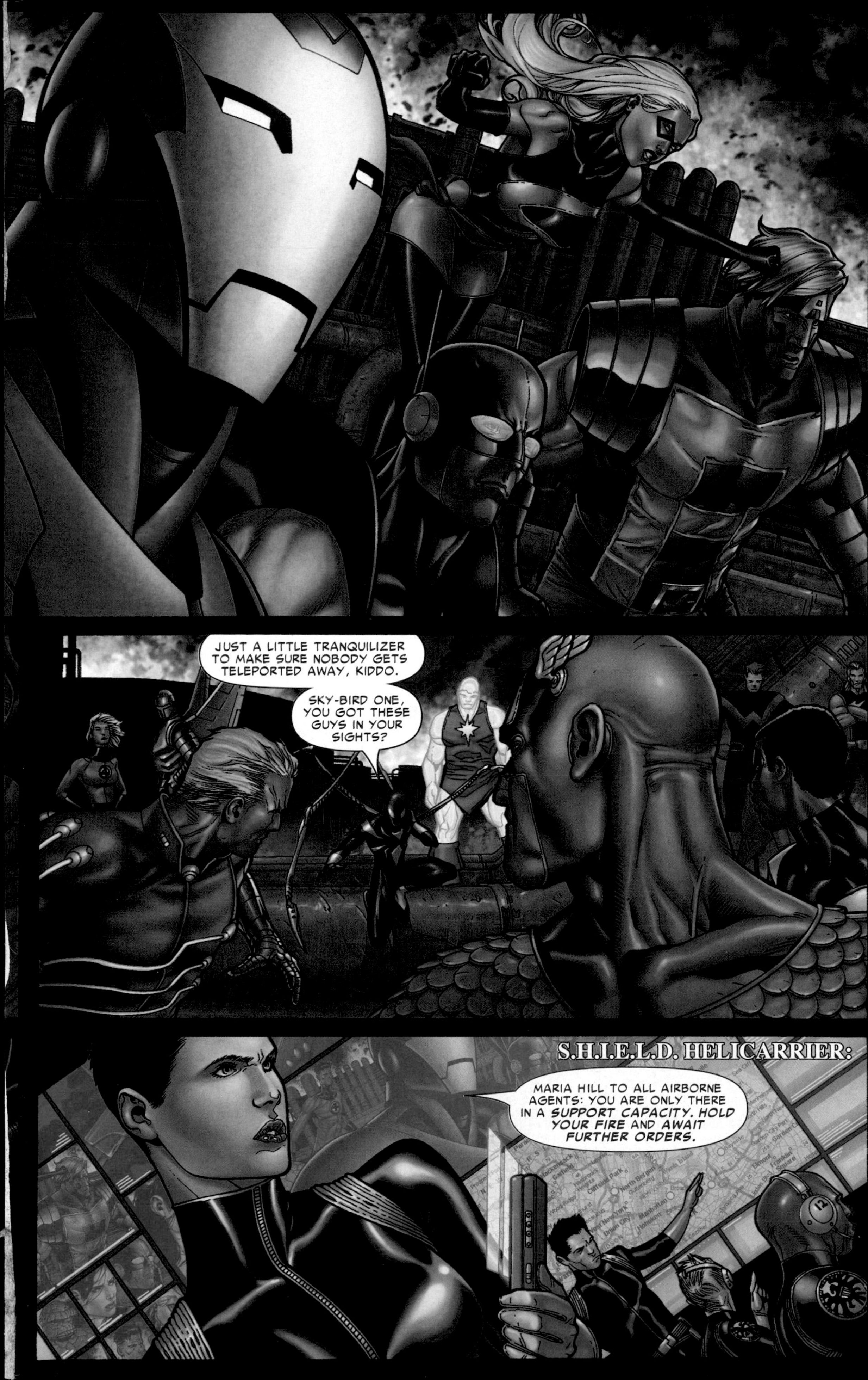

JUST A LITTLE TRANQUILIZER TO MAKE SURE NOBODY GETS TELEPORTED AWAY, KIDDO.
SKY-BIRD ONE, YOU GOT THESE GUYS IN YOUR SIGHTS?
S.H.I.E.L.D. HELICARRIER:
MARIA HILL TO ALL AIRBORNE AGENTS: YOU ARE ONLY THERE IN A *SUPPORT CAPACITY. HOLD YOUR FIRE* AND *AWAIT FURTHER ORDERS.*

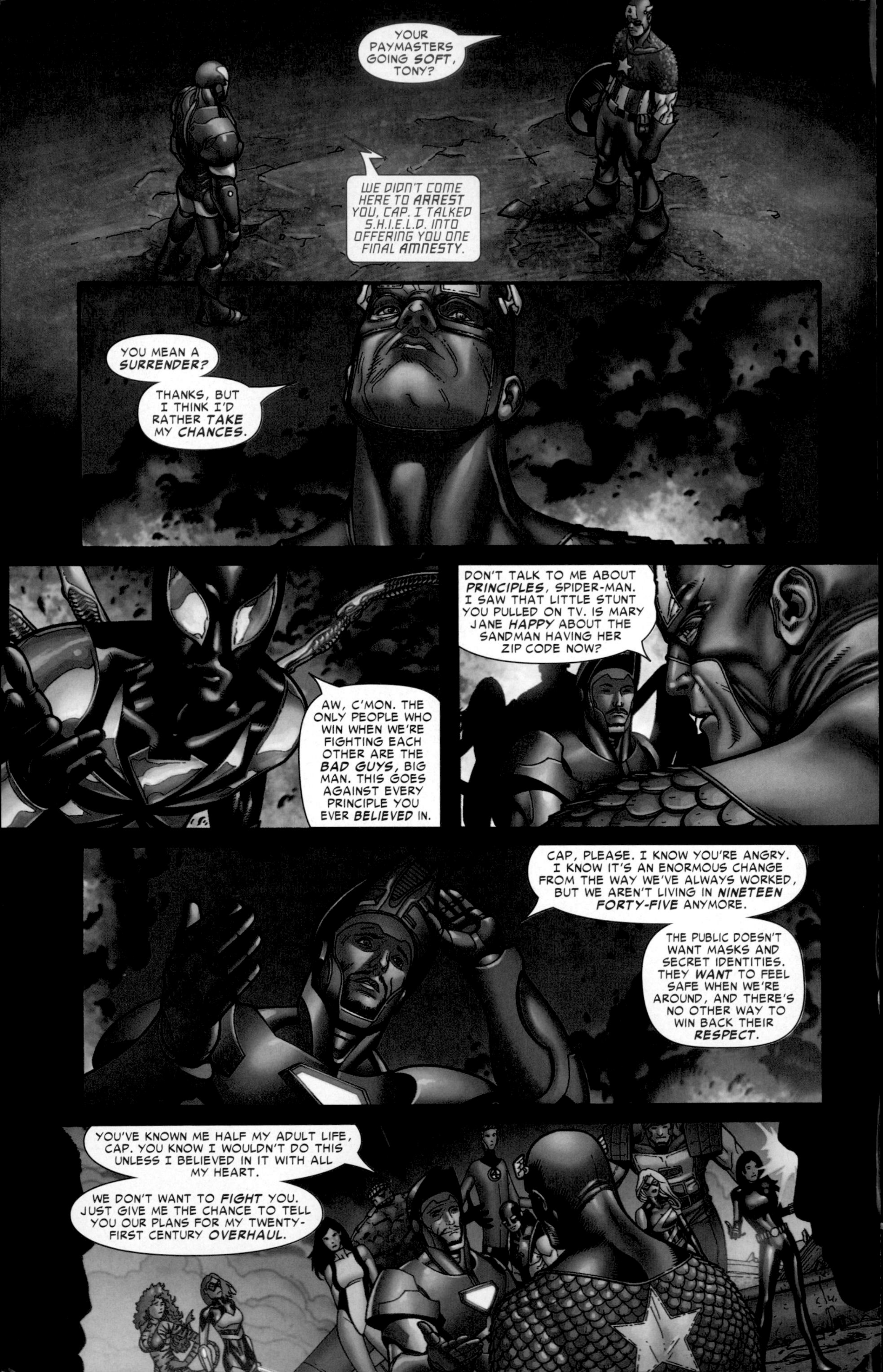
YOUR PAYMASTERS GOING SOFT, TONY?
WE DIDN'T COME HERE TO ARREST YOU, CAP. I TALKED S.H.I.E.L.D. INTO OFFERING YOU ONE FINAL AMNESTY.
YOU MEAN A SURRENDER?
THANKS, BUT I THINK I'D RATHER TAKE MY CHANCES.
AW, C'MON. THE ONLY PEOPLE WHO WIN WHEN WE'RE FIGHTING EACH OTHER ARE THE BAD GUYS, BIG MAN. THIS GOES AGAINST EVERY PRINCIPLE YOU EVER BELIEVED IN.
DON'T TALK TO ME ABOUT PRINCIPLES, SPIDER-MAN. I SAW THAT LITTLE STUNT YOU PULLED ON TV. IS MARY JANE HAPPY ABOUT THE SANDMAN HAVING HER ZIP CODE NOW?
CAP, PLEASE. I KNOW YOU'RE ANGRY. I KNOW IT'S AN ENORMOUS CHANGE FROM THE WAY WE'VE ALWAYS WORKED, BUT WE AREN'T LIVING IN NINETEEN FORTY-FIVE ANYMORE.
THE PUBLIC DOESN'T WANT MASKS AND SECRET IDENTITIES. THEY WANT TO FEEL SAFE WHEN WE'RE AROUND, AND THERE'S NO OTHER WAY TO WIN BACK THEIR RESPECT.
YOU'VE KNOWN ME HALF MY ADULT LIFE, CAP. YOU KNOW I WOULDN'T DO THIS UNLESS I BELIEVED IN IT WITH ALL MY HEART.
WE DON'T WANT TO FIGHT YOU. JUST GIVE ME THE CHANCE TO TELL YOU OUR PLANS FOR MY TWENTY-FIRST CENTURY OVERHAUL.

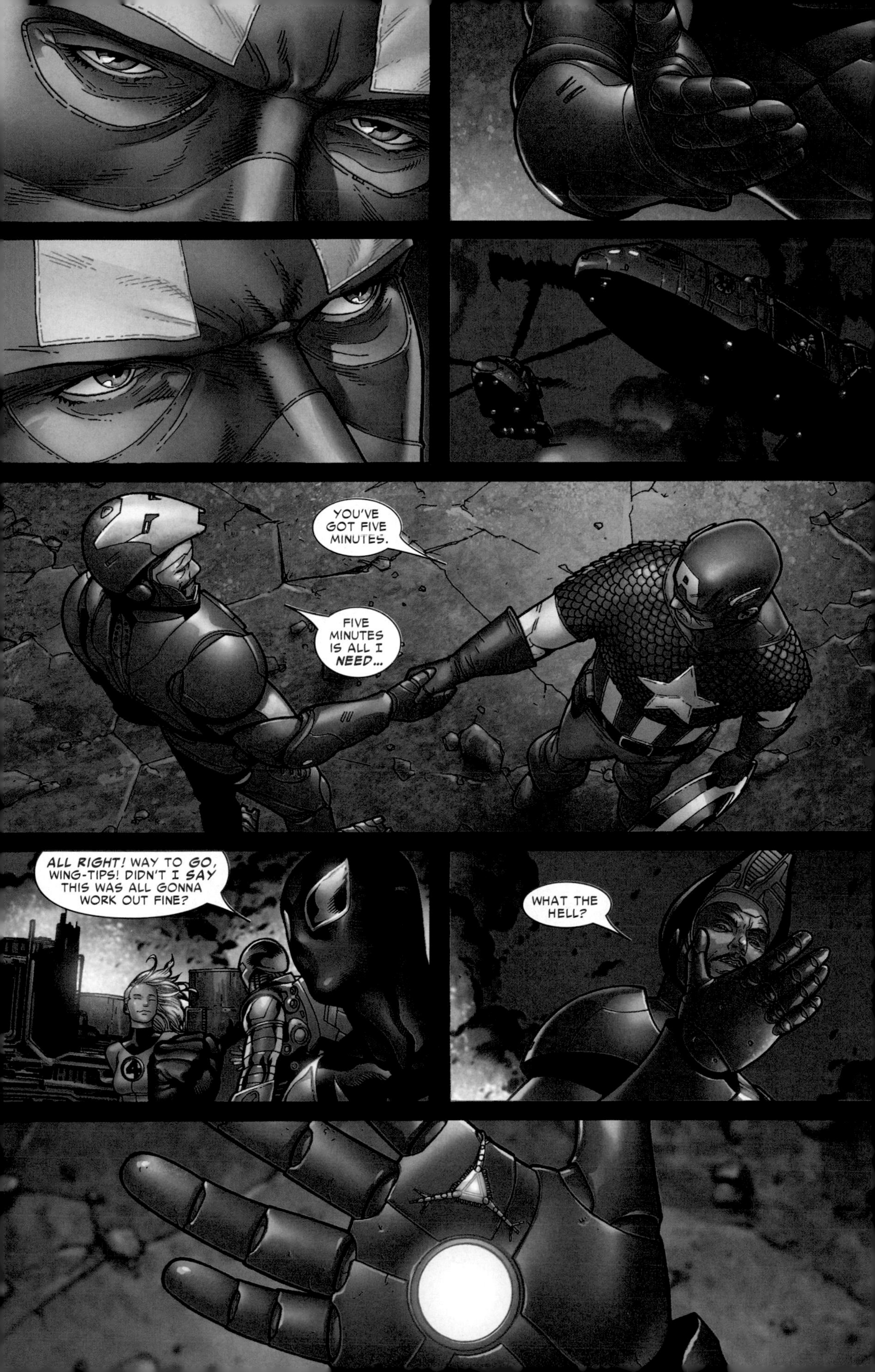
YOU'VE GOT FIVE MINUTES.
FIVE MINUTES IS ALL I NEED...
ALL RIGHT! WAY TO GO, WING-TIPS! DIDN'T I SAY THIS WAS ALL GONNA WORK OUT FINE?
WHAT THE HELL?

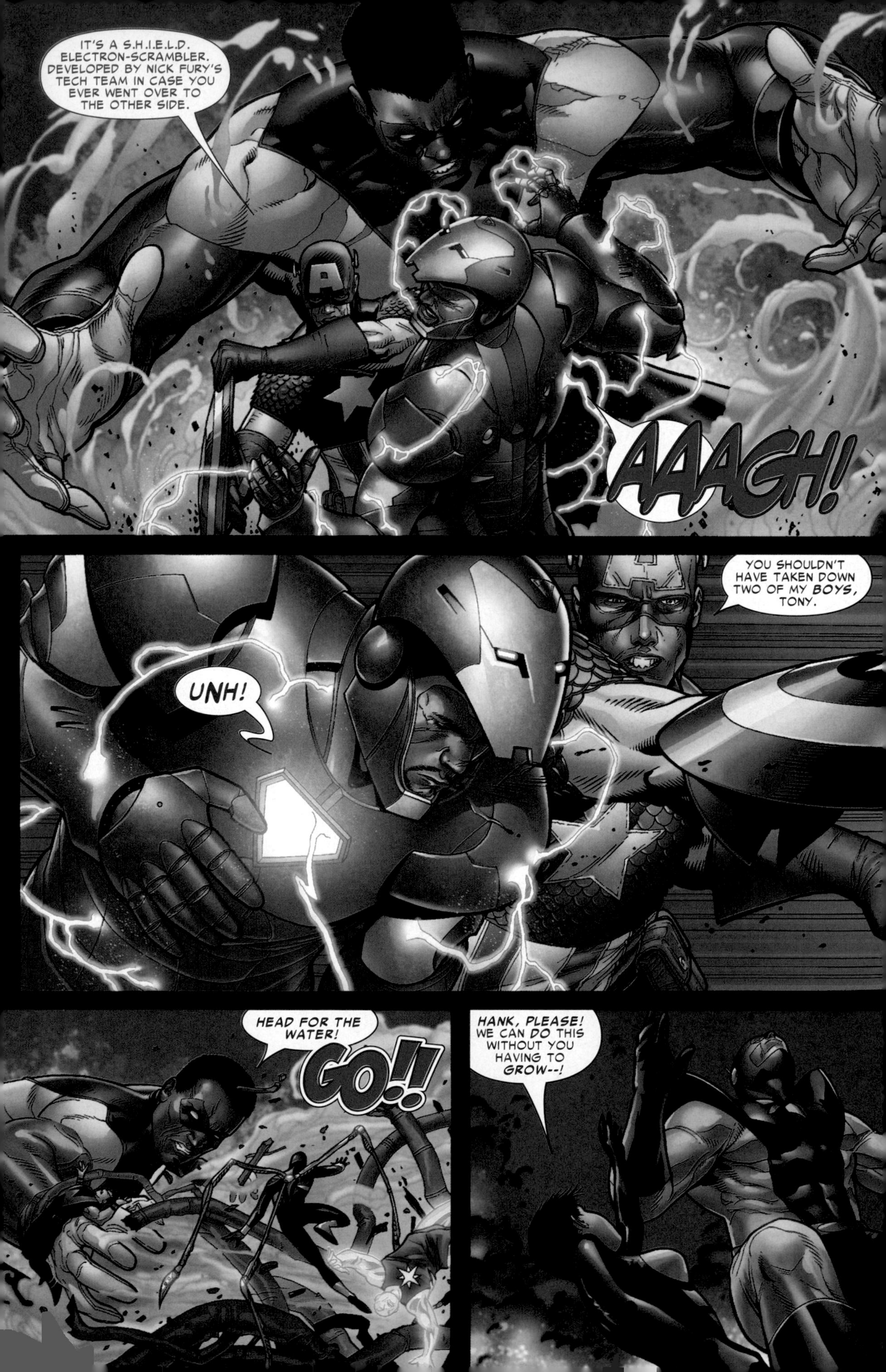
IT'S A S.H.I.E.L.D. ELECTRON-SCRAMBLER. DEVELOPED BY NICK FURY'S TECH TEAM IN CASE YOU EVER WENT OVER TO THE OTHER SIDE.
AAAGH!
YOU SHOULDN'T HAVE TAKEN DOWN TWO OF MY *BOYS*, TONY.
UNH!
HEAD FOR THE WATER!
GO!!
HANK, PLEASE! WE CAN DO THIS WITHOUT YOU HAVING TO GROW--!

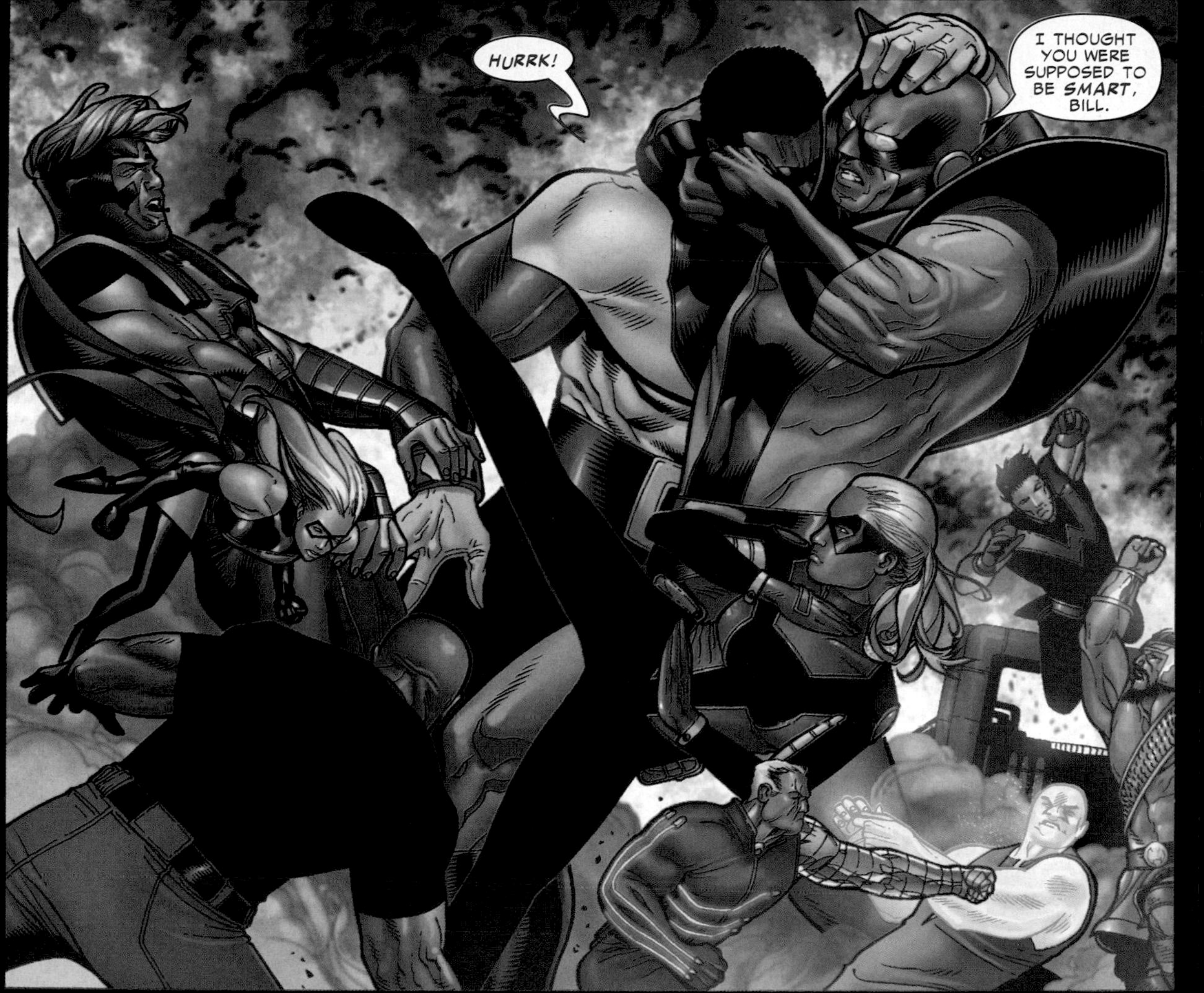
HURRK!
I THOUGHT YOU WERE SUPPOSED TO BE SMART, BILL.

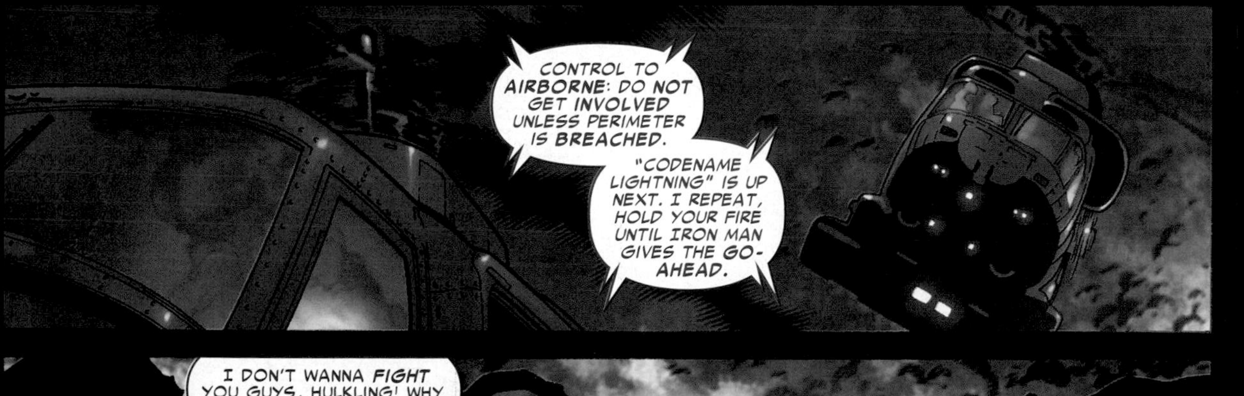
CONTROL TO AIRBORNE: DO NOT GET INVOLVED UNLESS PERIMETER IS BREACHED.
"CODENAME LIGHTNING" IS UP NEXT. I REPEAT, HOLD YOUR FIRE UNTIL IRON MAN GIVES THE GO-AHEAD.

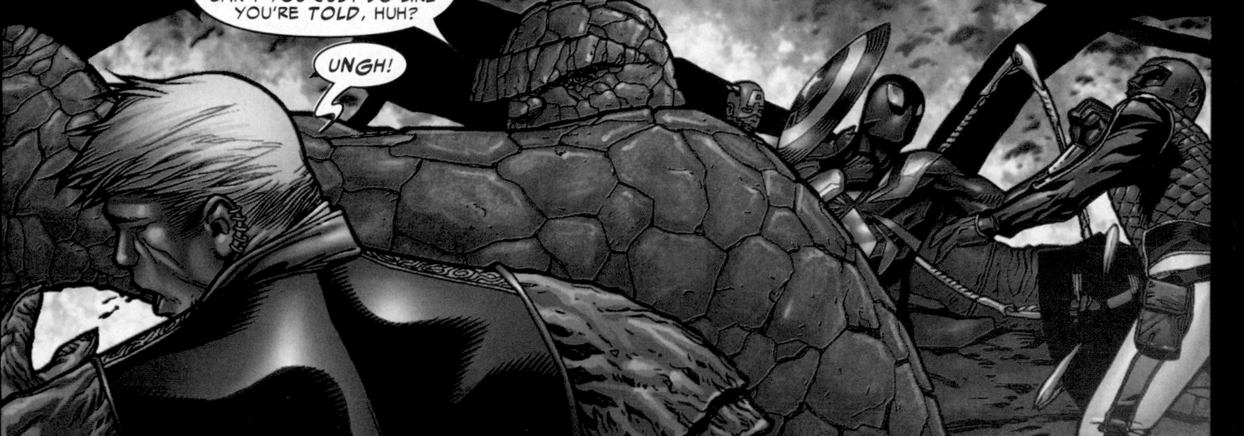
I DON'T WANNA FIGHT YOU GUYS, HULKLING! WHY CAN'T YOU JUST DO LIKE YOU'RE TOLD, HUH?
UNGH!

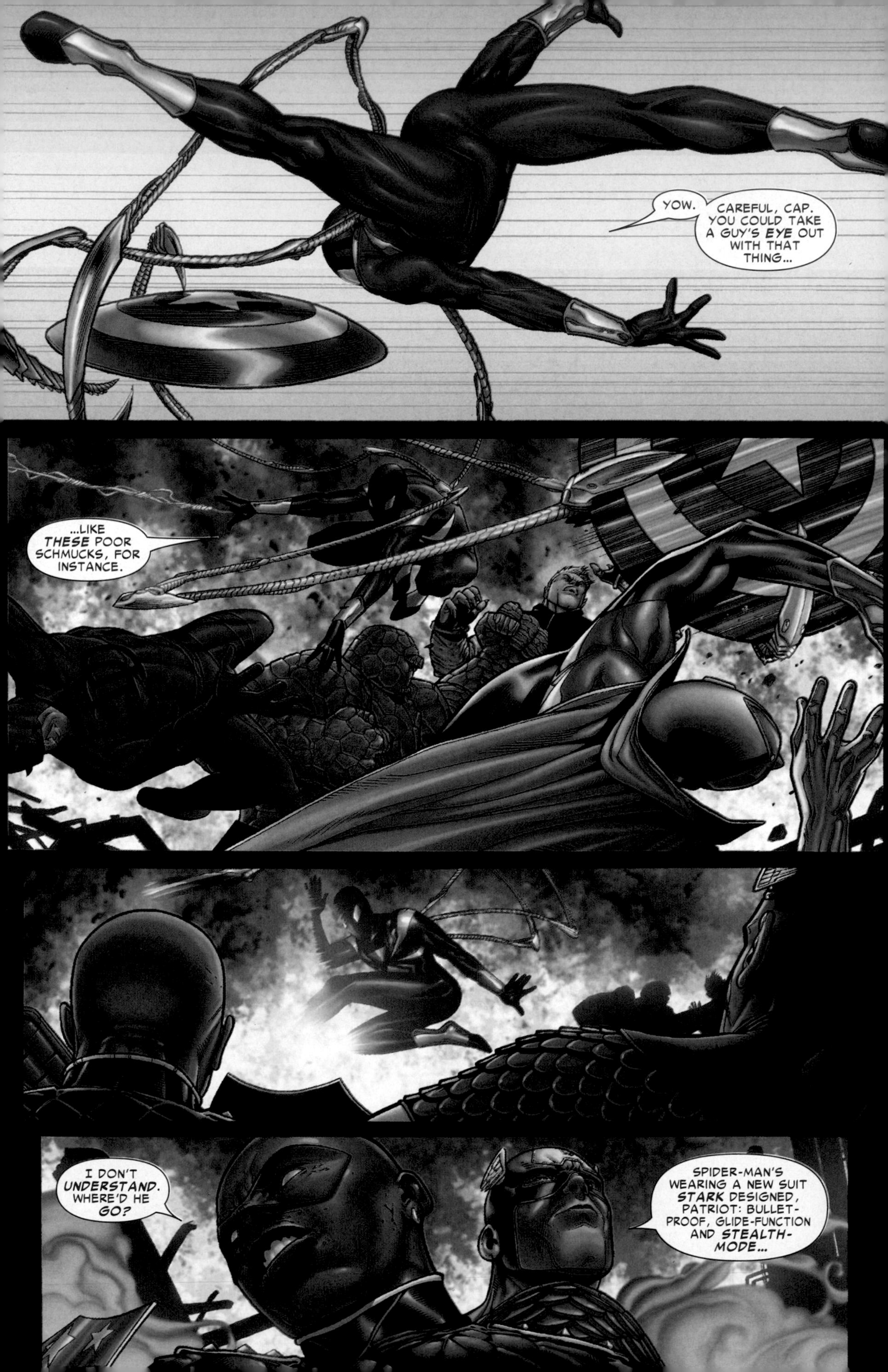

YOW.
CAREFUL, CAP. YOU COULD TAKE A GUY'S EYE OUT WITH THAT THING...
...LIKE THESE POOR SCHMUCKS, FOR INSTANCE.
I DON'T UNDERSTAND. WHERE'D HE GO?
SPIDER-MAN'S WEARING A NEW SUIT STARK DESIGNED, PATRIOT: BULLET-PROOF, GLIDE-FUNCTION AND STEALTH-MODE...

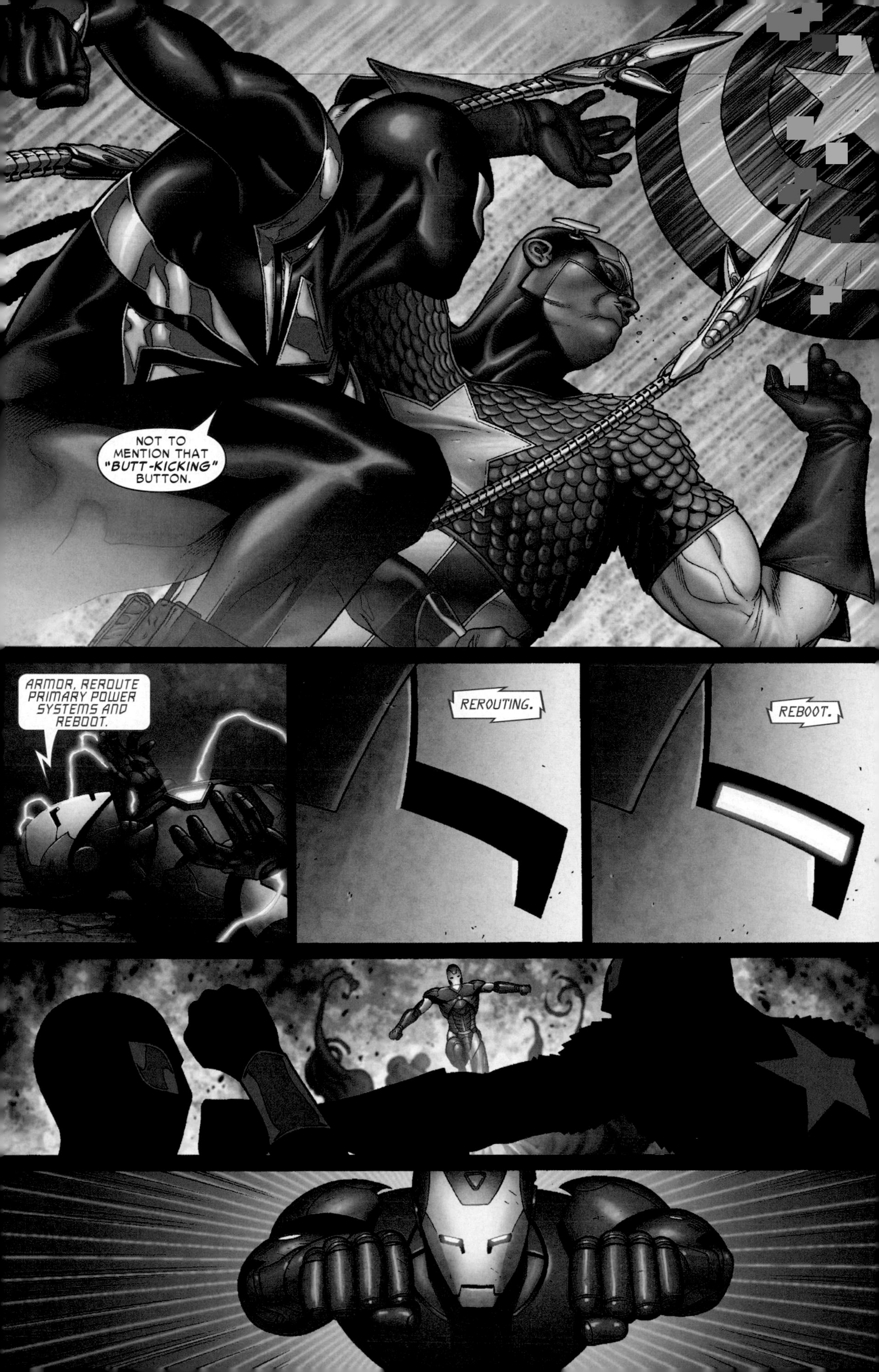
NOT TO MENTION THAT "BUTT-KICKING" BUTTON.
ARMOR, REROUTE PRIMARY POWER SYSTEMS AND REBOOT.
REROUTING.
REBOOT.

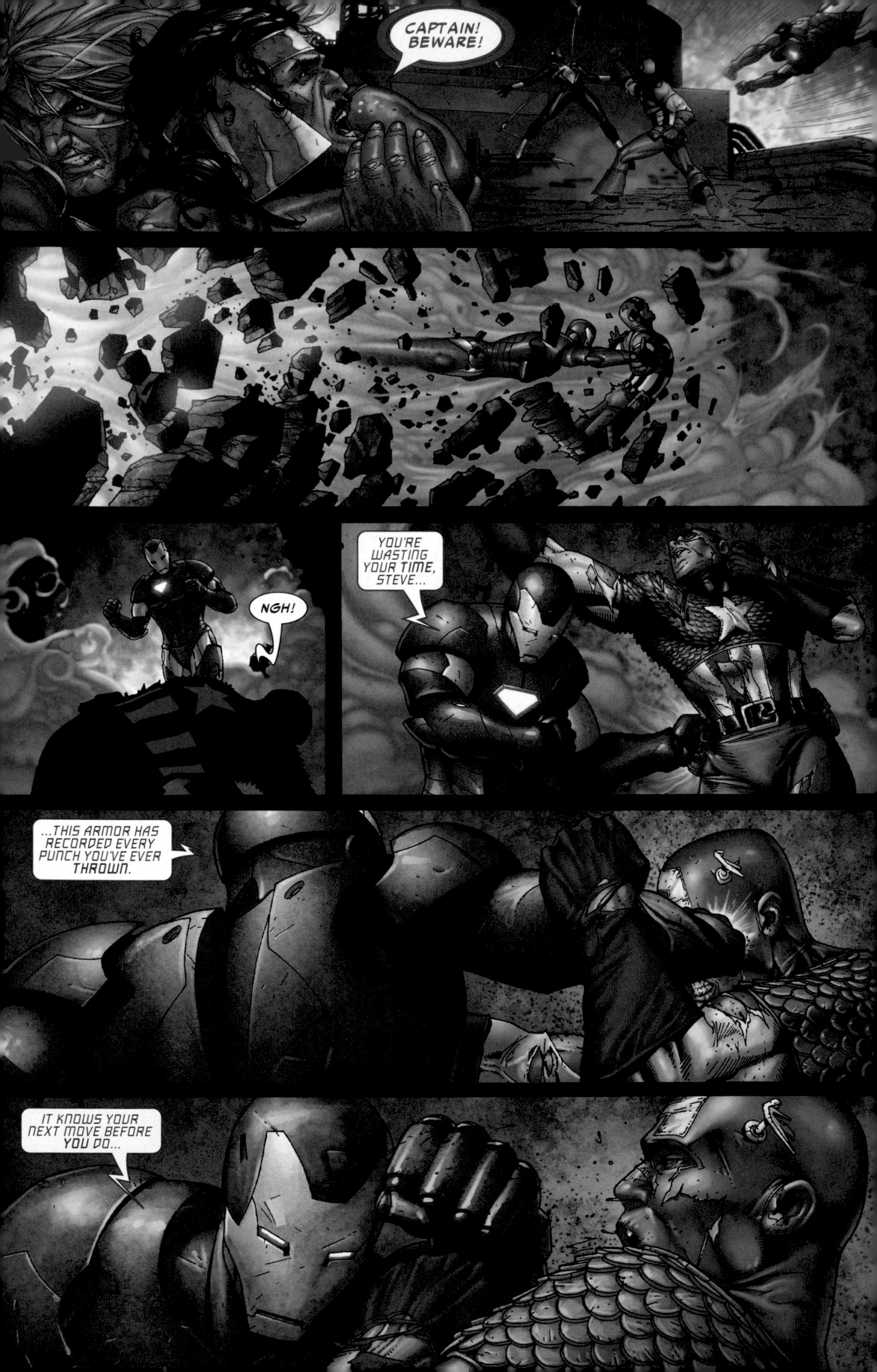
CAPTAIN! BEWARE!
NGH!
YOU'RE WASTING YOUR TIME, STEVE...
...THIS ARMOR HAS RECORDED EVERY PUNCH YOU'VE EVER THROWN.
IT KNOWS YOUR NEXT MOVE BEFORE YOU DO...

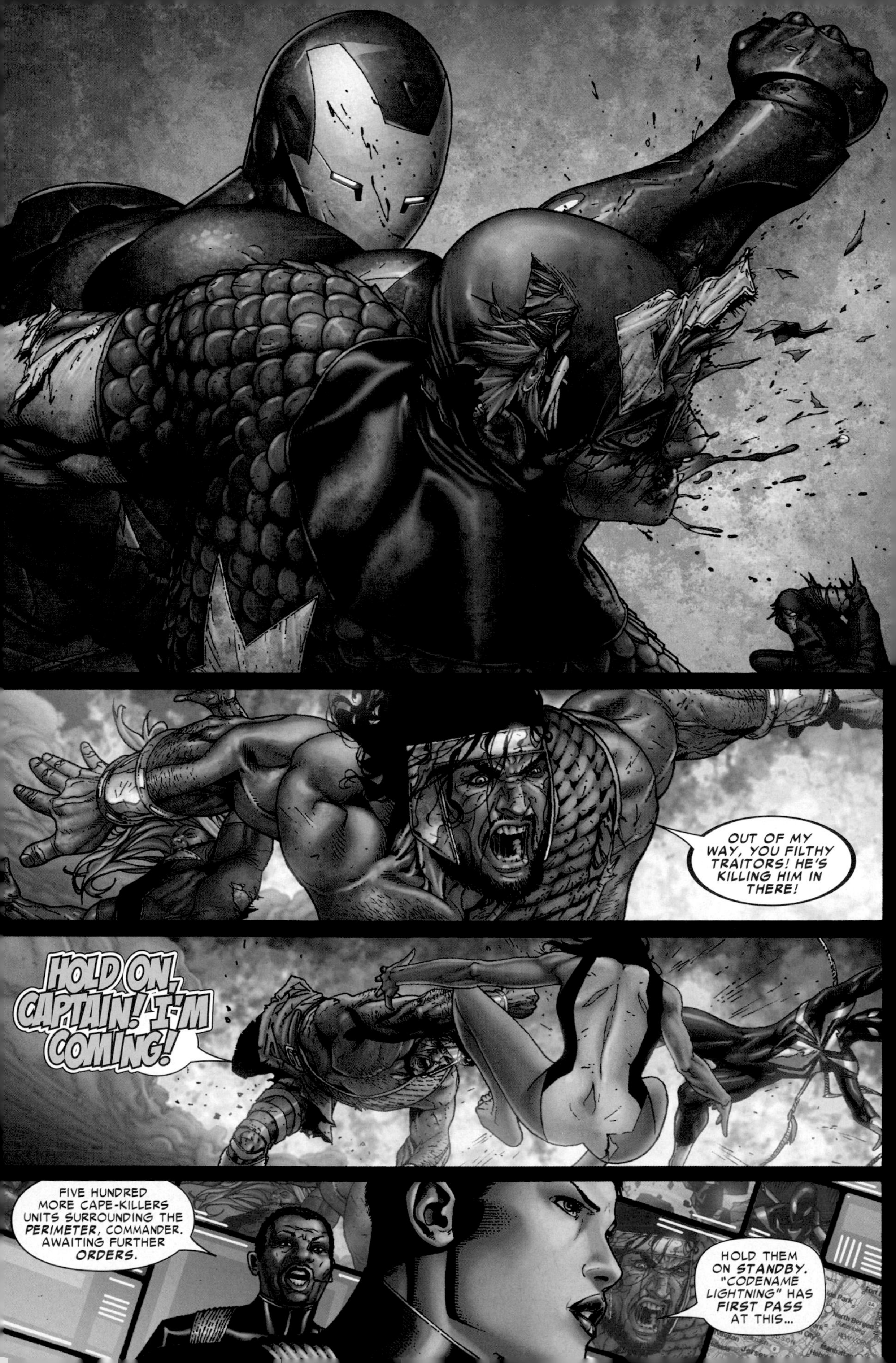
OUT OF MY WAY, YOU FILTHY TRAITORS! HE'S KILLING HIM IN THERE!
HOLD ON, CAPTAIN! I'M COMING!
FIVE HUNDRED MORE CAPE-KILLERS UNITS SURROUNDING THE PERIMETER, COMMANDER. AWAITING FURTHER ORDERS.
HOLD THEM ON STANDBY. "CODENAME LIGHTNING" HAS FIRST PASS AT THIS...

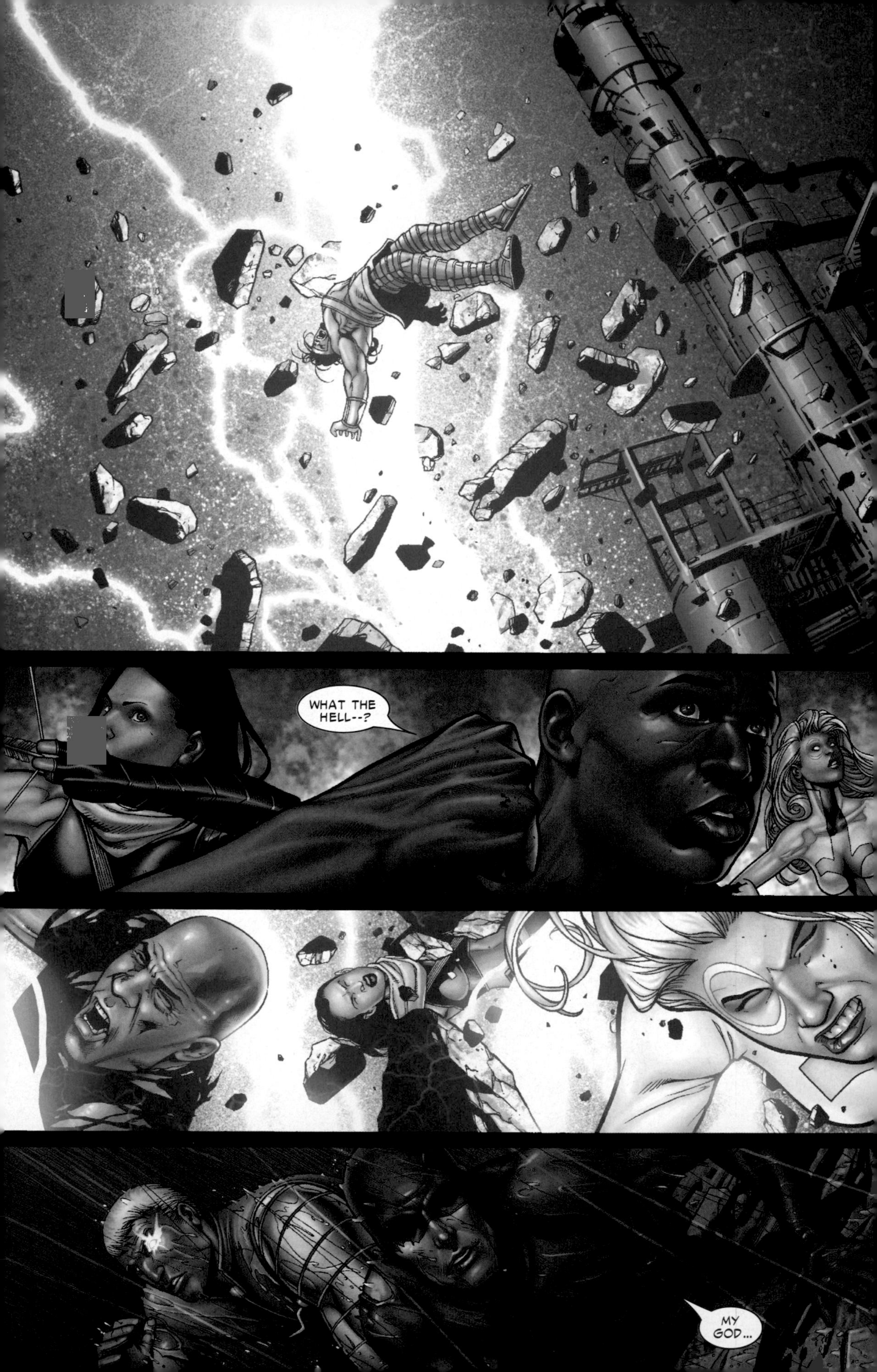
WHAT THE HELL--?
MY GOD...

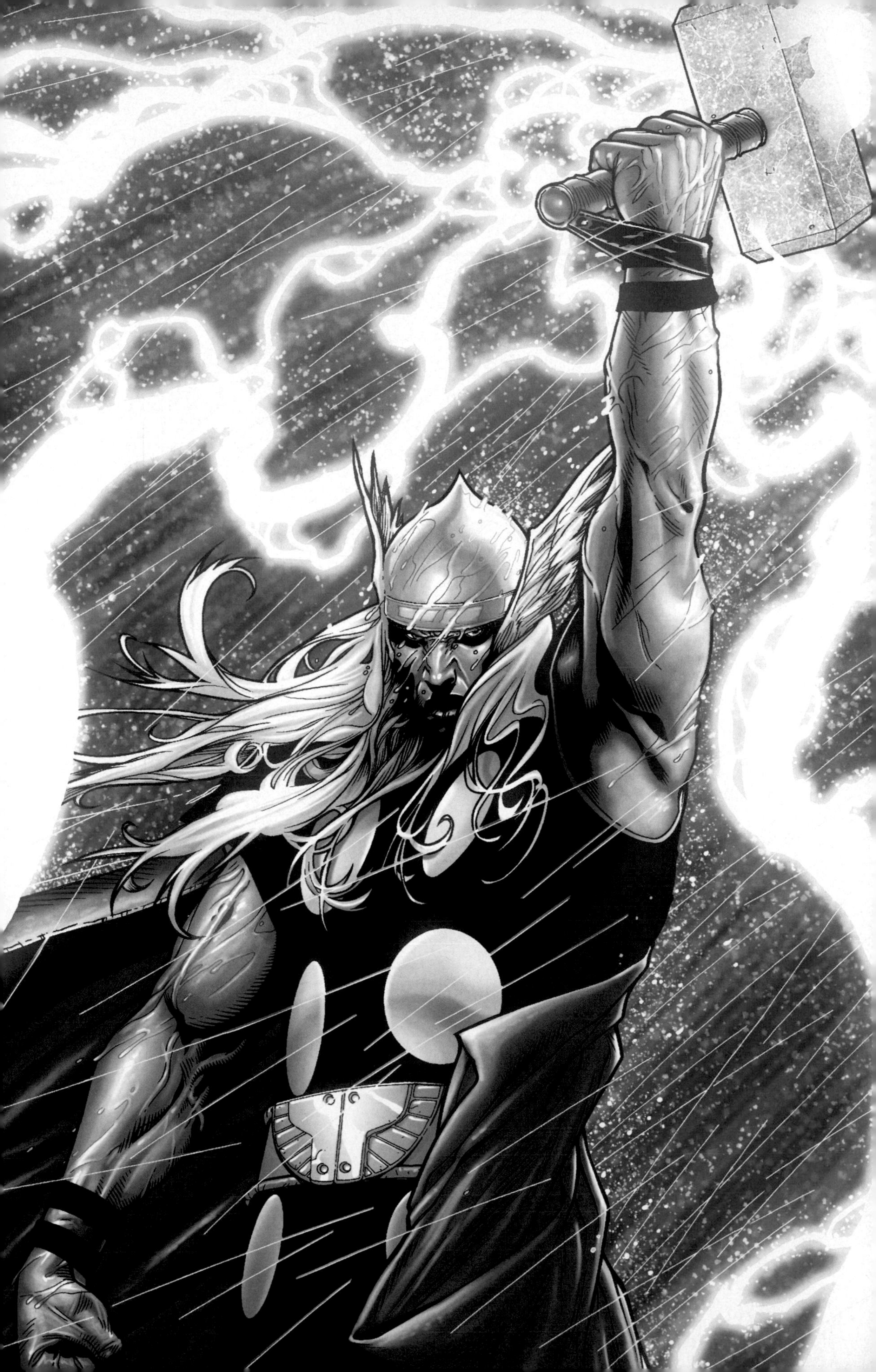

CIVIL WAR #4

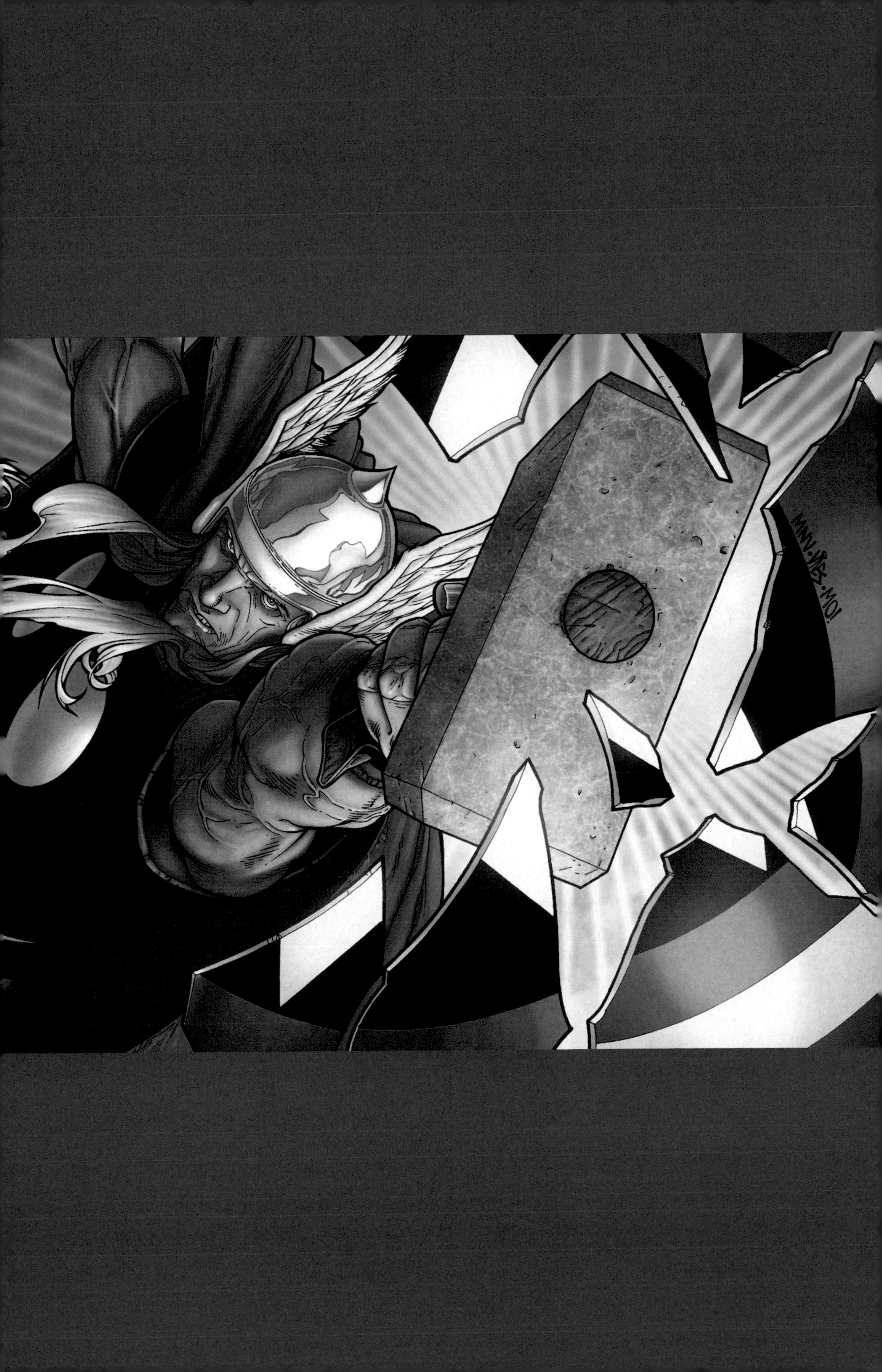

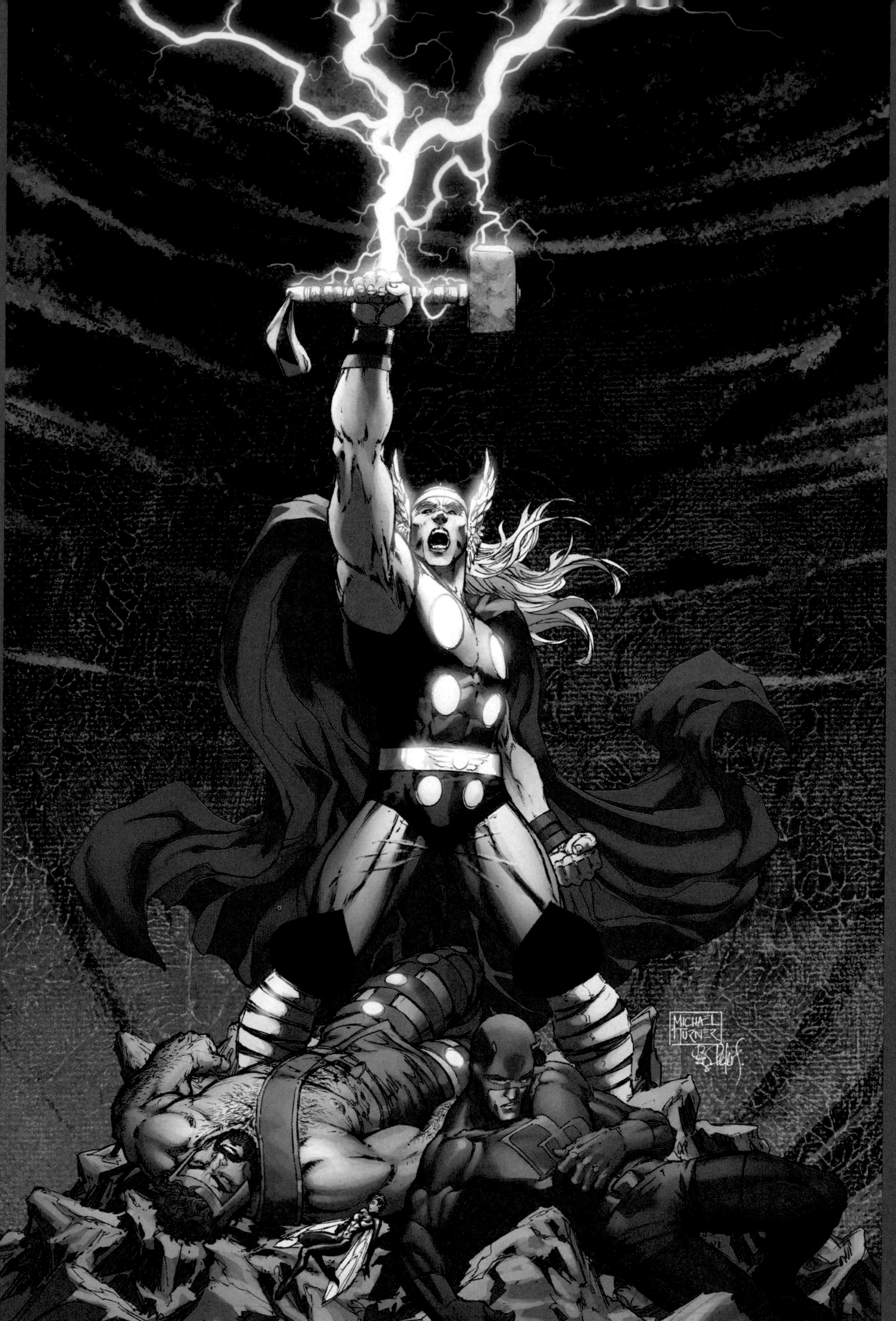
MICHAEL TURNER

CIVIL WAR #4 VARIANT BY MICHAEL TURNER & PETER STEIGERWALD

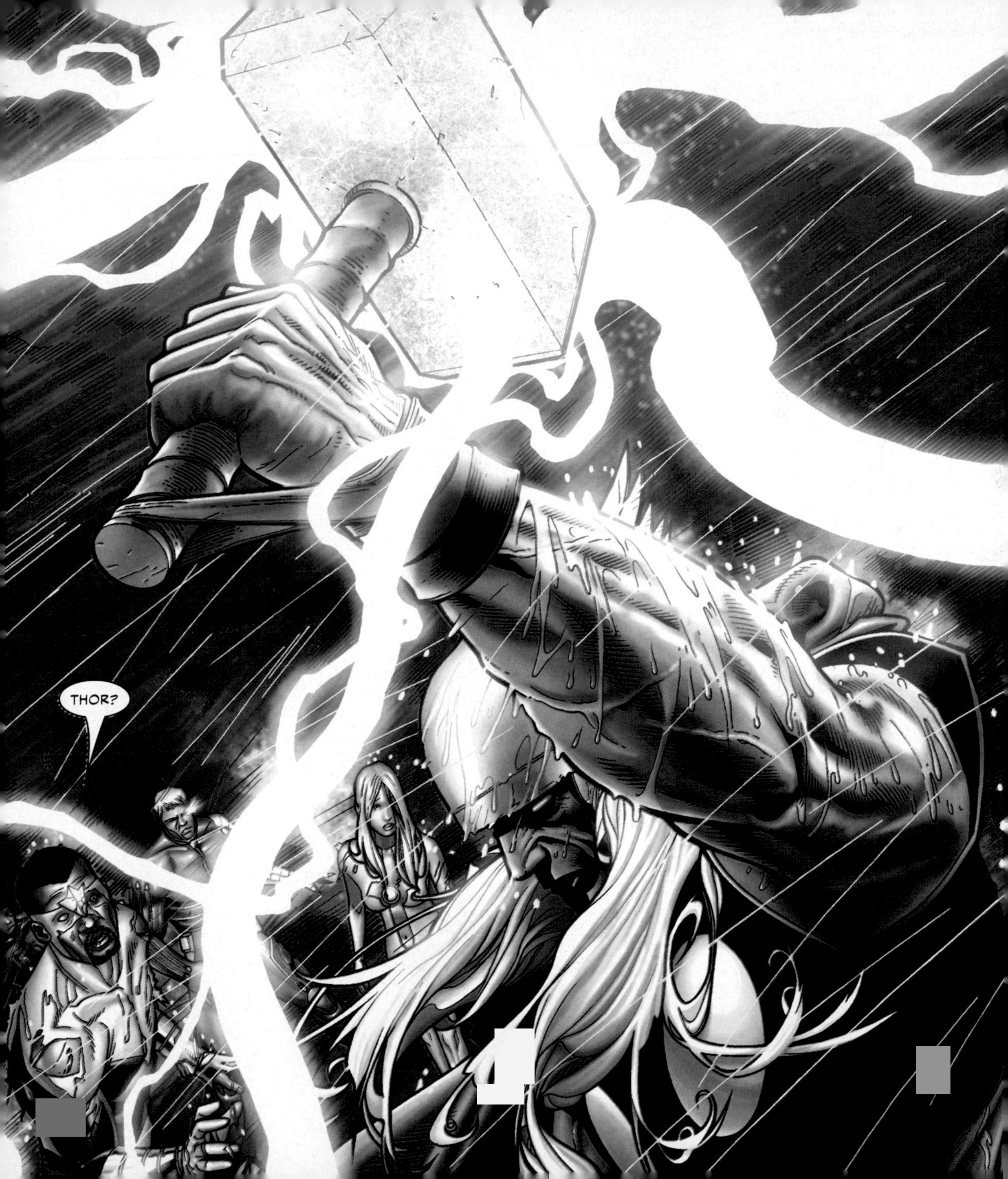
THOR?

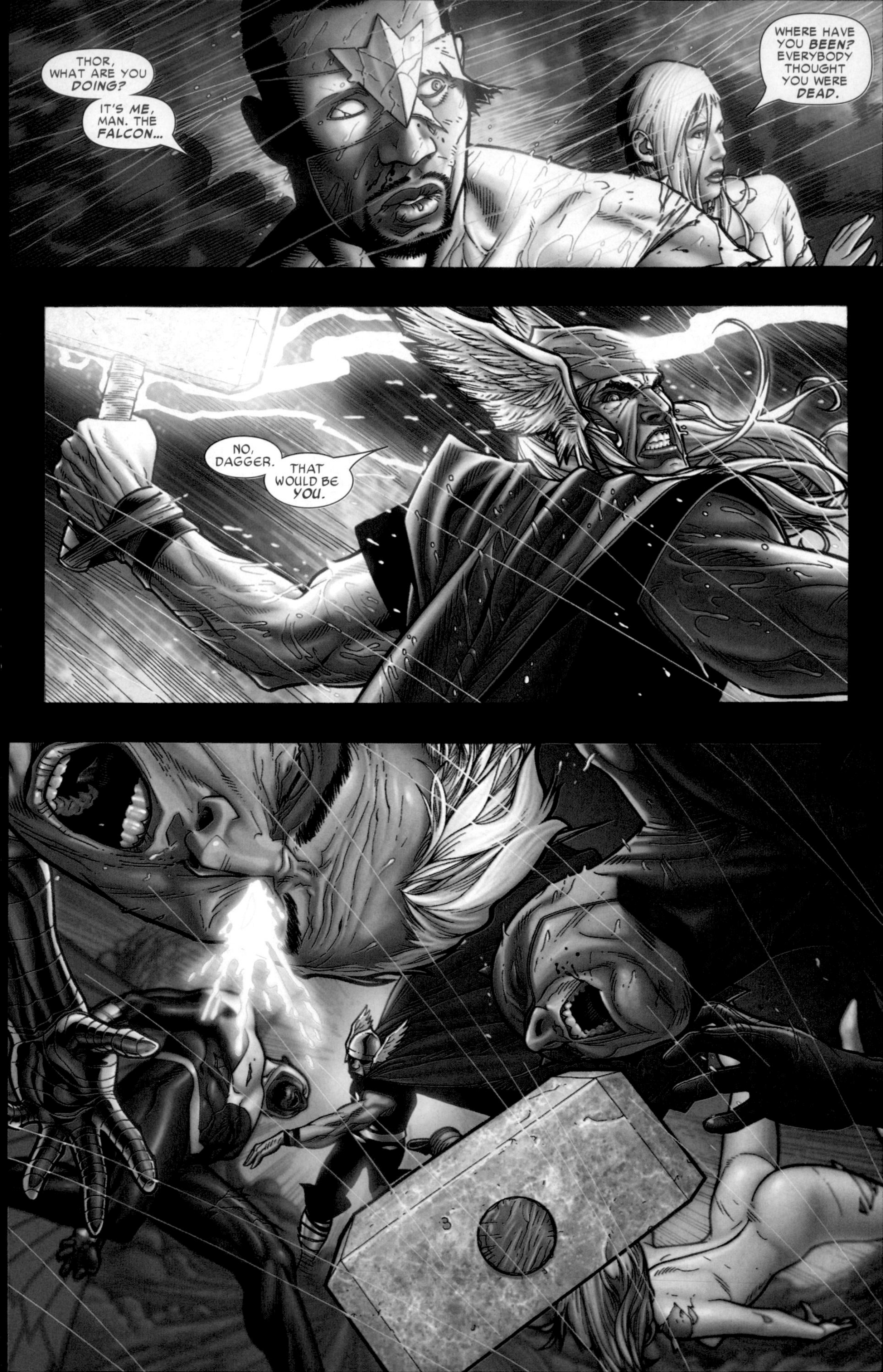
THOR, WHAT ARE YOU *DOING?*
IT'S *ME,* MAN. THE *FALCON...*
WHERE HAVE YOU *BEEN?* EVERYBODY THOUGHT YOU WERE *DEAD.*
NO, DAGGER.
THAT WOULD BE *YOU.*

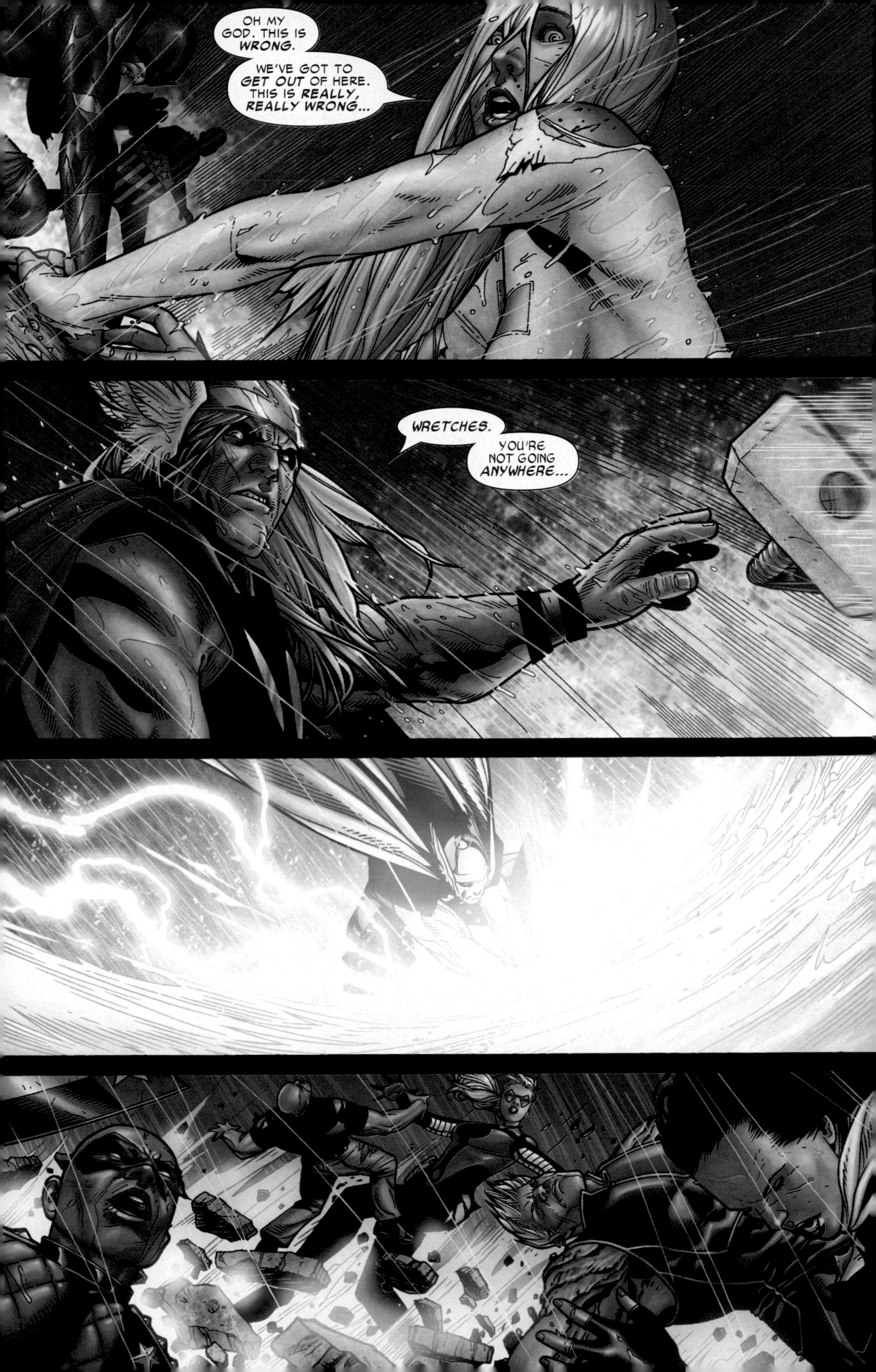
OH MY GOD. THIS IS WRONG.
WE'VE GOT TO GET OUT OF HERE. THIS IS REALLY, REALLY WRONG...
WRETCHES.
YOU'RE NOT GOING ANYWHERE...

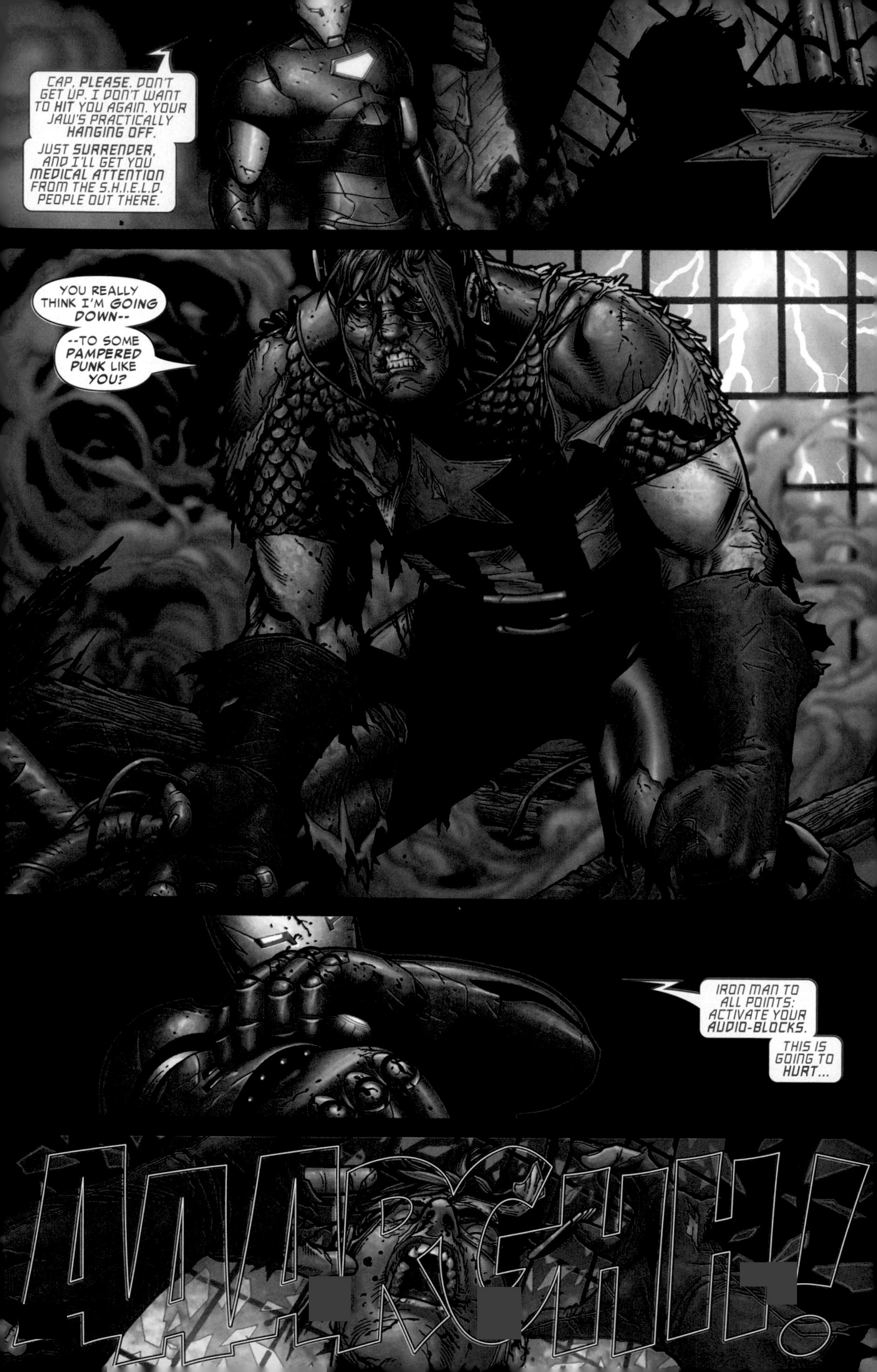
CAP, PLEASE. DON'T GET UP. I DON'T WANT TO HIT YOU AGAIN. YOUR JAW'S PRACTICALLY HANGING OFF.
JUST SURRENDER, AND I'LL GET YOU MEDICAL ATTENTION FROM THE S.H.I.E.L.D. PEOPLE OUT THERE.
YOU REALLY THINK I'M GOING DOWN--
--TO SOME PAMPERED PUNK LIKE YOU?
IRON MAN TO ALL POINTS: ACTIVATE YOUR AUDIO-BLOCKS.
THIS IS GOING TO HURT...

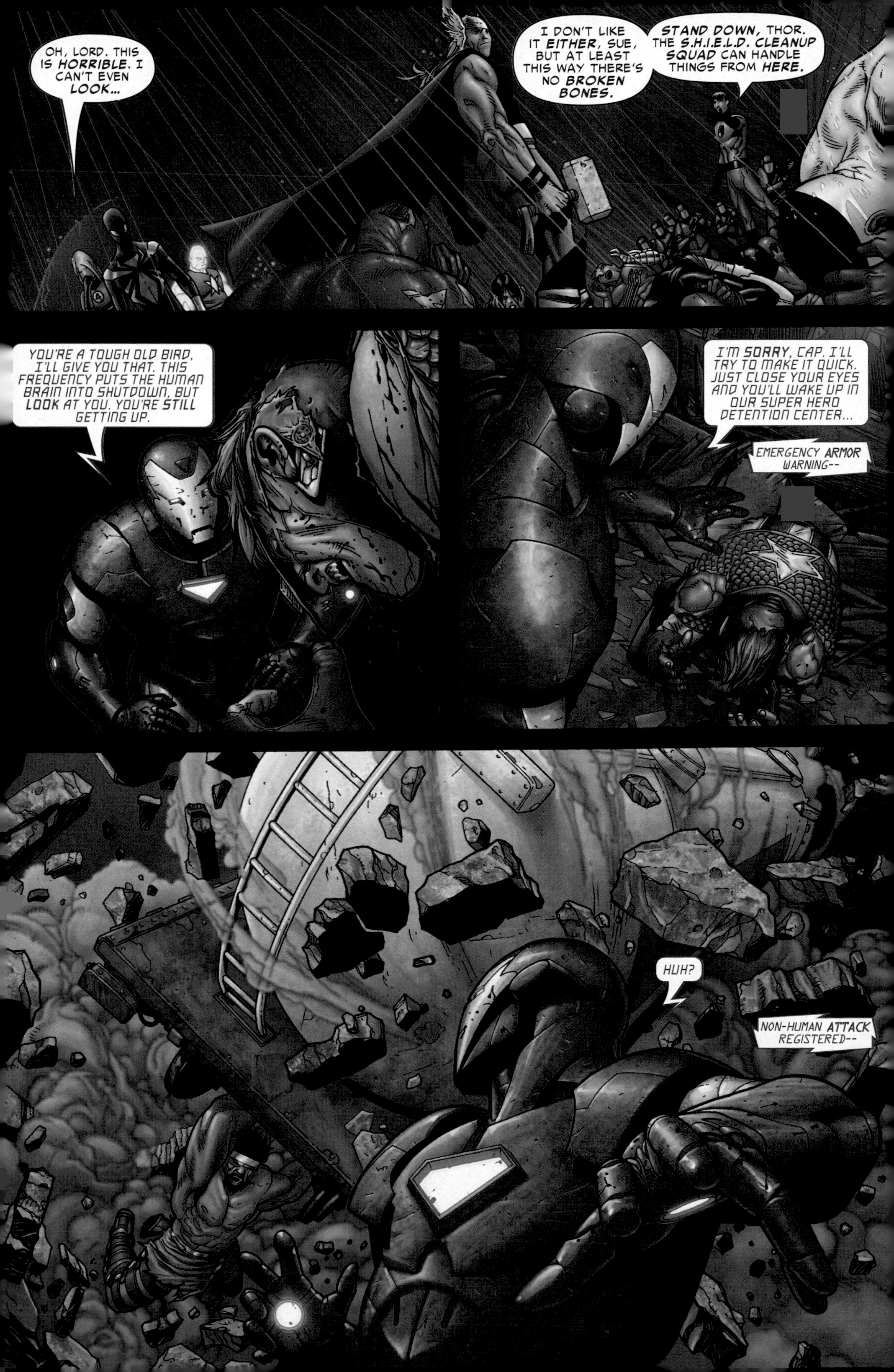
OH, LORD. THIS IS HORRIBLE. I CAN'T EVEN LOOK...
I DON'T LIKE IT EITHER, SUE, BUT AT LEAST THIS WAY THERE'S NO BROKEN BONES.
STAND DOWN, THOR. THE S.H.I.E.L.D. CLEANUP SQUAD CAN HANDLE THINGS FROM HERE.
YOU'RE A TOUGH OLD BIRD, I'LL GIVE YOU THAT. THIS FREQUENCY PUTS THE HUMAN BRAIN INTO SHUTDOWN, BUT LOOK AT YOU. YOU'RE STILL GETTING UP.
I'M SORRY, CAP. I'LL TRY TO MAKE IT QUICK. JUST CLOSE YOUR EYES AND YOU'LL WAKE UP IN OUR SUPER HERO DETENTION CENTER...
EMERGENCY ARMOR WARNING--
HUH?
NON-HUMAN ATTACK REGISTERED--

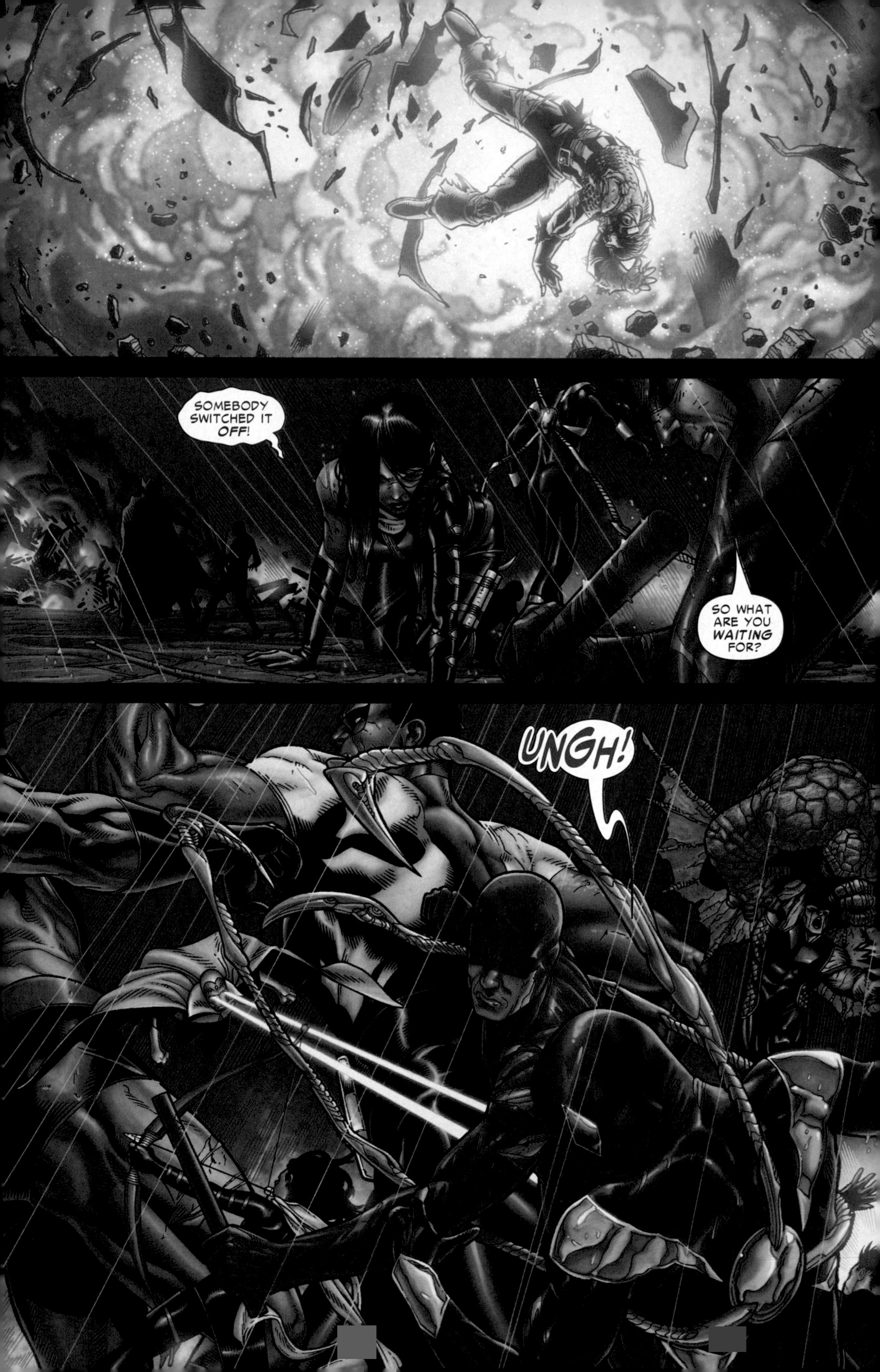
SOMEBODY SWITCHED IT OFF!
SO WHAT ARE YOU WAITING FOR?
UNGH!

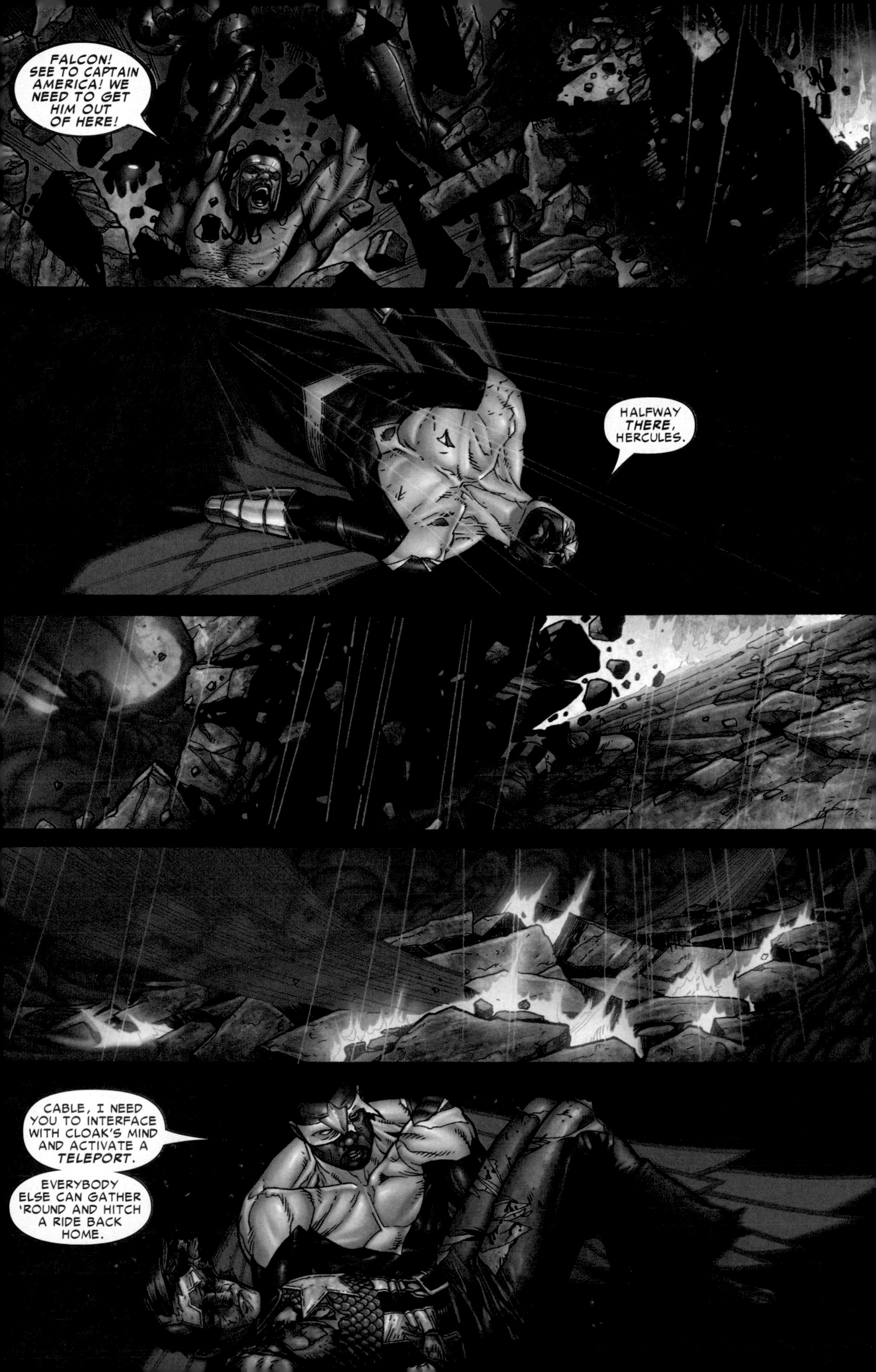
FALCON! SEE TO CAPTAIN AMERICA! WE NEED TO GET HIM OUT OF HERE!
HALFWAY *THERE*, HERCULES.
CABLE, I NEED YOU TO INTERFACE WITH CLOAK'S MIND AND ACTIVATE A *TELEPORT*.
EVERYBODY ELSE CAN GATHER 'ROUND AND HITCH A RIDE BACK HOME.

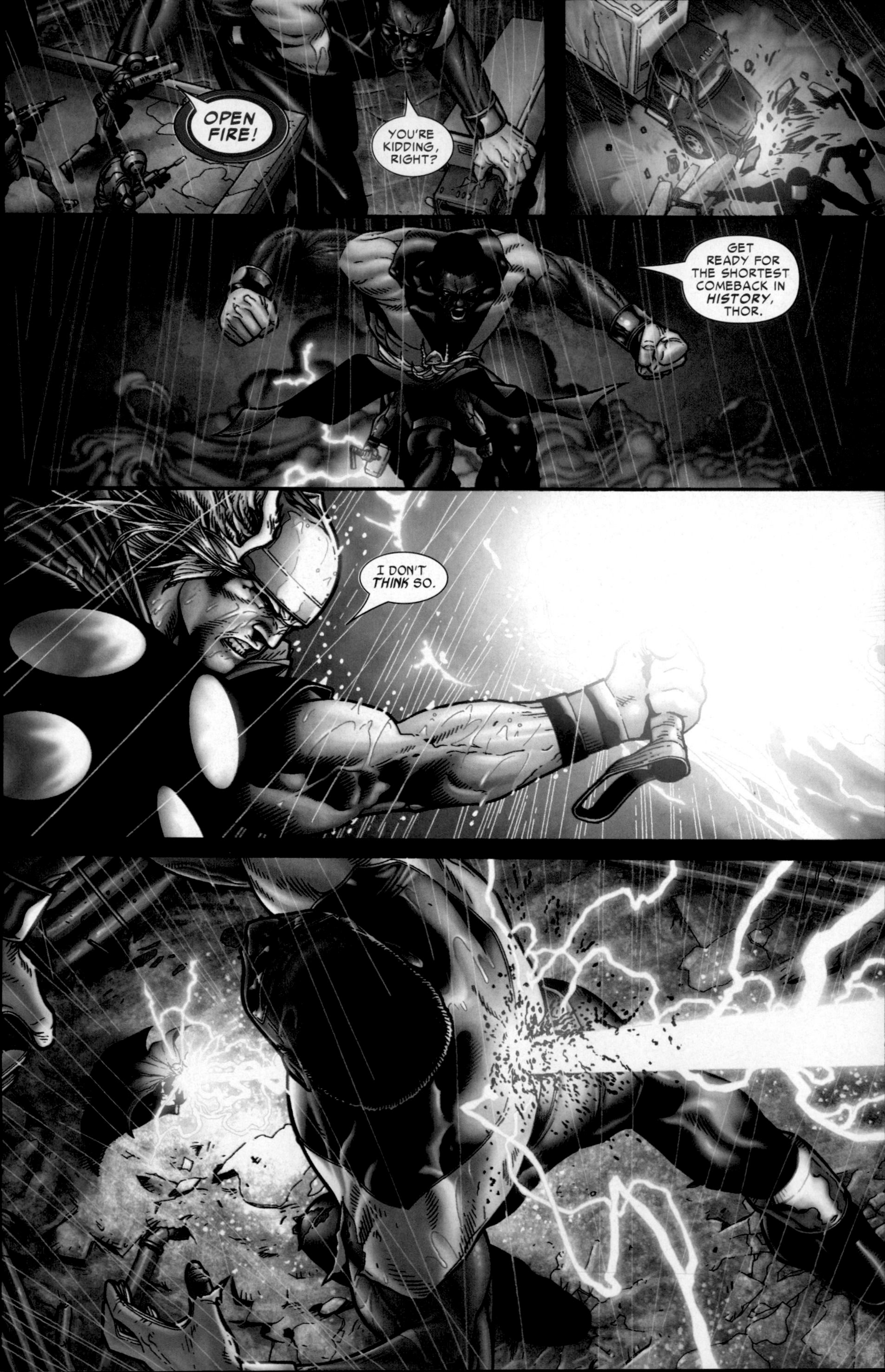
OPEN FIRE!
YOU'RE KIDDING, RIGHT?
GET READY FOR THE SHORTEST COMEBACK IN HISTORY, THOR.
I DON'T THINK SO.

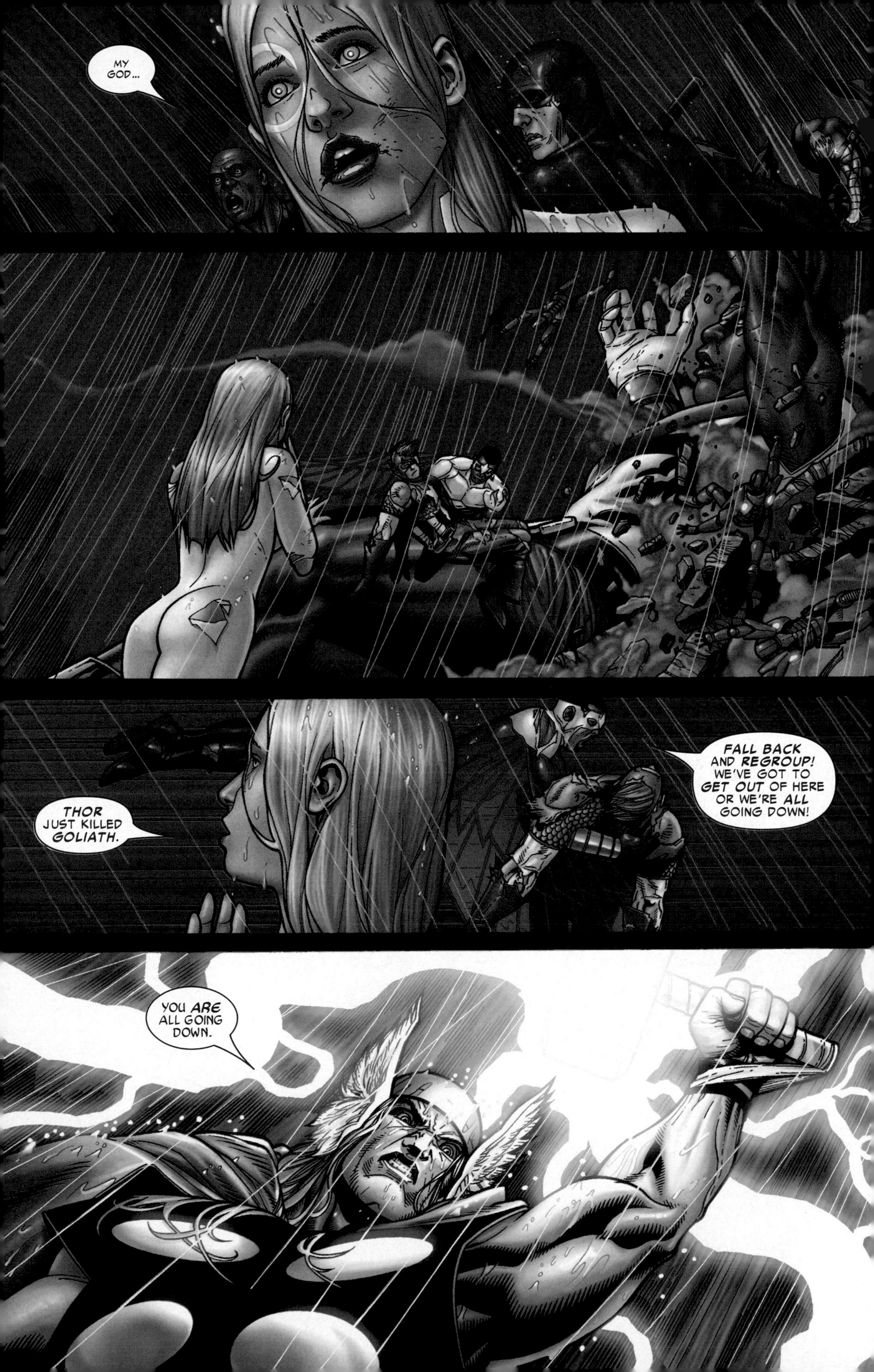
MY GOD...
THOR JUST KILLED GOLIATH.
FALL BACK AND REGROUP! WE'VE GOT TO GET OUT OF HERE OR WE'RE ALL GOING DOWN!
YOU ARE ALL GOING DOWN.

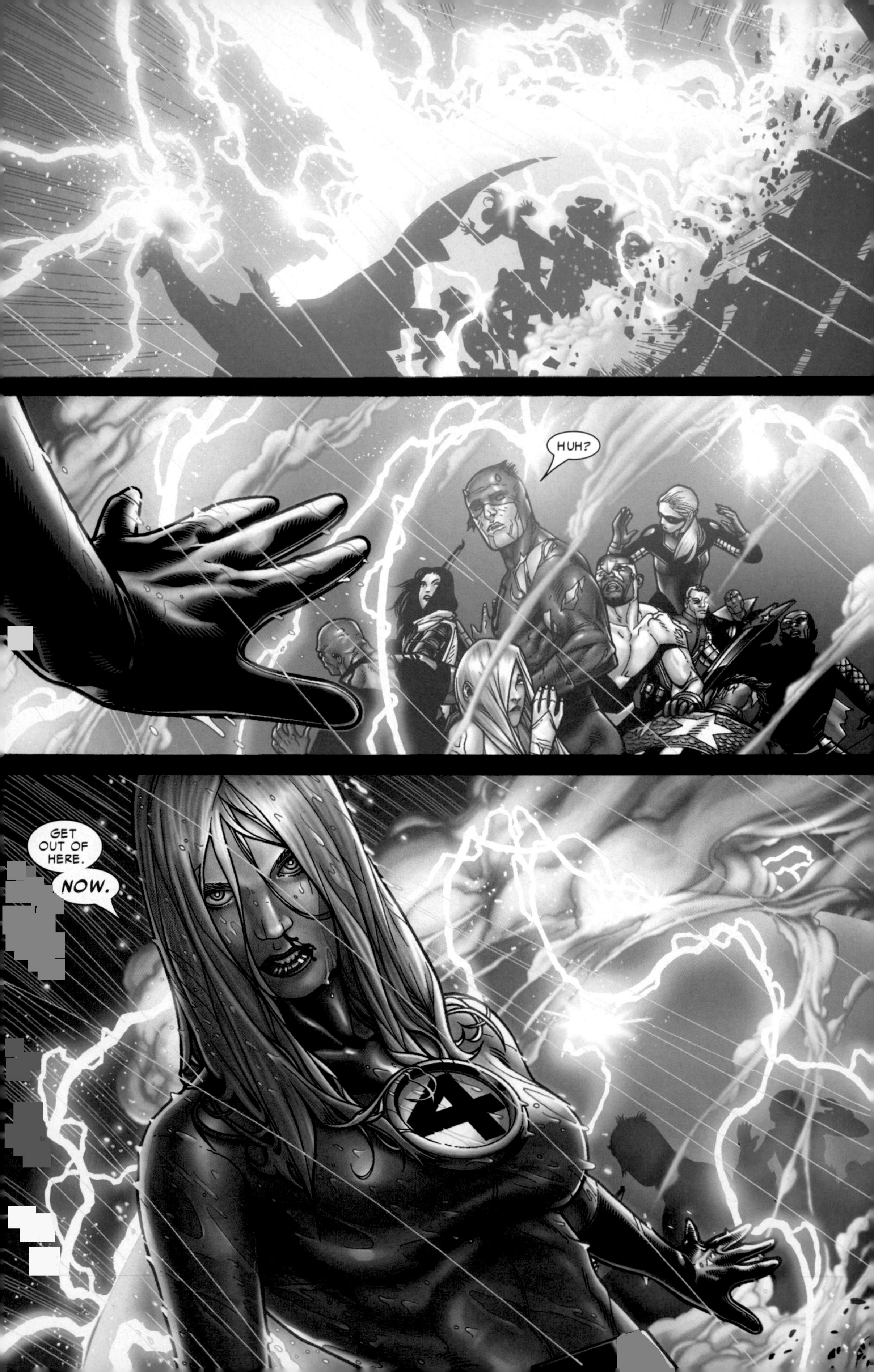
HUH?
GET OUT OF HERE.
NOW.

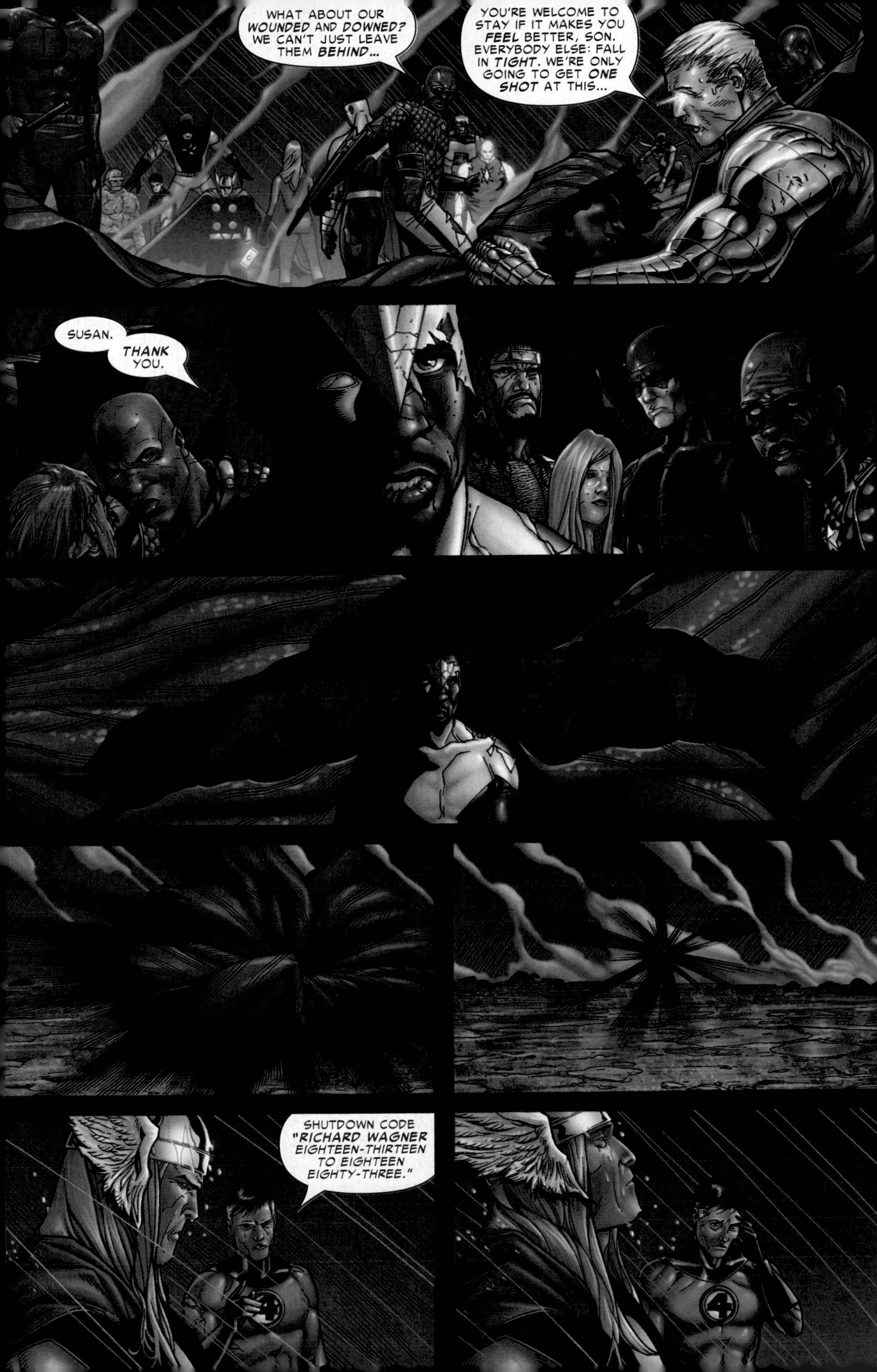
WHAT ABOUT OUR WOUNDED AND DOWNED? WE CAN'T JUST LEAVE THEM BEHIND...
YOU'RE WELCOME TO STAY IF IT MAKES YOU FEEL BETTER, SON. EVERYBODY ELSE: FALL IN TIGHT. WE'RE ONLY GOING TO GET ONE SHOT AT THIS...
SUSAN.
THANK YOU.
SHUTDOWN CODE "RICHARD WAGNER EIGHTEEN-THIRTEEN TO EIGHTEEN EIGHTY-THREE."

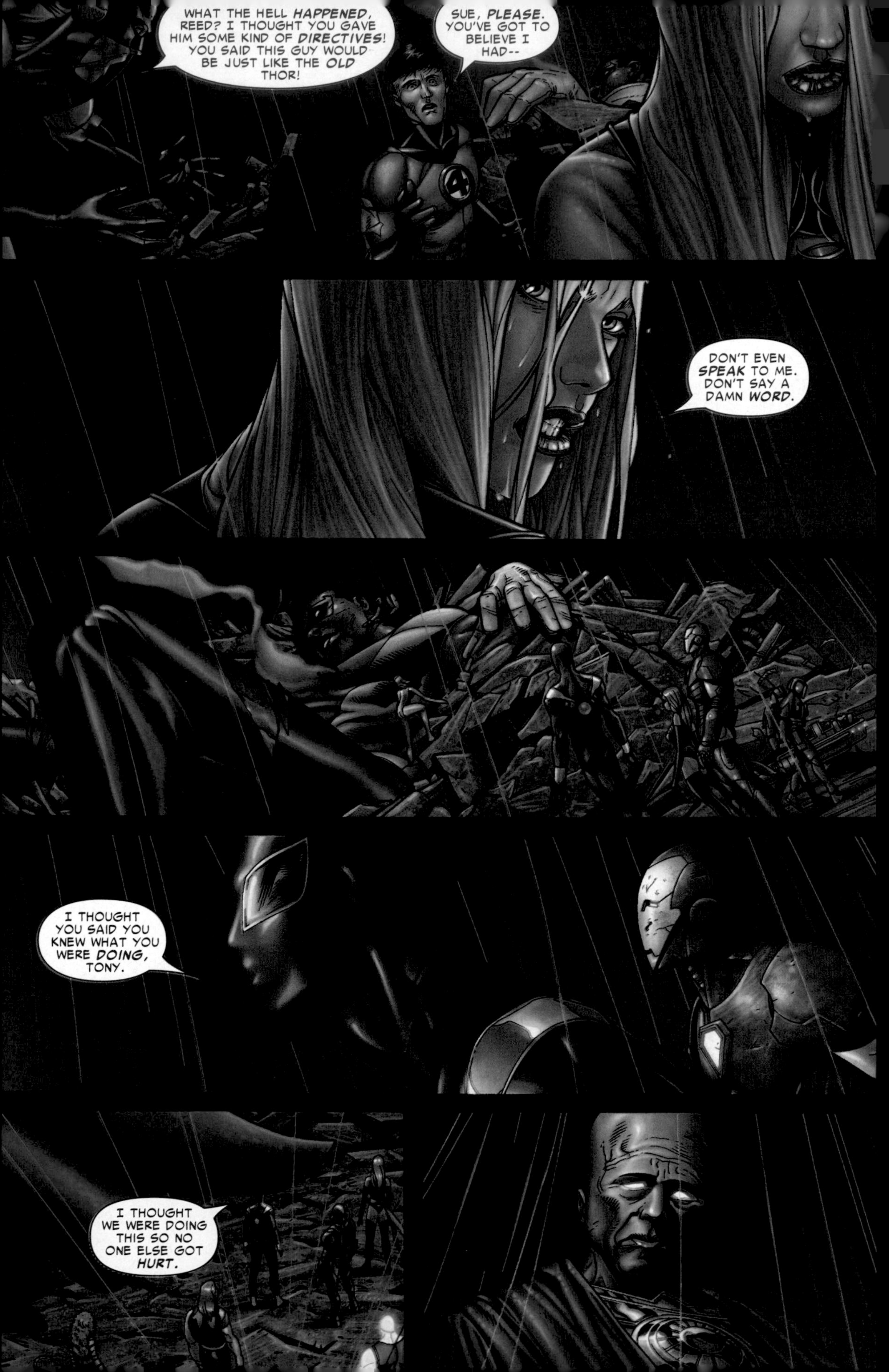
WHAT THE HELL HAPPENED, REED? I THOUGHT YOU GAVE HIM SOME KIND OF DIRECTIVES! YOU SAID THIS GUY WOULD BE JUST LIKE THE OLD THOR!
SUE, PLEASE. YOU'VE GOT TO BELIEVE I HAD--
DON'T EVEN SPEAK TO ME. DON'T SAY A DAMN WORD.
I THOUGHT YOU SAID YOU KNEW WHAT YOU WERE DOING, TONY.
I THOUGHT WE WERE DOING THIS SO NO ONE ELSE GOT HURT.

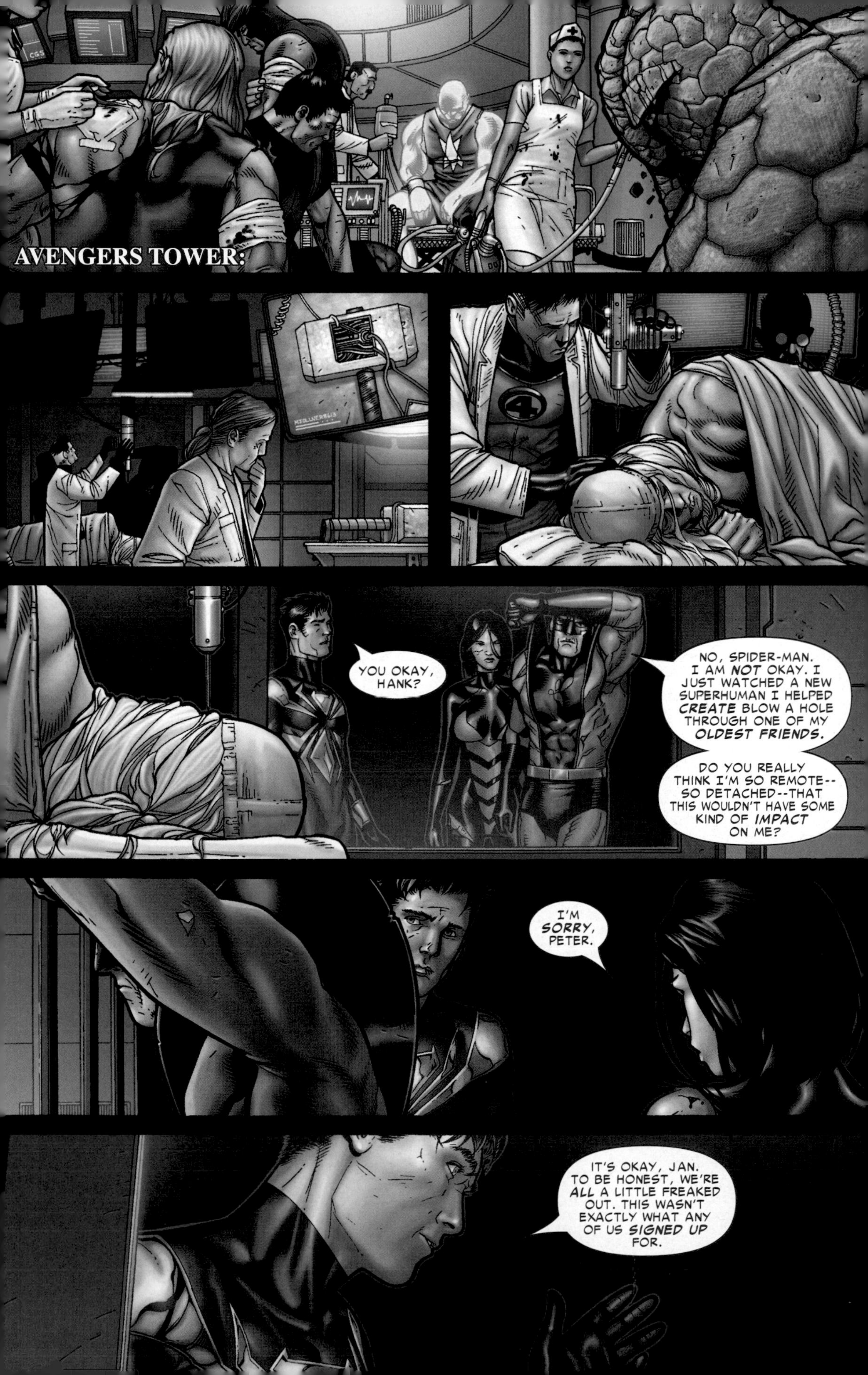
AVENGERS TOWER:
YOU OKAY, HANK?
NO, SPIDER-MAN. I AM NOT OKAY. I JUST WATCHED A NEW SUPERHUMAN I HELPED CREATE BLOW A HOLE THROUGH ONE OF MY OLDEST FRIENDS.
DO YOU REALLY THINK I'M SO REMOTE-- SO DETACHED--THAT THIS WOULDN'T HAVE SOME KIND OF IMPACT ON ME?
I'M SORRY, PETER.
IT'S OKAY, JAN. TO BE HONEST, WE'RE ALL A LITTLE FREAKED OUT. THIS WASN'T EXACTLY WHAT ANY OF US SIGNED UP FOR.

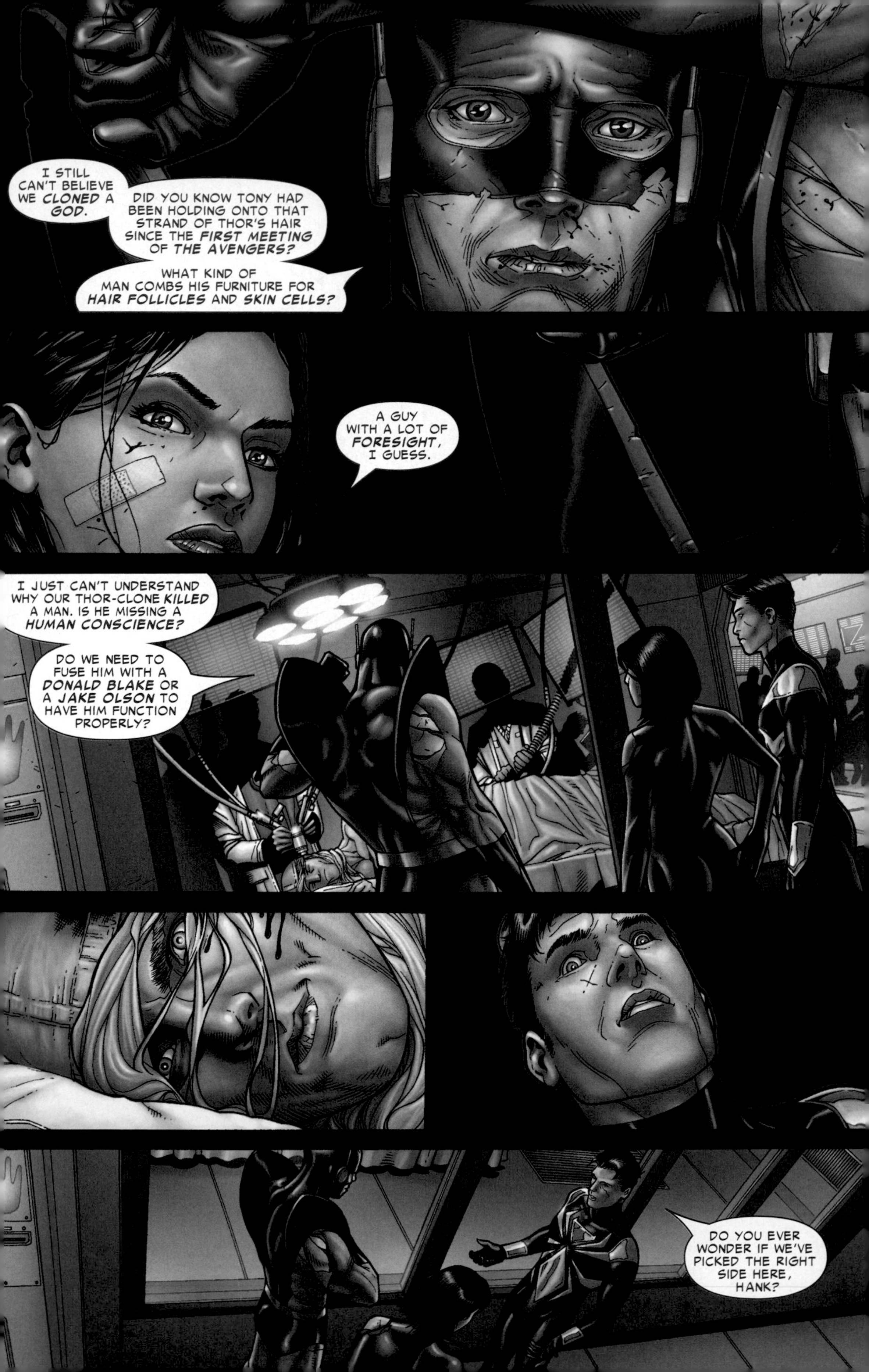
I STILL CAN'T BELIEVE WE CLONED A GOD.
DID YOU KNOW TONY HAD BEEN HOLDING ONTO THAT STRAND OF THOR'S HAIR SINCE THE FIRST MEETING OF THE AVENGERS?
WHAT KIND OF MAN COMBS HIS FURNITURE FOR HAIR FOLLICLES AND SKIN CELLS?
A GUY WITH A LOT OF FORESIGHT, I GUESS.
I JUST CAN'T UNDERSTAND WHY OUR THOR-CLONE KILLED A MAN. IS HE MISSING A HUMAN CONSCIENCE?
DO WE NEED TO FUSE HIM WITH A DONALD BLAKE OR A JAKE OLSON TO HAVE HIM FUNCTION PROPERLY?
DO YOU EVER WONDER IF WE'VE PICKED THE RIGHT SIDE HERE, HANK?

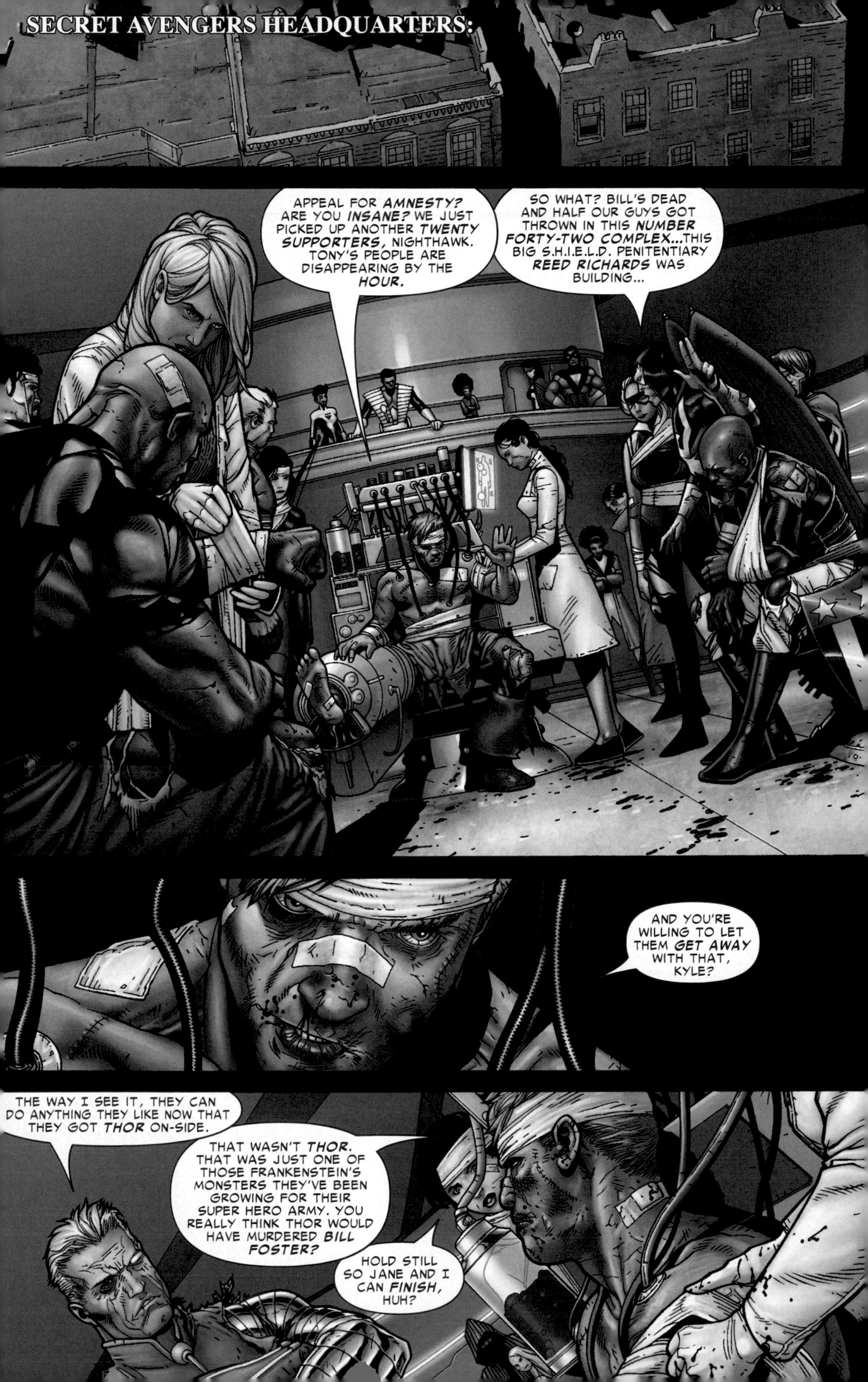
SECRET AVENGERS HEADQUARTERS:
APPEAL FOR AMNESTY? ARE YOU INSANE? WE JUST PICKED UP ANOTHER TWENTY SUPPORTERS, NIGHTHAWK. TONY'S PEOPLE ARE DISAPPEARING BY THE HOUR.
SO WHAT? BILL'S DEAD AND HALF OUR GUYS GOT THROWN IN THIS NUMBER FORTY-TWO COMPLEX...THIS BIG S.H.I.E.L.D. PENITENTIARY REED RICHARDS WAS BUILDING...
AND YOU'RE WILLING TO LET THEM GET AWAY WITH THAT, KYLE?
THE WAY I SEE IT, THEY CAN DO ANYTHING THEY LIKE NOW THAT THEY GOT THOR ON-SIDE.
THAT WASN'T THOR. THAT WAS JUST ONE OF THOSE FRANKENSTEIN'S MONSTERS THEY'VE BEEN GROWING FOR THEIR SUPER HERO ARMY. YOU REALLY THINK THOR WOULD HAVE MURDERED BILL FOSTER?
HOLD STILL SO JANE AND I CAN FINISH, HUH?

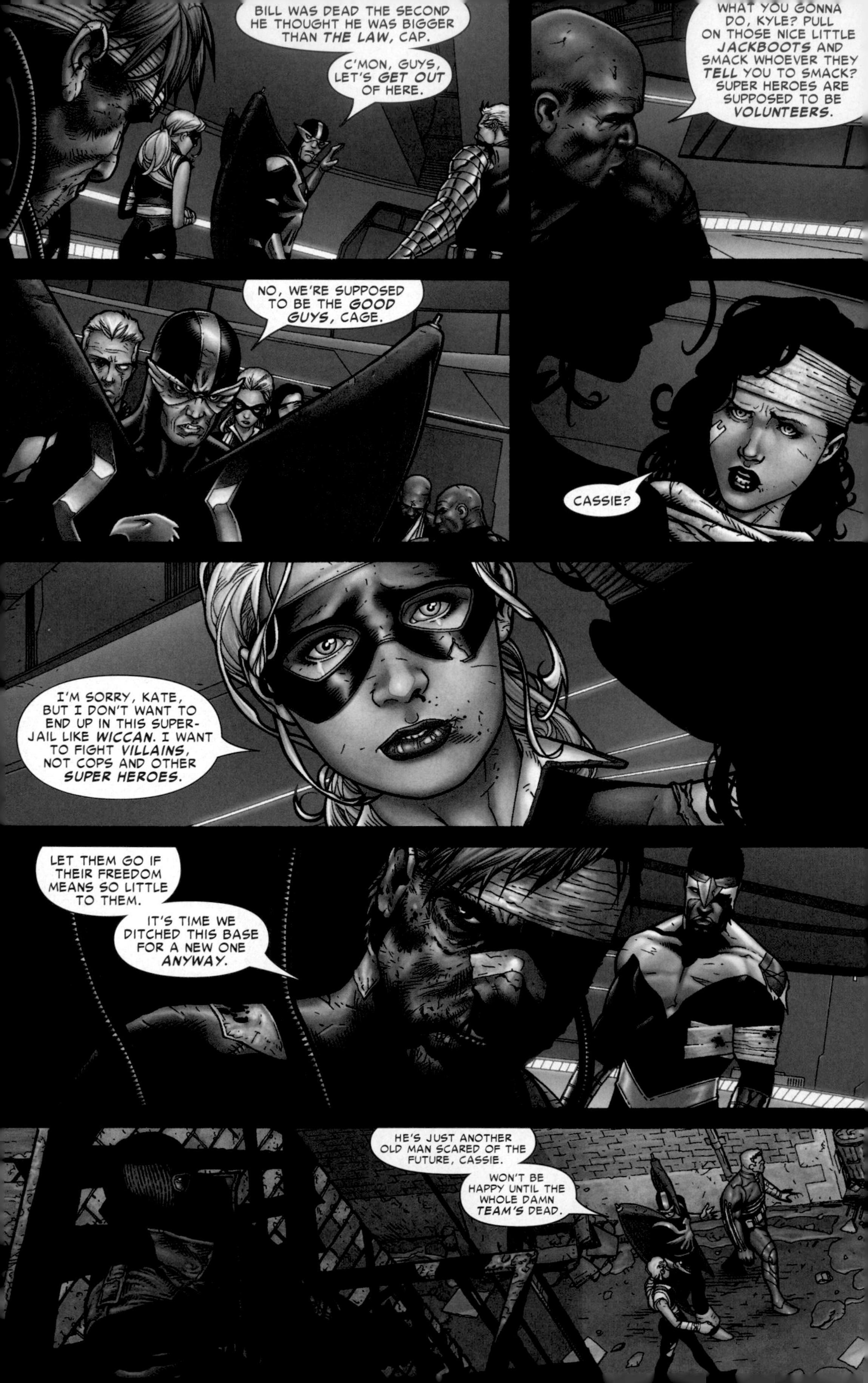
BILL WAS DEAD THE SECOND HE THOUGHT HE WAS BIGGER THAN THE LAW, CAP.
C'MON, GUYS, LET'S GET OUT OF HERE.
WHAT YOU GONNA DO, KYLE? PULL ON THOSE NICE LITTLE JACKBOOTS AND SMACK WHOEVER THEY TELL YOU TO SMACK? SUPER HEROES ARE SUPPOSED TO BE VOLUNTEERS.
NO, WE'RE SUPPOSED TO BE THE GOOD GUYS, CAGE.
CASSIE?
I'M SORRY, KATE, BUT I DON'T WANT TO END UP IN THIS SUPER-JAIL LIKE WICCAN. I WANT TO FIGHT VILLAINS, NOT COPS AND OTHER SUPER HEROES.
LET THEM GO IF THEIR FREEDOM MEANS SO LITTLE TO THEM.
IT'S TIME WE DITCHED THIS BASE FOR A NEW ONE ANYWAY.
HE'S JUST ANOTHER OLD MAN SCARED OF THE FUTURE, CASSIE.
WON'T BE HAPPY UNTIL THE WHOLE DAMN TEAM'S DEAD.

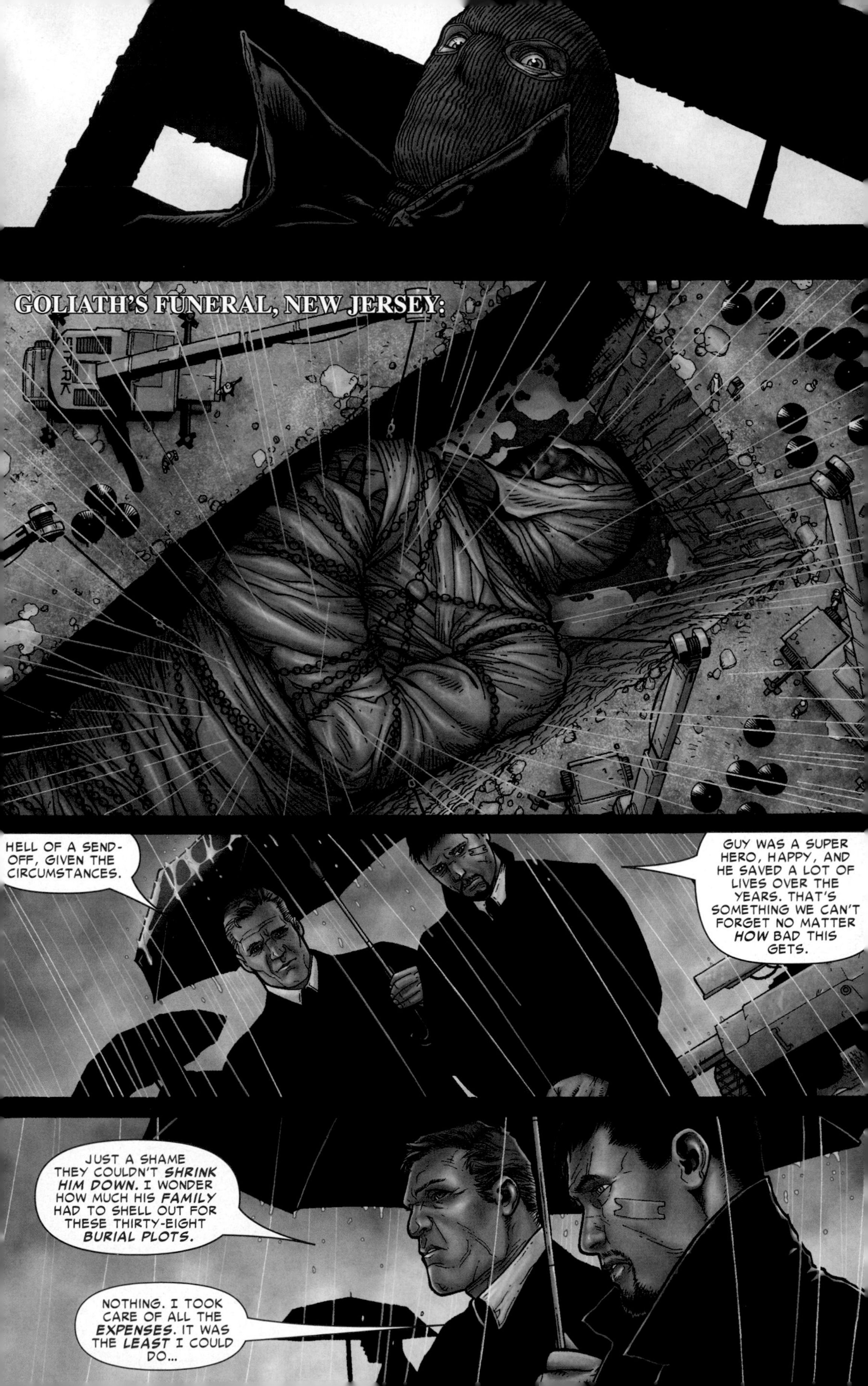
GOLIATH'S FUNERAL, NEW JERSEY:
HELL OF A SEND-OFF, GIVEN THE CIRCUMSTANCES.
GUY WAS A SUPER HERO, HAPPY, AND HE SAVED A LOT OF LIVES OVER THE YEARS. THAT'S SOMETHING WE CAN'T FORGET NO MATTER HOW BAD THIS GETS.
JUST A SHAME THEY COULDN'T SHRINK HIM DOWN. I WONDER HOW MUCH HIS FAMILY HAD TO SHELL OUT FOR THESE THIRTY-EIGHT BURIAL PLOTS.
NOTHING. I TOOK CARE OF ALL THE EXPENSES. IT WAS THE LEAST I COULD DO...

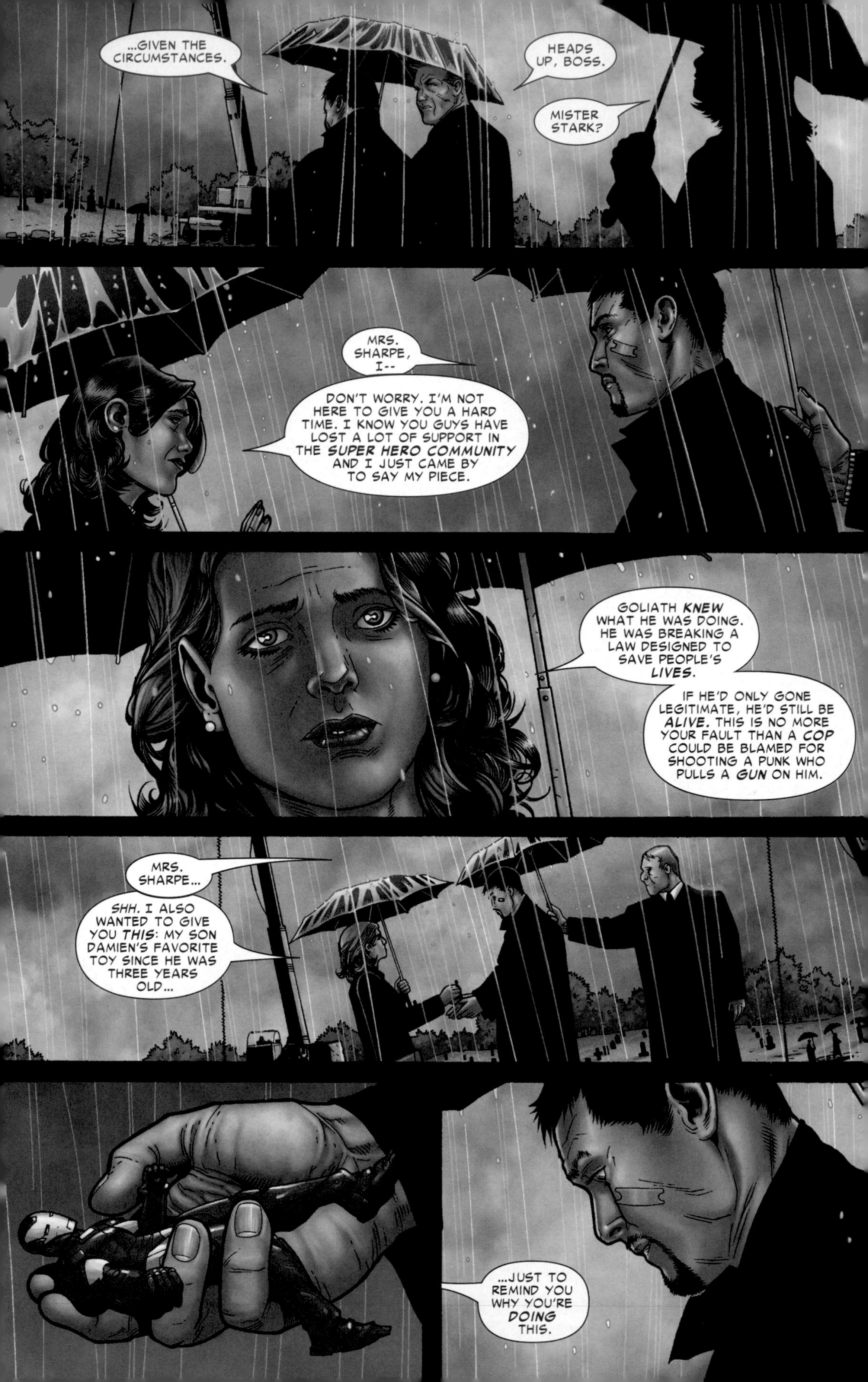
...GIVEN THE CIRCUMSTANCES.
HEADS UP, BOSS.
MISTER STARK?
MRS. SHARPE, I--
DON'T WORRY. I'M NOT HERE TO GIVE YOU A HARD TIME. I KNOW YOU GUYS HAVE LOST A LOT OF SUPPORT IN THE *SUPER HERO COMMUNITY* AND I JUST CAME BY TO SAY MY PIECE.
GOLIATH *KNEW* WHAT HE WAS DOING. HE WAS BREAKING A LAW DESIGNED TO SAVE PEOPLE'S *LIVES*.
IF HE'D ONLY GONE LEGITIMATE, HE'D STILL BE *ALIVE*. THIS IS NO MORE YOUR FAULT THAN A *COP* COULD BE BLAMED FOR SHOOTING A PUNK WHO PULLS A *GUN* ON HIM.
MRS. SHARPE...
SHH. I ALSO WANTED TO GIVE YOU *THIS*: MY SON DAMIEN'S FAVORITE TOY SINCE HE WAS THREE YEARS OLD...
...JUST TO REMIND YOU WHY YOU'RE *DOING* THIS.

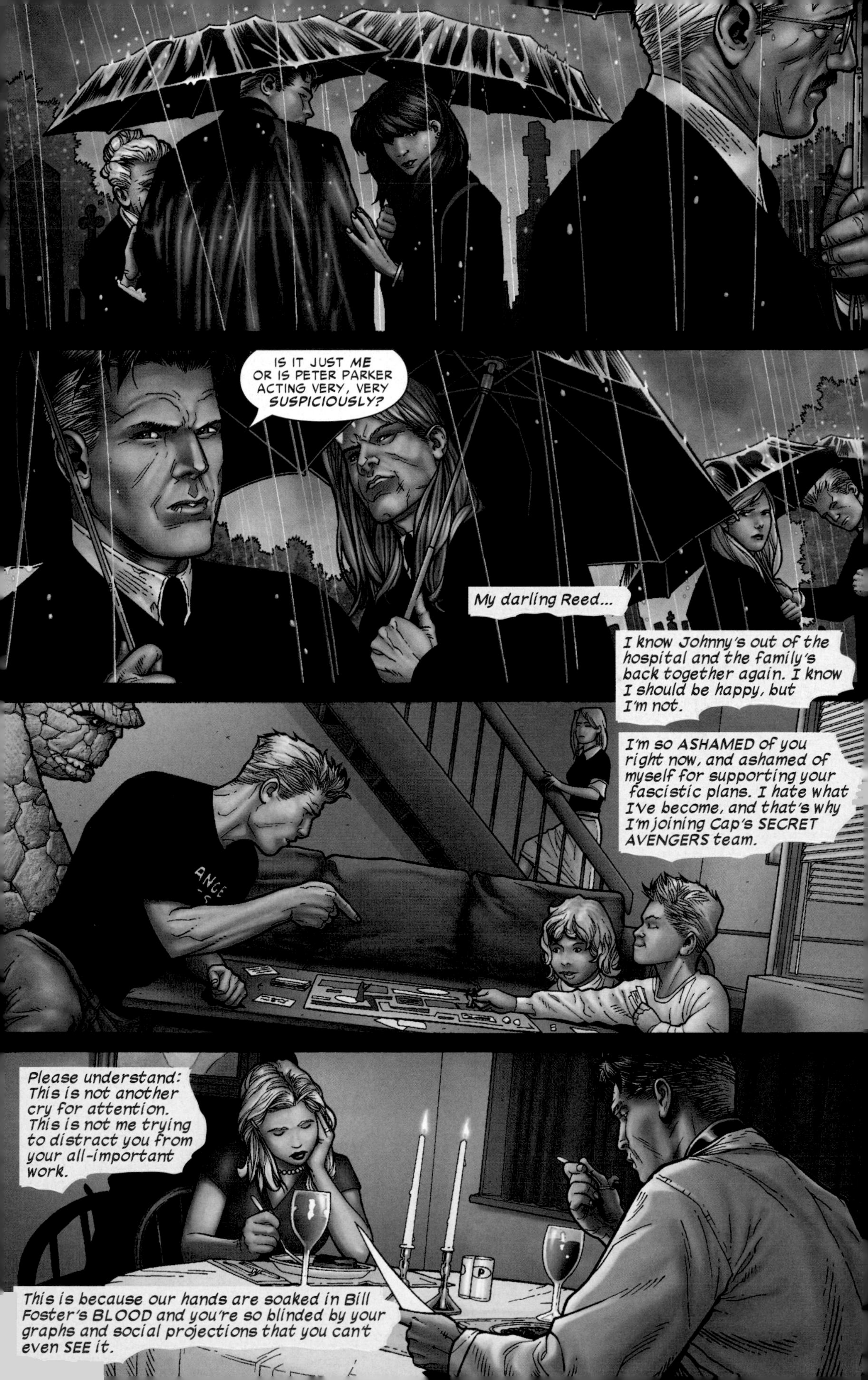
IS IT JUST ME OR IS PETER PARKER ACTING VERY, VERY SUSPICIOUSLY?
My darling Reed...
I know Johnny's out of the hospital and the family's back together again. I know I should be happy, but I'm not.
I'm so ASHAMED of you right now, and ashamed of myself for supporting your fascistic plans. I hate what I've become, and that's why I'm joining Cap's SECRET AVENGERS team.
Please understand: This is not another cry for attention. This is not me trying to distract you from your all-important work.
This is because our hands are soaked in Bill Foster's BLOOD and you're so blinded by your graphs and social projections that you can't even SEE it.

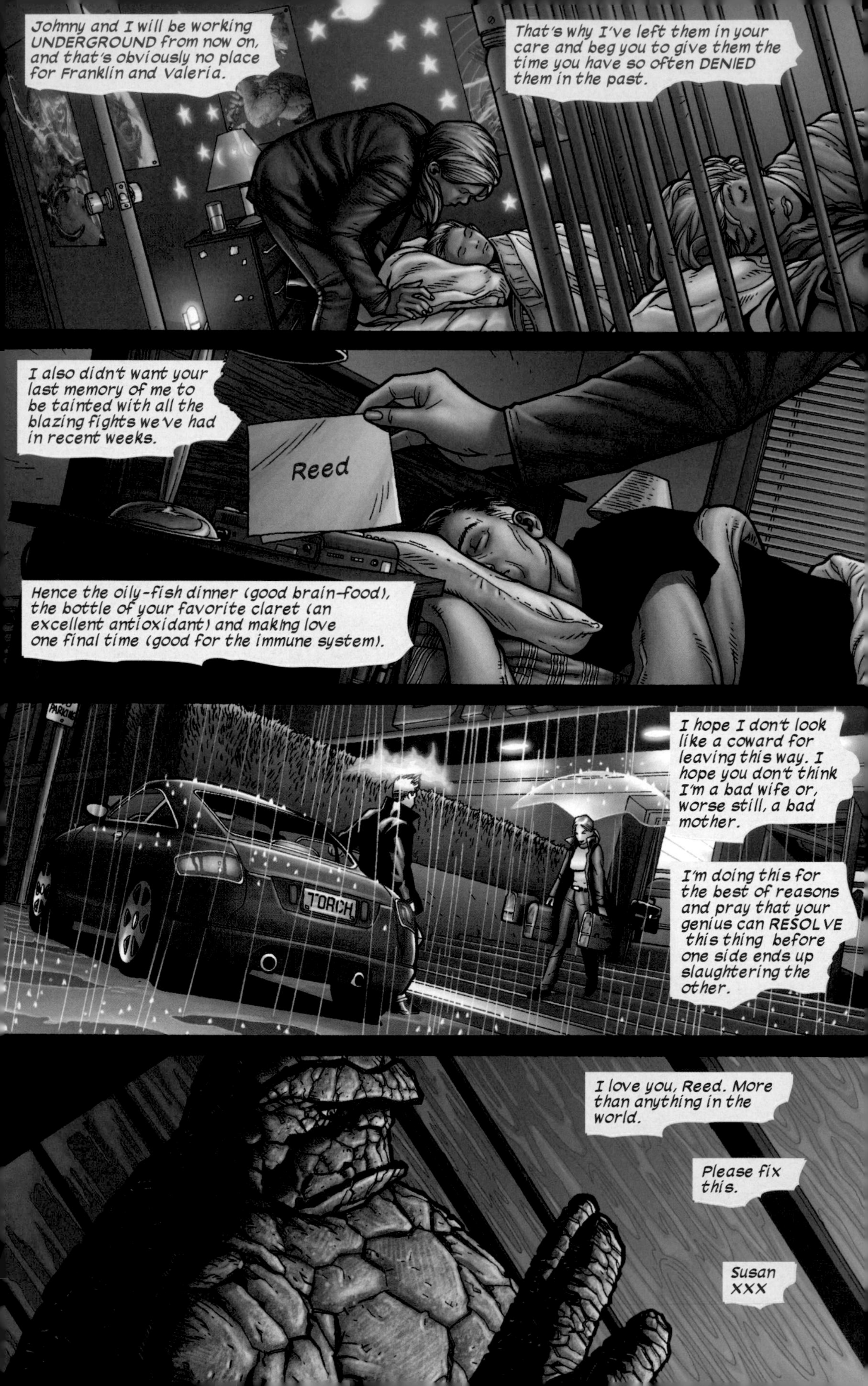
Johnny and I will be working UNDERGROUND from now on, and that's obviously no place for Franklin and Valeria.
That's why I've left them in your care and beg you to give them the time you have so often DENIED them in the past.
I also didn't want your last memory of me to be tainted with all the blazing fights we've had in recent weeks.
Reed
Hence the oily-fish dinner (good brain-food), the bottle of your favorite claret (an excellent antioxidant) and making love one final time (good for the immune system).
TORCH
I hope I don't look like a coward for leaving this way. I hope you don't think I'm a bad wife or, worse still, a bad mother.
I'm doing this for the best of reasons and pray that your genius can RESOLVE this thing before one side ends up slaughtering the other.
I love you, Reed. More than anything in the world.
Please fix this.
Susan
XXX

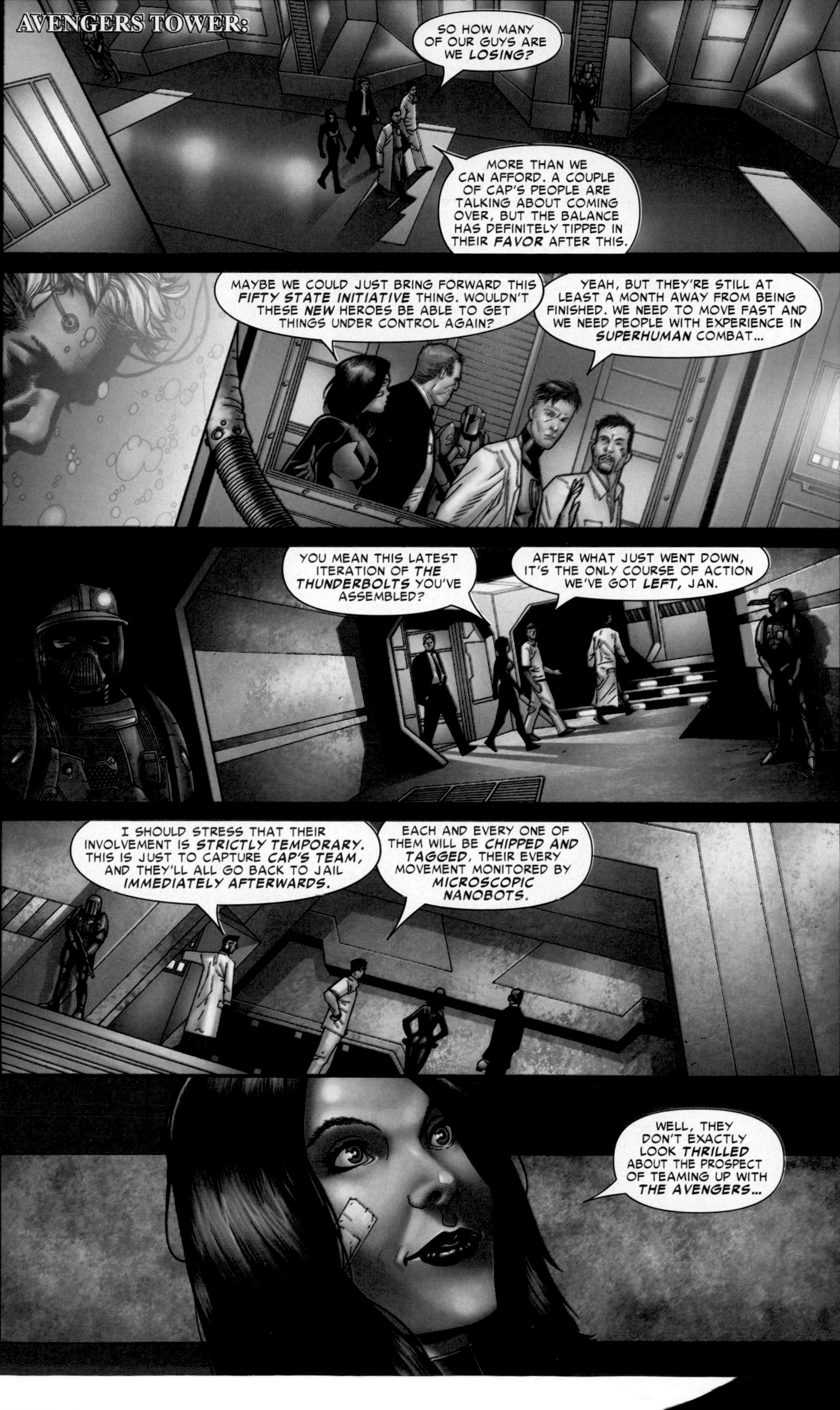
AVENGERS TOWER:
SO HOW MANY OF OUR GUYS ARE WE LOSING?
MORE THAN WE CAN AFFORD. A COUPLE OF CAP'S PEOPLE ARE TALKING ABOUT COMING OVER, BUT THE BALANCE HAS DEFINITELY TIPPED IN THEIR FAVOR AFTER THIS.
MAYBE WE COULD JUST BRING FORWARD THIS FIFTY STATE INITIATIVE THING. WOULDN'T THESE NEW HEROES BE ABLE TO GET THINGS UNDER CONTROL AGAIN?
YEAH, BUT THEY'RE STILL AT LEAST A MONTH AWAY FROM BEING FINISHED. WE NEED TO MOVE FAST AND WE NEED PEOPLE WITH EXPERIENCE IN SUPERHUMAN COMBAT...
YOU MEAN THIS LATEST ITERATION OF THE THUNDERBOLTS YOU'VE ASSEMBLED?
AFTER WHAT JUST WENT DOWN, IT'S THE ONLY COURSE OF ACTION WE'VE GOT LEFT, JAN.
I SHOULD STRESS THAT THEIR INVOLVEMENT IS STRICTLY TEMPORARY. THIS IS JUST TO CAPTURE CAP'S TEAM, AND THEY'LL ALL GO BACK TO JAIL IMMEDIATELY AFTERWARDS.
EACH AND EVERY ONE OF THEM WILL BE CHIPPED AND TAGGED, THEIR EVERY MOVEMENT MONITORED BY MICROSCOPIC NANOBOTS.
WELL, THEY DON'T EXACTLY LOOK THRILLED ABOUT THE PROSPECT OF TEAMING UP WITH THE AVENGERS...

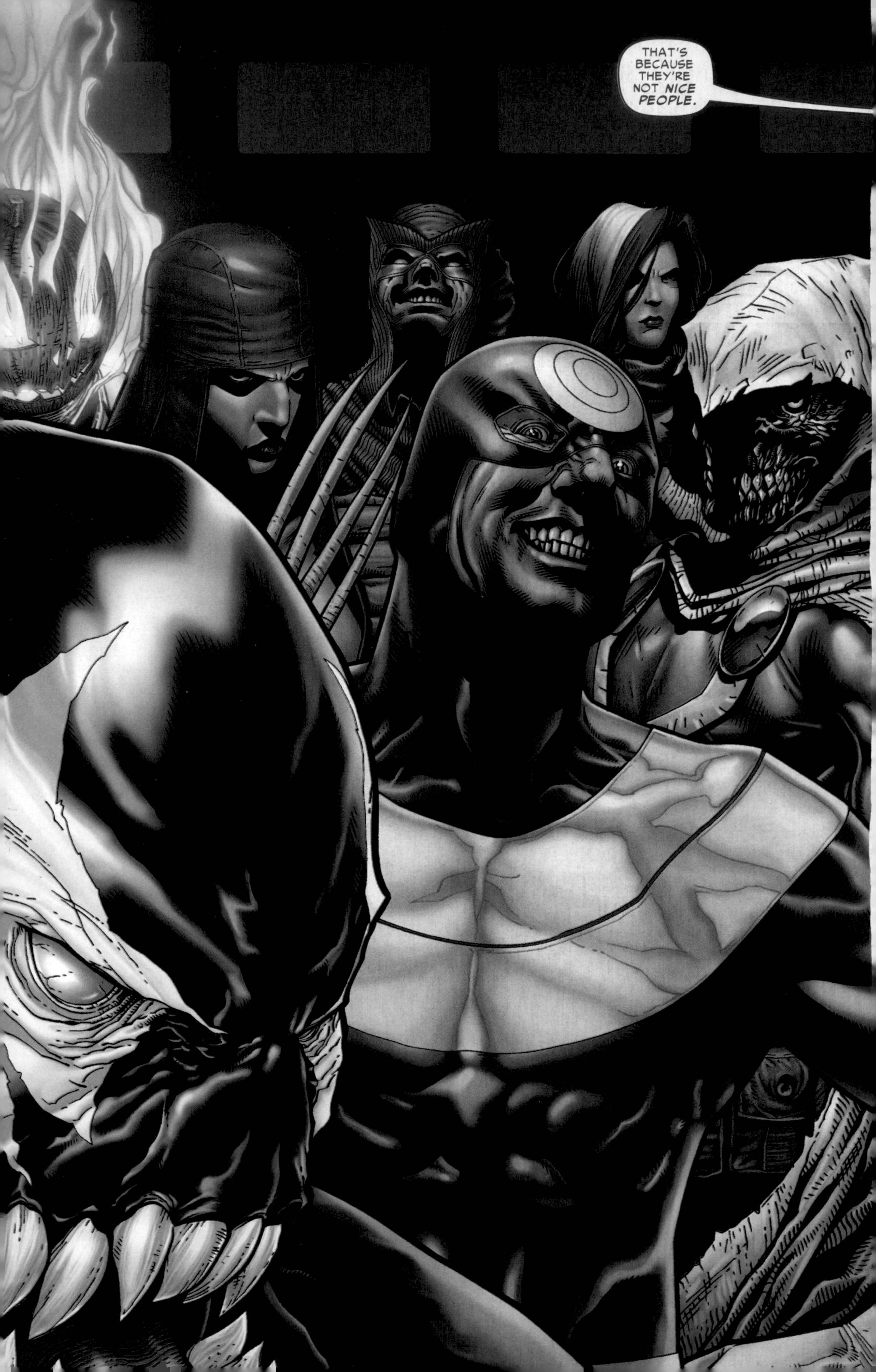
THAT'S BECAUSE THEY'RE NOT *NICE PEOPLE*.

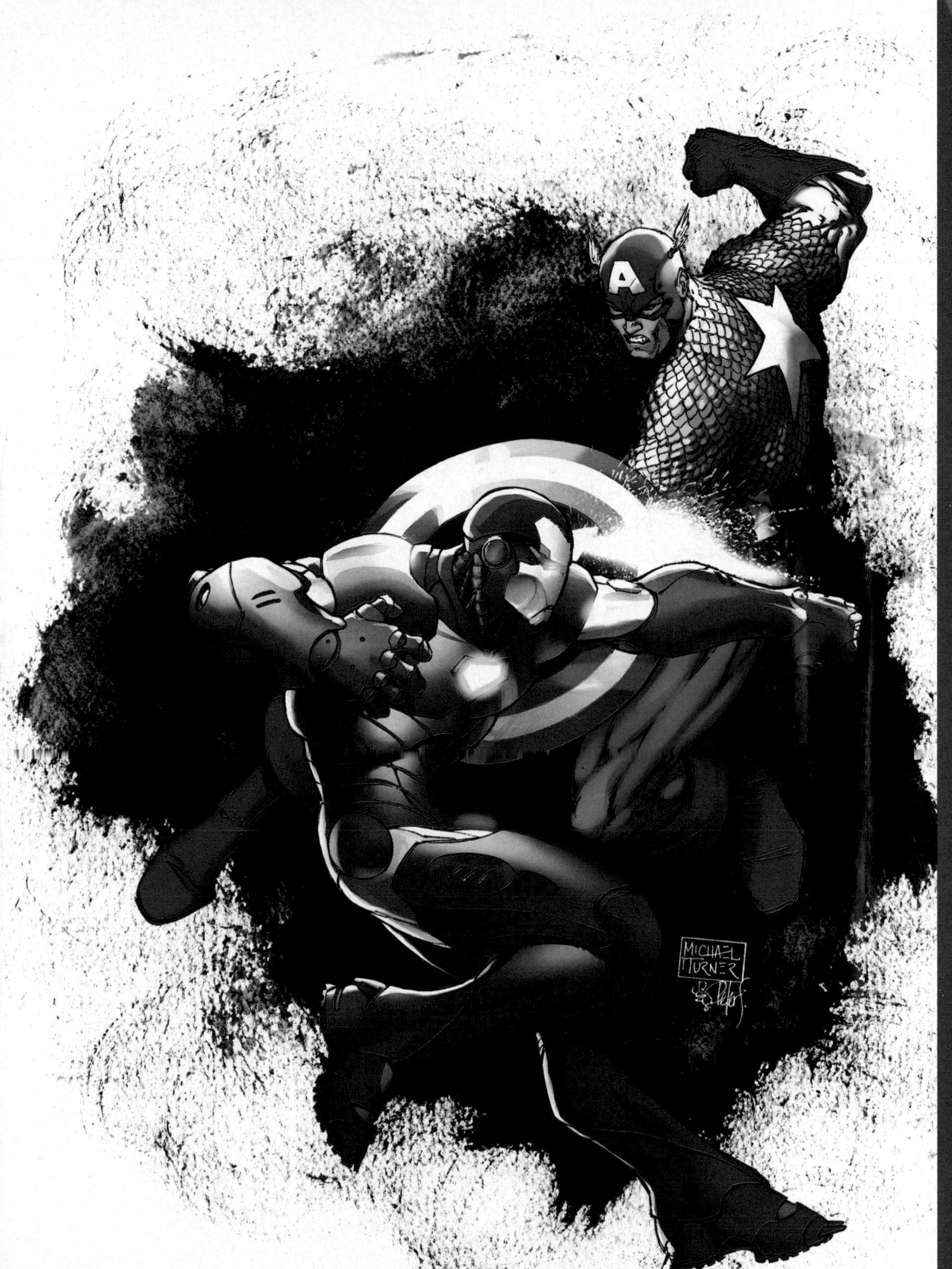
MICHAEL TURNER

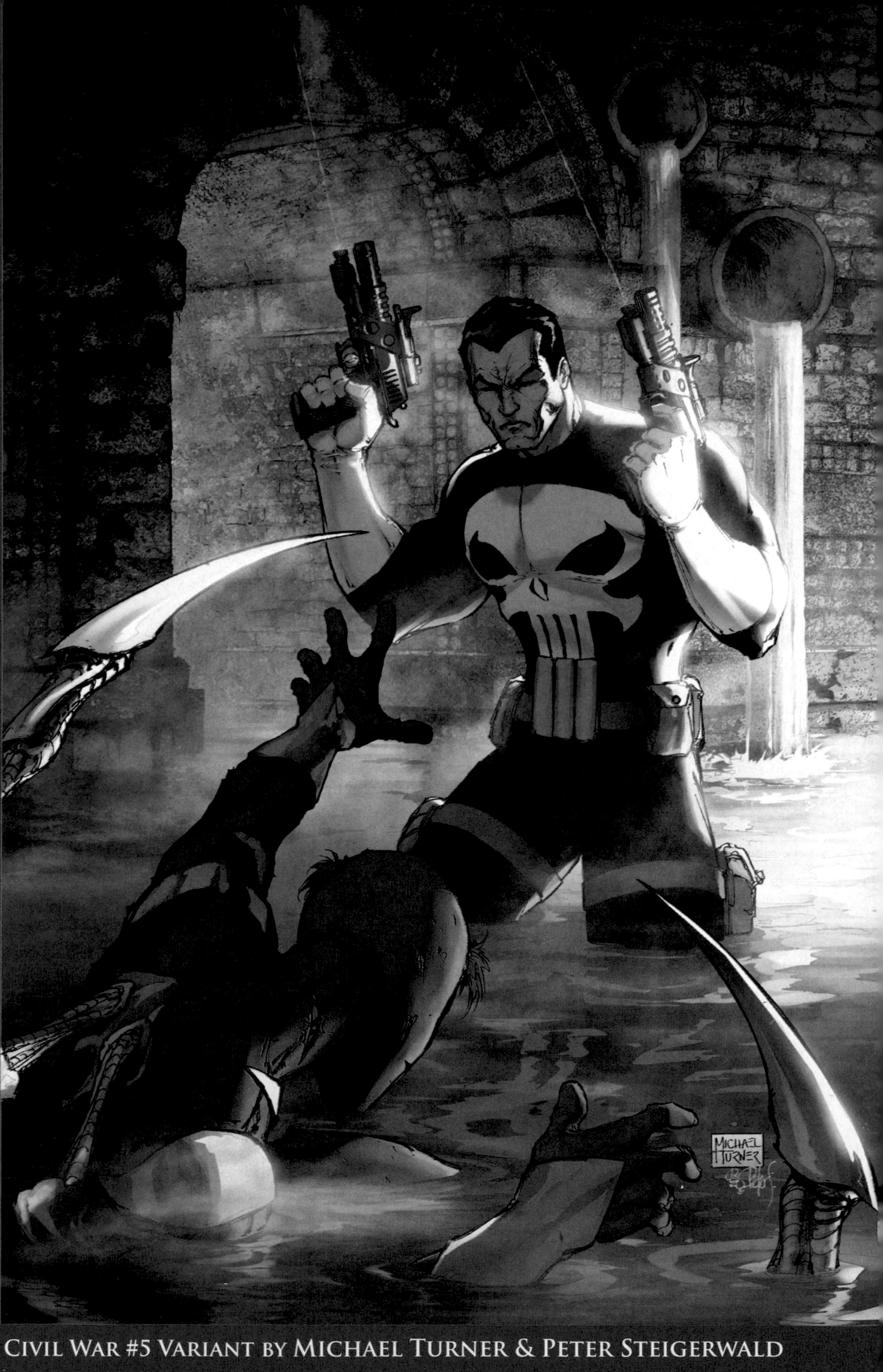
MICHAEL TURNER

Civil War #5 Variant by Michael Turner & Peter Steigerwald

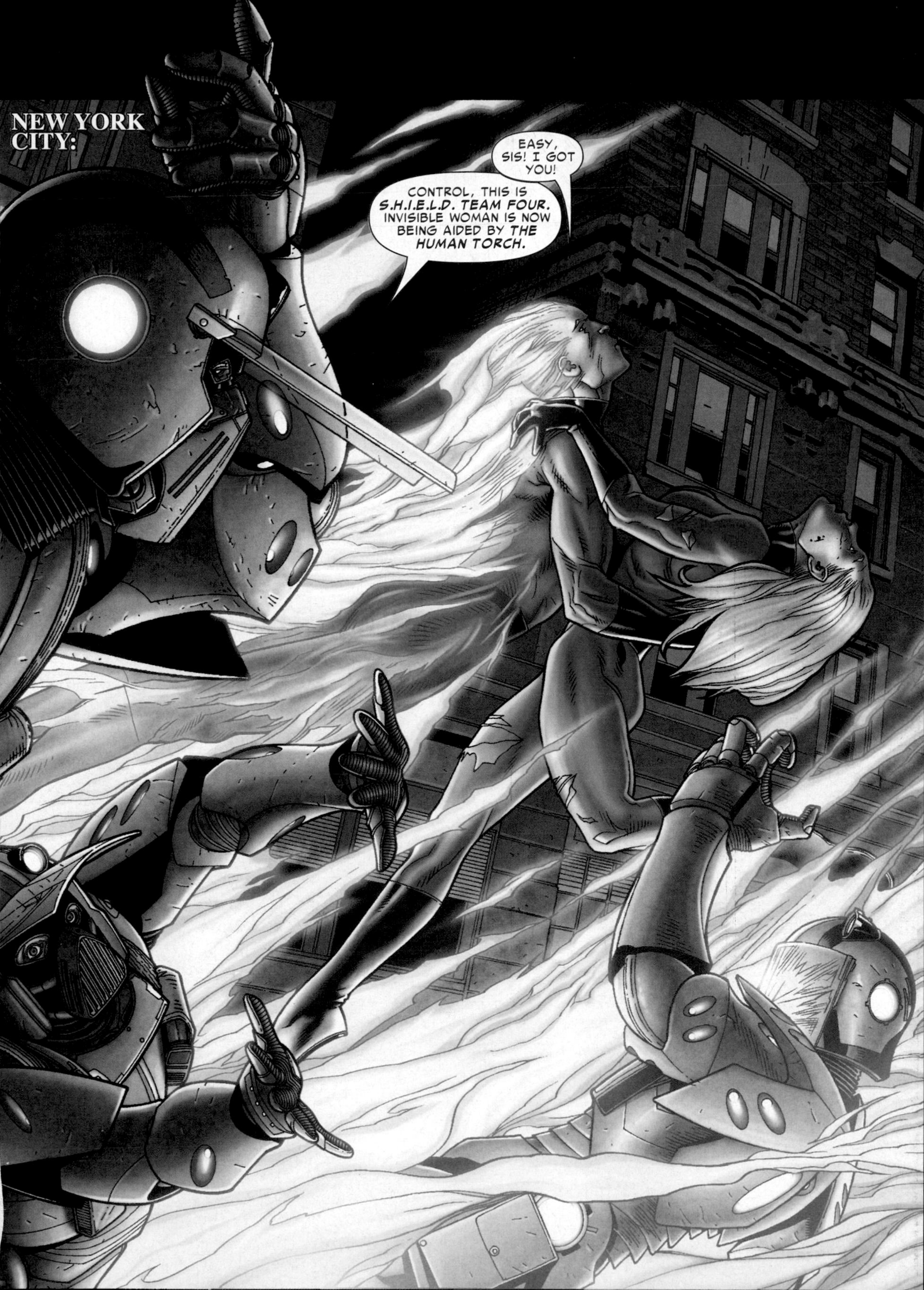
NEW YORK CITY:
CONTROL, THIS IS S.H.I.E.L.D. TEAM FOUR. INVISIBLE WOMAN IS NOW BEING AIDED BY THE HUMAN TORCH.
EASY, SIS! I GOT YOU!

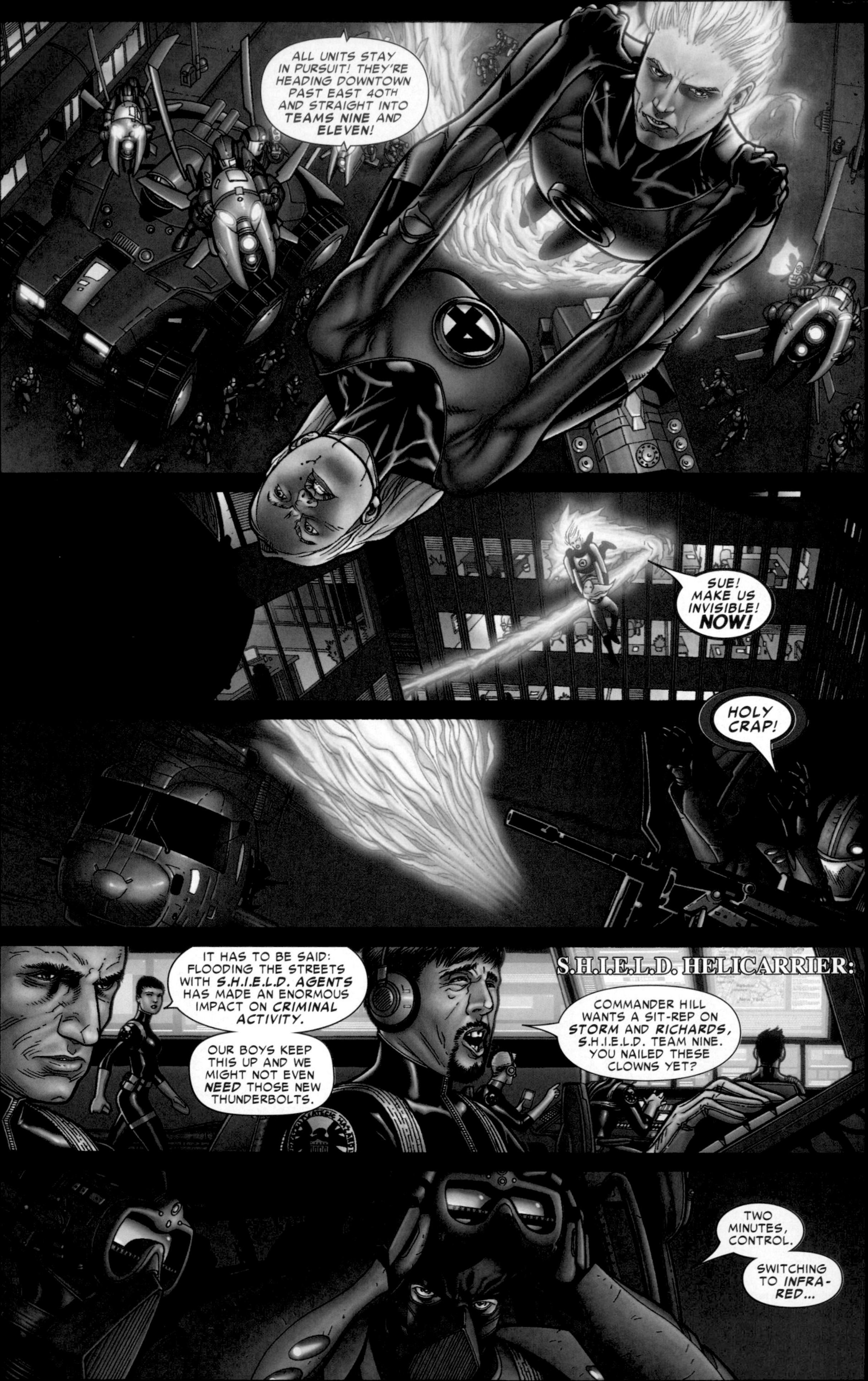
ALL UNITS STAY IN PURSUIT! THEY'RE HEADING DOWNTOWN PAST EAST 40TH AND STRAIGHT INTO TEAMS NINE AND ELEVEN!
SUE! MAKE US INVISIBLE! NOW!
HOLY CRAP!
S.H.I.E.L.D. HELICARRIER:
IT HAS TO BE SAID: FLOODING THE STREETS WITH S.H.I.E.L.D. AGENTS HAS MADE AN ENORMOUS IMPACT ON CRIMINAL ACTIVITY.
OUR BOYS KEEP THIS UP AND WE MIGHT NOT EVEN NEED THOSE NEW THUNDERBOLTS.
COMMANDER HILL WANTS A SIT-REP ON STORM AND RICHARDS, S.H.I.E.L.D. TEAM NINE. YOU NAILED THESE CLOWNS YET?
TWO MINUTES, CONTROL.
SWITCHING TO INFRA-RED...

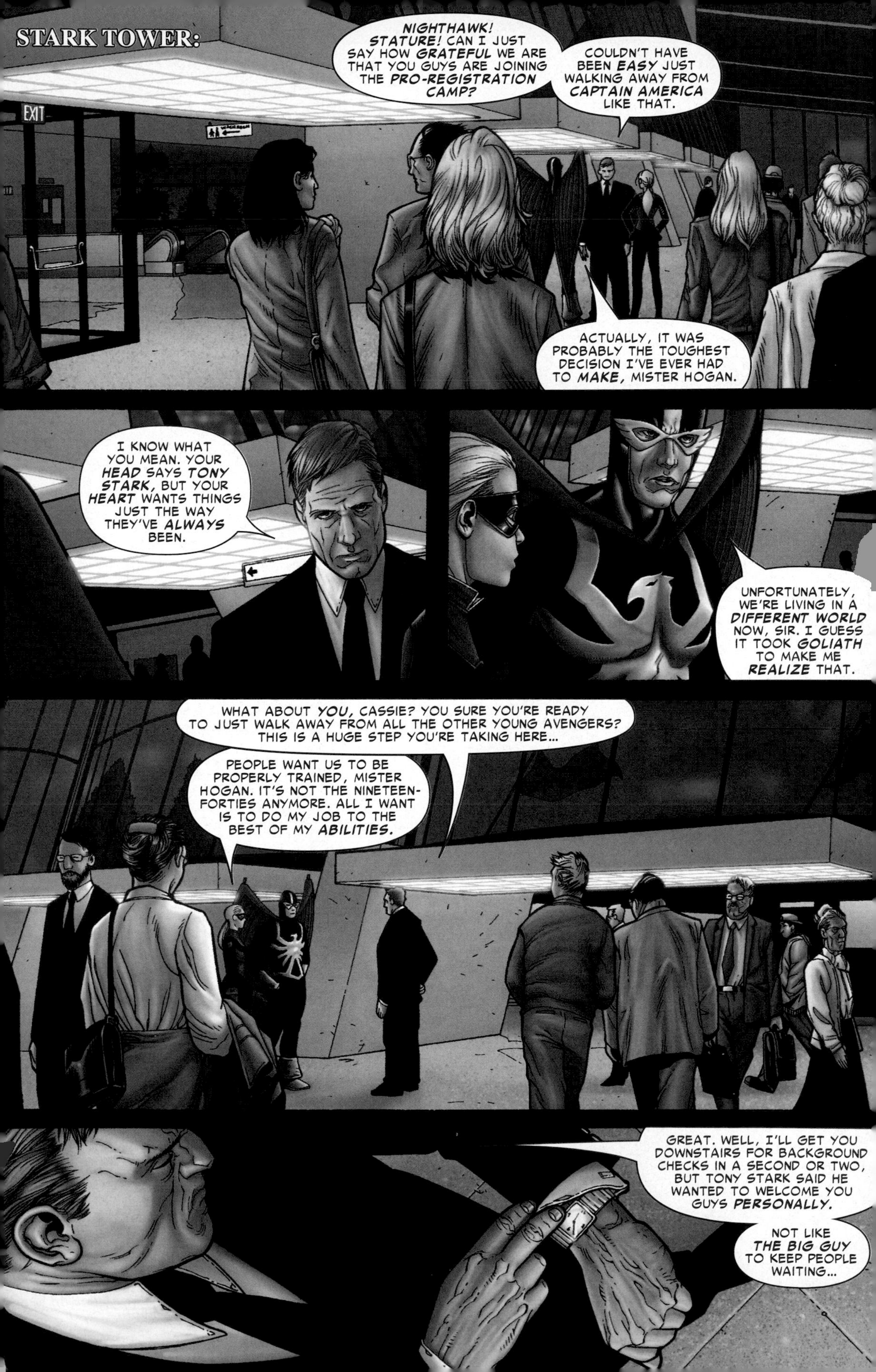
STARK TOWER:
NIGHTHAWK! STATURE! CAN I JUST SAY HOW GRATEFUL WE ARE THAT YOU GUYS ARE JOINING THE PRO-REGISTRATION CAMP?
COULDN'T HAVE BEEN EASY JUST WALKING AWAY FROM CAPTAIN AMERICA LIKE THAT.
EXIT
ACTUALLY, IT WAS PROBABLY THE TOUGHEST DECISION I'VE EVER HAD TO MAKE, MISTER HOGAN.
I KNOW WHAT YOU MEAN. YOUR HEAD SAYS TONY STARK, BUT YOUR HEART WANTS THINGS JUST THE WAY THEY'VE ALWAYS BEEN.
UNFORTUNATELY, WE'RE LIVING IN A DIFFERENT WORLD NOW, SIR. I GUESS IT TOOK GOLIATH TO MAKE ME REALIZE THAT.
WHAT ABOUT YOU, CASSIE? YOU SURE YOU'RE READY TO JUST WALK AWAY FROM ALL THE OTHER YOUNG AVENGERS? THIS IS A HUGE STEP YOU'RE TAKING HERE...
PEOPLE WANT US TO BE PROPERLY TRAINED, MISTER HOGAN. IT'S NOT THE NINETEEN-FORTIES ANYMORE. ALL I WANT IS TO DO MY JOB TO THE BEST OF MY ABILITIES.
GREAT. WELL, I'LL GET YOU DOWNSTAIRS FOR BACKGROUND CHECKS IN A SECOND OR TWO, BUT TONY STARK SAID HE WANTED TO WELCOME YOU GUYS PERSONALLY.
NOT LIKE THE BIG GUY TO KEEP PEOPLE WAITING...

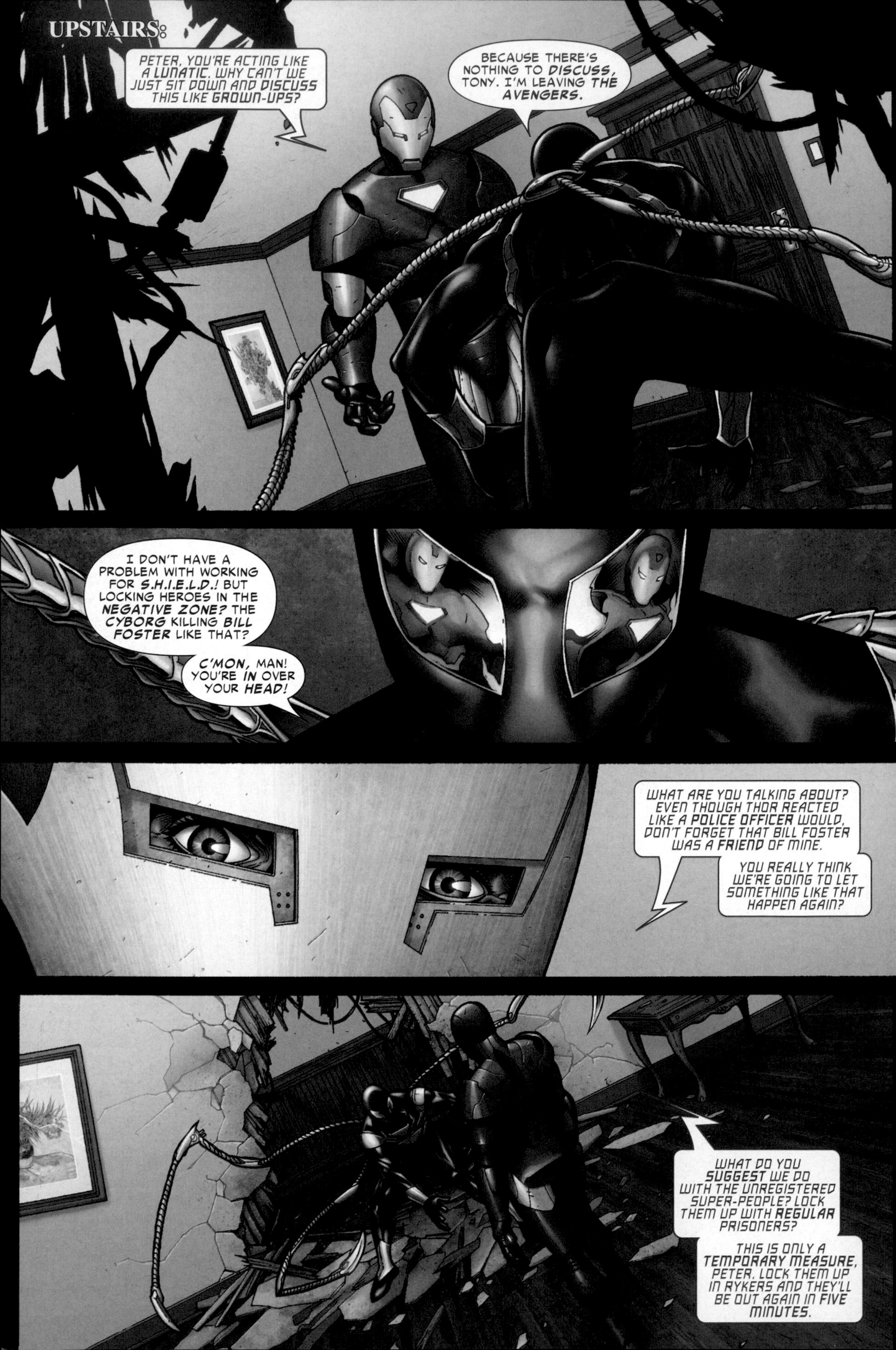
UPSTAIRS:
PETER, YOU'RE ACTING LIKE A LUNATIC. WHY CAN'T WE JUST SIT DOWN AND DISCUSS THIS LIKE GROWN-UPS?
BECAUSE THERE'S NOTHING TO DISCUSS, TONY. I'M LEAVING THE AVENGERS.
I DON'T HAVE A PROBLEM WITH WORKING FOR S.H.I.E.L.D.! BUT LOCKING HEROES IN THE NEGATIVE ZONE? THE CYBORG KILLING BILL FOSTER LIKE THAT?
C'MON, MAN! YOU'RE IN OVER YOUR HEAD!
WHAT ARE YOU TALKING ABOUT? EVEN THOUGH THOR REACTED LIKE A POLICE OFFICER WOULD, DON'T FORGET THAT BILL FOSTER WAS A FRIEND OF MINE.
YOU REALLY THINK WE'RE GOING TO LET SOMETHING LIKE THAT HAPPEN AGAIN?
WHAT DO YOU SUGGEST WE DO WITH THE UNREGISTERED SUPER-PEOPLE? LOCK THEM UP WITH REGULAR PRISONERS?
THIS IS ONLY A TEMPORARY MEASURE, PETER. LOCK THEM UP IN RYKERS AND THEY'LL BE OUT AGAIN IN FIVE MINUTES.

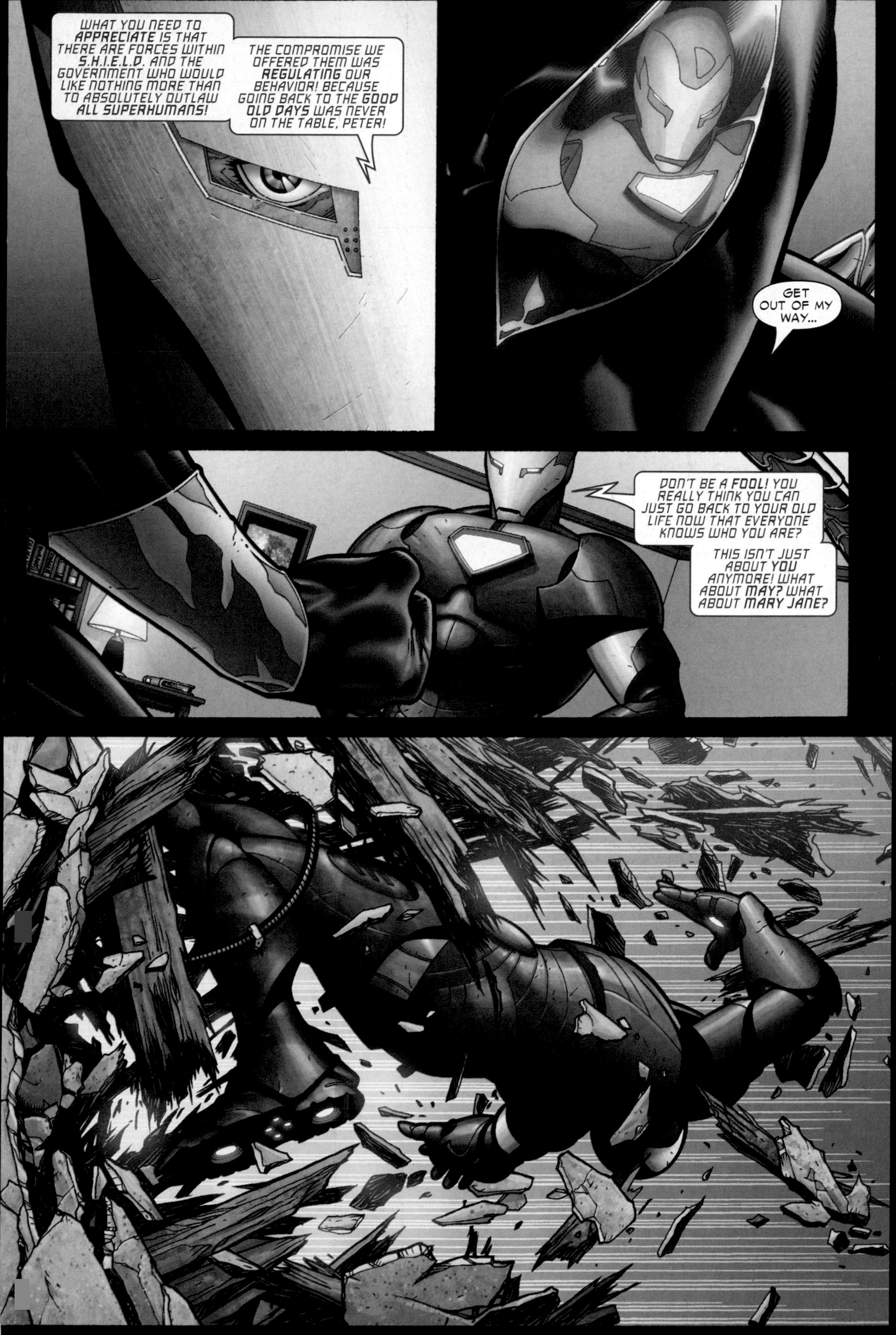
WHAT YOU NEED TO APPRECIATE IS THAT THERE ARE FORCES WITHIN S.H.I.E.L.D. AND THE GOVERNMENT WHO WOULD LIKE NOTHING MORE THAN TO ABSOLUTELY OUTLAW ALL SUPERHUMANS!
THE COMPROMISE WE OFFERED THEM WAS REGULATING OUR BEHAVIOR! BECAUSE GOING BACK TO THE GOOD OLD DAYS WAS NEVER ON THE TABLE, PETER!
GET OUT OF MY WAY...
DON'T BE A FOOL! YOU REALLY THINK YOU CAN JUST GO BACK TO YOUR OLD LIFE NOW THAT EVERYONE KNOWS WHO YOU ARE?
THIS ISN'T JUST ABOUT YOU ANYMORE! WHAT ABOUT MAY? WHAT ABOUT MARY JANE?

AUNT MAY AND MARY JANE ARE AS FAR AWAY AS POSSIBLE.

I'M DISAPPOINTED IN YOU, PETER...

NOT

AS

DISAPPOINTED

AS

I

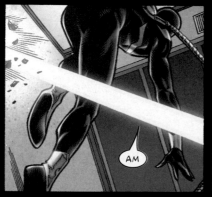

AM

IN

MYSELF--

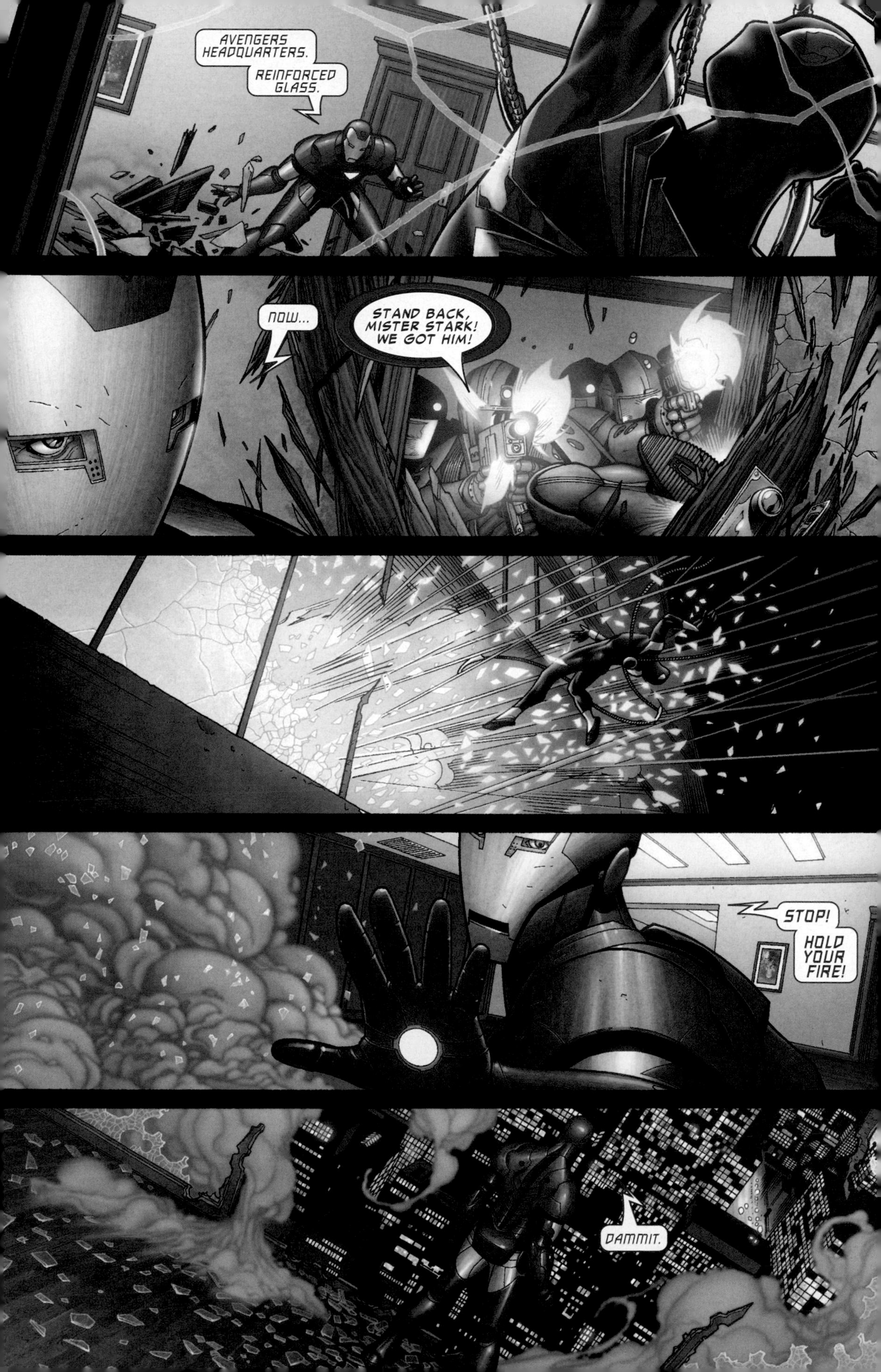
AVENGERS HEADQUARTERS.
REINFORCED GLASS.
NOW...
STAND BACK, MISTER STARK! WE GOT HIM!
STOP!
HOLD YOUR FIRE!
DAMMIT.

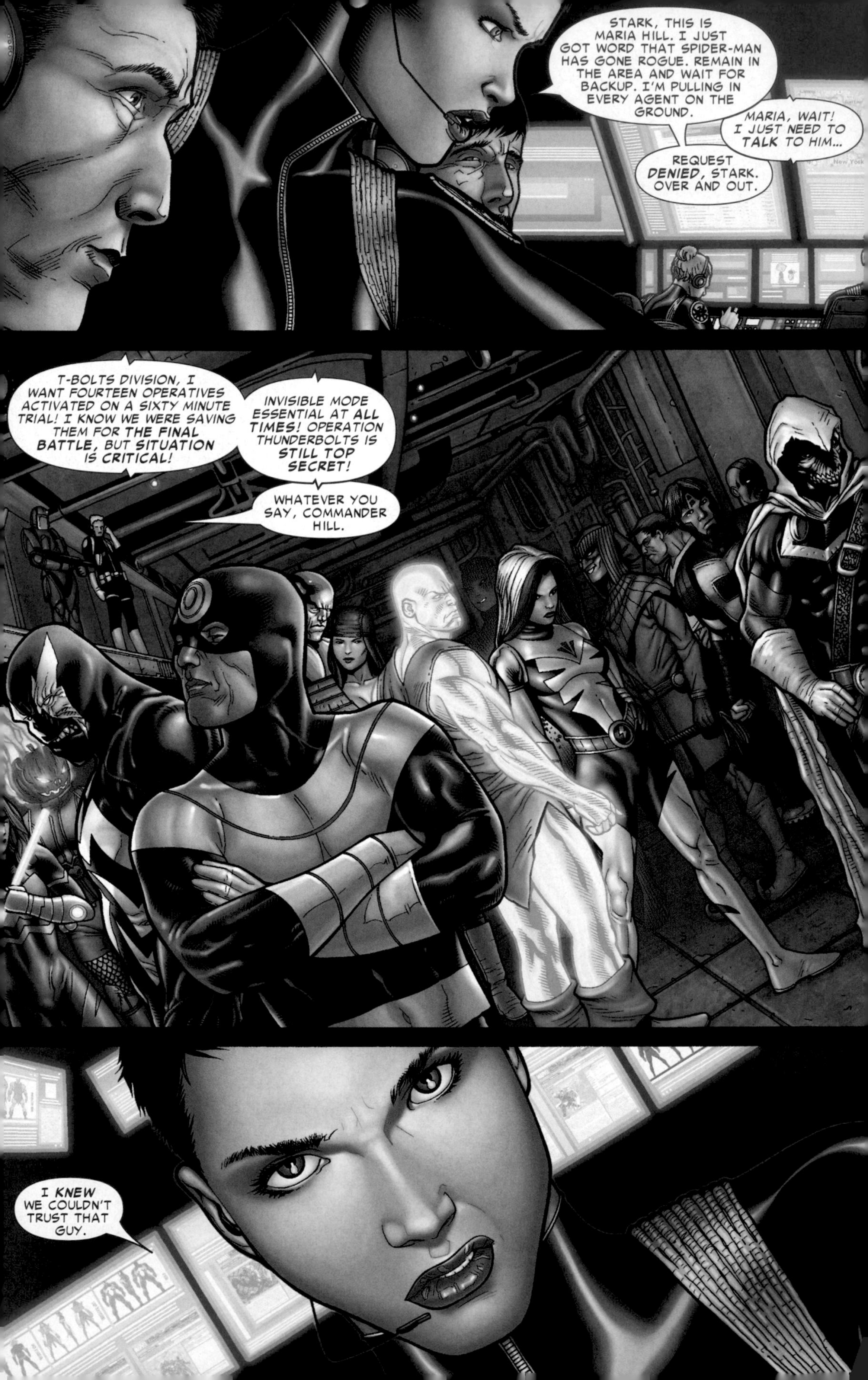

STARK, THIS IS MARIA HILL. I JUST GOT WORD THAT SPIDER-MAN HAS GONE ROGUE. REMAIN IN THE AREA AND WAIT FOR BACKUP. I'M PULLING IN EVERY AGENT ON THE GROUND.
MARIA, WAIT! I JUST NEED TO TALK TO HIM...
REQUEST DENIED, STARK. OVER AND OUT.
T-BOLTS DIVISION, I WANT FOURTEEN OPERATIVES ACTIVATED ON A SIXTY MINUTE TRIAL! I KNOW WE WERE SAVING THEM FOR THE FINAL BATTLE, BUT SITUATION IS CRITICAL!
INVISIBLE MODE ESSENTIAL AT ALL TIMES! OPERATION THUNDERBOLTS IS STILL TOP SECRET!
WHATEVER YOU SAY, COMMANDER HILL.
I KNEW WE COULDN'T TRUST THAT GUY.

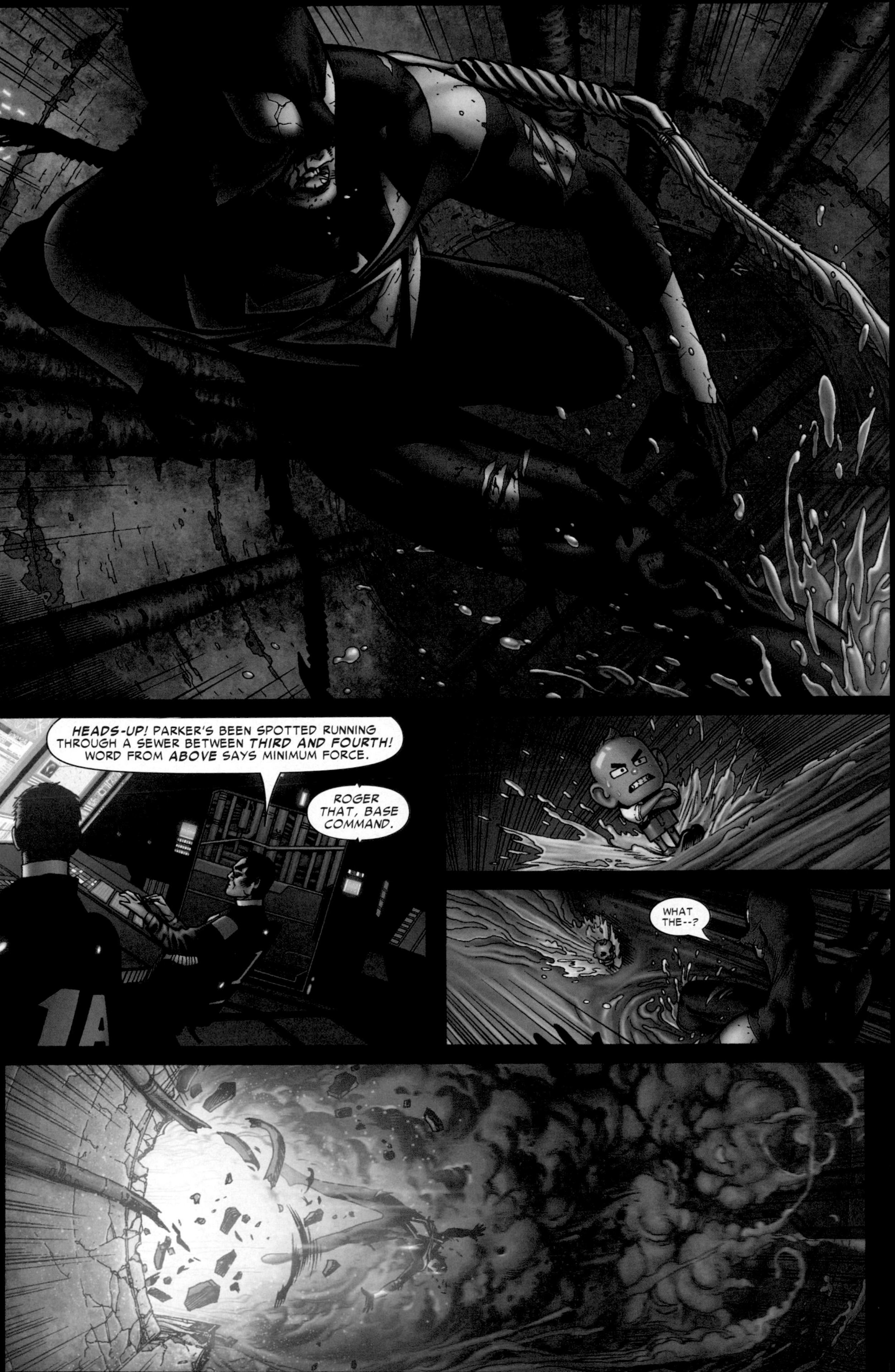
HEADS-UP! PARKER'S BEEN SPOTTED RUNNING THROUGH A SEWER BETWEEN THIRD AND FOURTH! WORD FROM ABOVE SAYS MINIMUM FORCE.
ROGER THAT, BASE COMMAND.
WHAT THE--?

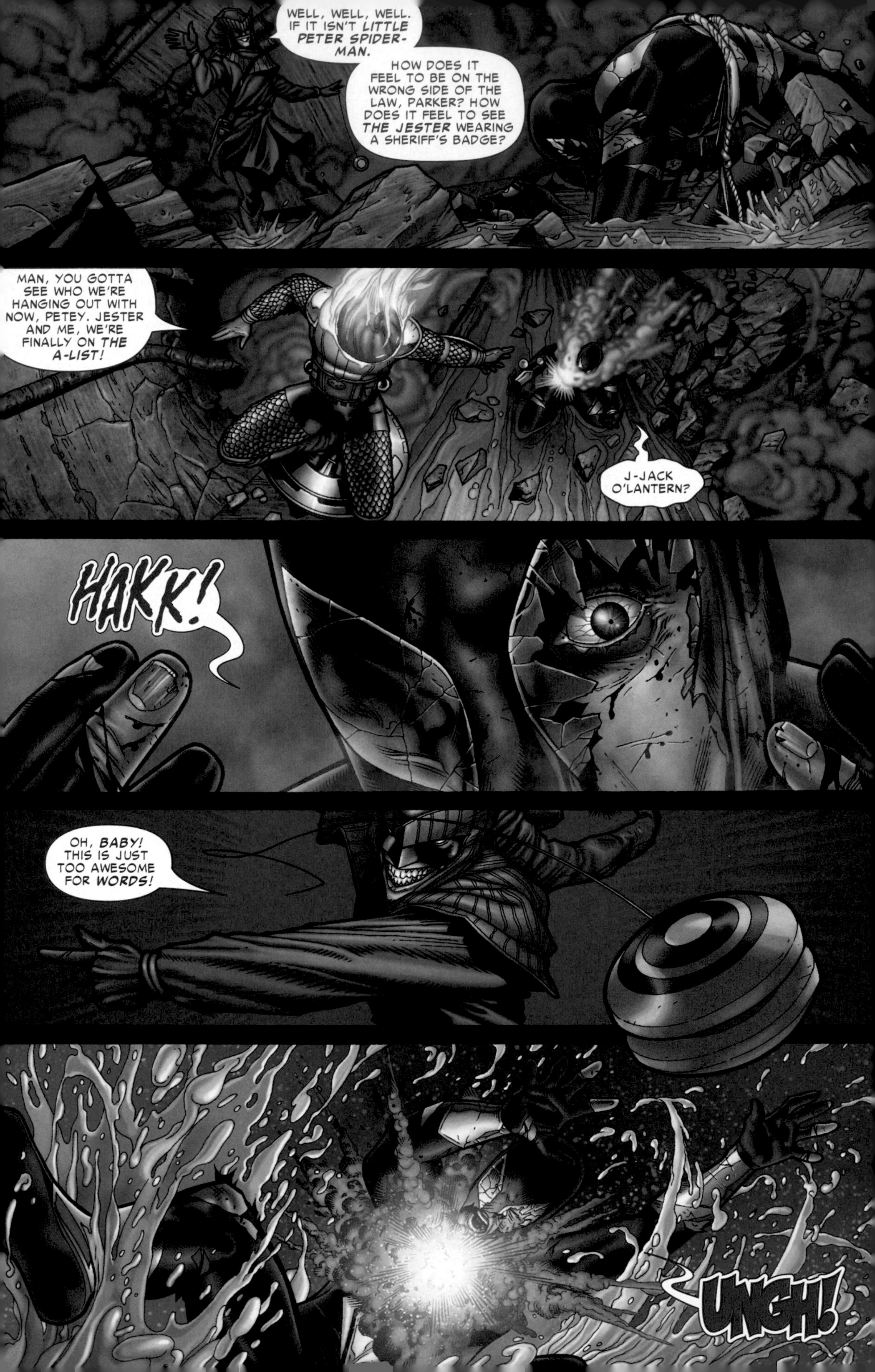

WELL, WELL, WELL. IF IT ISN'T *LITTLE PETER SPIDER-MAN.*
HOW DOES IT FEEL TO BE ON THE WRONG SIDE OF THE LAW, PARKER? HOW DOES IT FEEL TO SEE *THE JESTER* WEARING A SHERIFF'S BADGE?
MAN, YOU GOTTA SEE WHO WE'RE HANGING OUT WITH NOW, PETEY. JESTER AND ME, WE'RE FINALLY ON *THE A-LIST!*
J-JACK O'LANTERN?
HAKK!
OH, *BABY!* THIS IS JUST TOO AWESOME FOR *WORDS!*
UNGH!

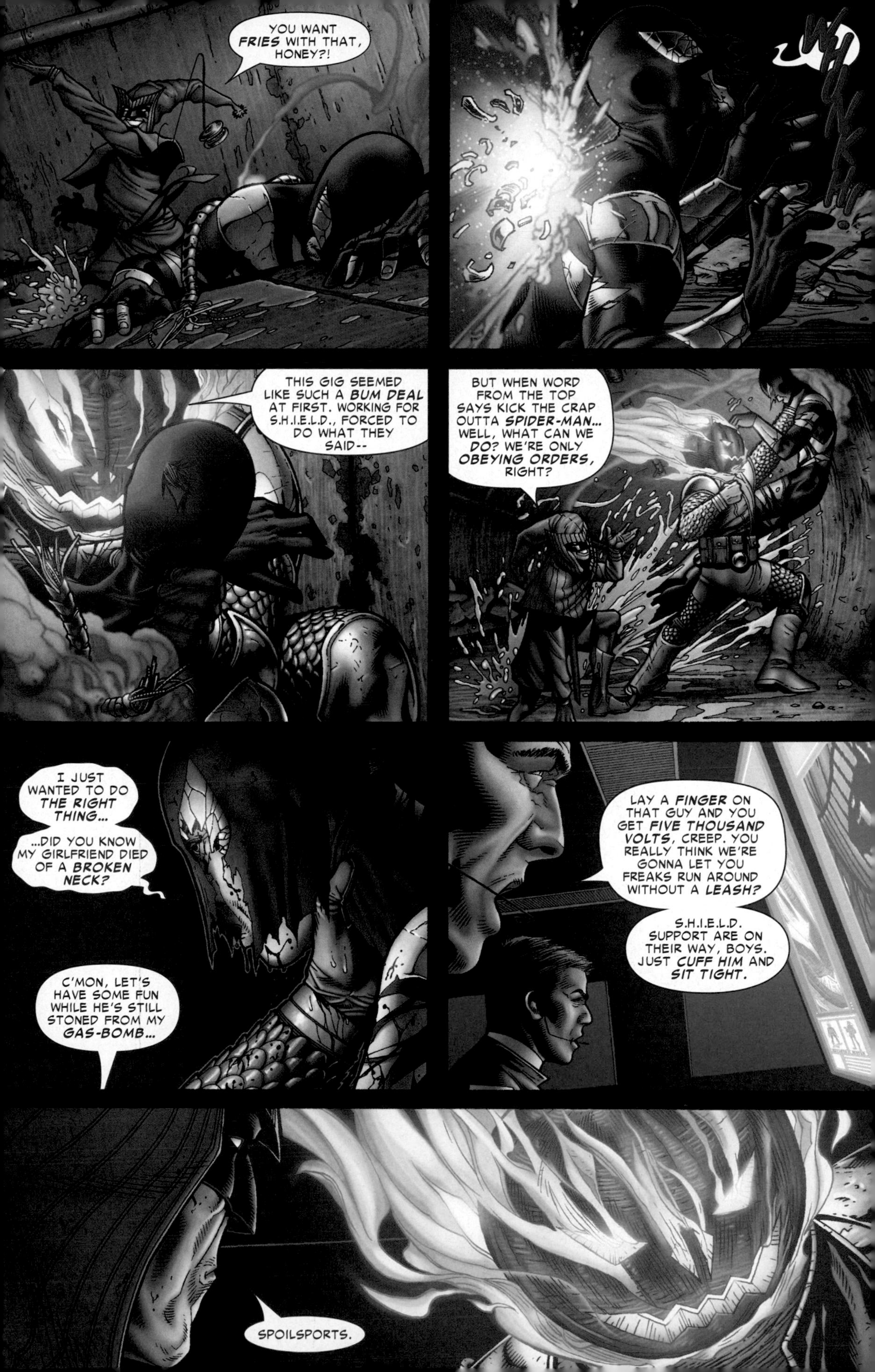
YOU WANT FRIES WITH THAT, HONEY?!
WHUNKHH
THIS GIG SEEMED LIKE SUCH A BUM DEAL AT FIRST. WORKING FOR S.H.I.E.L.D., FORCED TO DO WHAT THEY SAID--
BUT WHEN WORD FROM THE TOP SAYS KICK THE CRAP OUTTA SPIDER-MAN... WELL, WHAT CAN WE DO? WE'RE ONLY OBEYING ORDERS, RIGHT?
I JUST WANTED TO DO THE RIGHT THING...
...DID YOU KNOW MY GIRLFRIEND DIED OF A BROKEN NECK?
C'MON, LET'S HAVE SOME FUN WHILE HE'S STILL STONED FROM MY GAS-BOMB...
LAY A FINGER ON THAT GUY AND YOU GET FIVE THOUSAND VOLTS, CREEP. YOU REALLY THINK WE'RE GONNA LET YOU FREAKS RUN AROUND WITHOUT A LEASH?
S.H.I.E.L.D. SUPPORT ARE ON THEIR WAY, BOYS. JUST CUFF HIM AND SIT TIGHT.
SPOILSPORTS.

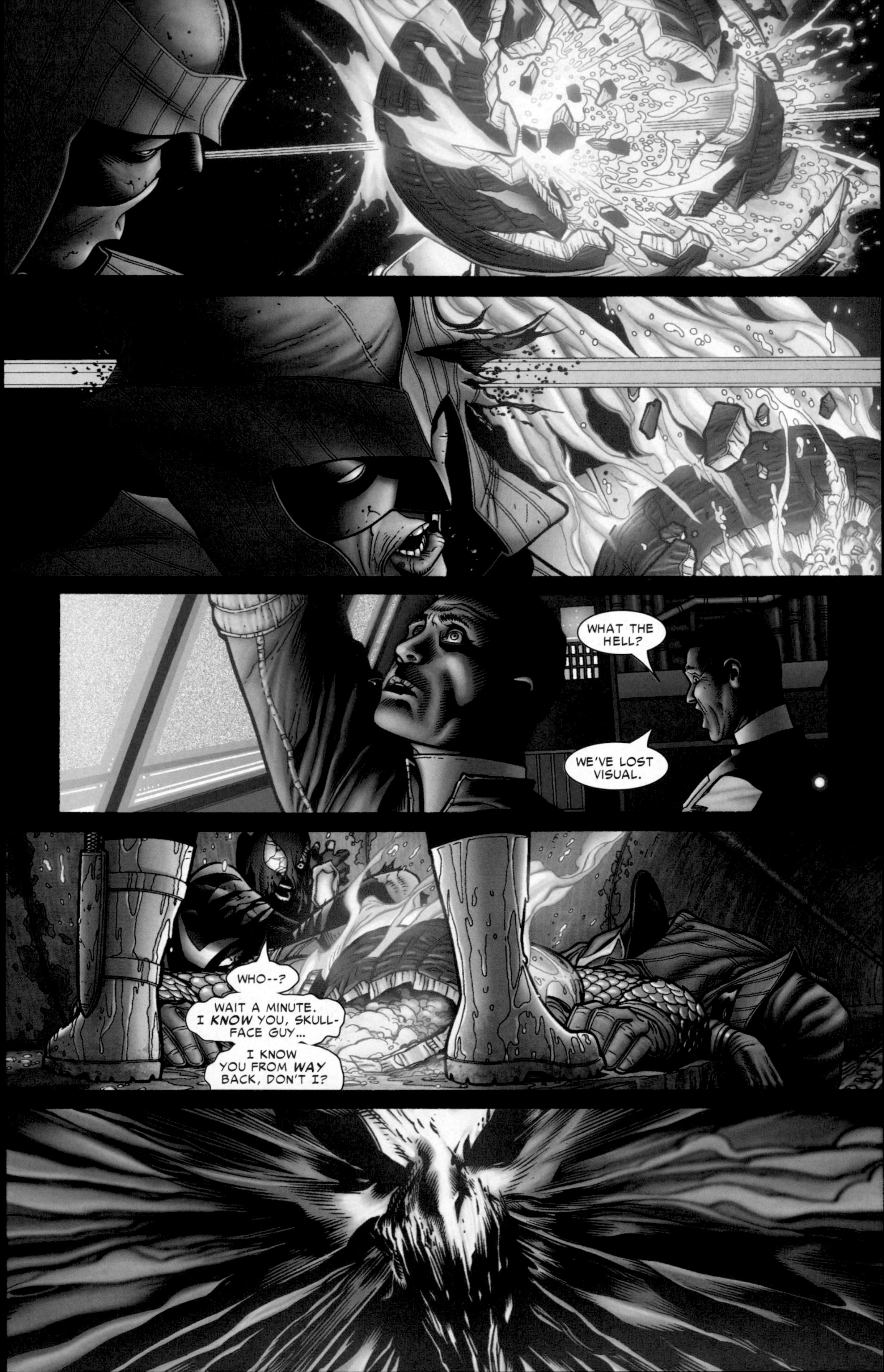
WHAT THE HELL?
WE'VE LOST VISUAL.
WHO--?
WAIT A MINUTE. I **KNOW** YOU, SKULL-FACE GUY...
I KNOW YOU FROM **WAY** BACK, DON'T I?

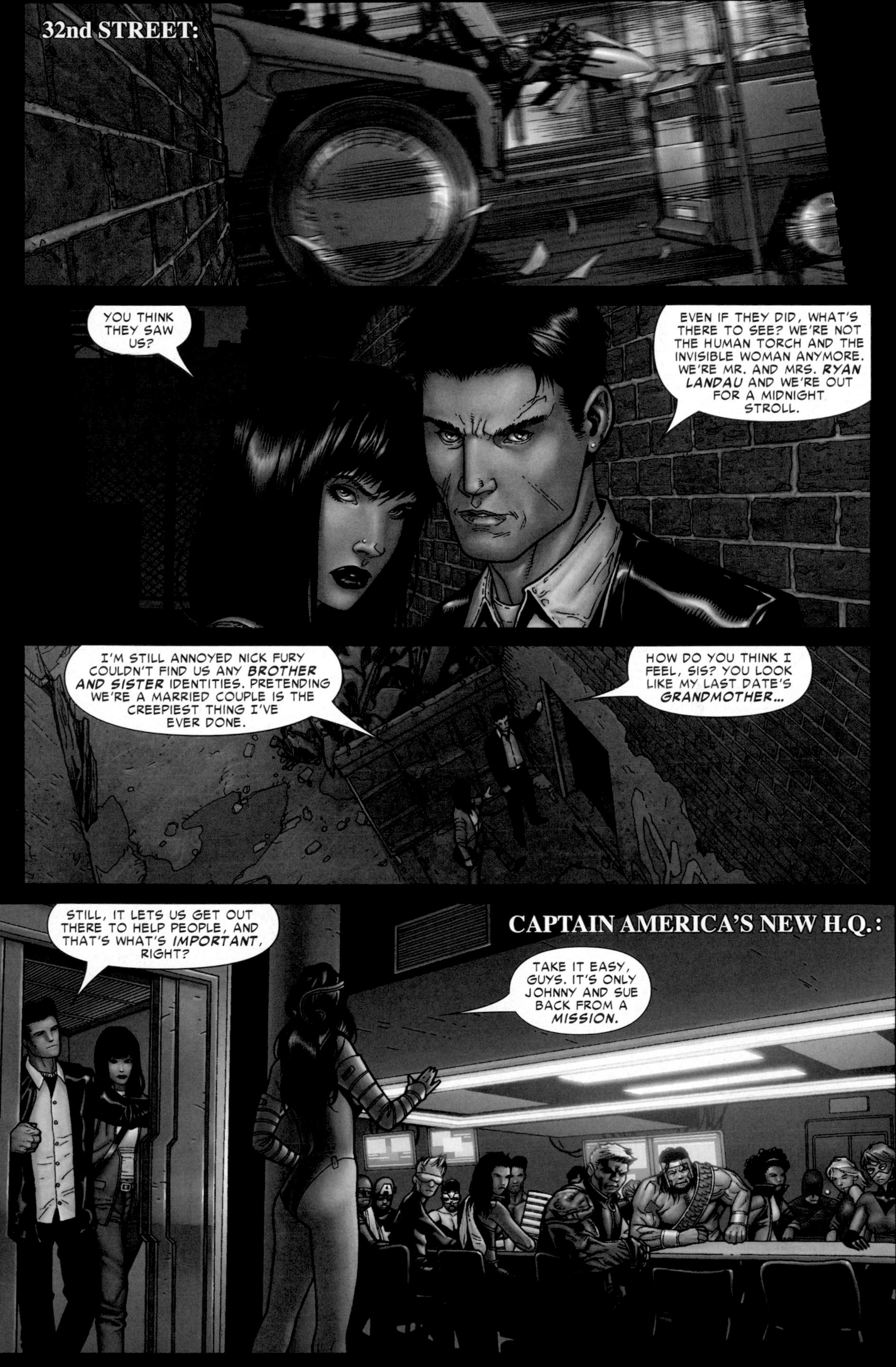
32nd STREET:
YOU THINK THEY SAW US?
EVEN IF THEY DID, WHAT'S THERE TO SEE? WE'RE NOT THE HUMAN TORCH AND THE INVISIBLE WOMAN ANYMORE. WE'RE MR. AND MRS. RYAN LANDAU AND WE'RE OUT FOR A MIDNIGHT STROLL.
I'M STILL ANNOYED NICK FURY COULDN'T FIND US ANY BROTHER AND SISTER IDENTITIES. PRETENDING WE'RE A MARRIED COUPLE IS THE CREEPIEST THING I'VE EVER DONE.
HOW DO YOU THINK I FEEL, SIS? YOU LOOK LIKE MY LAST DATE'S GRANDMOTHER...
STILL, IT LETS US GET OUT THERE TO HELP PEOPLE, AND THAT'S WHAT'S IMPORTANT, RIGHT?
CAPTAIN AMERICA'S NEW H.Q.:
TAKE IT EASY, GUYS. IT'S ONLY JOHNNY AND SUE BACK FROM A MISSION.

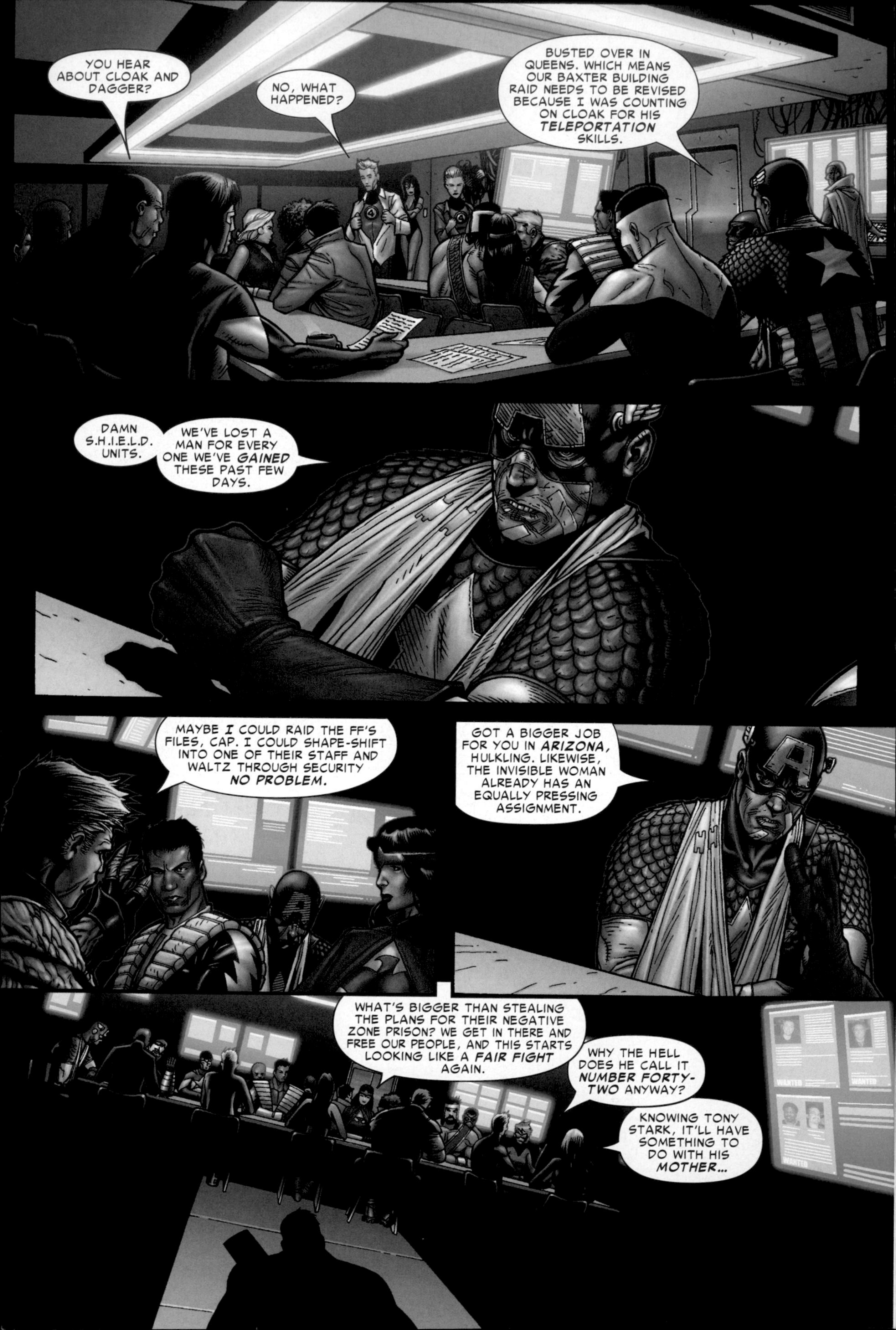
YOU HEAR ABOUT CLOAK AND DAGGER?
NO, WHAT HAPPENED?
BUSTED OVER IN QUEENS. WHICH MEANS OUR BAXTER BUILDING RAID NEEDS TO BE REVISED BECAUSE I WAS COUNTING ON CLOAK FOR HIS TELEPORTATION SKILLS.
DAMN S.H.I.E.L.D. UNITS.
WE'VE LOST A MAN FOR EVERY ONE WE'VE GAINED THESE PAST FEW DAYS.
MAYBE I COULD RAID THE FF'S FILES, CAP. I COULD SHAPE-SHIFT INTO ONE OF THEIR STAFF AND WALTZ THROUGH SECURITY NO PROBLEM.
GOT A BIGGER JOB FOR YOU IN ARIZONA, HULKLING. LIKEWISE, THE INVISIBLE WOMAN ALREADY HAS AN EQUALLY PRESSING ASSIGNMENT.
WHAT'S BIGGER THAN STEALING THE PLANS FOR THEIR NEGATIVE ZONE PRISON? WE GET IN THERE AND FREE OUR PEOPLE, AND THIS STARTS LOOKING LIKE A FAIR FIGHT AGAIN.
WHY THE HELL DOES HE CALL IT NUMBER FORTY-TWO ANYWAY?
KNOWING TONY STARK, IT'LL HAVE SOMETHING TO DO WITH HIS MOTHER...

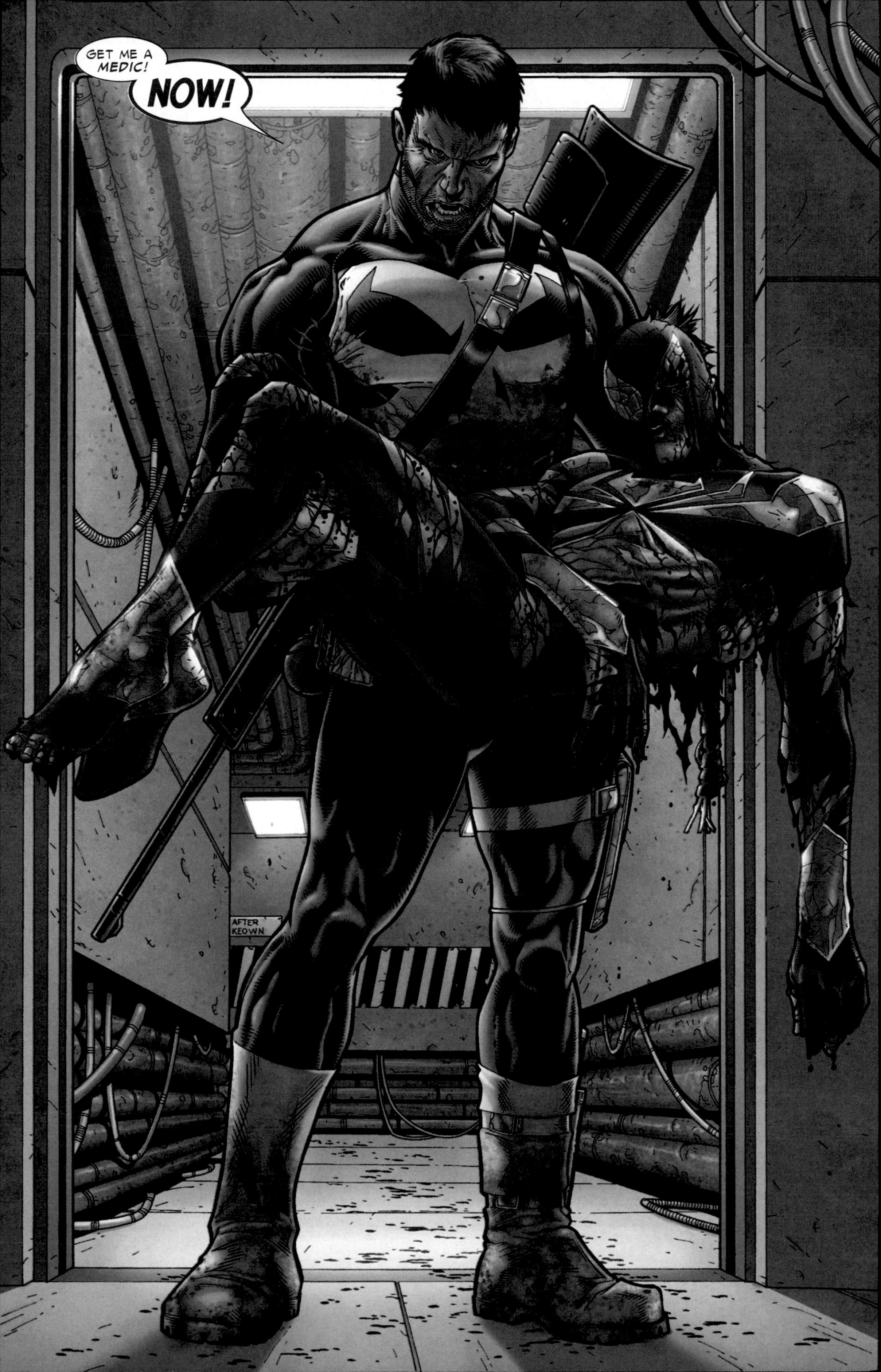
GET ME A MEDIC!
NOW!
AFTER KEOWN

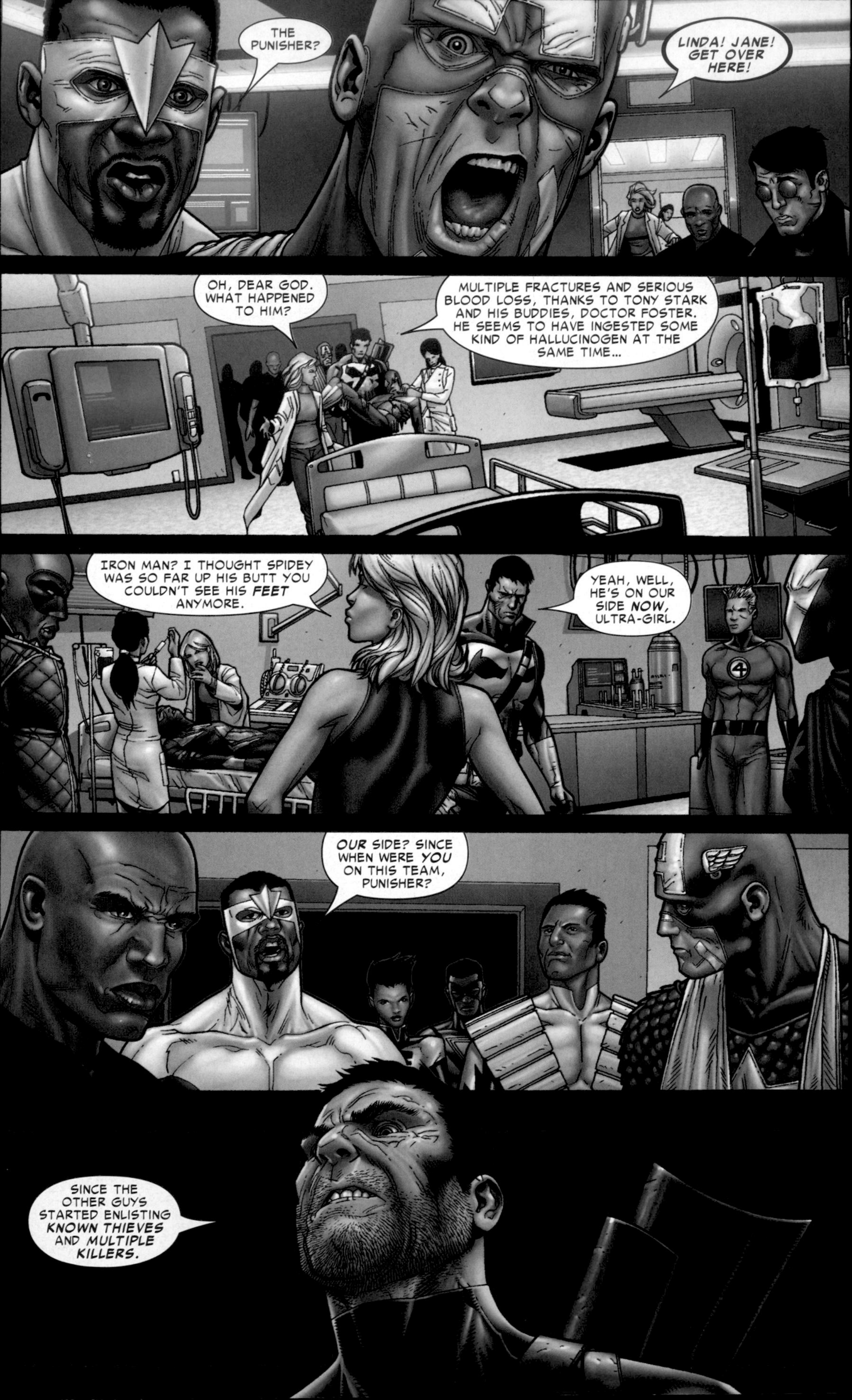
THE PUNISHER?
LINDA! JANE! GET OVER HERE!
OH, DEAR GOD. WHAT HAPPENED TO HIM?
MULTIPLE FRACTURES AND SERIOUS BLOOD LOSS, THANKS TO TONY STARK AND HIS BUDDIES, DOCTOR FOSTER. HE SEEMS TO HAVE INGESTED SOME KIND OF HALLUCINOGEN AT THE SAME TIME...
IRON MAN? I THOUGHT SPIDEY WAS SO FAR UP HIS BUTT YOU COULDN'T SEE HIS *FEET* ANYMORE.
YEAH, WELL, HE'S ON OUR SIDE *NOW*, ULTRA-GIRL.
OUR SIDE? SINCE WHEN WERE *YOU* ON THIS TEAM, PUNISHER?
SINCE THE OTHER GUYS STARTED ENLISTING *KNOWN THIEVES* AND *MULTIPLE KILLERS*.

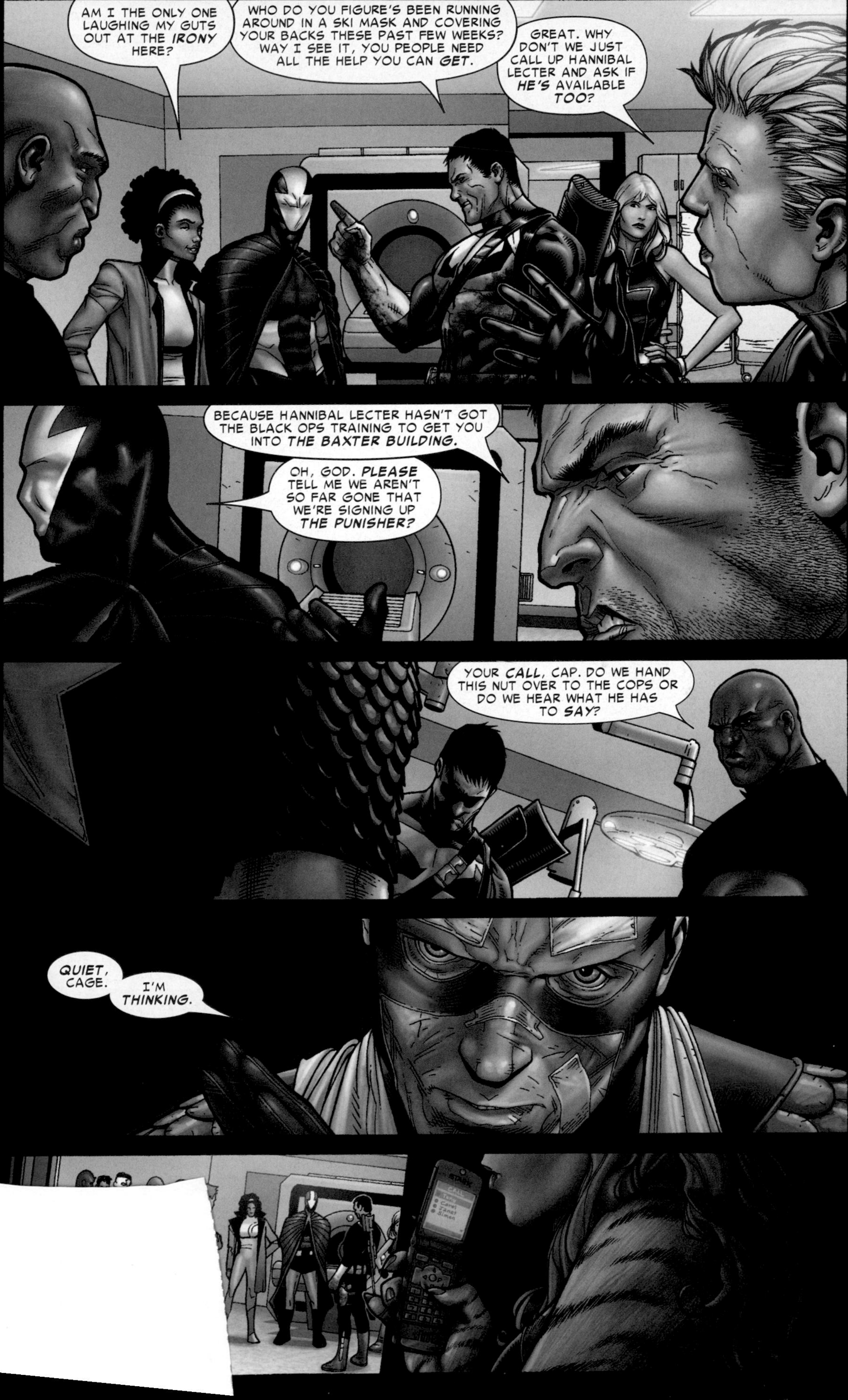

AM I THE ONLY ONE LAUGHING MY GUTS OUT AT THE IRONY HERE?
WHO DO YOU FIGURE'S BEEN RUNNING AROUND IN A SKI MASK AND COVERING YOUR BACKS THESE PAST FEW WEEKS? WAY I SEE IT, YOU PEOPLE NEED ALL THE HELP YOU CAN GET.
GREAT. WHY DON'T WE JUST CALL UP HANNIBAL LECTER AND ASK IF HE'S AVAILABLE TOO?
BECAUSE HANNIBAL LECTER HASN'T GOT THE BLACK OPS TRAINING TO GET YOU INTO THE BAXTER BUILDING.
OH, GOD. PLEASE TELL ME WE AREN'T SO FAR GONE THAT WE'RE SIGNING UP THE PUNISHER?
YOUR CALL, CAP. DO WE HAND THIS NUT OVER TO THE COPS OR DO WE HEAR WHAT HE HAS TO SAY?
QUIET, CAGE.
I'M THINKING.

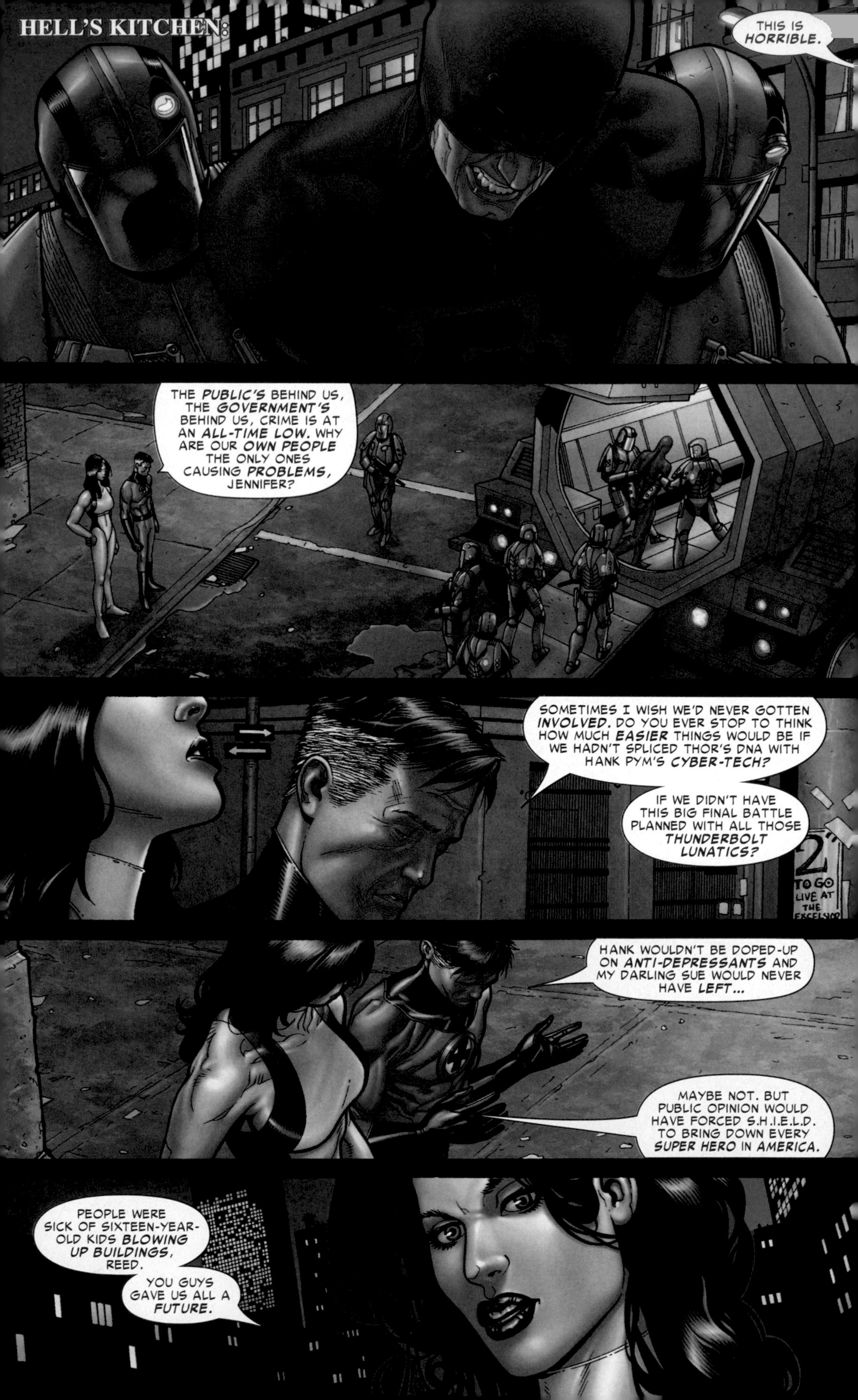
HELL'S KITCHEN:
THIS IS HORRIBLE.
THE PUBLIC'S BEHIND US, THE GOVERNMENT'S BEHIND US, CRIME IS AT AN ALL-TIME LOW. WHY ARE OUR OWN PEOPLE THE ONLY ONES CAUSING PROBLEMS, JENNIFER?
SOMETIMES I WISH WE'D NEVER GOTTEN INVOLVED. DO YOU EVER STOP TO THINK HOW MUCH EASIER THINGS WOULD BE IF WE HADN'T SPLICED THOR'S DNA WITH HANK PYM'S CYBER-TECH?
IF WE DIDN'T HAVE THIS BIG FINAL BATTLE PLANNED WITH ALL THOSE THUNDERBOLT LUNATICS?
2 TO GO LIVE AT THE
HANK WOULDN'T BE DOPED-UP ON ANTI-DEPRESSANTS AND MY DARLING SUE WOULD NEVER HAVE LEFT...
MAYBE NOT. BUT PUBLIC OPINION WOULD HAVE FORCED S.H.I.E.L.D. TO BRING DOWN EVERY SUPER HERO IN AMERICA.
PEOPLE WERE SICK OF SIXTEEN-YEAR-OLD KIDS BLOWING UP BUILDINGS, REED.
YOU GUYS GAVE US ALL A FUTURE.

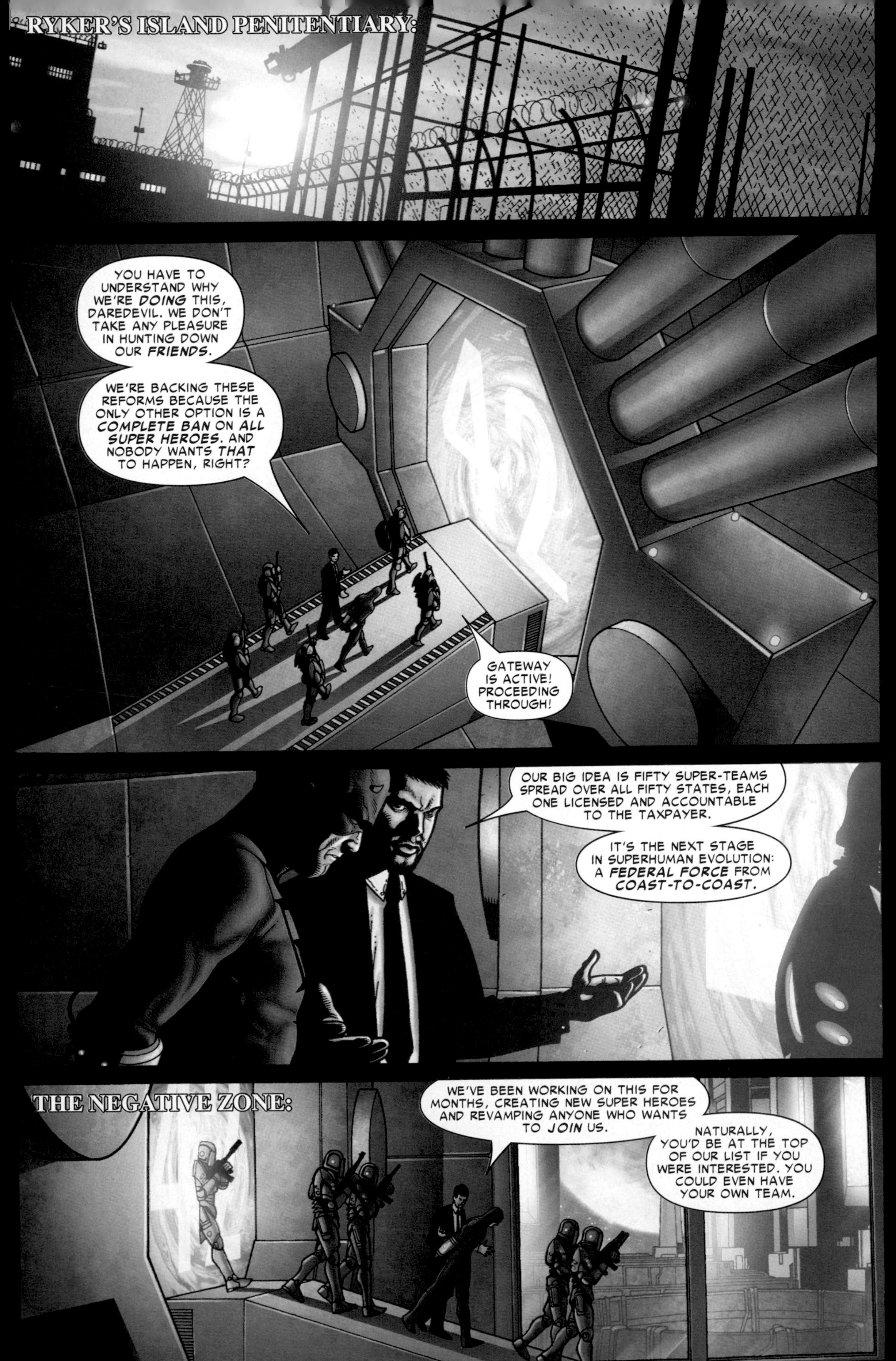
RYKER'S ISLAND PENITENTIARY:
YOU HAVE TO UNDERSTAND WHY WE'RE DOING THIS, DAREDEVIL. WE DON'T TAKE ANY PLEASURE IN HUNTING DOWN OUR FRIENDS.
WE'RE BACKING THESE REFORMS BECAUSE THE ONLY OTHER OPTION IS A COMPLETE BAN ON ALL SUPER HEROES. AND NOBODY WANTS THAT TO HAPPEN, RIGHT?
GATEWAY IS ACTIVE! PROCEEDING THROUGH!
OUR BIG IDEA IS FIFTY SUPER-TEAMS SPREAD OVER ALL FIFTY STATES, EACH ONE LICENSED AND ACCOUNTABLE TO THE TAXPAYER.
IT'S THE NEXT STAGE IN SUPERHUMAN EVOLUTION: A FEDERAL FORCE FROM COAST-TO-COAST.
THE NEGATIVE ZONE:
WE'VE BEEN WORKING ON THIS FOR MONTHS, CREATING NEW SUPER HEROES AND REVAMPING ANYONE WHO WANTS TO JOIN US.
NATURALLY, YOU'D BE AT THE TOP OF OUR LIST IF YOU WERE INTERESTED. YOU COULD EVEN HAVE YOUR OWN TEAM.

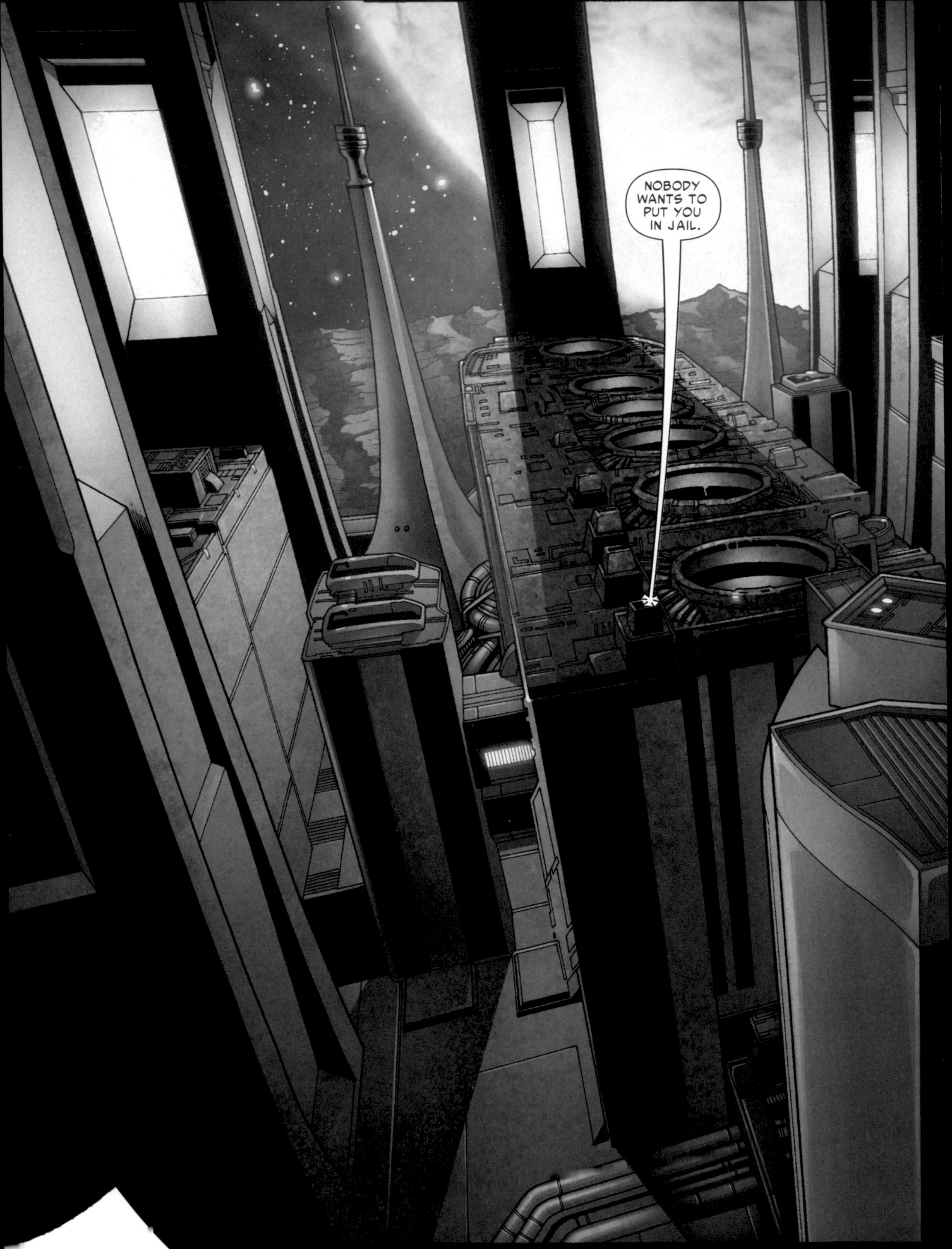
NOBODY WANTS TO PUT YOU IN JAIL.

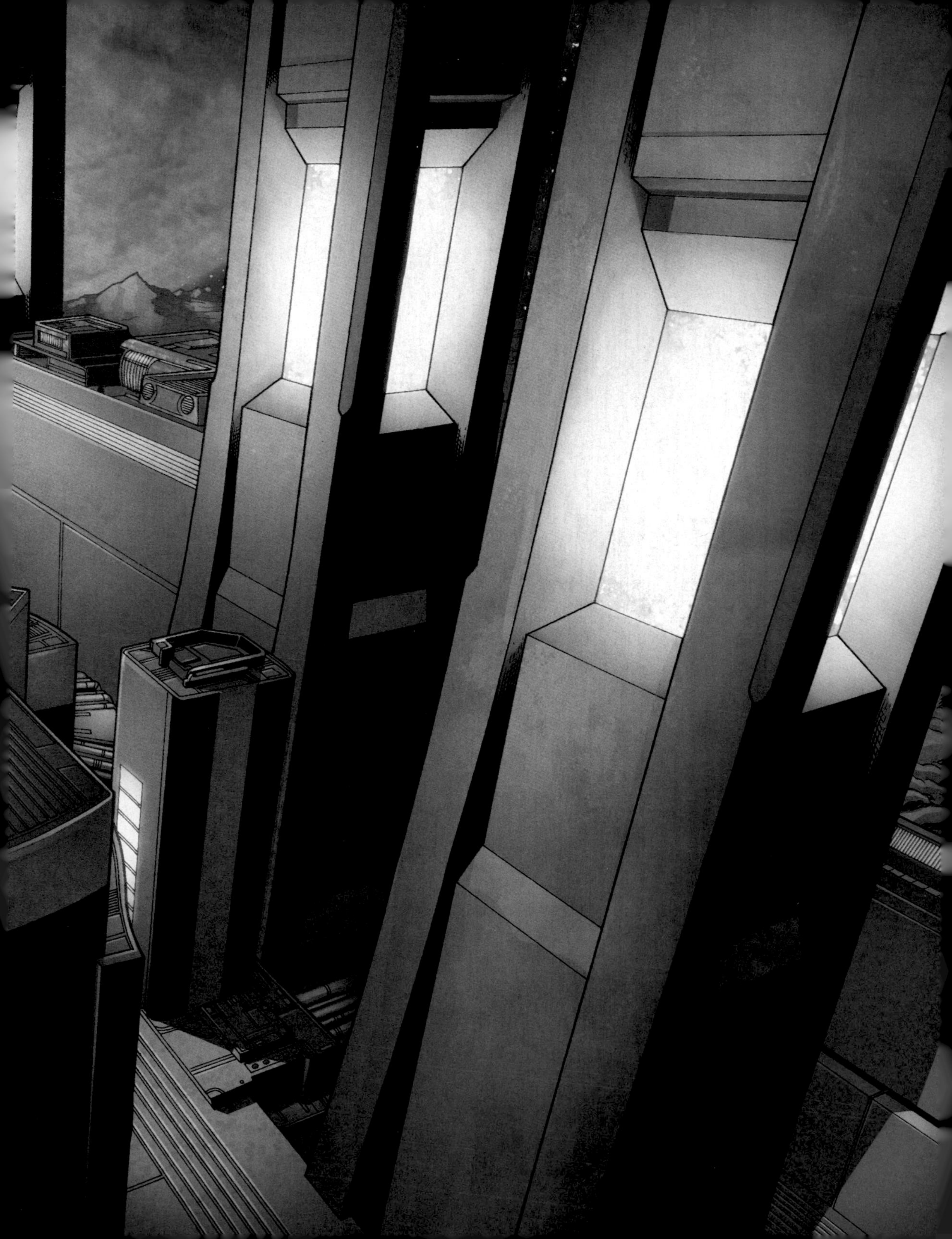

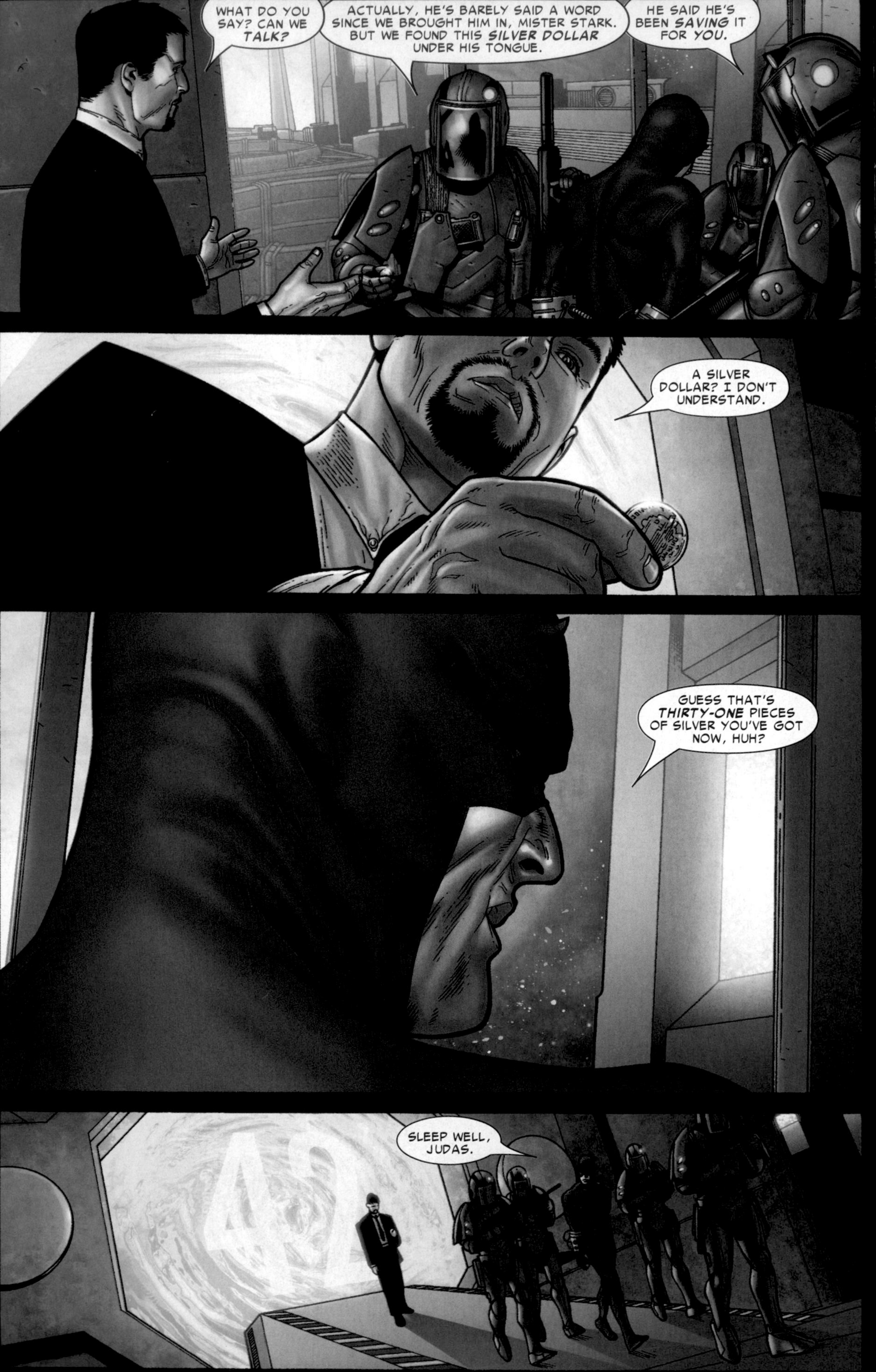
WHAT DO YOU SAY? CAN WE TALK?
ACTUALLY, HE'S BARELY SAID A WORD SINCE WE BROUGHT HIM IN, MISTER STARK. BUT WE FOUND THIS SILVER DOLLAR UNDER HIS TONGUE.
HE SAID HE'S BEEN SAVING IT FOR YOU.
A SILVER DOLLAR? I DON'T UNDERSTAND.
GUESS THAT'S THIRTY-ONE PIECES OF SILVER YOU'VE GOT NOW, HUH?
SLEEP WELL, JUDAS.
42

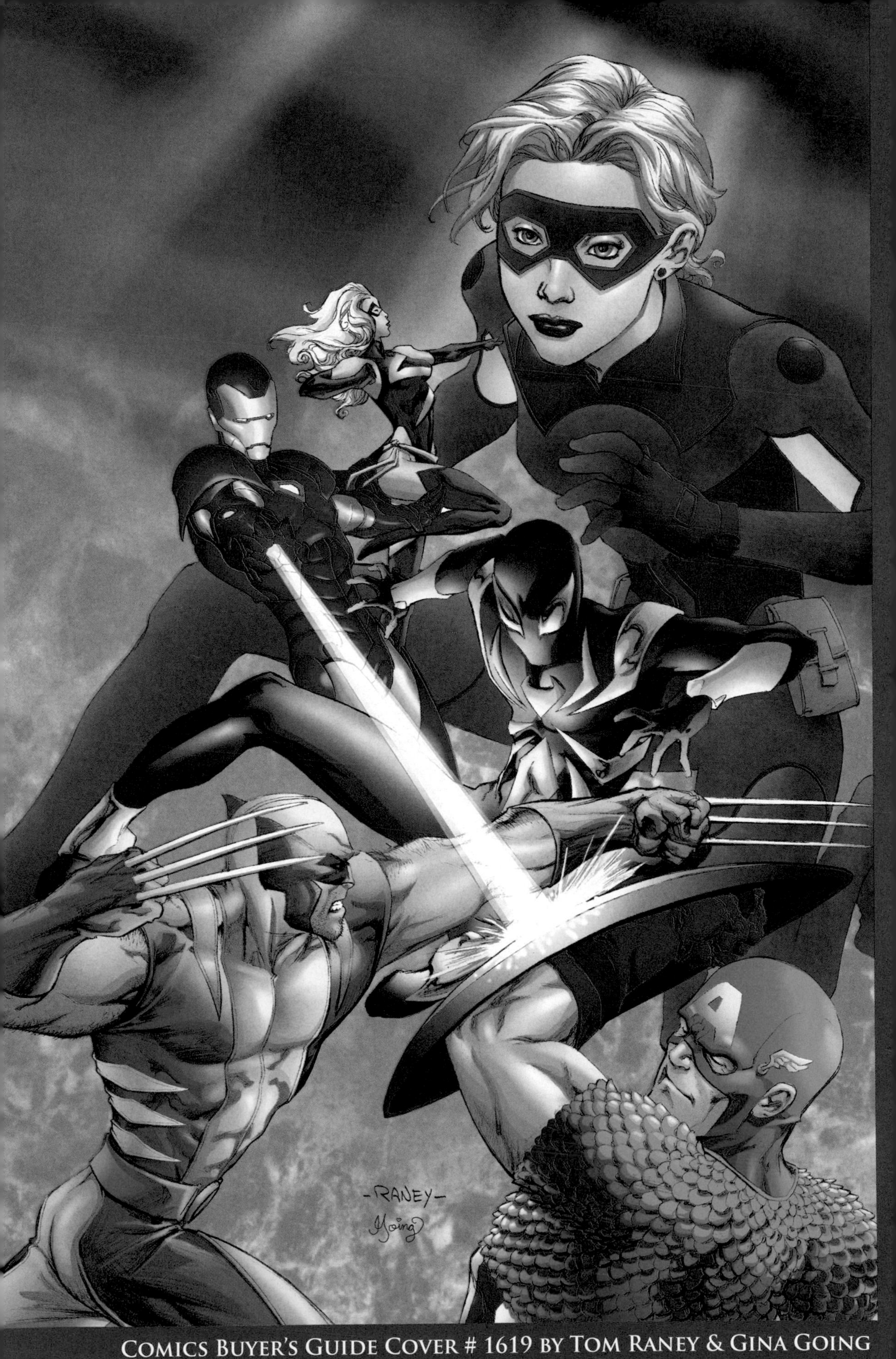
-RANEY-
Going

Comics Buyer's Guide Cover # 1619 by Tom Raney & Gina Going

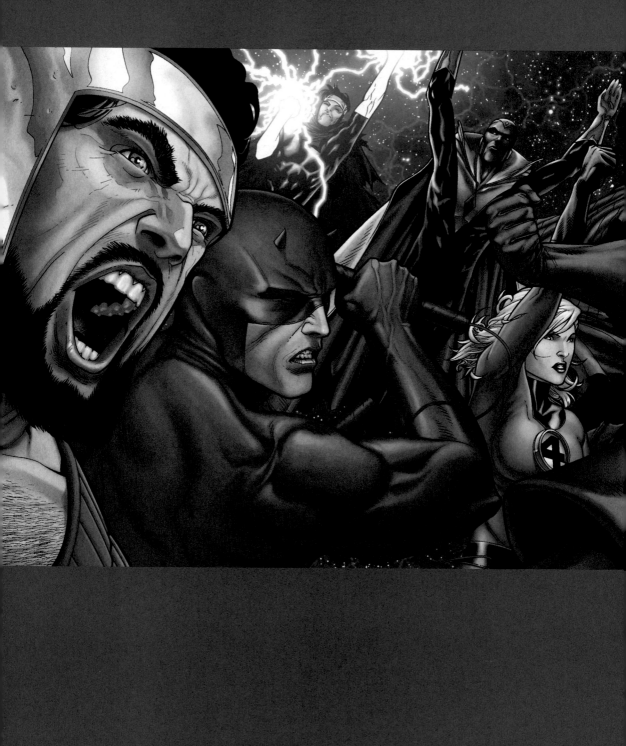

CIVIL WAR #6

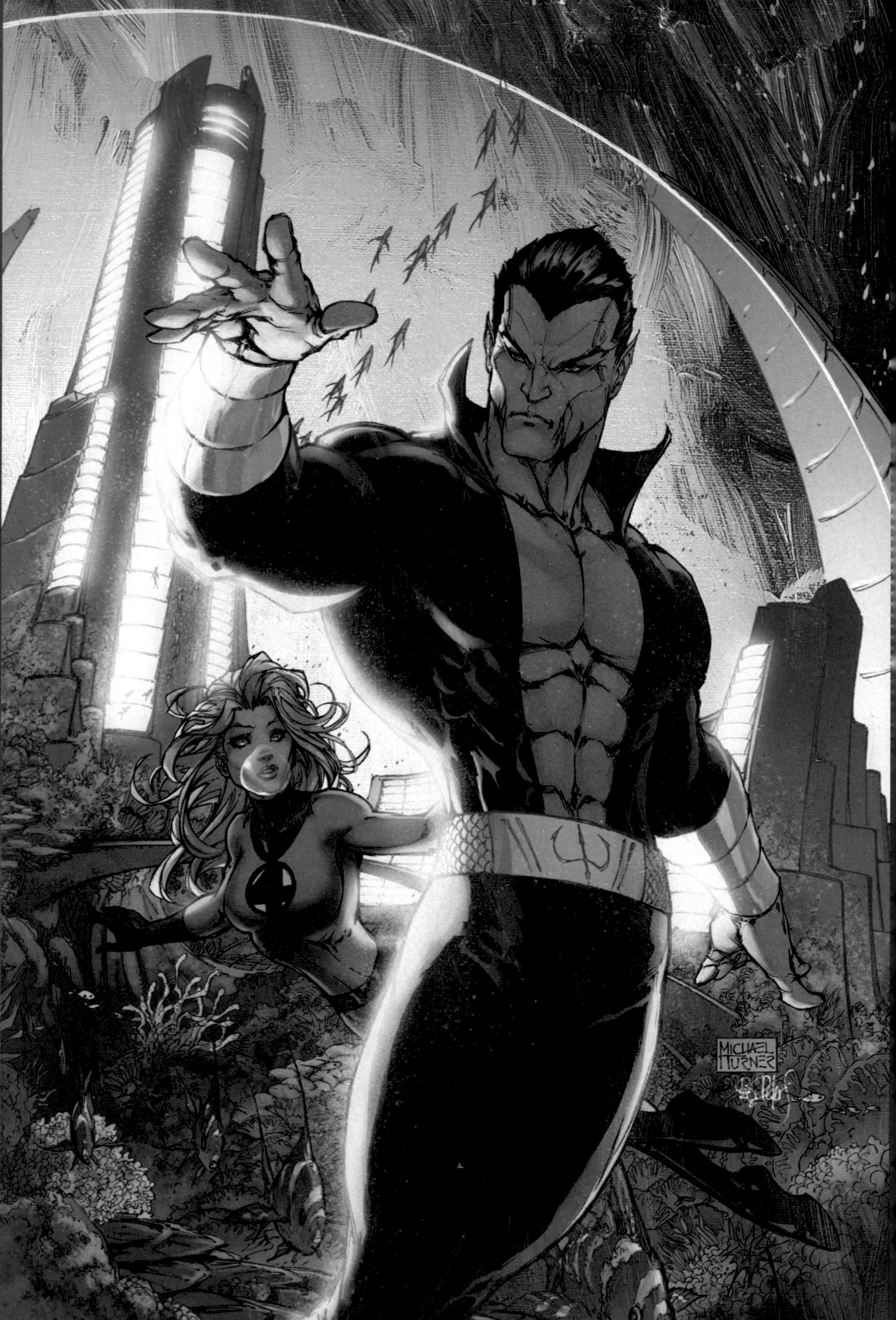
MICHAEL TURNER

CIVIL WAR #6 VARIANT BY MICHAEL TURNER & PETER STEIGERWALD

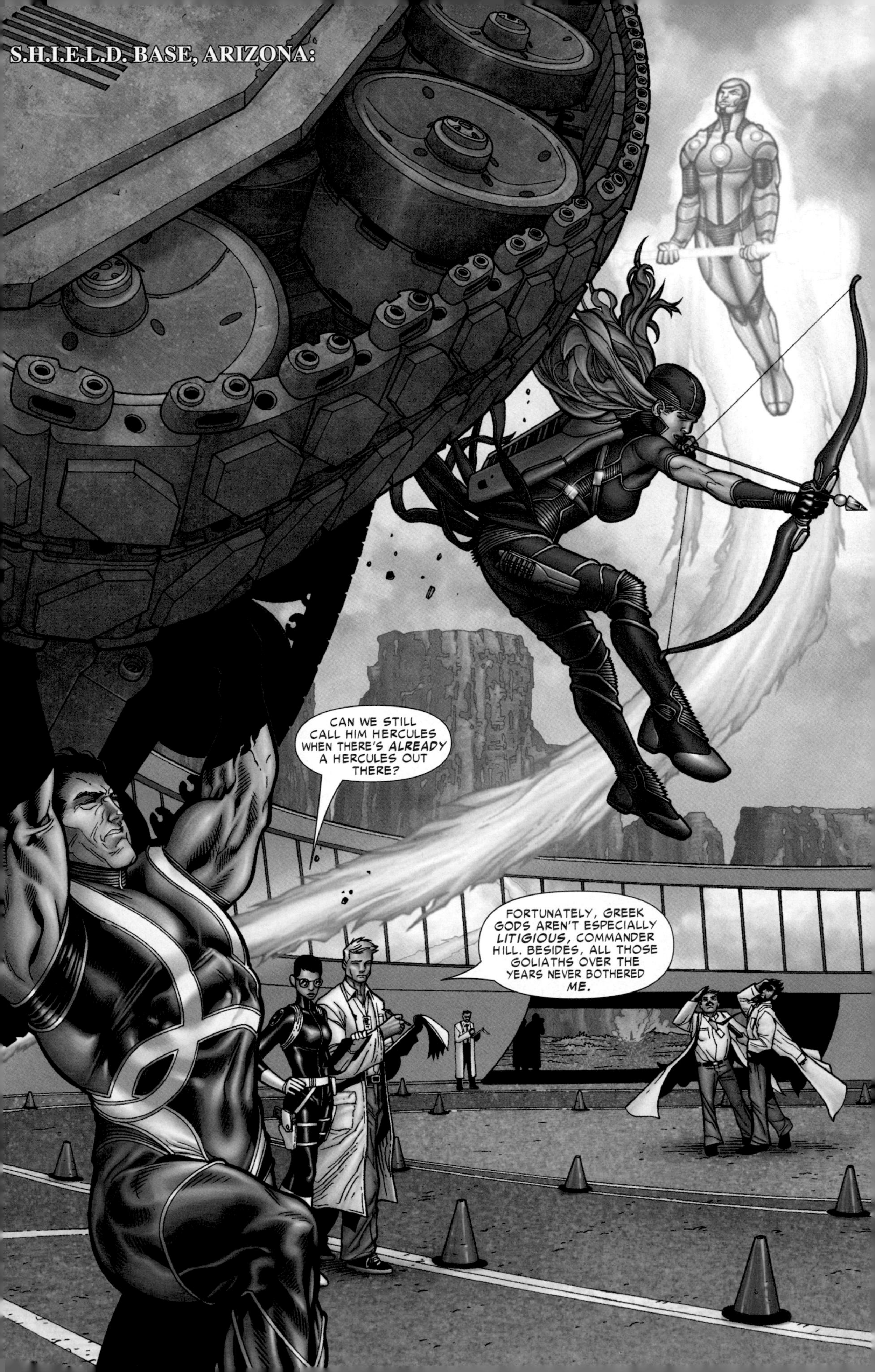
S.H.I.E.L.D. BASE, ARIZONA:
CAN WE STILL CALL HIM HERCULES WHEN THERE'S ALREADY A HERCULES OUT THERE?
FORTUNATELY, GREEK GODS AREN'T ESPECIALLY LITIGIOUS, COMMANDER HILL. BESIDES, ALL THOSE GOLIATHS OVER THE YEARS NEVER BOTHERED ME.

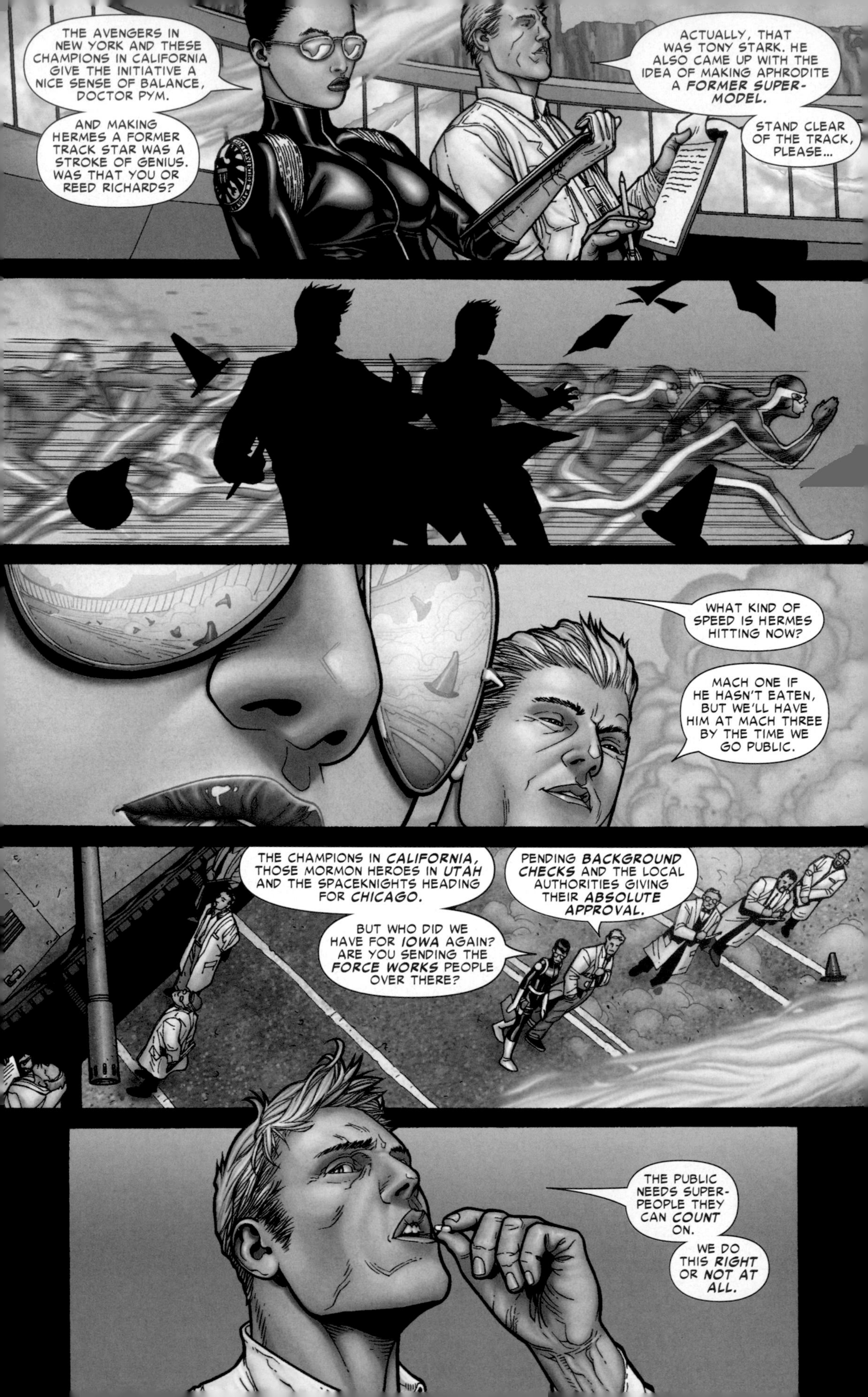
THE AVENGERS IN NEW YORK AND THESE CHAMPIONS IN CALIFORNIA GIVE THE INITIATIVE A NICE SENSE OF BALANCE, DOCTOR PYM.
AND MAKING HERMES A FORMER TRACK STAR WAS A STROKE OF GENIUS. WAS THAT YOU OR REED RICHARDS?
ACTUALLY, THAT WAS TONY STARK. HE ALSO CAME UP WITH THE IDEA OF MAKING APHRODITE A *FORMER SUPER-MODEL.*
STAND CLEAR OF THE TRACK, PLEASE...
WHAT KIND OF SPEED IS HERMES HITTING NOW?
MACH ONE IF HE HASN'T EATEN, BUT WE'LL HAVE HIM AT MACH THREE BY THE TIME WE GO PUBLIC.
THE CHAMPIONS IN *CALIFORNIA*, THOSE MORMON HEROES IN *UTAH* AND THE SPACEKNIGHTS HEADING FOR *CHICAGO.*
BUT WHO DID WE HAVE FOR *IOWA* AGAIN? ARE YOU SENDING THE *FORCE WORKS* PEOPLE OVER THERE?
PENDING *BACKGROUND CHECKS* AND THE LOCAL AUTHORITIES GIVING THEIR *ABSOLUTE APPROVAL.*
THE PUBLIC NEEDS SUPER-PEOPLE THEY CAN *COUNT* ON.
WE DO THIS *RIGHT* OR *NOT AT ALL.*

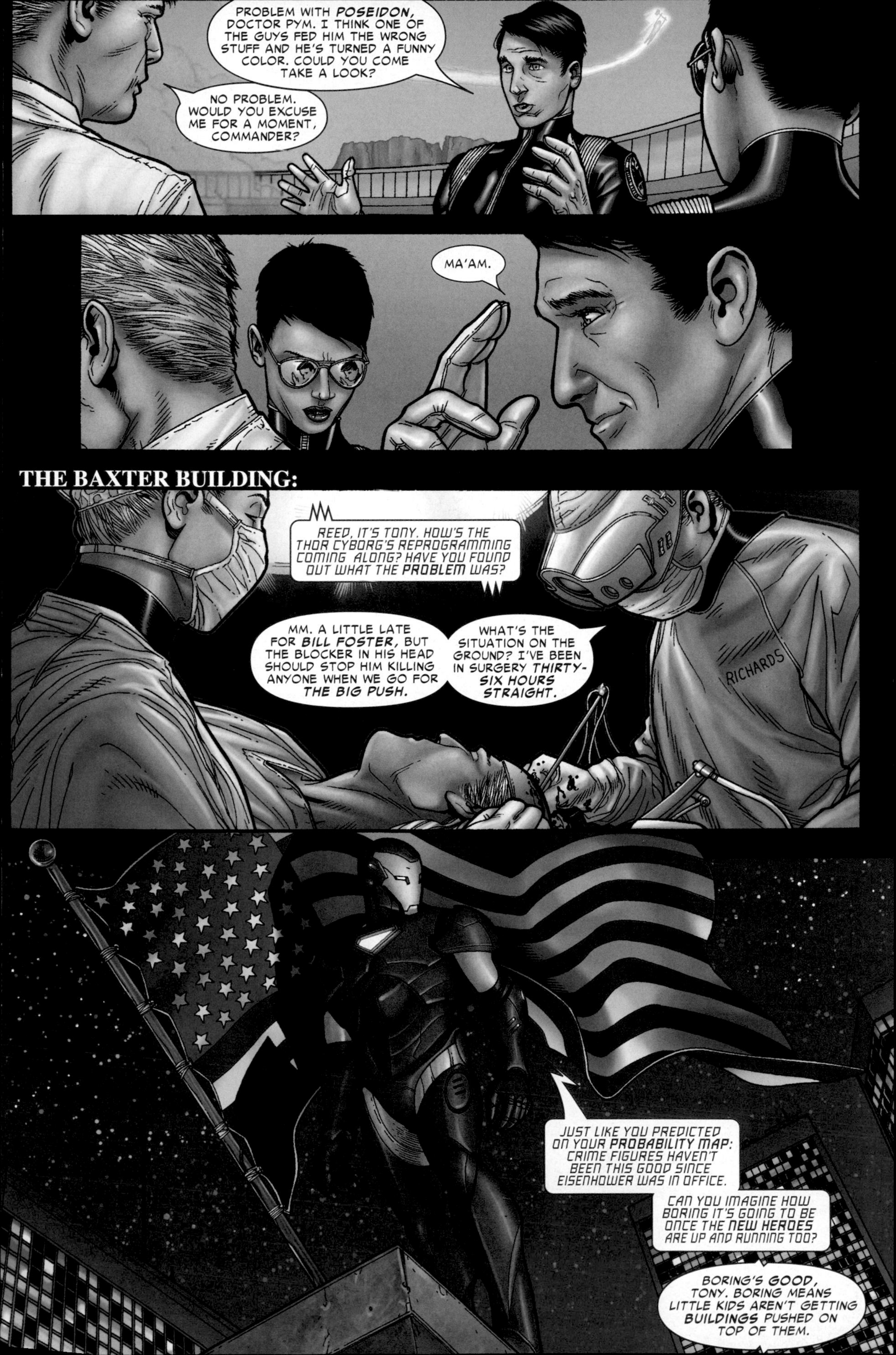
PROBLEM WITH POSEIDON, DOCTOR PYM. I THINK ONE OF THE GUYS FED HIM THE WRONG STUFF AND HE'S TURNED A FUNNY COLOR. COULD YOU COME TAKE A LOOK?
NO PROBLEM. WOULD YOU EXCUSE ME FOR A MOMENT, COMMANDER?
MA'AM.
THE BAXTER BUILDING:
REED, IT'S TONY. HOW'S THE THOR CYBORG'S REPROGRAMMING COMING ALONG? HAVE YOU FOUND OUT WHAT THE PROBLEM WAS?
MM. A LITTLE LATE FOR BILL FOSTER, BUT THE BLOCKER IN HIS HEAD SHOULD STOP HIM KILLING ANYONE WHEN WE GO FOR THE BIG PUSH.
WHAT'S THE SITUATION ON THE GROUND? I'VE BEEN IN SURGERY THIRTY-SIX HOURS STRAIGHT.
RICHARDS
JUST LIKE YOU PREDICTED ON YOUR PROBABILITY MAP: CRIME FIGURES HAVEN'T BEEN THIS GOOD SINCE EISENHOWER WAS IN OFFICE.
CAN YOU IMAGINE HOW BORING IT'S GOING TO BE ONCE THE NEW HEROES ARE UP AND RUNNING TOO?
BORING'S GOOD, TONY. BORING MEANS LITTLE KIDS AREN'T GETTING BUILDINGS PUSHED ON TOP OF THEM.

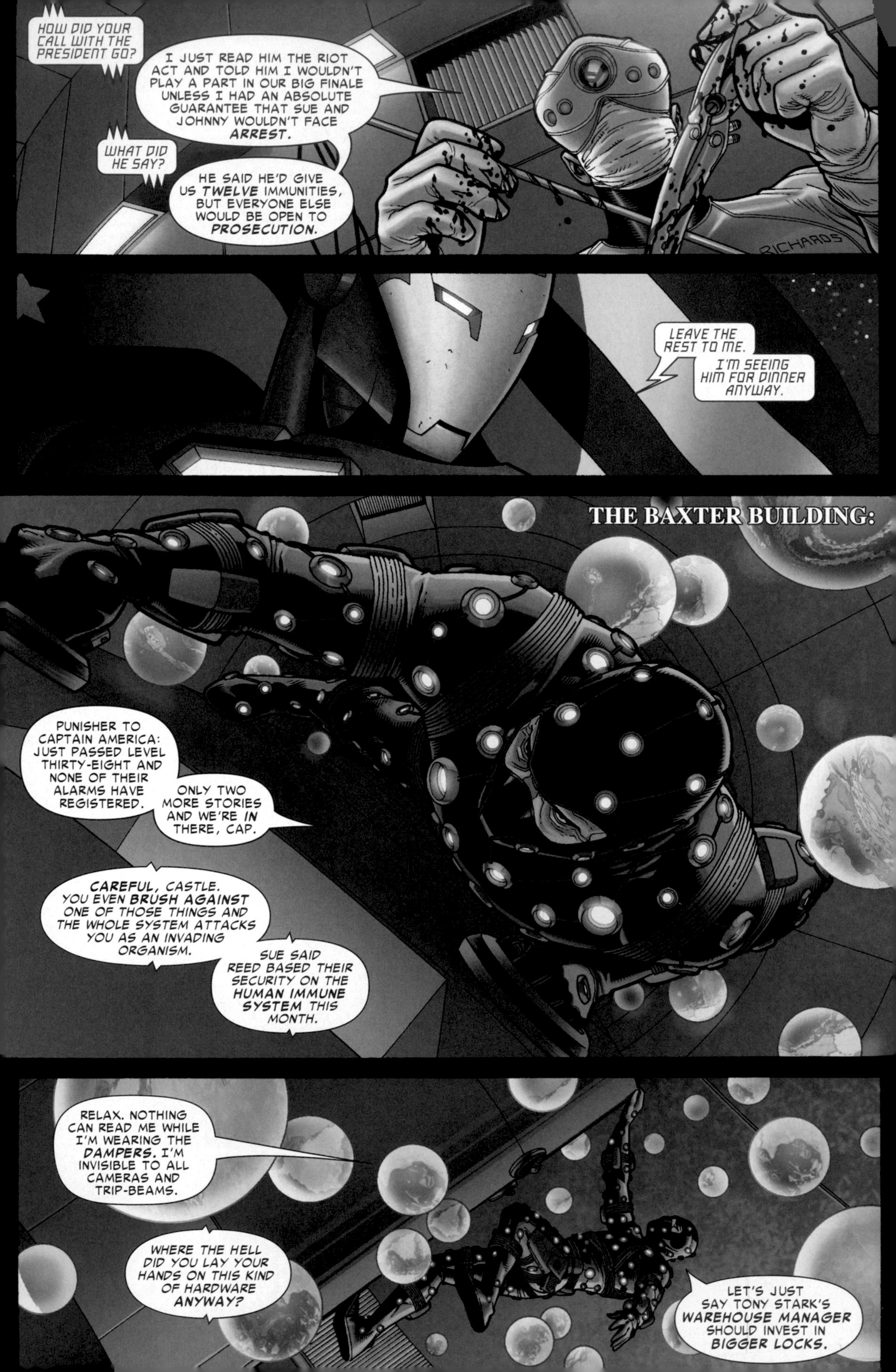

HOW DID YOUR CALL WITH THE PRESIDENT GO?
I JUST READ HIM THE RIOT ACT AND TOLD HIM I WOULDN'T PLAY A PART IN OUR BIG FINALE UNLESS I HAD AN ABSOLUTE GUARANTEE THAT SUE AND JOHNNY WOULDN'T FACE ARREST.
WHAT DID HE SAY?
HE SAID HE'D GIVE US TWELVE IMMUNITIES, BUT EVERYONE ELSE WOULD BE OPEN TO PROSECUTION.
RICHARDS
LEAVE THE REST TO ME.
I'M SEEING HIM FOR DINNER ANYWAY.
THE BAXTER BUILDING:
PUNISHER TO CAPTAIN AMERICA: JUST PASSED LEVEL THIRTY-EIGHT AND NONE OF THEIR ALARMS HAVE REGISTERED.
ONLY TWO MORE STORIES AND WE'RE IN THERE, CAP.
CAREFUL, CASTLE. YOU EVEN BRUSH AGAINST ONE OF THOSE THINGS AND THE WHOLE SYSTEM ATTACKS YOU AS AN INVADING ORGANISM.
SUE SAID REED BASED THEIR SECURITY ON THE HUMAN IMMUNE SYSTEM THIS MONTH.
RELAX. NOTHING CAN READ ME WHILE I'M WEARING THE DAMPERS. I'M INVISIBLE TO ALL CAMERAS AND TRIP-BEAMS.
WHERE THE HELL DID YOU LAY YOUR HANDS ON THIS KIND OF HARDWARE ANYWAY?
LET'S JUST SAY TONY STARK'S WAREHOUSE MANAGER SHOULD INVEST IN BIGGER LOCKS.

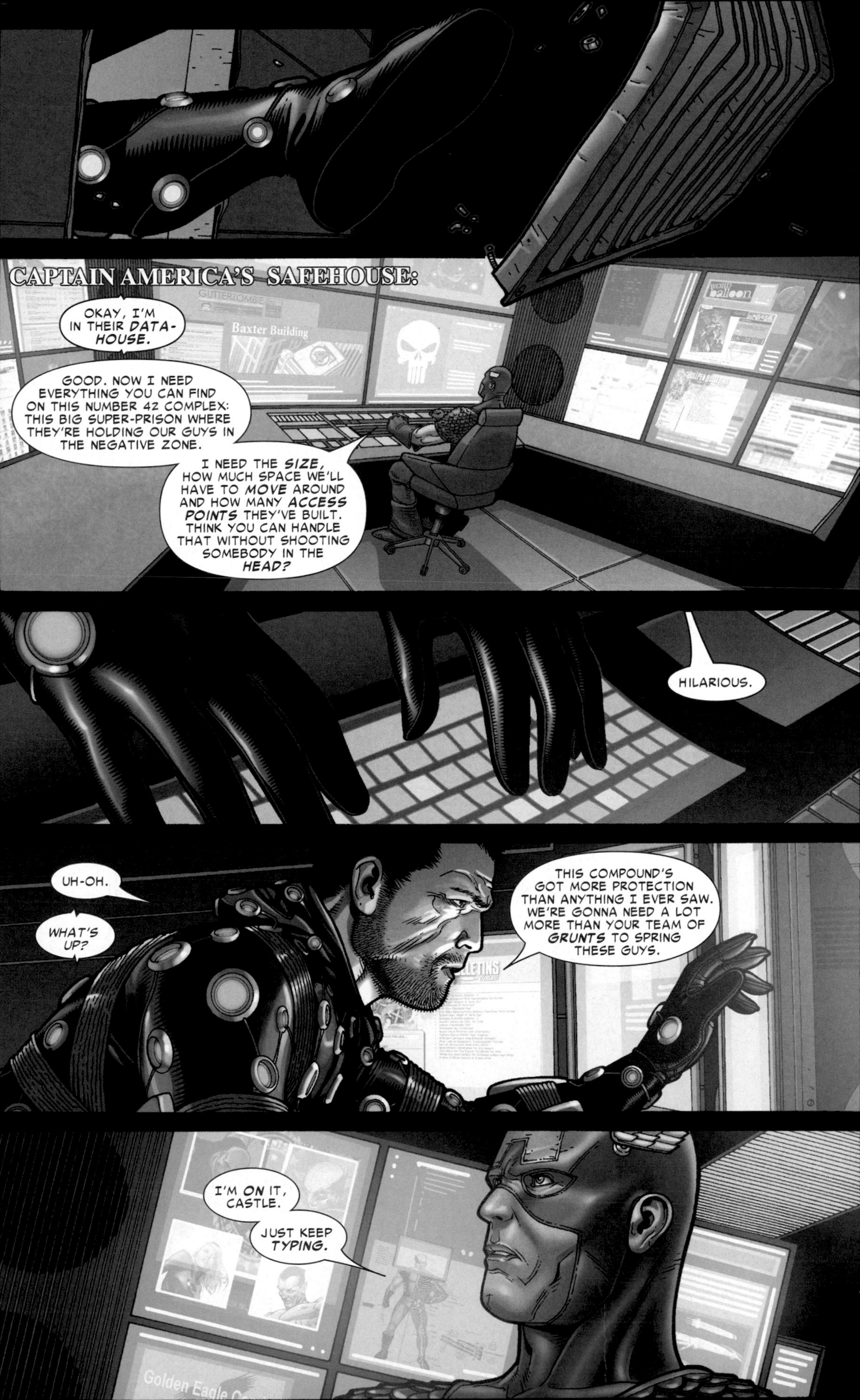
CAPTAIN AMERICA'S SAFEHOUSE:
OKAY, I'M IN THEIR DATA-HOUSE.
GOOD. NOW I NEED EVERYTHING YOU CAN FIND ON THIS NUMBER 42 COMPLEX: THIS BIG SUPER-PRISON WHERE THEY'RE HOLDING OUR GUYS IN THE NEGATIVE ZONE.
I NEED THE SIZE, HOW MUCH SPACE WE'LL HAVE TO MOVE AROUND AND HOW MANY ACCESS POINTS THEY'VE BUILT. THINK YOU CAN HANDLE THAT WITHOUT SHOOTING SOMEBODY IN THE HEAD?
Baxter Building
HILARIOUS.
UH-OH.
WHAT'S UP?
THIS COMPOUND'S GOT MORE PROTECTION THAN ANYTHING I EVER SAW. WE'RE GONNA NEED A LOT MORE THAN YOUR TEAM OF GRUNTS TO SPRING THESE GUYS.
I'M ON IT, CASTLE.
JUST KEEP TYPING.

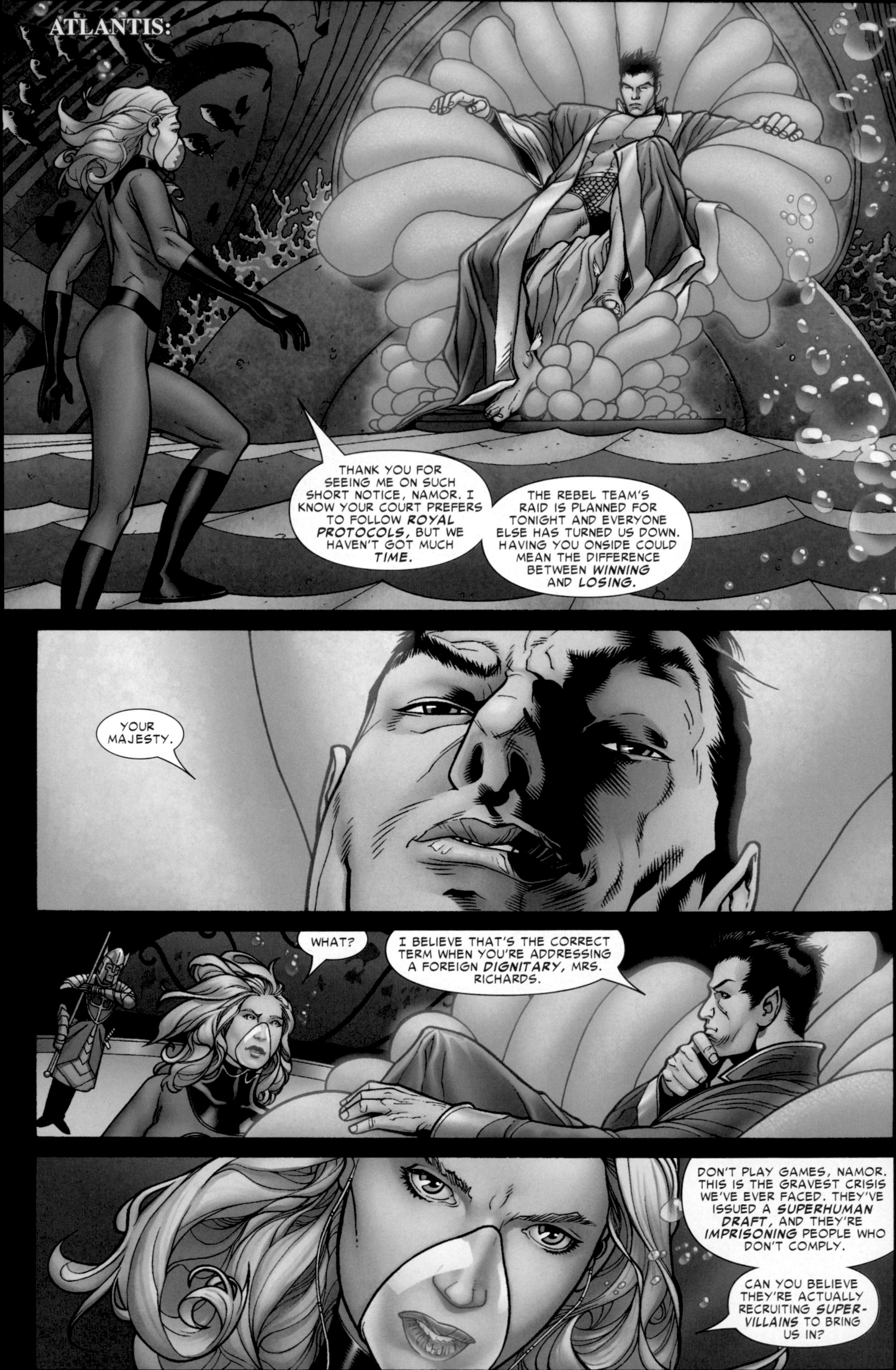
ATLANTIS:
THANK YOU FOR SEEING ME ON SUCH SHORT NOTICE, NAMOR. I KNOW YOUR COURT PREFERS TO FOLLOW ROYAL PROTOCOLS, BUT WE HAVEN'T GOT MUCH TIME.
THE REBEL TEAM'S RAID IS PLANNED FOR TONIGHT AND EVERYONE ELSE HAS TURNED US DOWN. HAVING YOU ONSIDE COULD MEAN THE DIFFERENCE BETWEEN WINNING AND LOSING.
YOUR MAJESTY.
WHAT?
I BELIEVE THAT'S THE CORRECT TERM WHEN YOU'RE ADDRESSING A FOREIGN DIGNITARY, MRS. RICHARDS.
DON'T PLAY GAMES, NAMOR. THIS IS THE GRAVEST CRISIS WE'VE EVER FACED. THEY'VE ISSUED A SUPERHUMAN DRAFT, AND THEY'RE IMPRISONING PEOPLE WHO DON'T COMPLY.
CAN YOU BELIEVE THEY'RE ACTUALLY RECRUITING SUPER-VILLAINS TO BRING US IN?

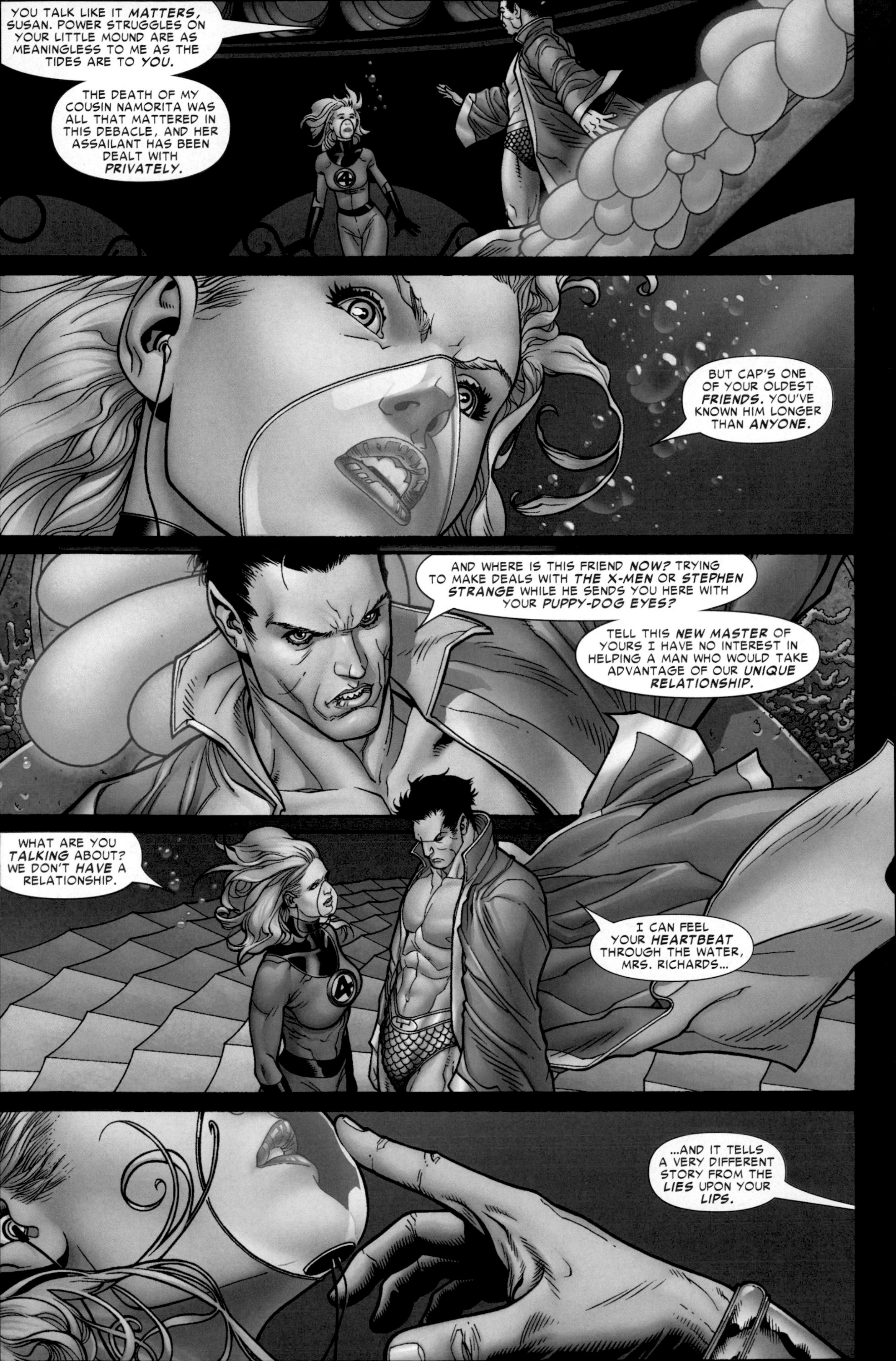
YOU TALK LIKE IT MATTERS, SUSAN. POWER STRUGGLES ON YOUR LITTLE MOUND ARE AS MEANINGLESS TO ME AS THE TIDES ARE TO YOU.
THE DEATH OF MY COUSIN NAMORITA WAS ALL THAT MATTERED IN THIS DEBACLE, AND HER ASSAILANT HAS BEEN DEALT WITH PRIVATELY.
BUT CAP'S ONE OF YOUR OLDEST FRIENDS. YOU'VE KNOWN HIM LONGER THAN ANYONE.
AND WHERE IS THIS FRIEND NOW? TRYING TO MAKE DEALS WITH THE X-MEN OR STEPHEN STRANGE WHILE HE SENDS YOU HERE WITH YOUR PUPPY-DOG EYES?
TELL THIS NEW MASTER OF YOURS I HAVE NO INTEREST IN HELPING A MAN WHO WOULD TAKE ADVANTAGE OF OUR UNIQUE RELATIONSHIP.
WHAT ARE YOU TALKING ABOUT? WE DON'T HAVE A RELATIONSHIP.
I CAN FEEL YOUR HEARTBEAT THROUGH THE WATER, MRS. RICHARDS...
...AND IT TELLS A VERY DIFFERENT STORY FROM THE LIES UPON YOUR LIPS.

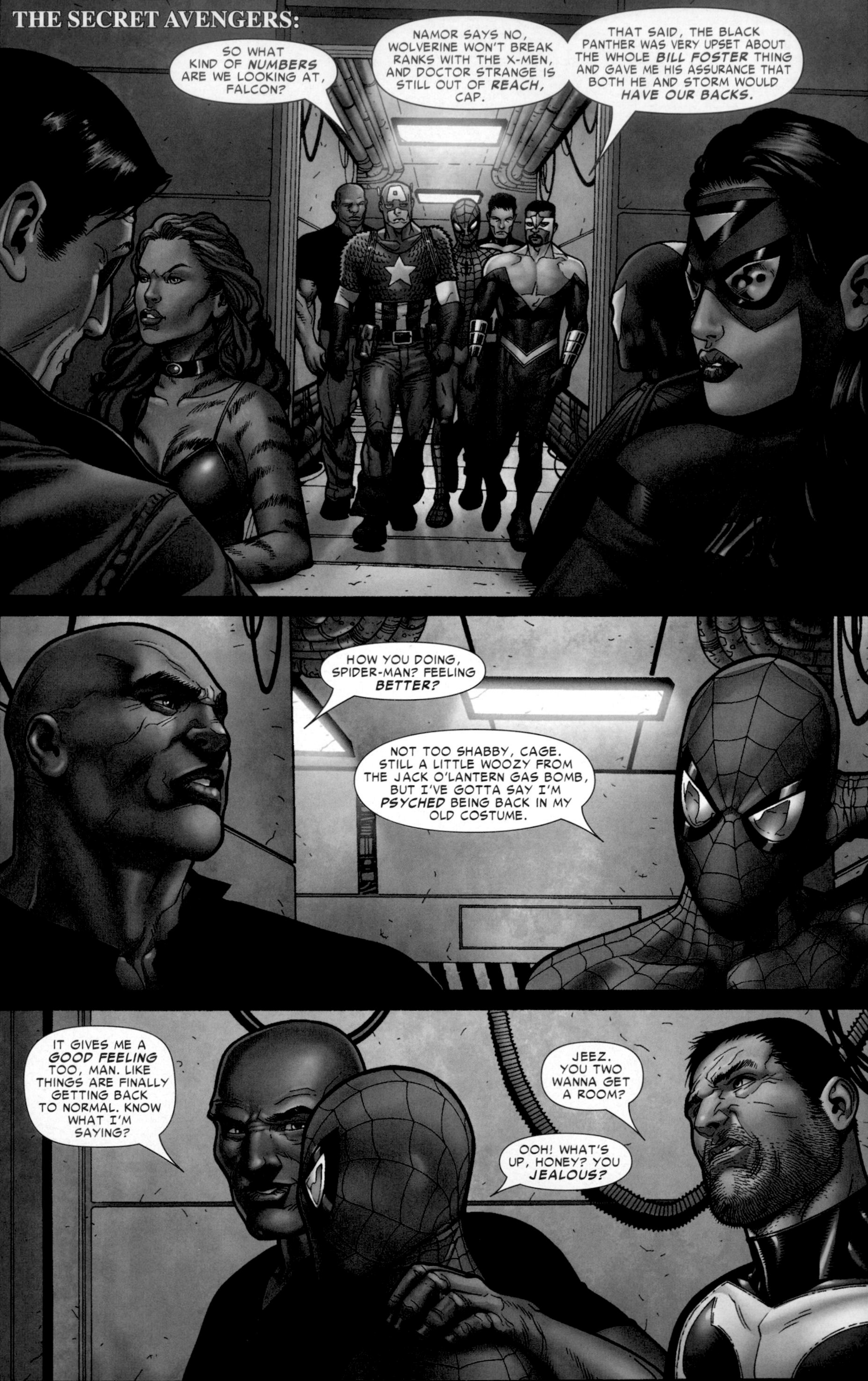
THE SECRET AVENGERS:
SO WHAT KIND OF NUMBERS ARE WE LOOKING AT, FALCON?
NAMOR SAYS NO, WOLVERINE WON'T BREAK RANKS WITH THE X-MEN, AND DOCTOR STRANGE IS STILL OUT OF REACH, CAP.
THAT SAID, THE BLACK PANTHER WAS VERY UPSET ABOUT THE WHOLE BILL FOSTER THING AND GAVE ME HIS ASSURANCE THAT BOTH HE AND STORM WOULD HAVE OUR BACKS.
HOW YOU DOING, SPIDER-MAN? FEELING BETTER?
NOT TOO SHABBY, CAGE. STILL A LITTLE WOOZY FROM THE JACK O'LANTERN GAS BOMB, BUT I'VE GOTTA SAY I'M PSYCHED BEING BACK IN MY OLD COSTUME.
IT GIVES ME A GOOD FEELING TOO, MAN. LIKE THINGS ARE FINALLY GETTING BACK TO NORMAL. KNOW WHAT I'M SAYING?
JEEZ. YOU TWO WANNA GET A ROOM?
OOH! WHAT'S UP, HONEY? YOU JEALOUS?

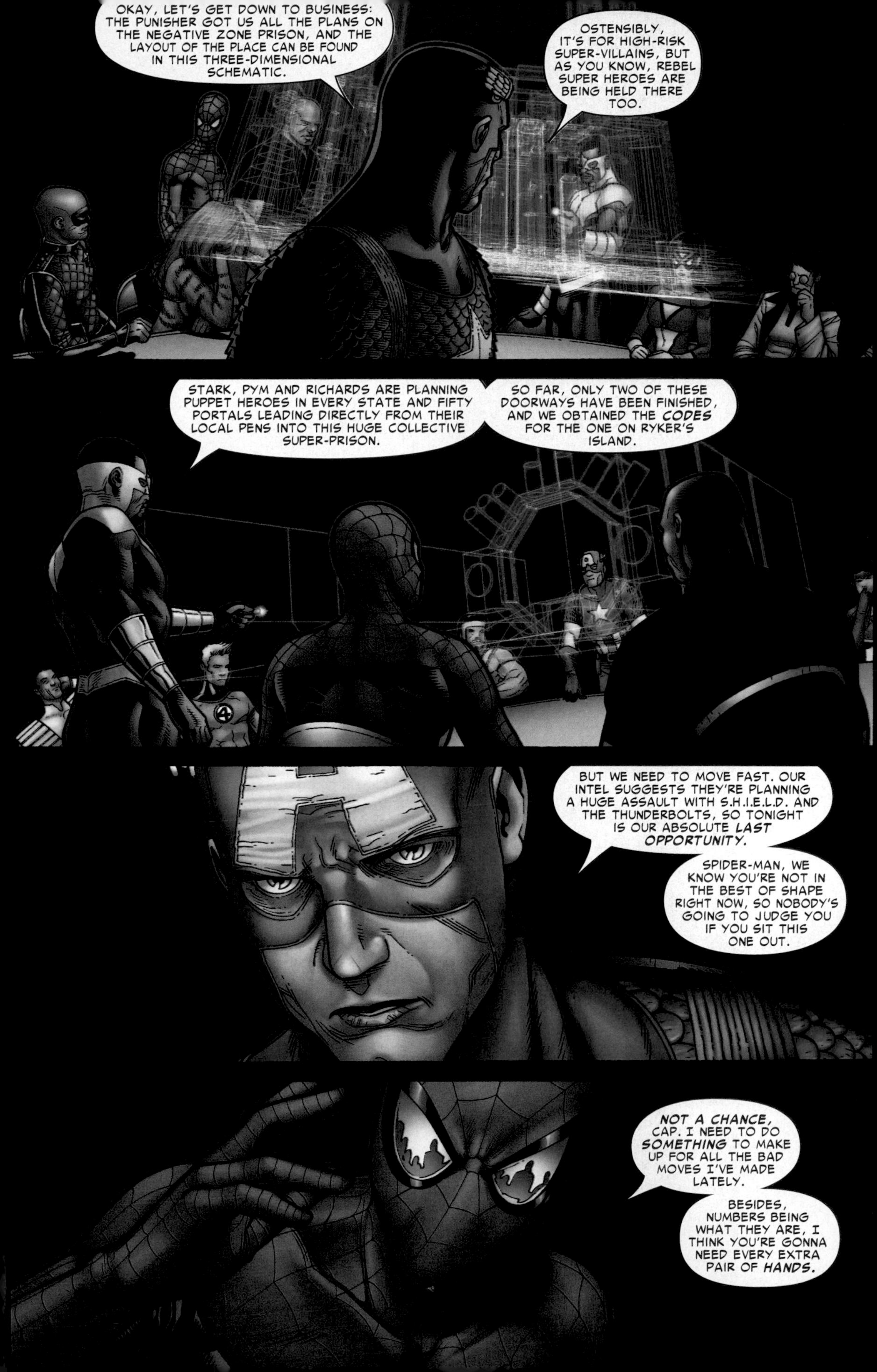
OKAY, LET'S GET DOWN TO BUSINESS: THE PUNISHER GOT US ALL THE PLANS ON THE NEGATIVE ZONE PRISON, AND THE LAYOUT OF THE PLACE CAN BE FOUND IN THIS THREE-DIMENSIONAL SCHEMATIC.
OSTENSIBLY, IT'S FOR HIGH-RISK SUPER-VILLAINS, BUT AS YOU KNOW, REBEL SUPER HEROES ARE BEING HELD THERE TOO.
STARK, PYM AND RICHARDS ARE PLANNING PUPPET HEROES IN EVERY STATE AND FIFTY PORTALS LEADING DIRECTLY FROM THEIR LOCAL PENS INTO THIS HUGE COLLECTIVE SUPER-PRISON.
SO FAR, ONLY TWO OF THESE DOORWAYS HAVE BEEN FINISHED, AND WE OBTAINED THE *CODES* FOR THE ONE ON RYKER'S ISLAND.
BUT WE NEED TO MOVE FAST. OUR INTEL SUGGESTS THEY'RE PLANNING A HUGE ASSAULT WITH S.H.I.E.L.D. AND THE THUNDERBOLTS, SO TONIGHT IS OUR ABSOLUTE *LAST OPPORTUNITY*.
SPIDER-MAN, WE KNOW YOU'RE NOT IN THE BEST OF SHAPE RIGHT NOW, SO NOBODY'S GOING TO JUDGE YOU IF YOU SIT THIS ONE OUT.
NOT A CHANCE, CAP. I NEED TO DO *SOMETHING* TO MAKE UP FOR ALL THE BAD MOVES I'VE MADE LATELY.
BESIDES, NUMBERS BEING WHAT THEY ARE, I THINK YOU'RE GONNA NEED EVERY EXTRA PAIR OF *HANDS*.

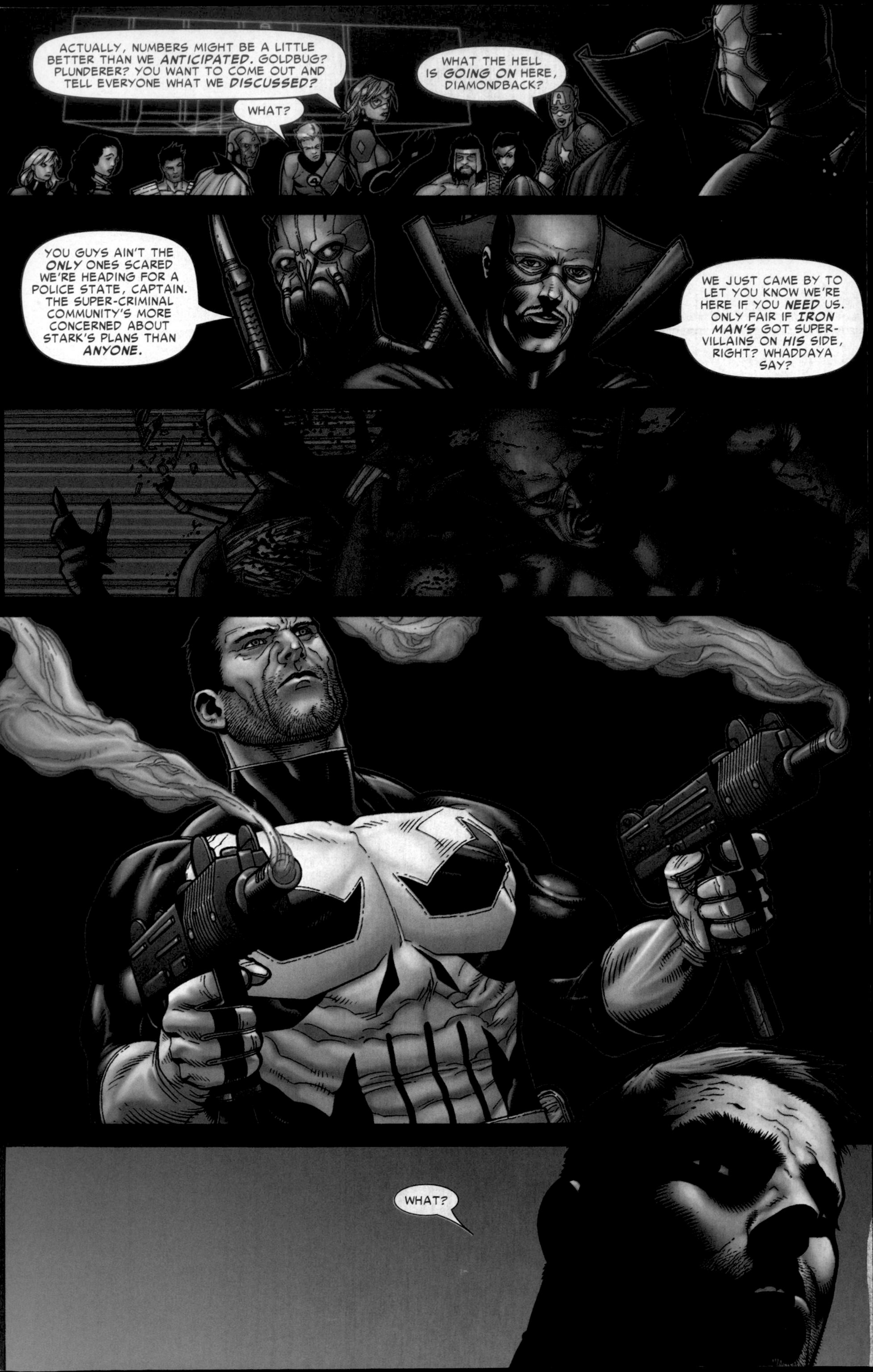
ACTUALLY, NUMBERS MIGHT BE A LITTLE BETTER THAN WE ANTICIPATED. GOLDBUG? PLUNDERER? YOU WANT TO COME OUT AND TELL EVERYONE WHAT WE DISCUSSED?
WHAT?
WHAT THE HELL IS GOING ON HERE, DIAMONDBACK?
YOU GUYS AIN'T THE ONLY ONES SCARED WE'RE HEADING FOR A POLICE STATE, CAPTAIN. THE SUPER-CRIMINAL COMMUNITY'S MORE CONCERNED ABOUT STARK'S PLANS THAN ANYONE.
WE JUST CAME BY TO LET YOU KNOW WE'RE HERE IF YOU NEED US. ONLY FAIR IF IRON MAN'S GOT SUPER-VILLAINS ON HIS SIDE, RIGHT? WHADDAYA SAY?
WHAT?

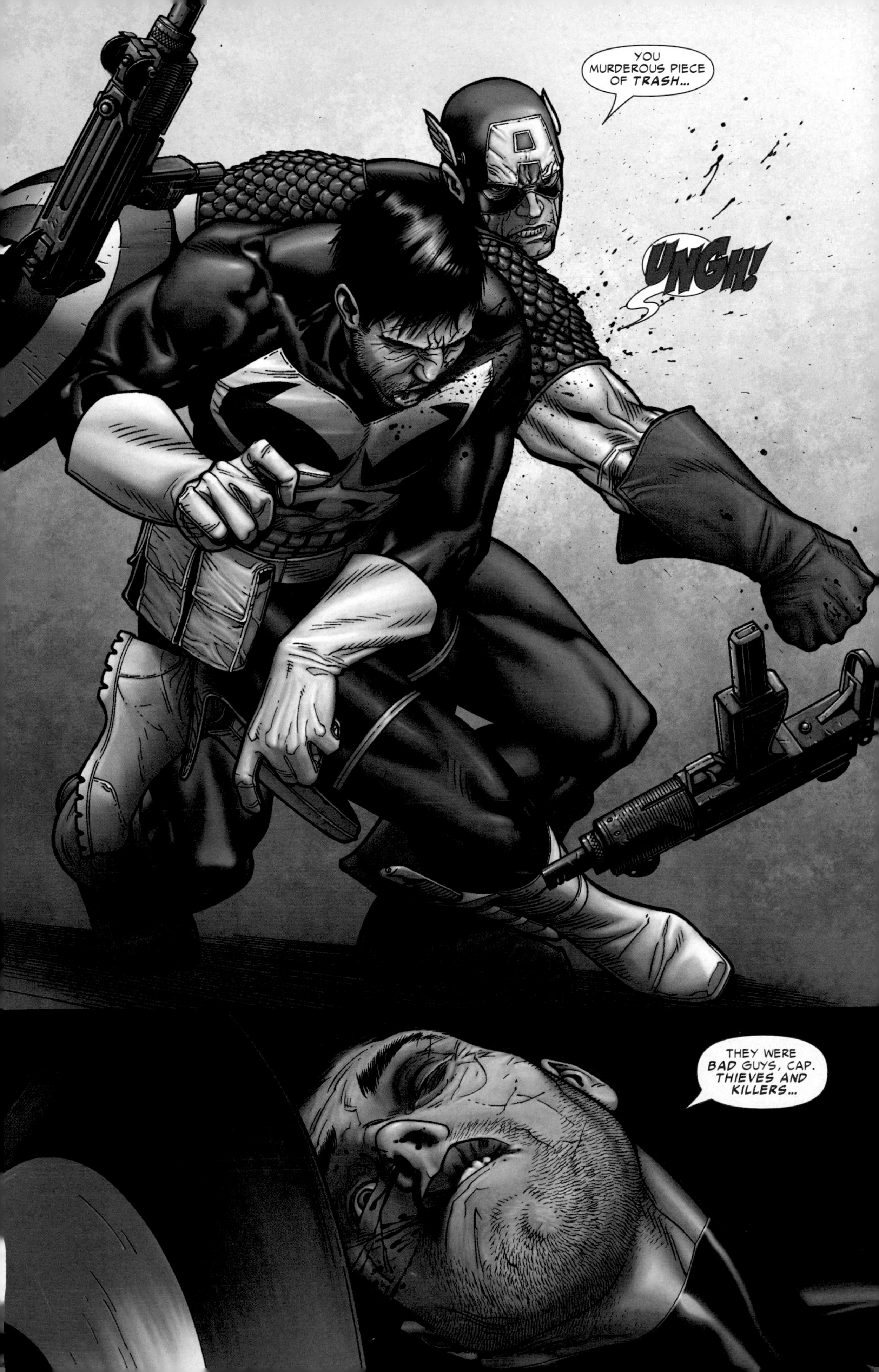
YOU MURDEROUS PIECE OF TRASH...
UNGH!
THEY WERE BAD GUYS, CAP. THIEVES AND KILLERS...

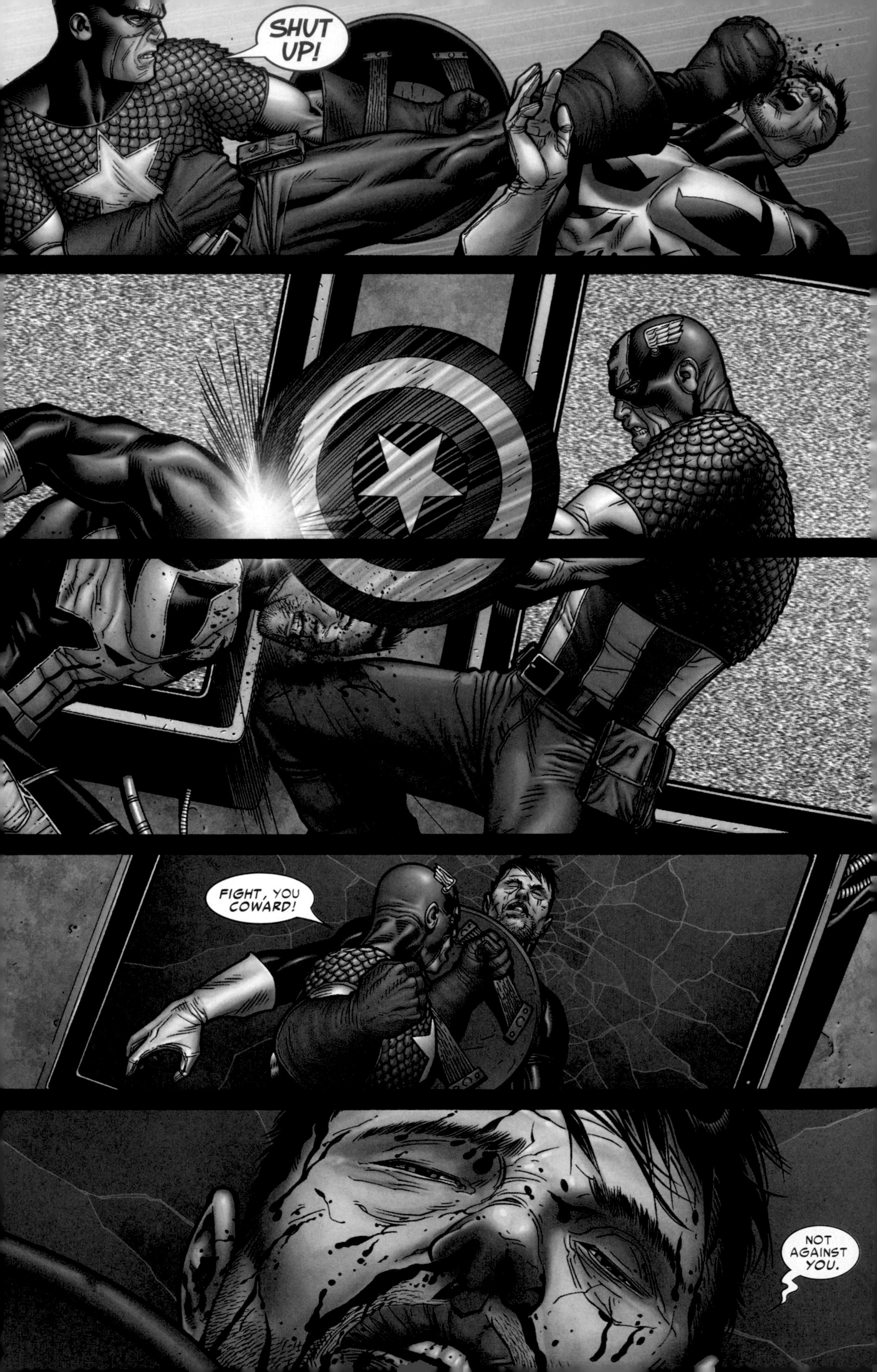
SHUT UP!
FIGHT, YOU COWARD!
NOT AGAINST YOU.

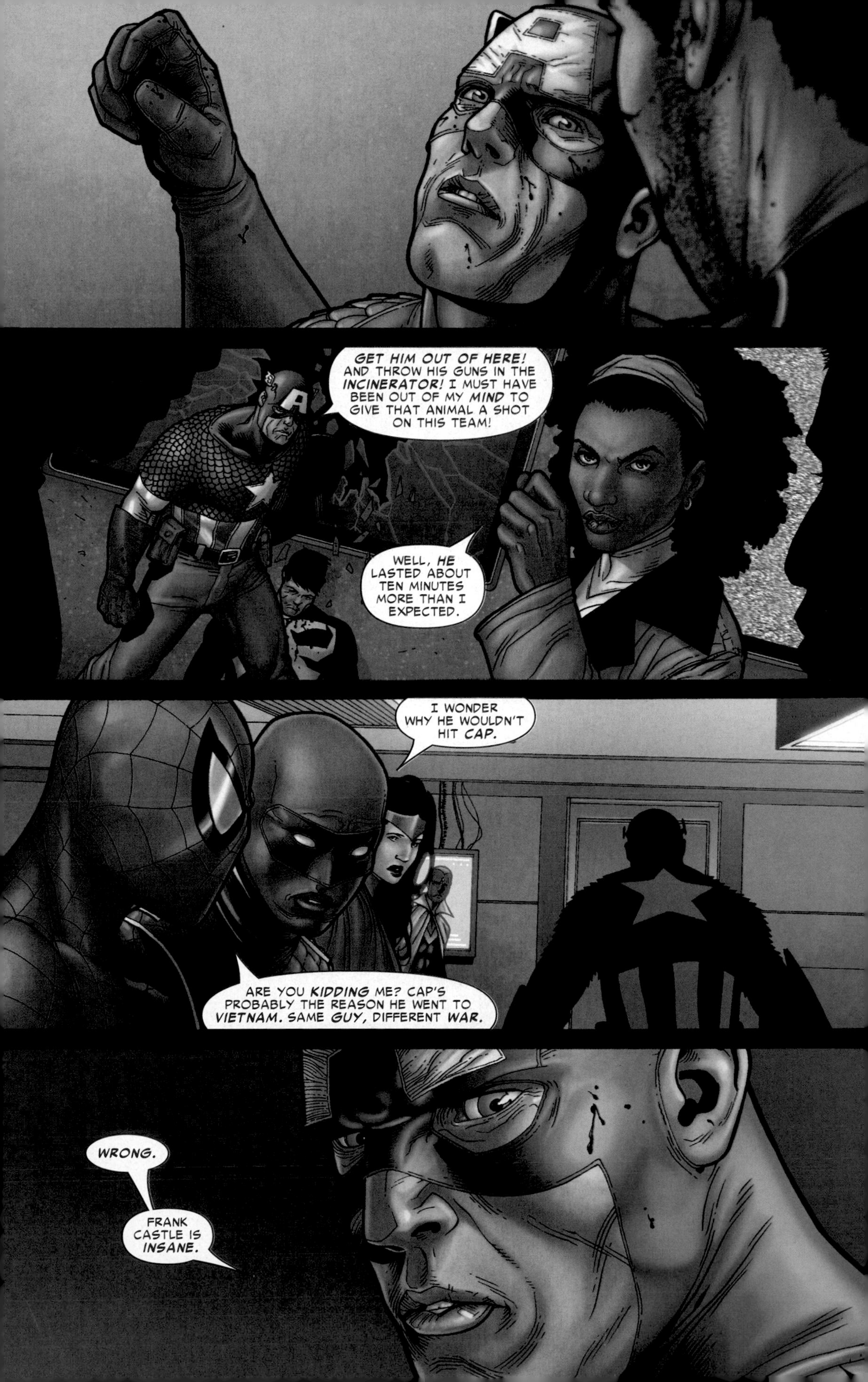

GET HIM OUT OF HERE! AND THROW HIS GUNS IN THE INCINERATOR! I MUST HAVE BEEN OUT OF MY MIND TO GIVE THAT ANIMAL A SHOT ON THIS TEAM!
WELL, HE LASTED ABOUT TEN MINUTES MORE THAN I EXPECTED.
I WONDER WHY HE WOULDN'T HIT CAP.
ARE YOU KIDDING ME? CAP'S PROBABLY THE REASON HE WENT TO VIETNAM. SAME GUY, DIFFERENT WAR.
WRONG.
FRANK CASTLE IS INSANE.

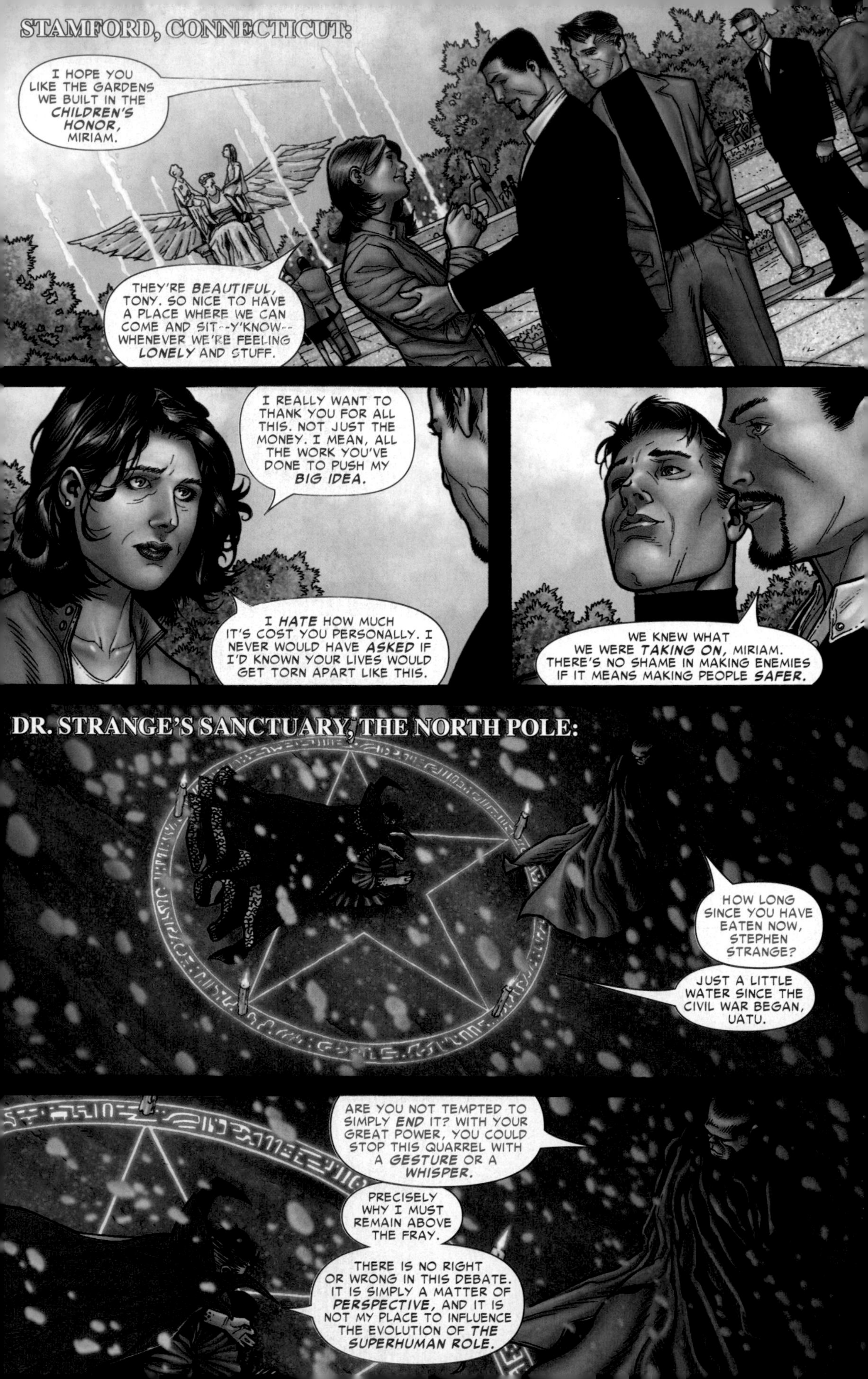
STAMFORD, CONNECTICUT:
I HOPE YOU LIKE THE GARDENS WE BUILT IN THE CHILDREN'S HONOR, MIRIAM.
THEY'RE BEAUTIFUL, TONY. SO NICE TO HAVE A PLACE WHERE WE CAN COME AND SIT--Y'KNOW--WHENEVER WE'RE FEELING LONELY AND STUFF.
I REALLY WANT TO THANK YOU FOR ALL THIS. NOT JUST THE MONEY. I MEAN, ALL THE WORK YOU'VE DONE TO PUSH MY BIG IDEA.
I HATE HOW MUCH IT'S COST YOU PERSONALLY. I NEVER WOULD HAVE ASKED IF I'D KNOWN YOUR LIVES WOULD GET TORN APART LIKE THIS.
WE KNEW WHAT WE WERE TAKING ON, MIRIAM. THERE'S NO SHAME IN MAKING ENEMIES IF IT MEANS MAKING PEOPLE SAFER.
DR. STRANGE'S SANCTUARY, THE NORTH POLE:
HOW LONG SINCE YOU HAVE EATEN NOW, STEPHEN STRANGE?
JUST A LITTLE WATER SINCE THE CIVIL WAR BEGAN, UATU.
ARE YOU NOT TEMPTED TO SIMPLY END IT? WITH YOUR GREAT POWER, YOU COULD STOP THIS QUARREL WITH A GESTURE OR A WHISPER.
PRECISELY WHY I MUST REMAIN ABOVE THE FRAY.
THERE IS NO RIGHT OR WRONG IN THIS DEBATE. IT IS SIMPLY A MATTER OF PERSPECTIVE, AND IT IS NOT MY PLACE TO INFLUENCE THE EVOLUTION OF THE SUPERHUMAN ROLE.

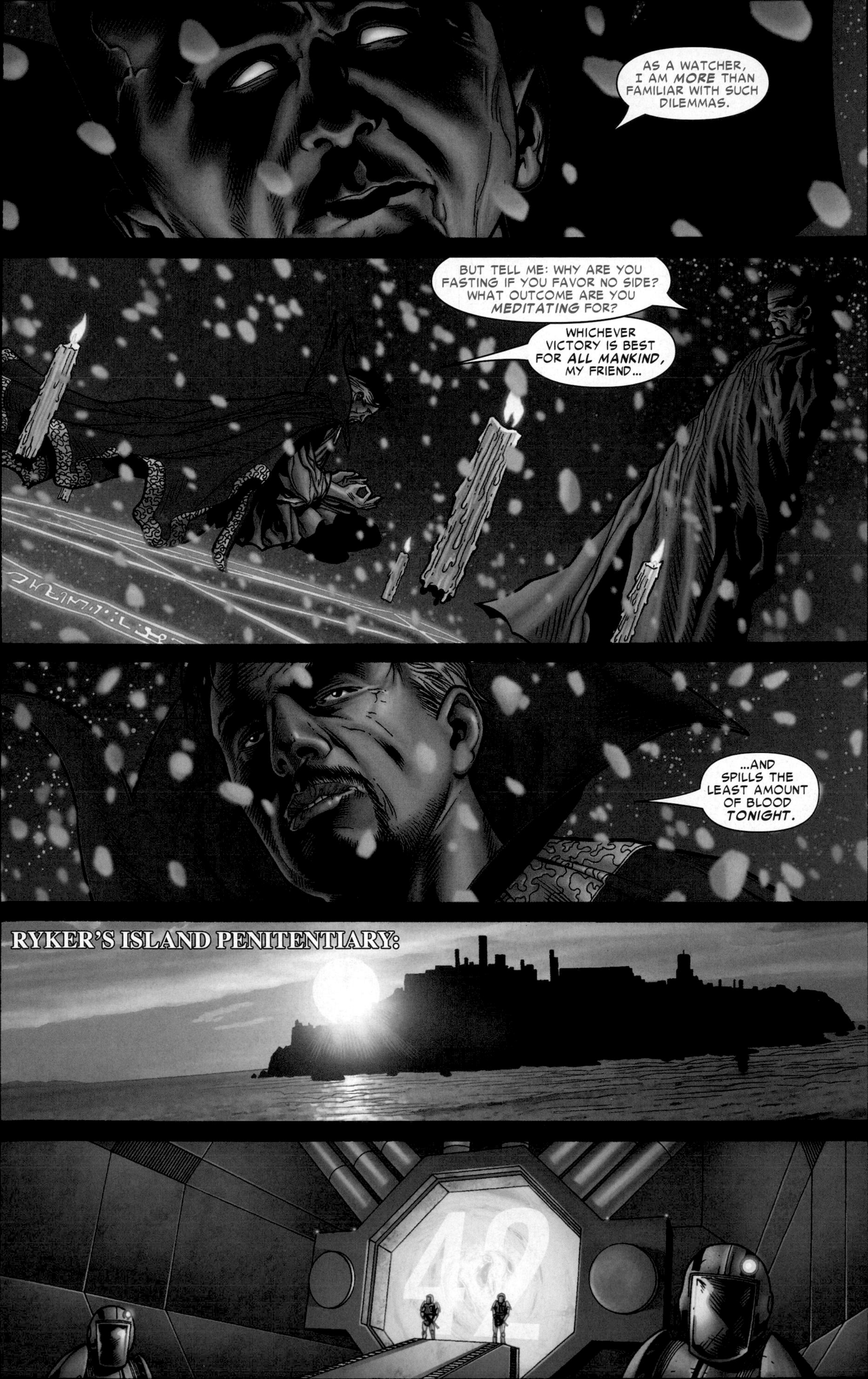
AS A WATCHER, I AM MORE THAN FAMILIAR WITH SUCH DILEMMAS.
BUT TELL ME: WHY ARE YOU FASTING IF YOU FAVOR NO SIDE? WHAT OUTCOME ARE YOU MEDITATING FOR?
WHICHEVER VICTORY IS BEST FOR ALL MANKIND, MY FRIEND...
...AND SPILLS THE LEAST AMOUNT OF BLOOD TONIGHT.
RYKER'S ISLAND PENITENTIARY:
42

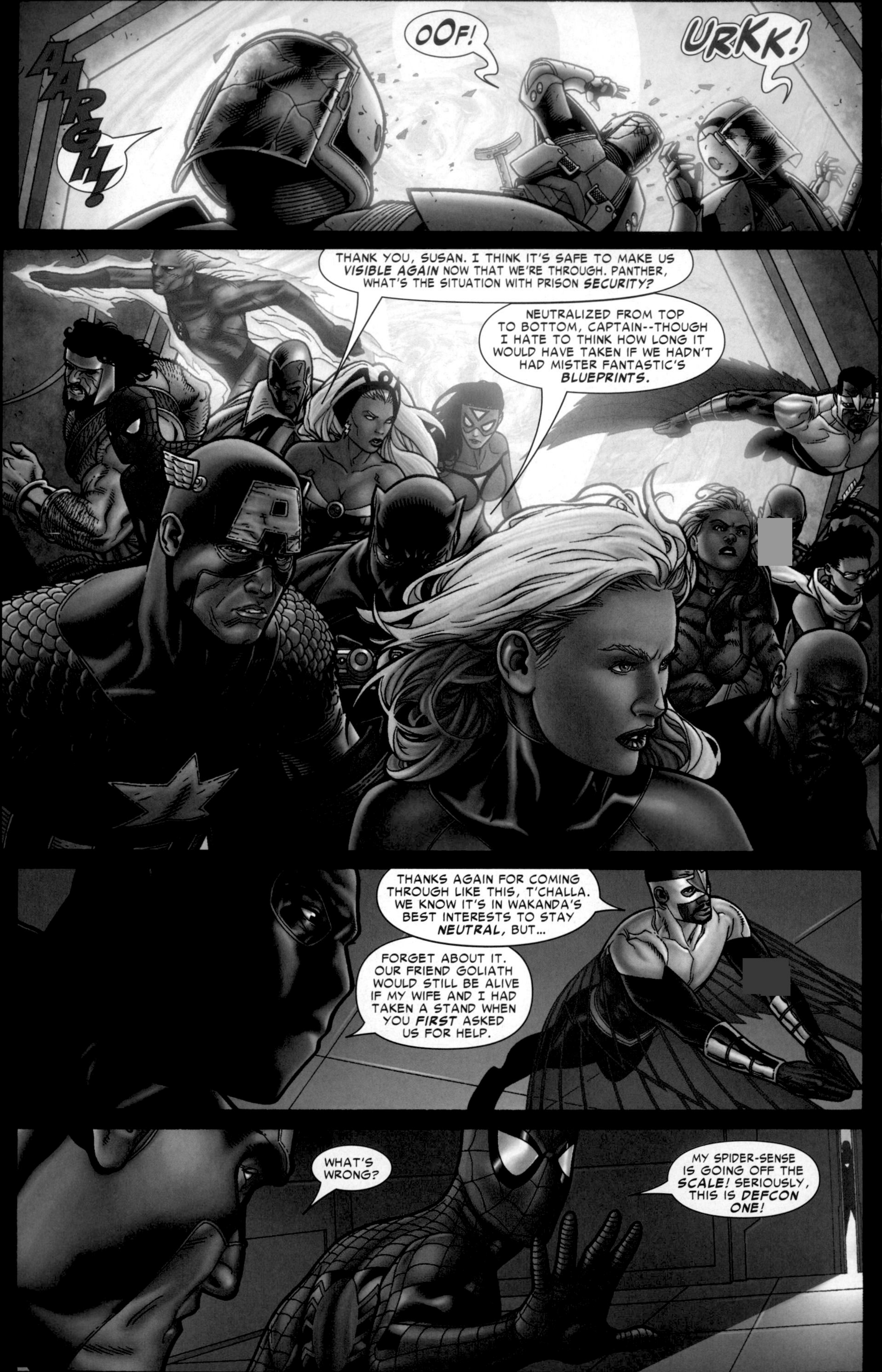
AARGH!
OOF!
URKK!
THANK YOU, SUSAN. I THINK IT'S SAFE TO MAKE US VISIBLE AGAIN NOW THAT WE'RE THROUGH. PANTHER, WHAT'S THE SITUATION WITH PRISON SECURITY?
NEUTRALIZED FROM TOP TO BOTTOM, CAPTAIN--THOUGH I HATE TO THINK HOW LONG IT WOULD HAVE TAKEN IF WE HADN'T HAD MISTER FANTASTIC'S BLUEPRINTS.
THANKS AGAIN FOR COMING THROUGH LIKE THIS, T'CHALLA. WE KNOW IT'S IN WAKANDA'S BEST INTERESTS TO STAY NEUTRAL, BUT...
FORGET ABOUT IT. OUR FRIEND GOLIATH WOULD STILL BE ALIVE IF MY WIFE AND I HAD TAKEN A STAND WHEN YOU FIRST ASKED US FOR HELP.
WHAT'S WRONG?
MY SPIDER-SENSE IS GOING OFF THE SCALE! SERIOUSLY, THIS IS DEFCON ONE!

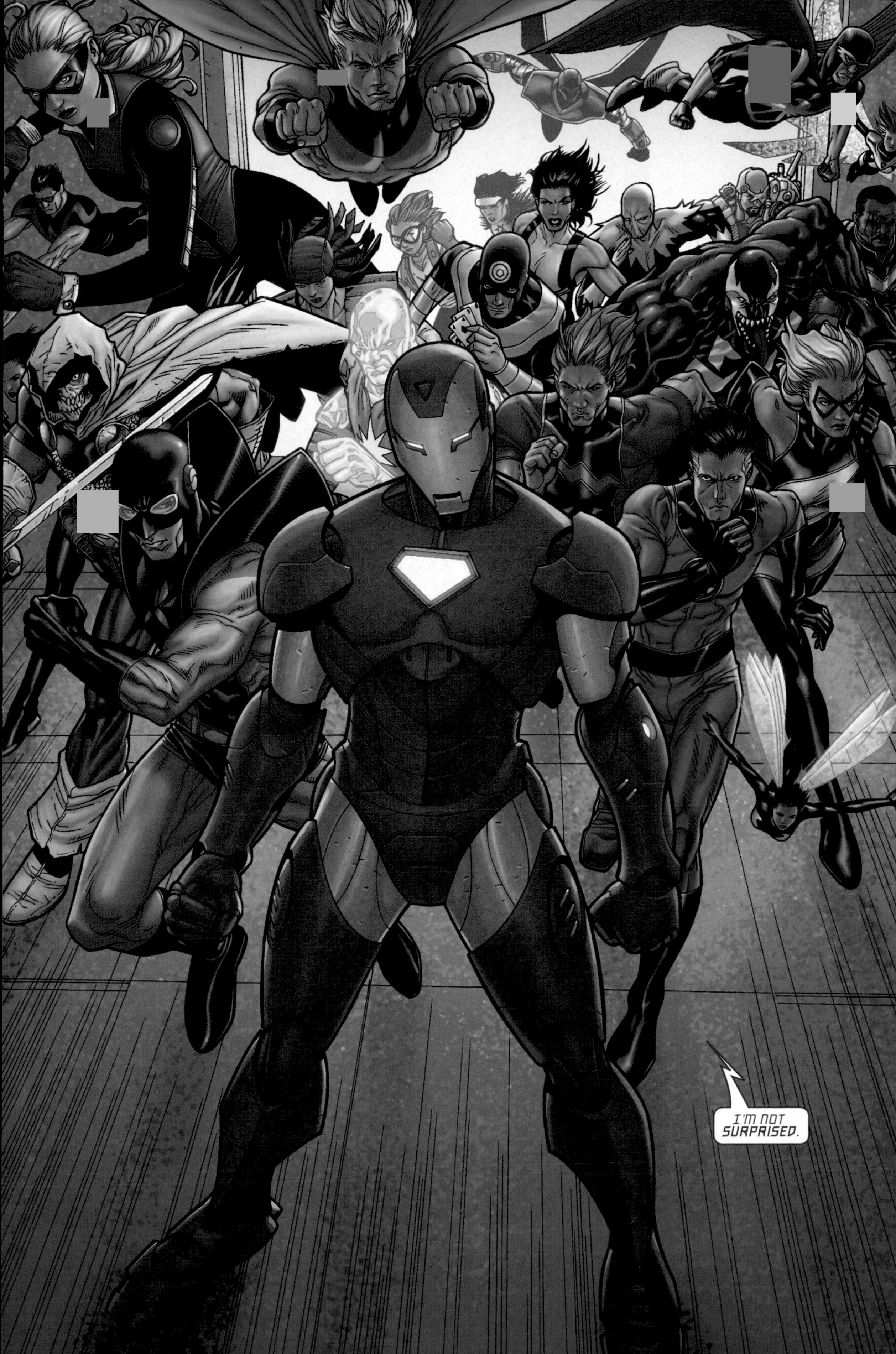
I'M NOT SURPRISED.

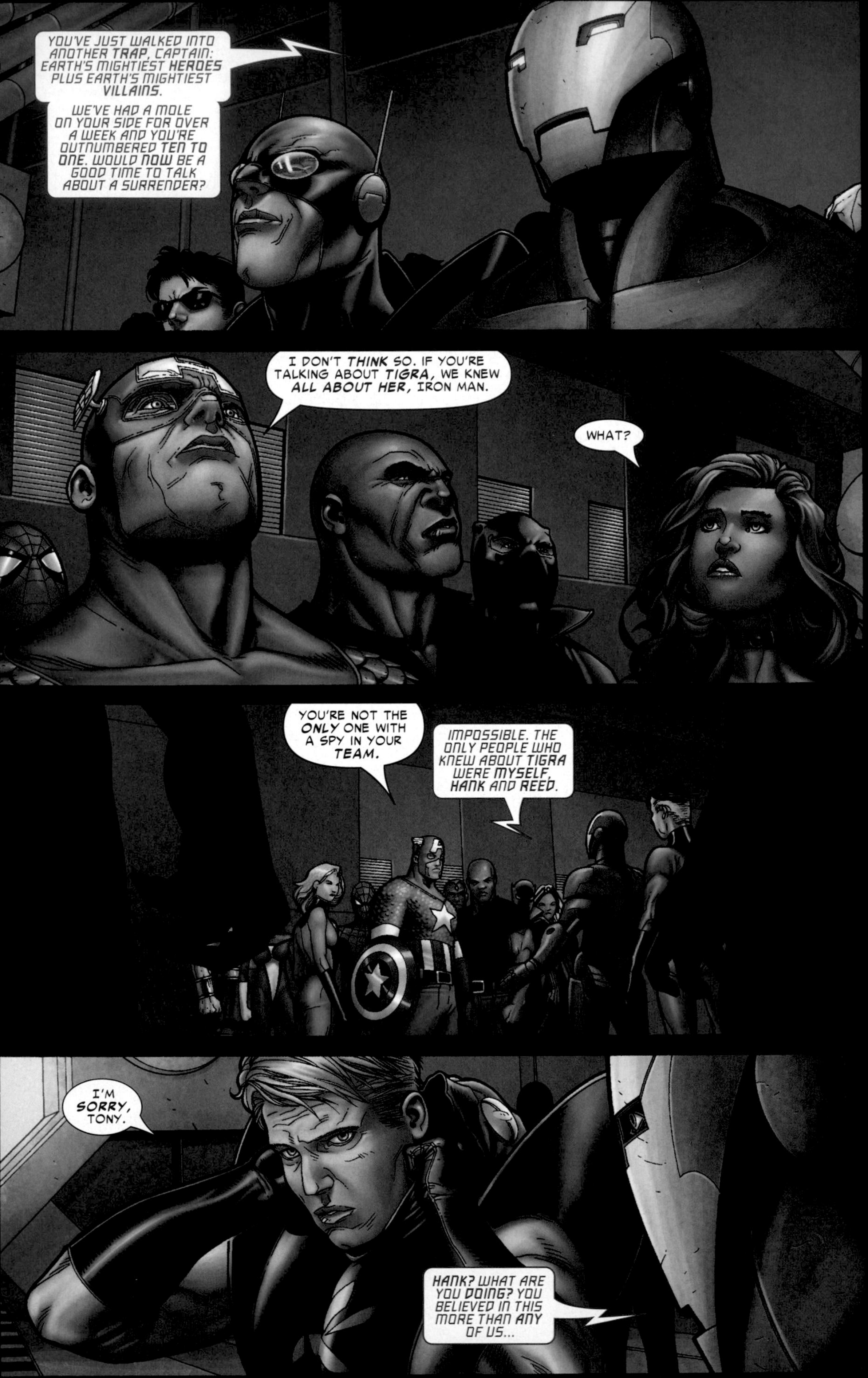
YOU'VE JUST WALKED INTO ANOTHER TRAP, CAPTAIN: EARTH'S MIGHTIEST HEROES PLUS EARTH'S MIGHTIEST VILLAINS.
WE'VE HAD A MOLE ON YOUR SIDE FOR OVER A WEEK AND YOU'RE OUTNUMBERED TEN TO ONE. WOULD NOW BE A GOOD TIME TO TALK ABOUT A SURRENDER?
I DON'T THINK SO. IF YOU'RE TALKING ABOUT TIGRA, WE KNEW ALL ABOUT HER, IRON MAN.
WHAT?
YOU'RE NOT THE ONLY ONE WITH A SPY IN YOUR TEAM.
IMPOSSIBLE. THE ONLY PEOPLE WHO KNEW ABOUT TIGRA WERE MYSELF, HANK AND REED.
I'M SORRY, TONY.
HANK? WHAT ARE YOU DOING? YOU BELIEVED IN THIS MORE THAN ANY OF US...

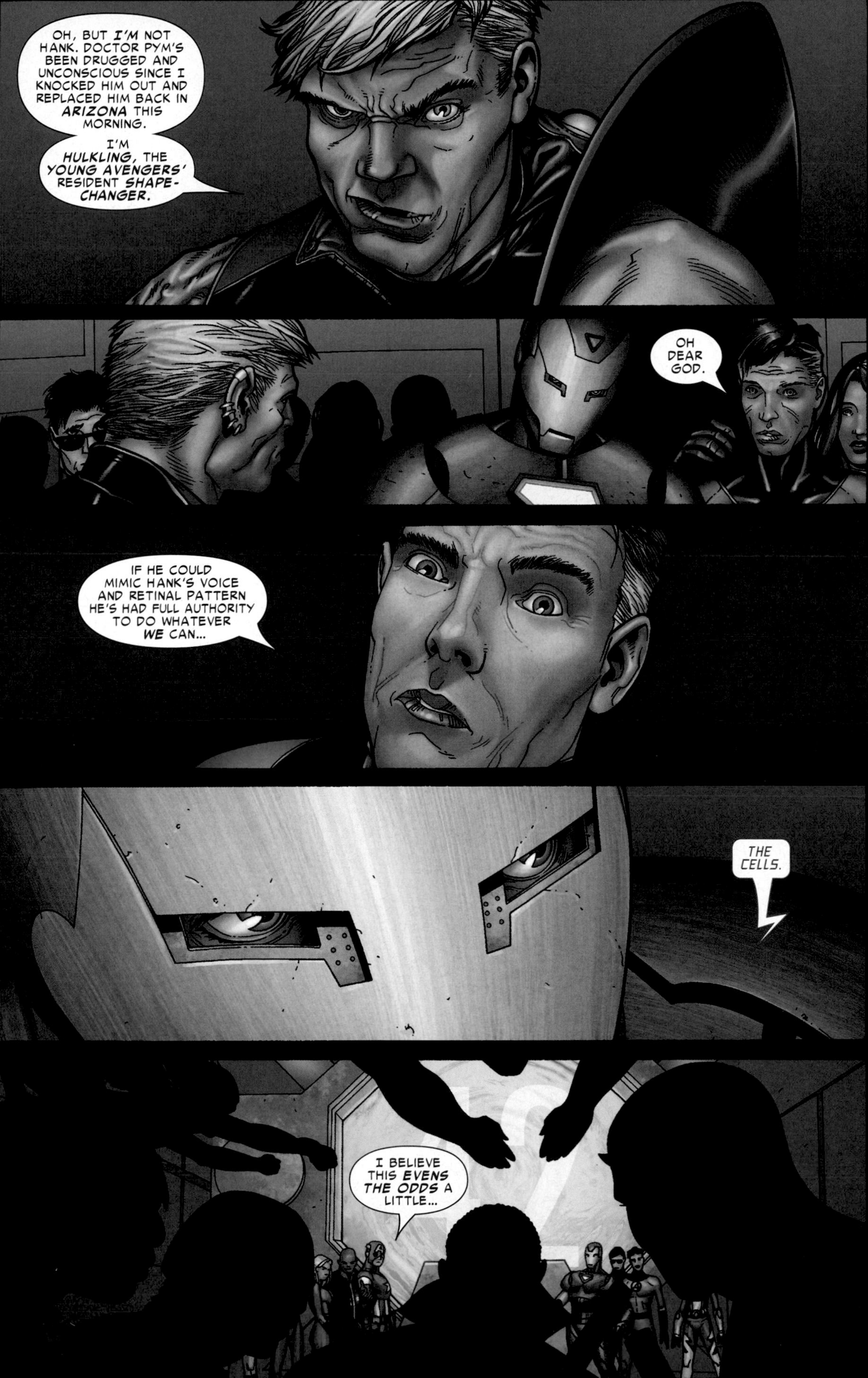
OH, BUT I'M NOT HANK. DOCTOR PYM'S BEEN DRUGGED AND UNCONSCIOUS SINCE I KNOCKED HIM OUT AND REPLACED HIM BACK IN ARIZONA THIS MORNING.
I'M HULKLING, THE YOUNG AVENGERS' RESIDENT SHAPE-CHANGER.
OH DEAR GOD.
IF HE COULD MIMIC HANK'S VOICE AND RETINAL PATTERN HE'S HAD FULL AUTHORITY TO DO WHATEVER WE CAN...
THE CELLS.
I BELIEVE THIS EVENS THE ODDS A LITTLE...

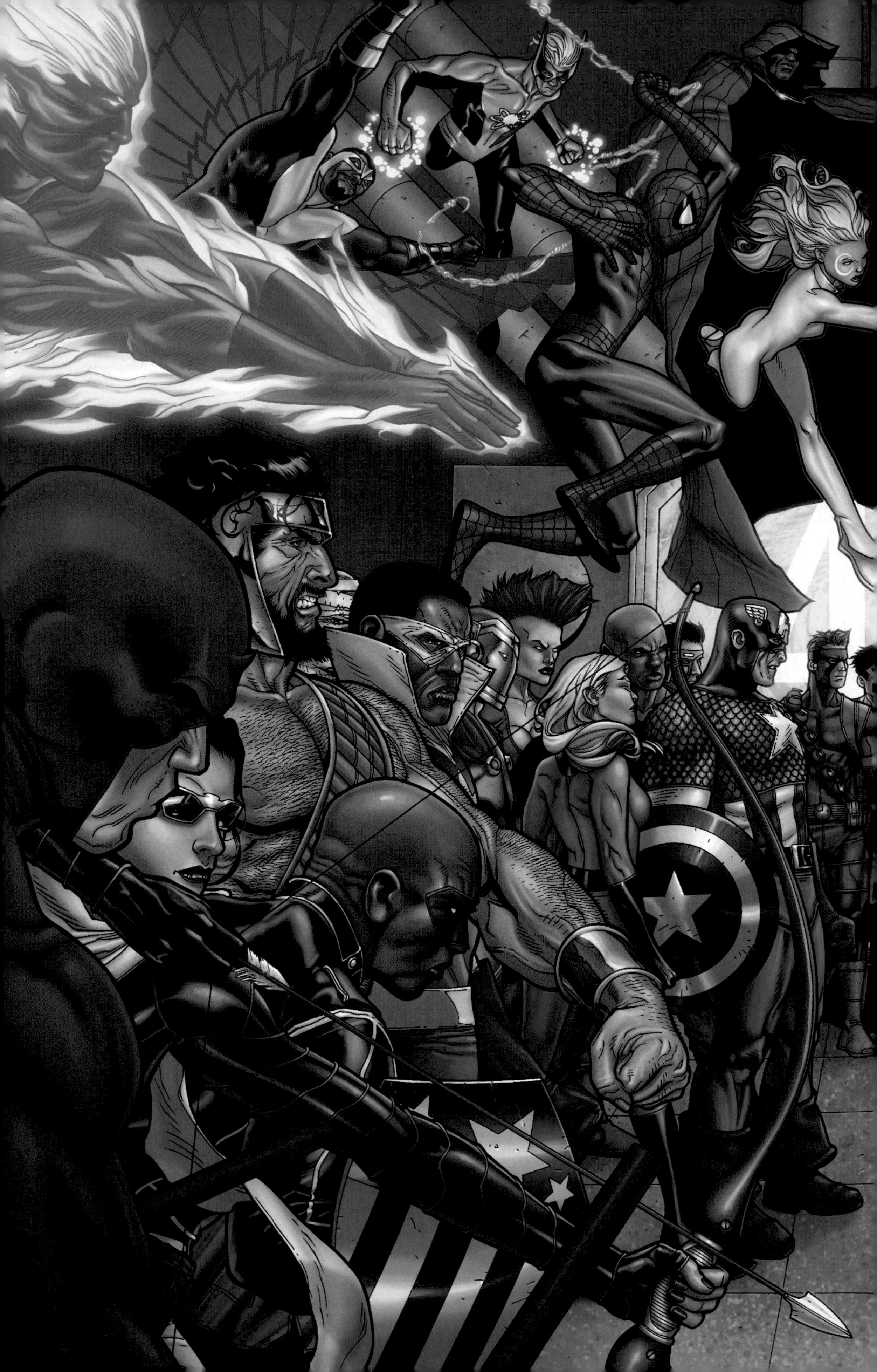

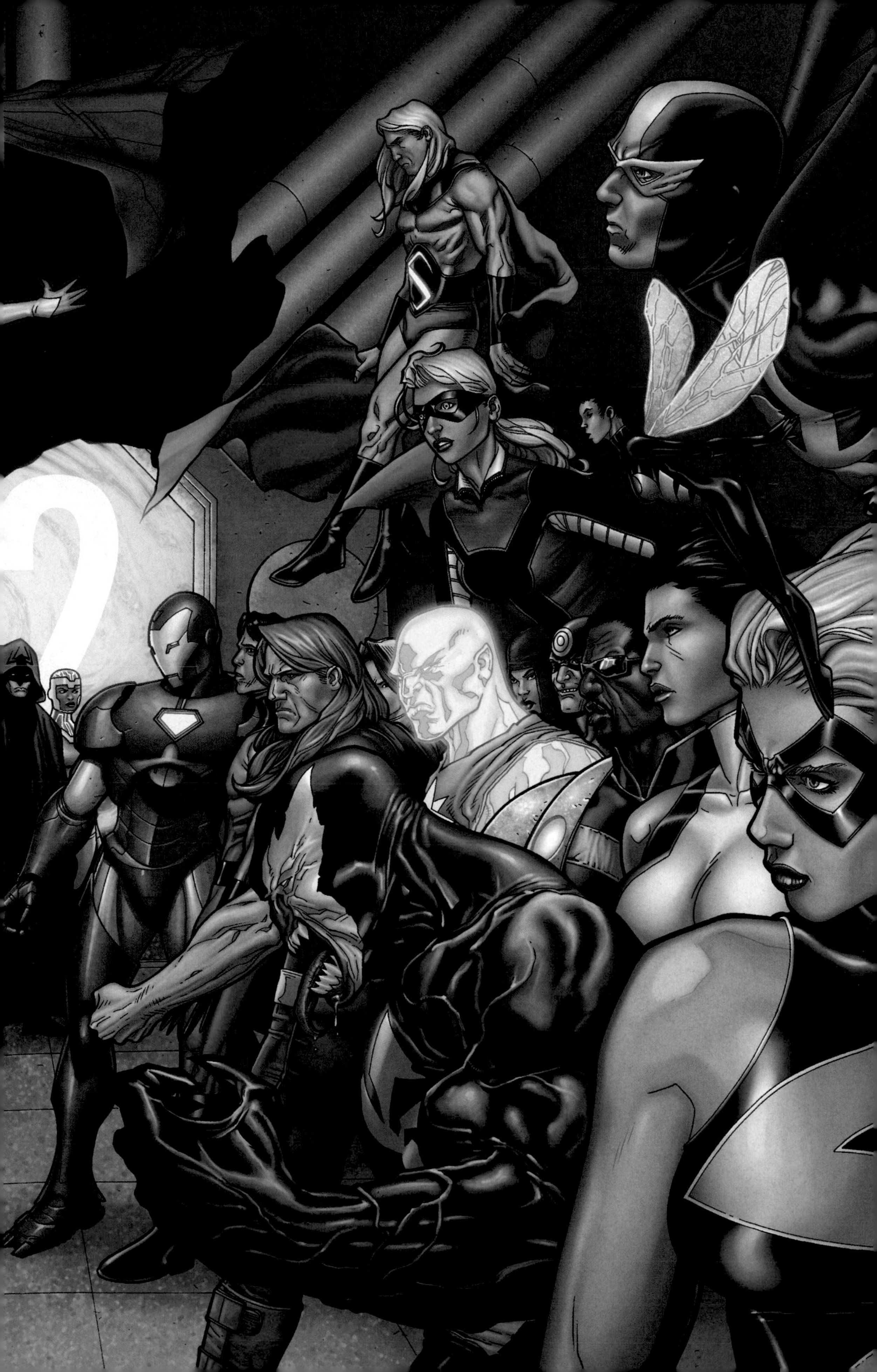

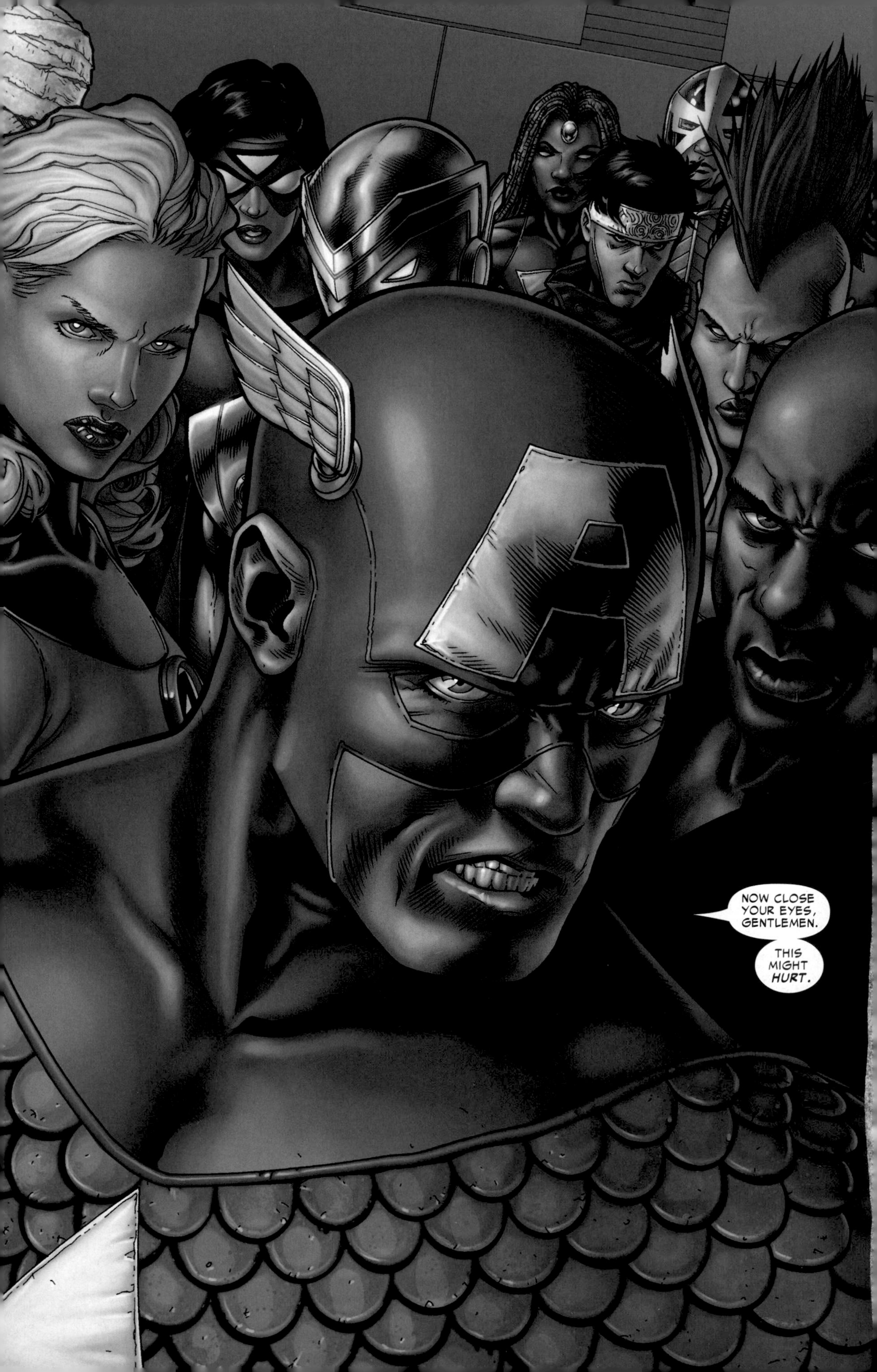
NOW CLOSE YOUR EYES, GENTLEMEN.
THIS MIGHT HURT.

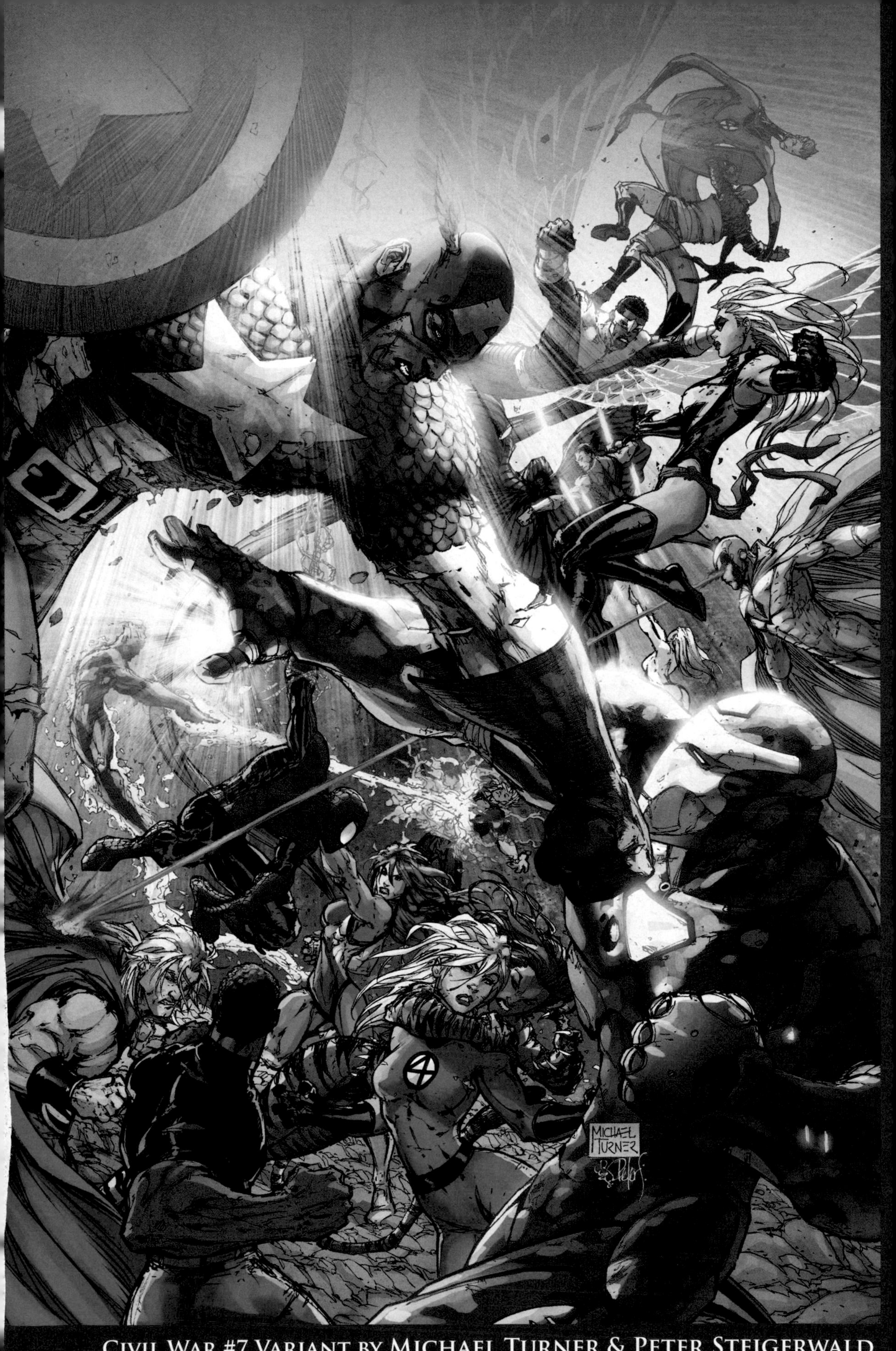
MICHAEL TURNER

Civil War #7 Variant by Michael Turner & Peter Steigerwald

CIVIL WAR #7

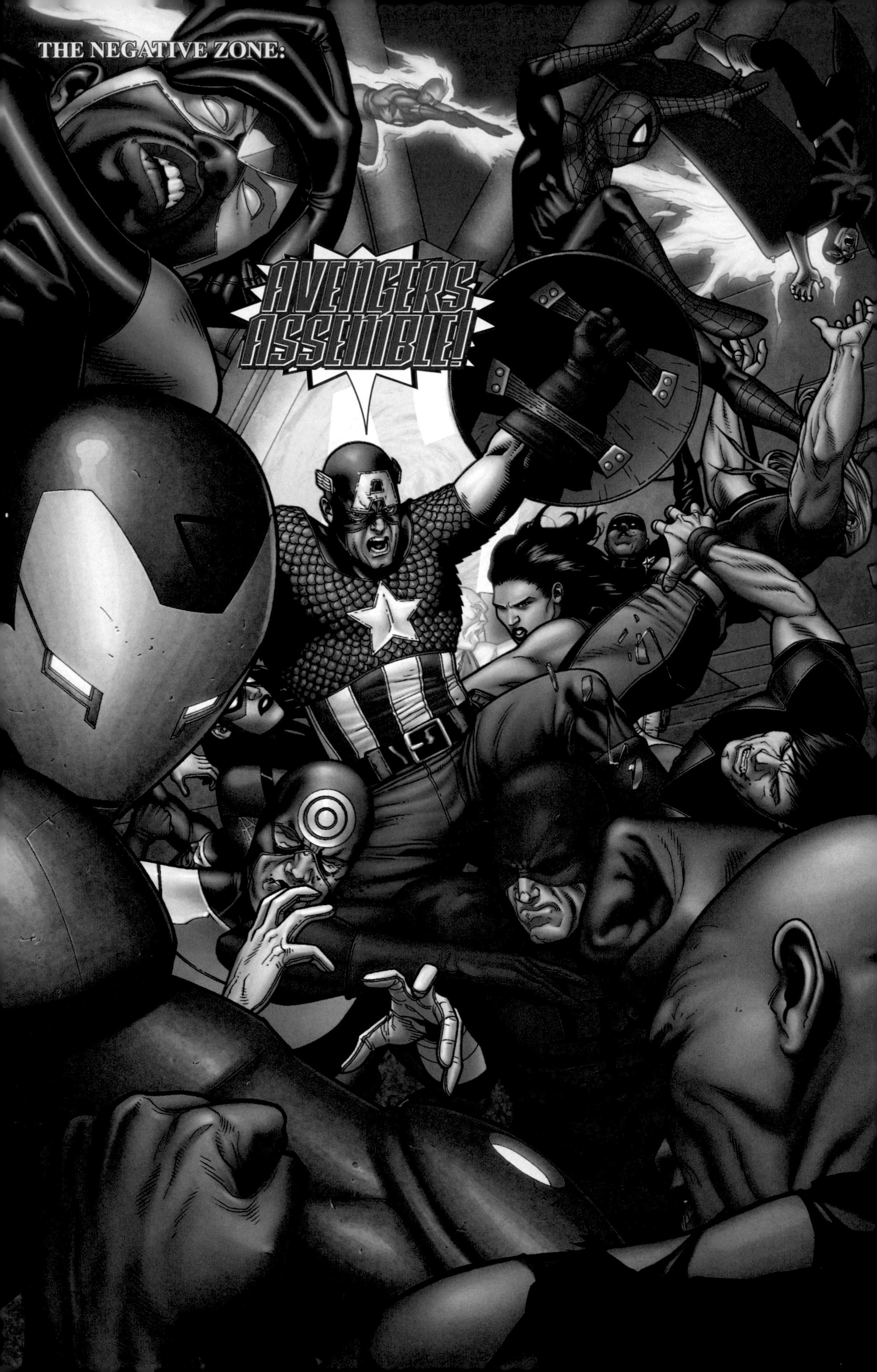
THE NEGATIVE ZONE:
AVENGERS ASSEMBLE!

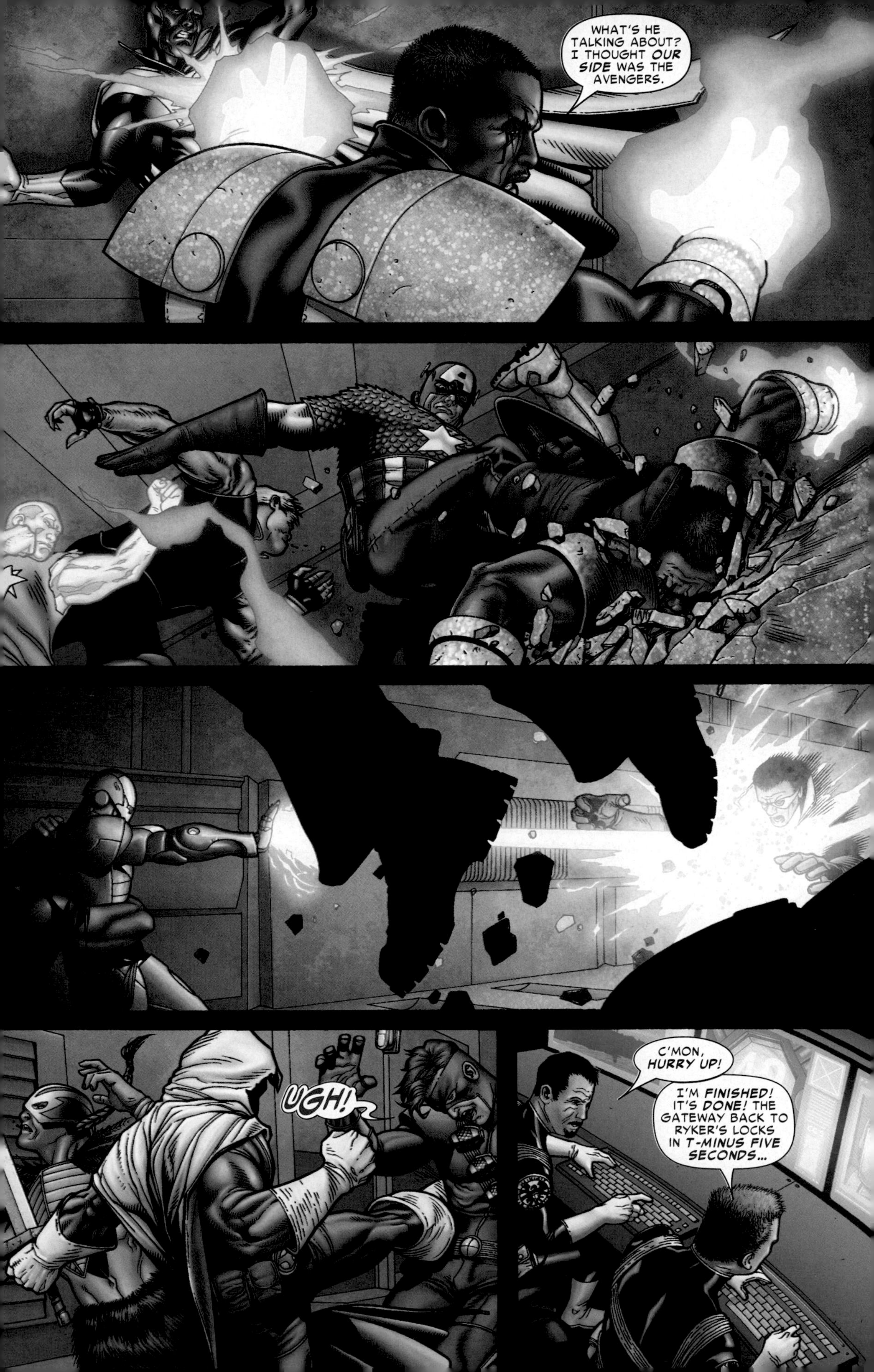
WHAT'S HE TALKING ABOUT? I THOUGHT OUR SIDE WAS THE AVENGERS.
UGH!
C'MON, HURRY UP!
I'M FINISHED! IT'S DONE! THE GATEWAY BACK TO RYKER'S LOCKS IN T-MINUS FIVE SECONDS...

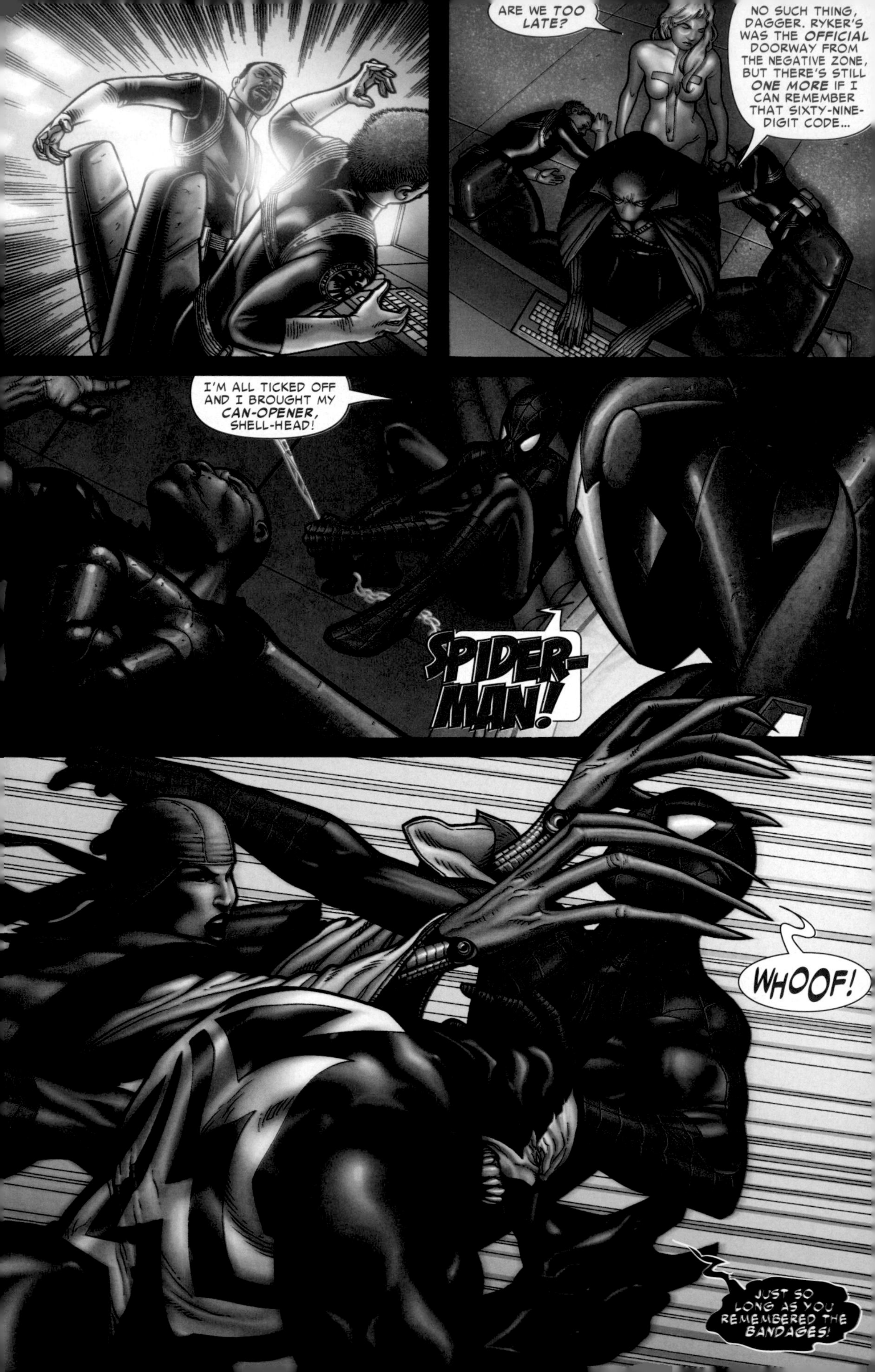
ARE WE TOO LATE?
NO SUCH THING, DAGGER. RYKER'S WAS THE OFFICIAL DOORWAY FROM THE NEGATIVE ZONE, BUT THERE'S STILL ONE MORE IF I CAN REMEMBER THAT SIXTY-NINE-DIGIT CODE...
I'M ALL TICKED OFF AND I BROUGHT MY CAN-OPENER, SHELL-HEAD!
SPIDER-MAN!
WHOOF!
JUST SO LONG AS YOU REMEMBERED THE BANDAGES!

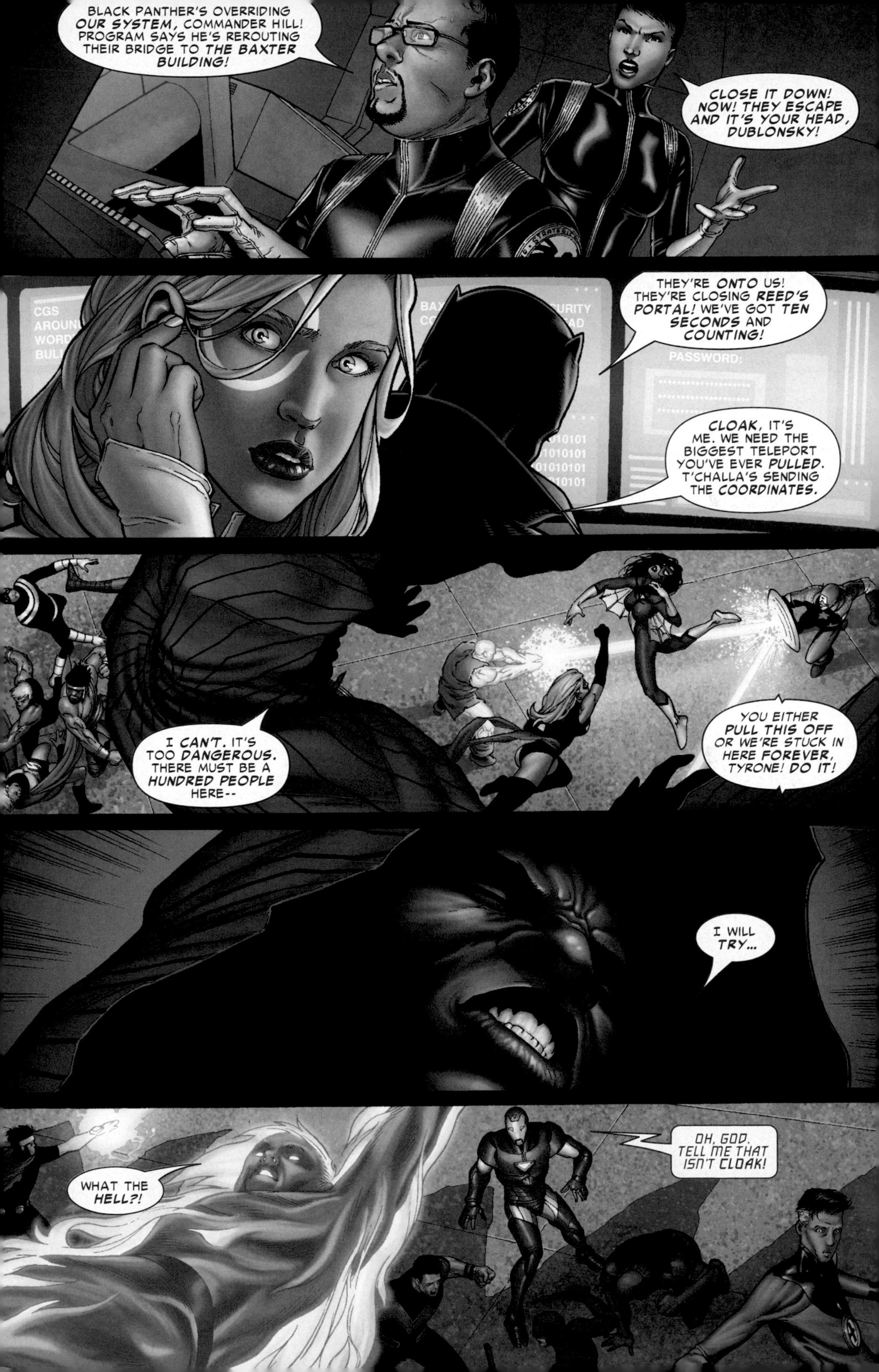
BLACK PANTHER'S OVERRIDING OUR SYSTEM, COMMANDER HILL! PROGRAM SAYS HE'S REROUTING THEIR BRIDGE TO THE BAXTER BUILDING!
CLOSE IT DOWN! NOW! THEY ESCAPE AND IT'S YOUR HEAD, DUBLONSKY!
THEY'RE ONTO US! THEY'RE CLOSING REED'S PORTAL! WE'VE GOT TEN SECONDS AND COUNTING!
PASSWORD:
CLOAK, IT'S ME. WE NEED THE BIGGEST TELEPORT YOU'VE EVER PULLED. T'CHALLA'S SENDING THE COORDINATES.
I CAN'T. IT'S TOO DANGEROUS. THERE MUST BE A HUNDRED PEOPLE HERE--
YOU EITHER PULL THIS OFF OR WE'RE STUCK IN HERE FOREVER, TYRONE! DO IT!
I WILL TRY...
WHAT THE HELL?!
OH, GOD. TELL ME THAT ISN'T CLOAK!

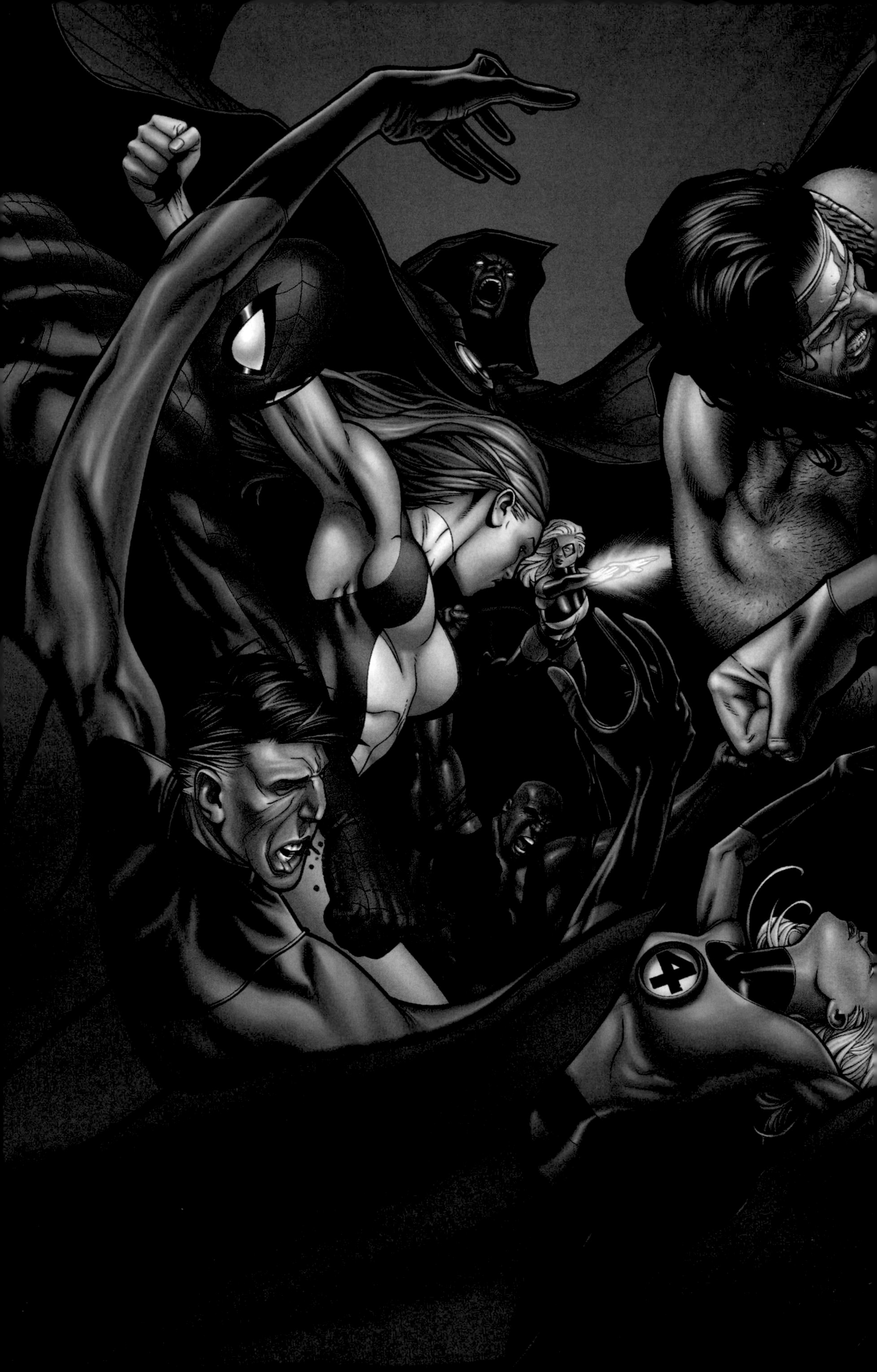

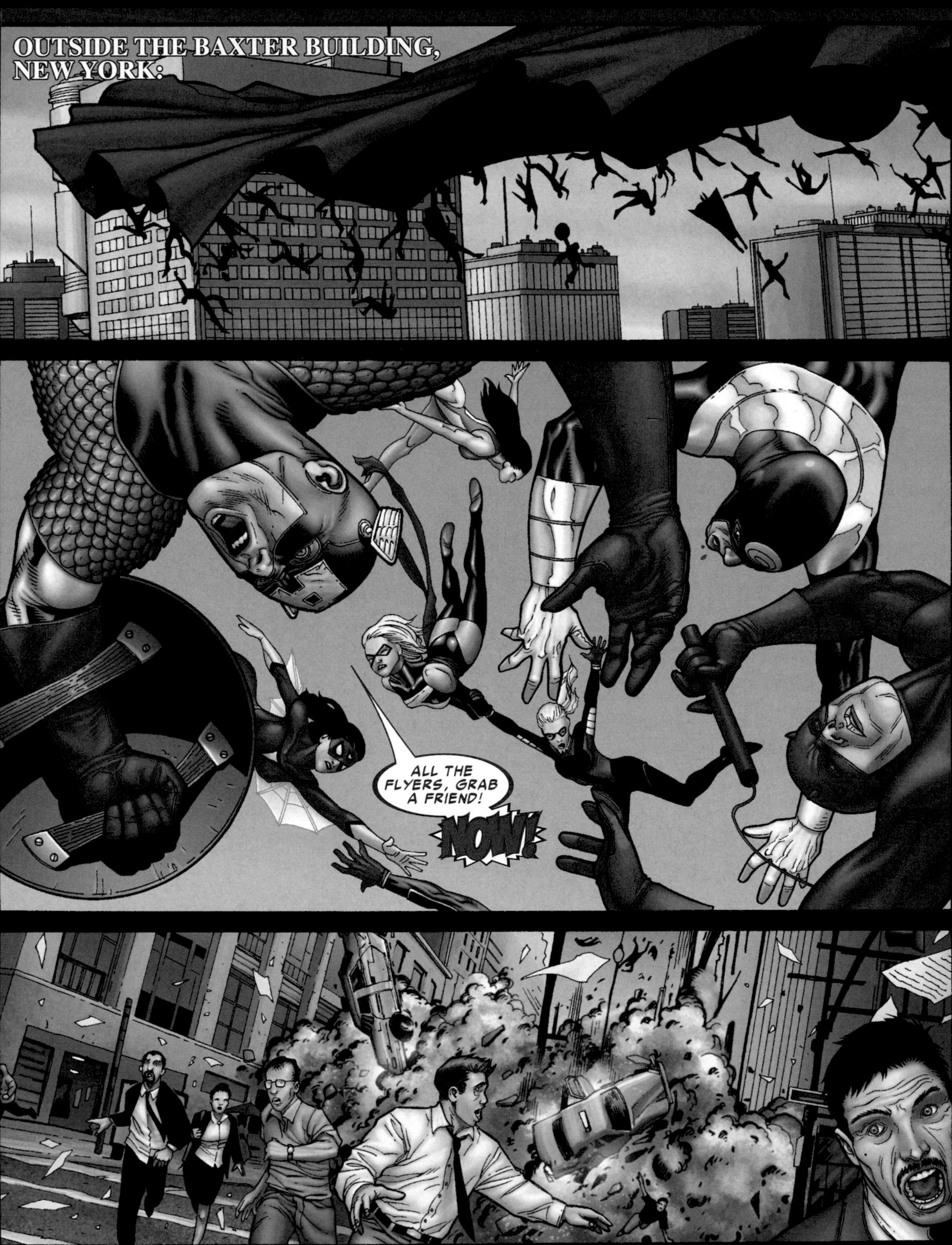
OUTSIDE THE BAXTER BUILDING, NEW YORK:
ALL THE FLYERS, GRAB A FRIEND!
NOW!

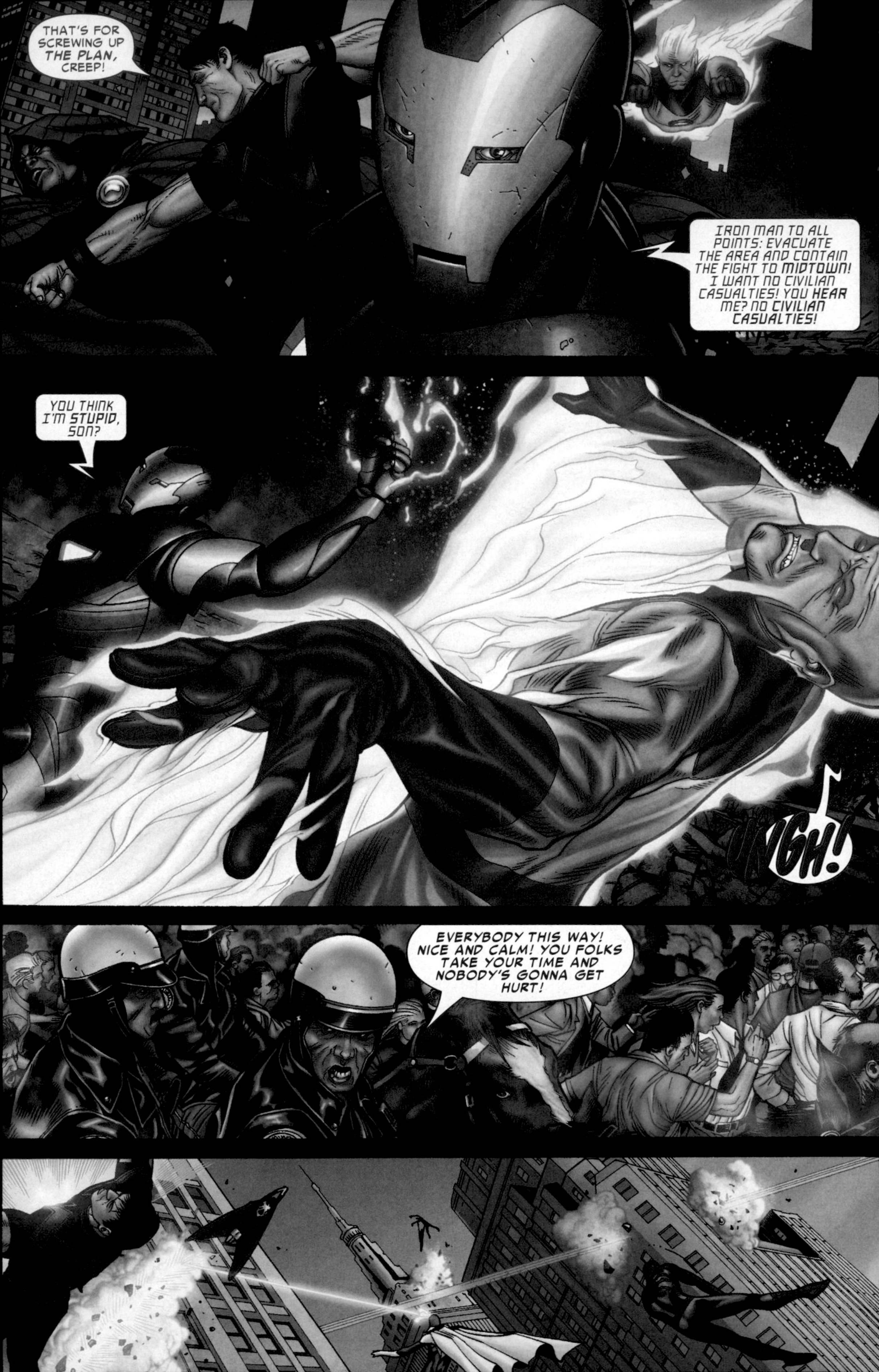
THAT'S FOR SCREWING UP THE PLAN, CREEP!
IRON MAN TO ALL POINTS: EVACUATE THE AREA AND CONTAIN THE FIGHT TO MIDTOWN! I WANT NO CIVILIAN CASUALTIES! YOU HEAR ME? NO CIVILIAN CASUALTIES!
YOU THINK I'M STUPID, SON?
UNGH!
EVERYBODY THIS WAY! NICE AND CALM! YOU FOLKS TAKE YOUR TIME AND NOBODY'S GONNA GET HURT!

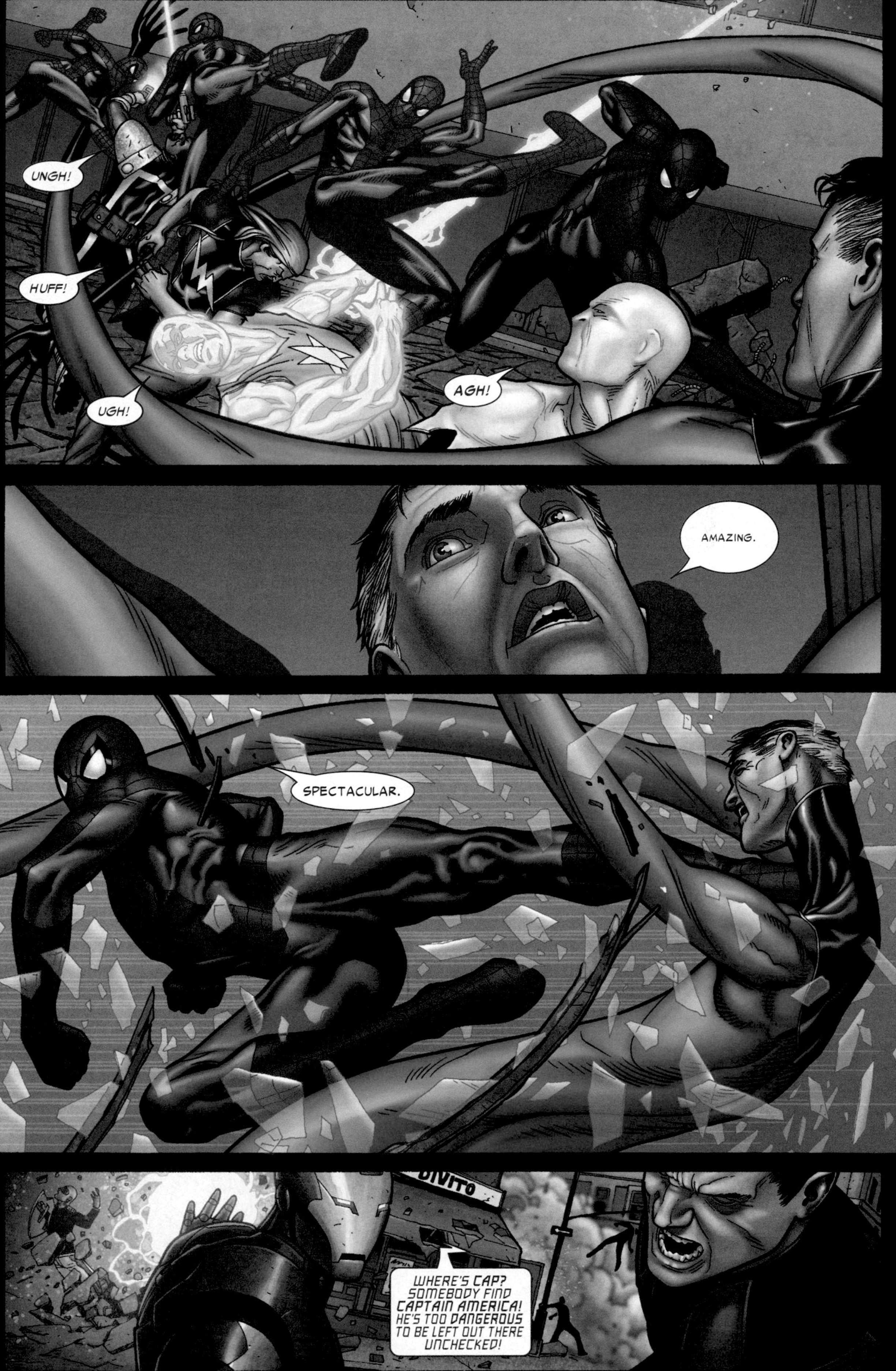
UNGH!
HUFF!
UGH!
AGH!
AMAZING.
SPECTACULAR.
WHERE'S CAP? SOMEBODY FIND CAPTAIN AMERICA! HE'S TOO DANGEROUS TO BE LEFT OUT THERE UNCHECKED!

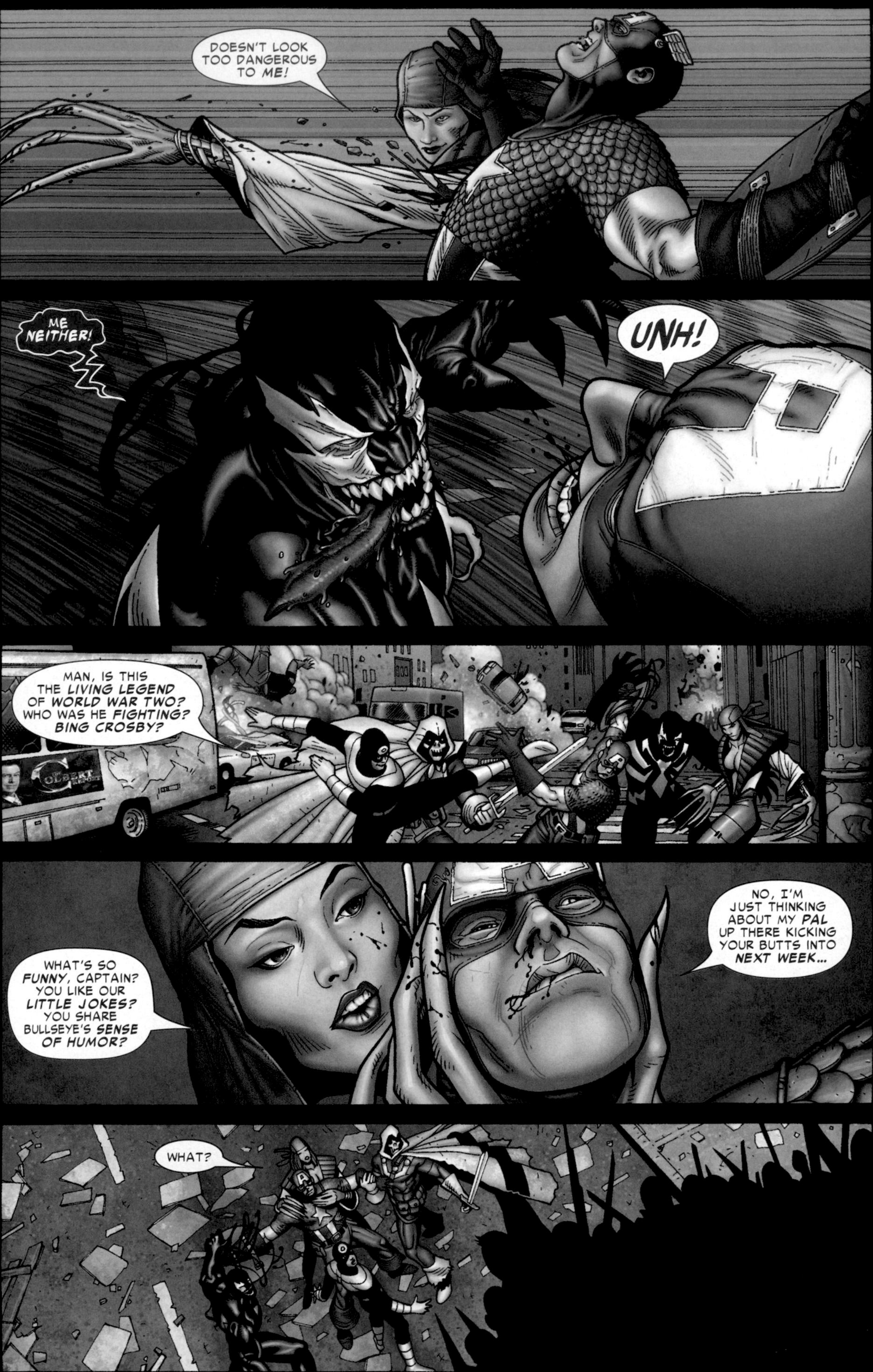
DOESN'T LOOK TOO DANGEROUS TO ME!
ME NEITHER!
UNH!
MAN, IS THIS THE LIVING LEGEND OF WORLD WAR TWO? WHO WAS HE FIGHTING? BING CROSBY?
WHAT'S SO FUNNY, CAPTAIN? YOU LIKE OUR LITTLE JOKES? YOU SHARE BULLSEYE'S SENSE OF HUMOR?
NO, I'M JUST THINKING ABOUT MY PAL UP THERE KICKING YOUR BUTTS INTO NEXT WEEK...
WHAT?

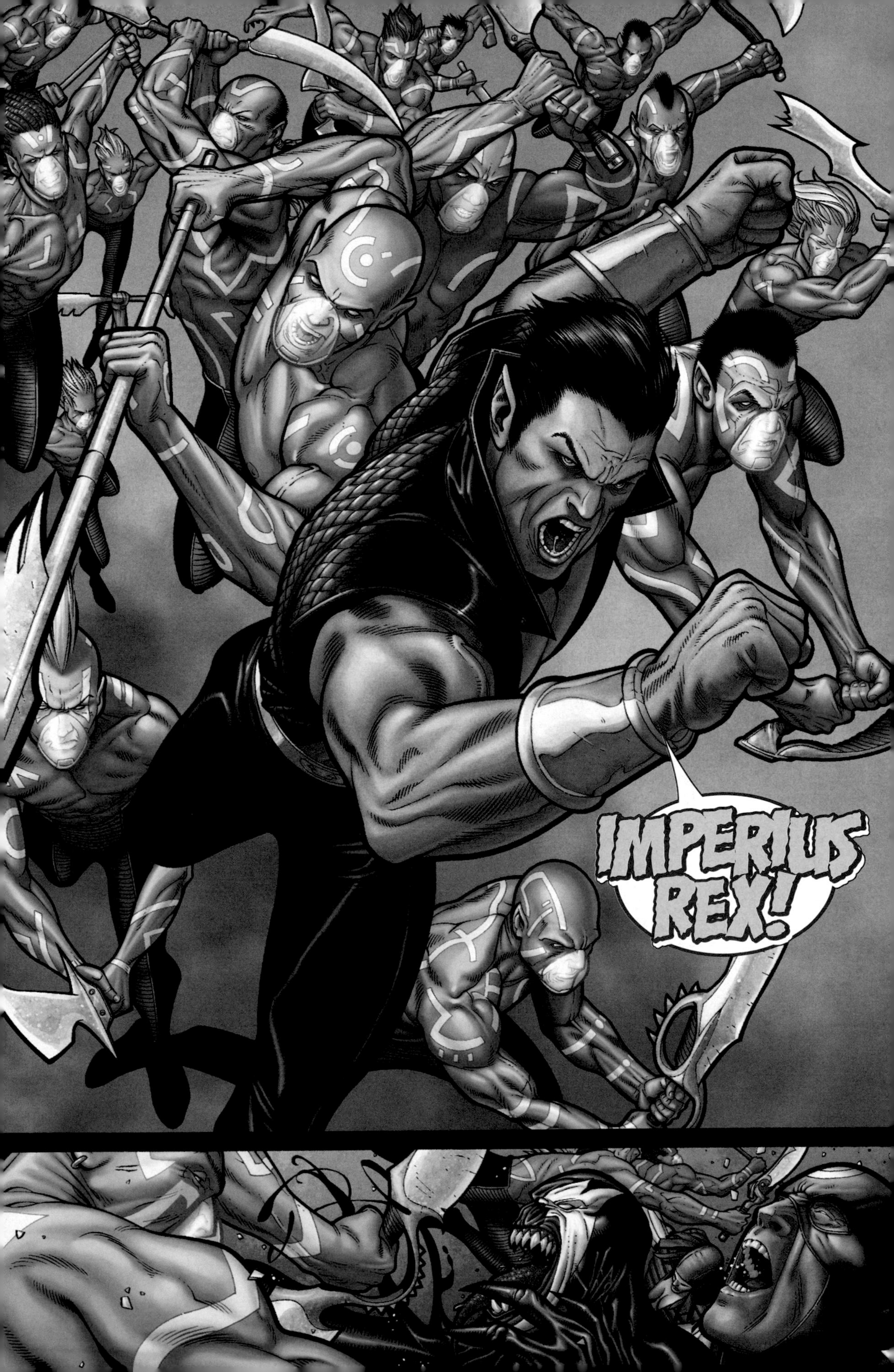
IMPERIUS REX!

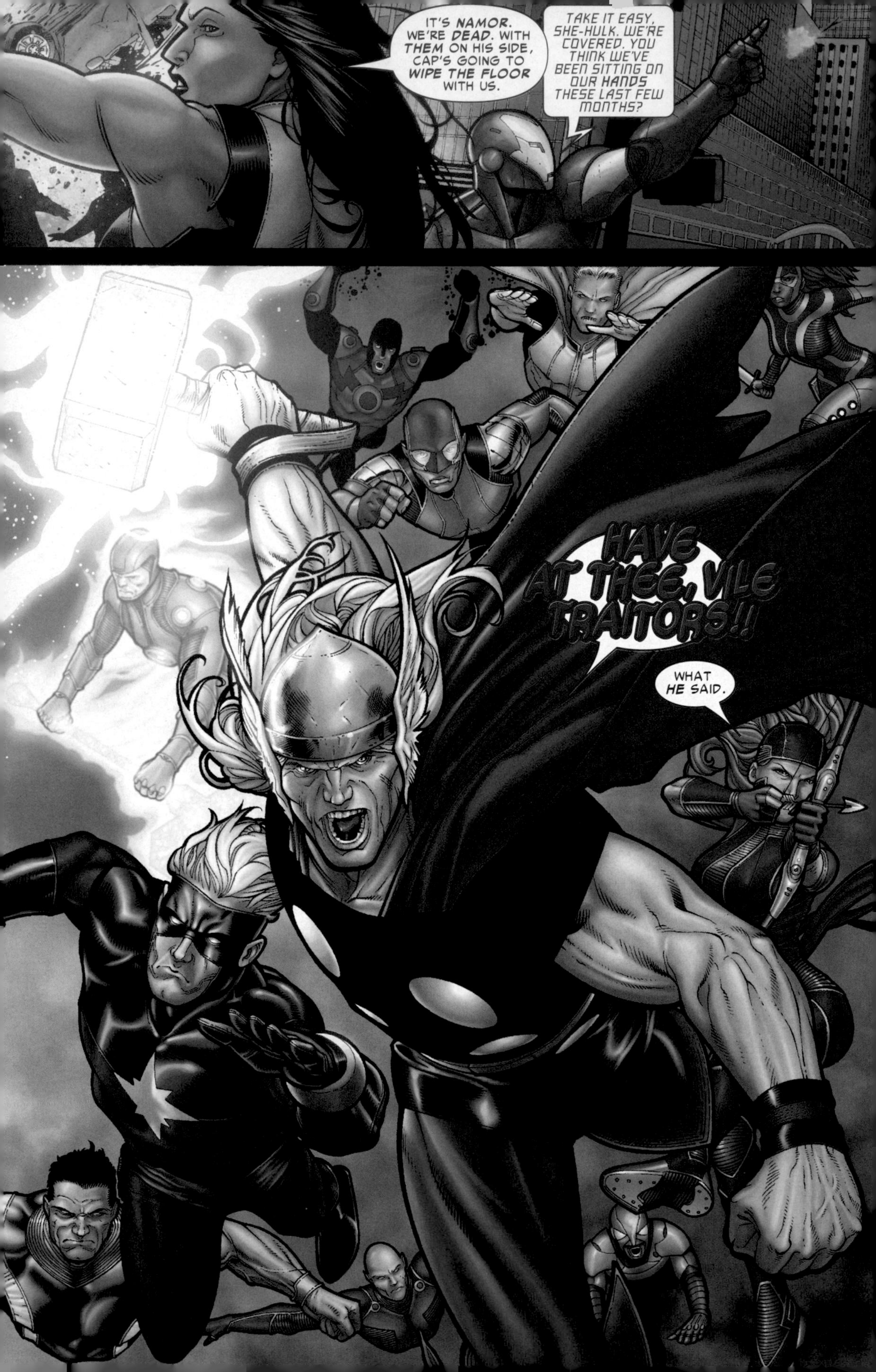
IT'S NAMOR. WE'RE DEAD. WITH THEM ON HIS SIDE, CAP'S GOING TO WIPE THE FLOOR WITH US.
TAKE IT EASY, SHE-HULK. WE'RE COVERED. YOU THINK WE'VE BEEN SITTING ON OUR HANDS THESE LAST FEW MONTHS?
HAVE AT THEE, VILE TRAITORS!!
WHAT HE SAID.

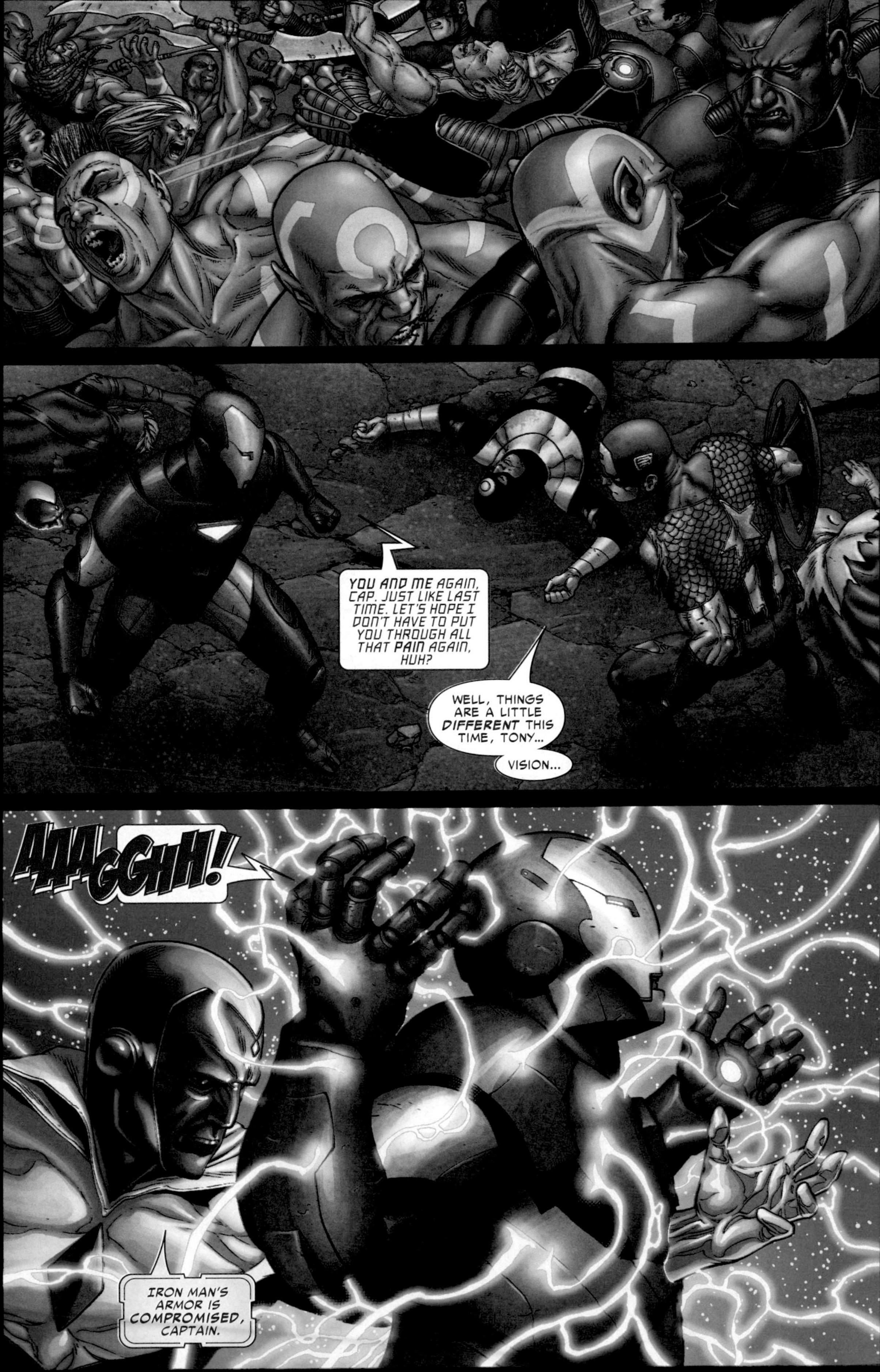
YOU AND ME AGAIN, CAP. JUST LIKE LAST TIME. LET'S HOPE I DON'T HAVE TO PUT YOU THROUGH ALL THAT PAIN AGAIN, HUH?
WELL, THINGS ARE A LITTLE DIFFERENT THIS TIME, TONY...
VISION...
AAAGGHH!
IRON MAN'S ARMOR IS COMPROMISED, CAPTAIN.

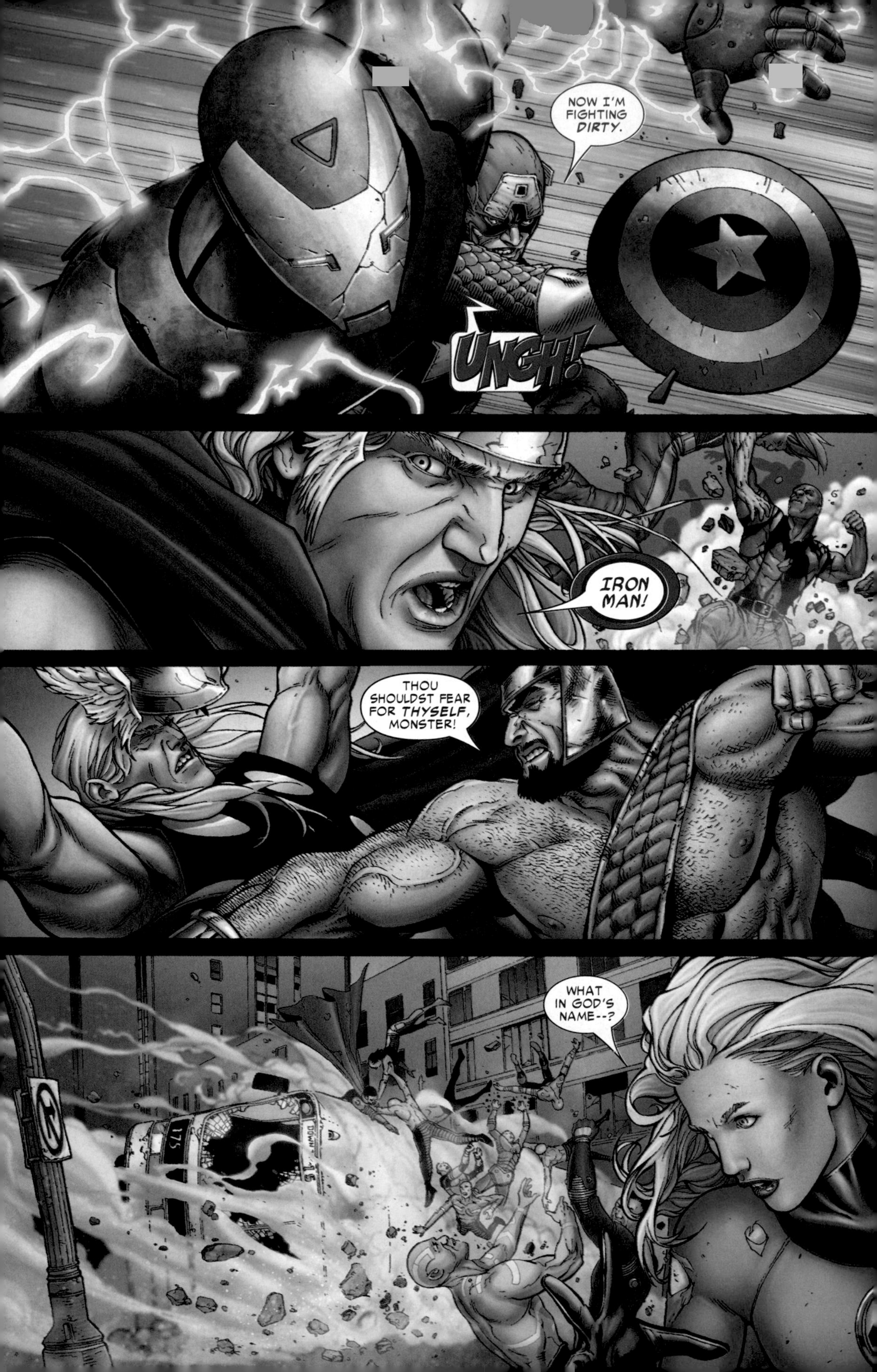
NOW I'M FIGHTING DIRTY.
UNGH!
IRON MAN!
THOU SHOULDST FEAR FOR THYSELF, MONSTER!
WHAT IN GOD'S NAME--?

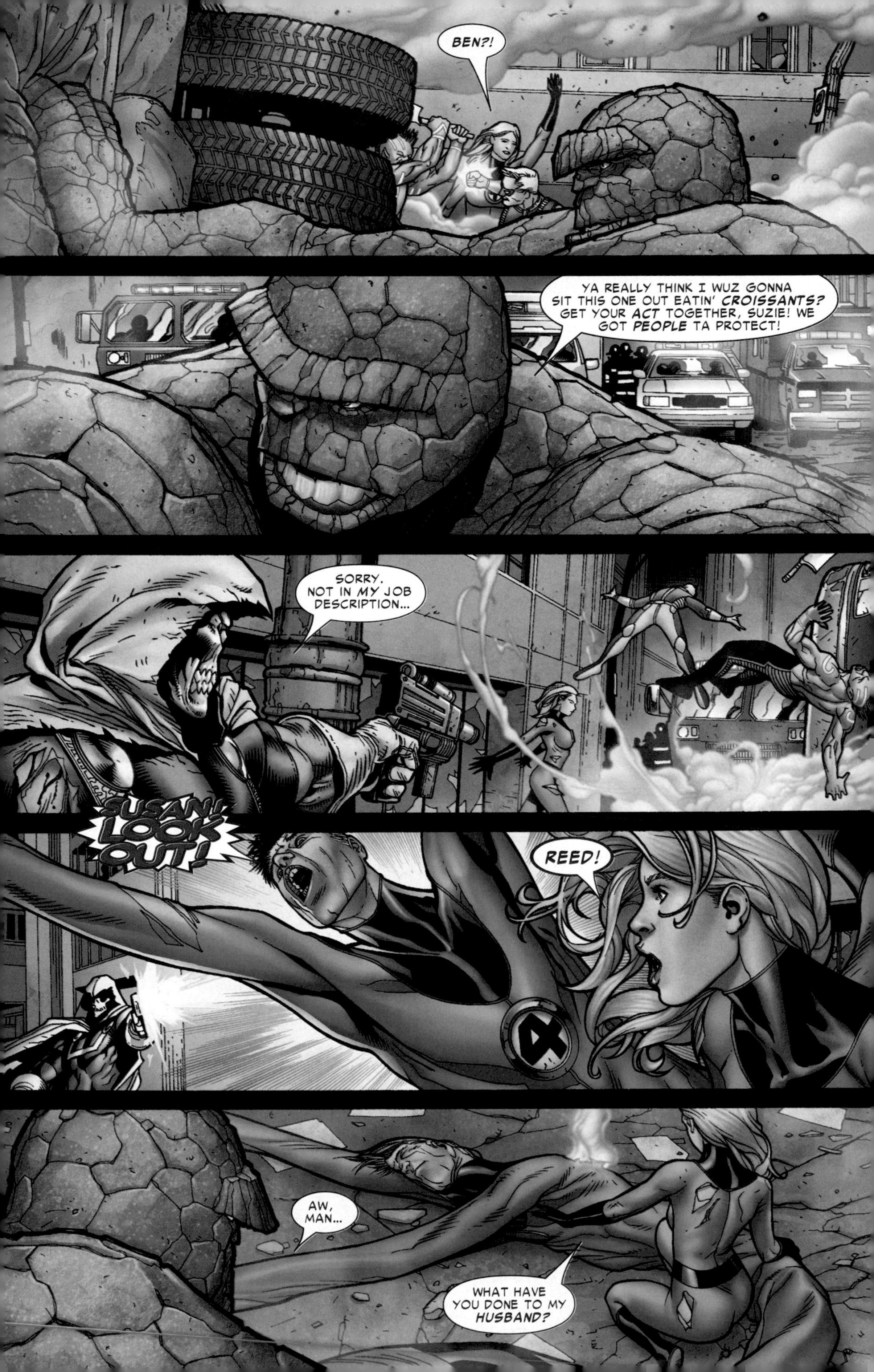
BEN?!
YA REALLY THINK I WUZ GONNA SIT THIS ONE OUT EATIN' CROISSANTS? GET YOUR ACT TOGETHER, SUZIE! WE GOT PEOPLE TA PROTECT!
SORRY. NOT IN MY JOB DESCRIPTION...
SUSAN! LOOK OUT!
REED!
AW, MAN...
WHAT HAVE YOU DONE TO MY HUSBAND?

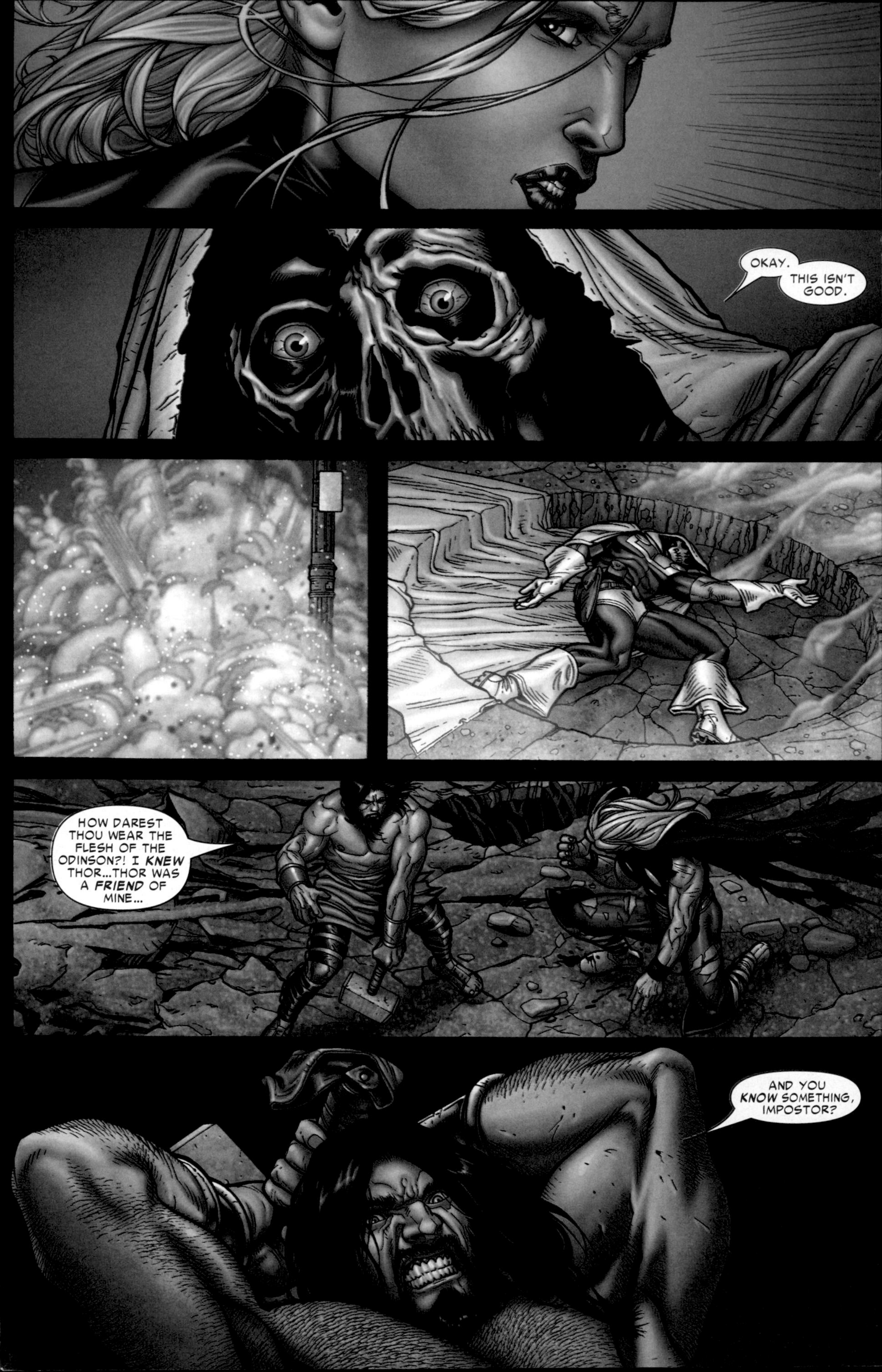
OKAY. THIS ISN'T GOOD.
HOW DAREST THOU WEAR THE FLESH OF THE ODINSON?! I KNEW THOR...THOR WAS A FRIEND OF MINE...
AND YOU KNOW SOMETHING, IMPOSTOR?

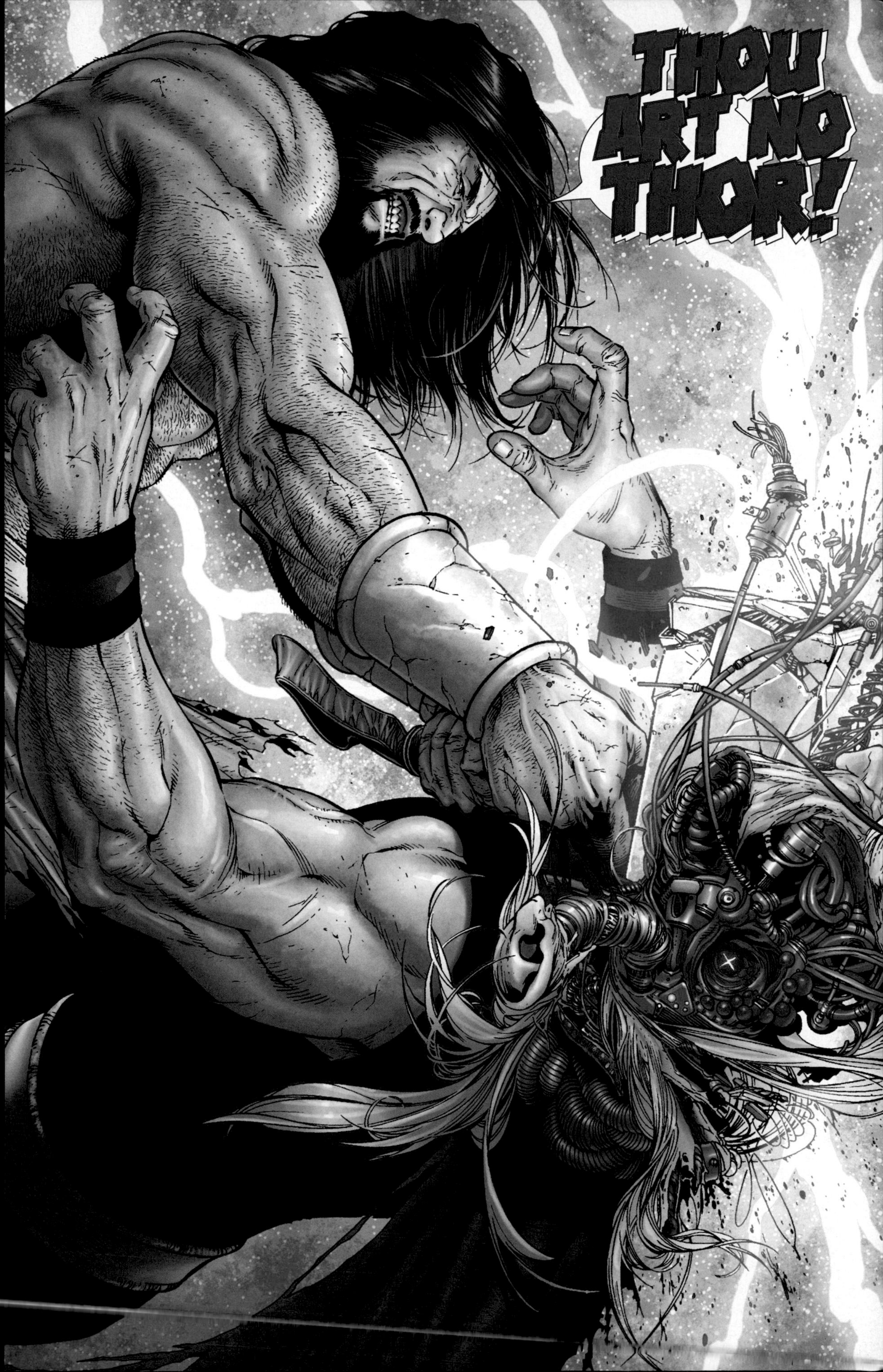
THOU ART NO THOR!

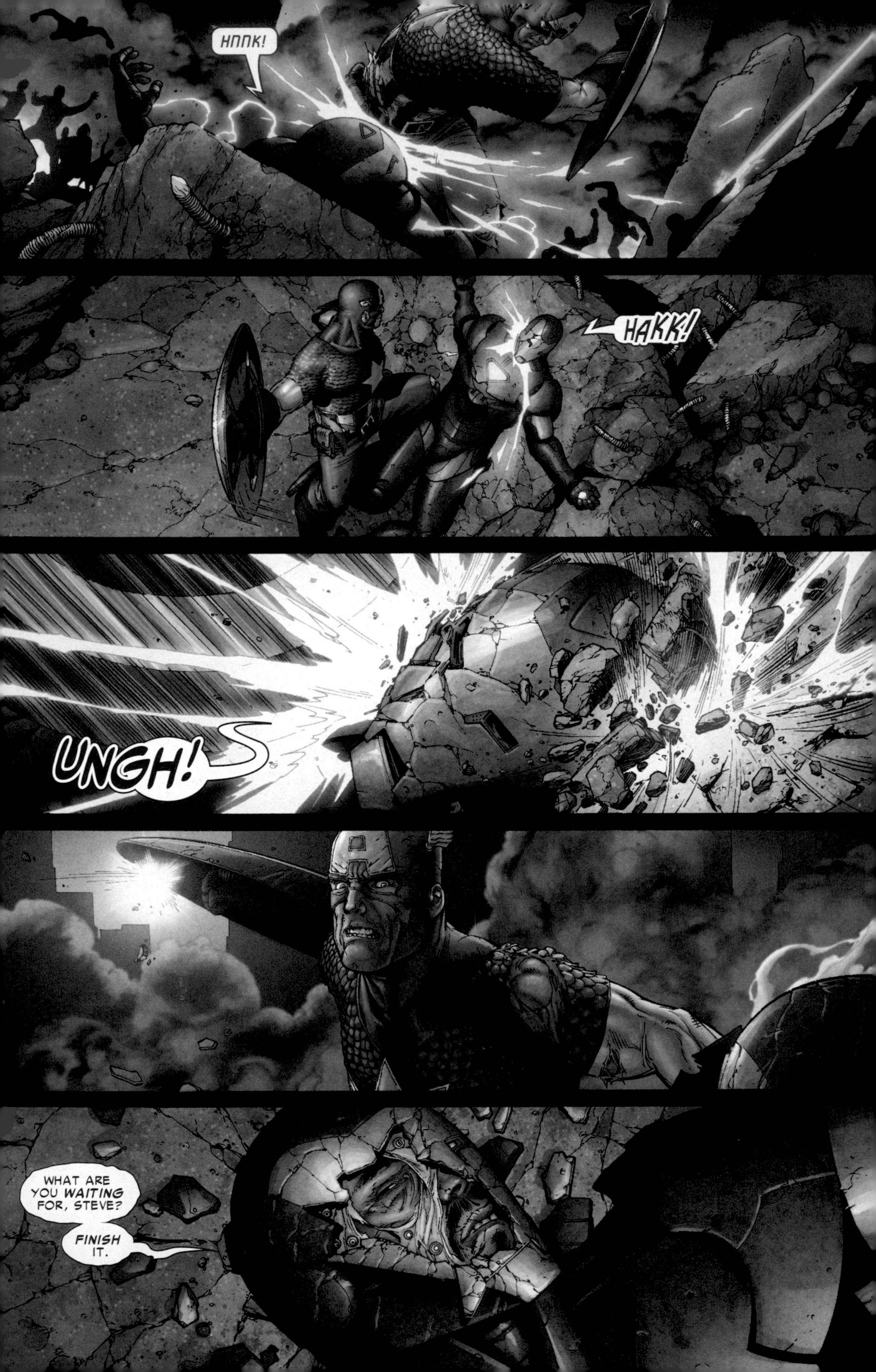
HNNK!
HAKK!
UNGH!
WHAT ARE YOU WAITING FOR, STEVE?
FINISH IT.

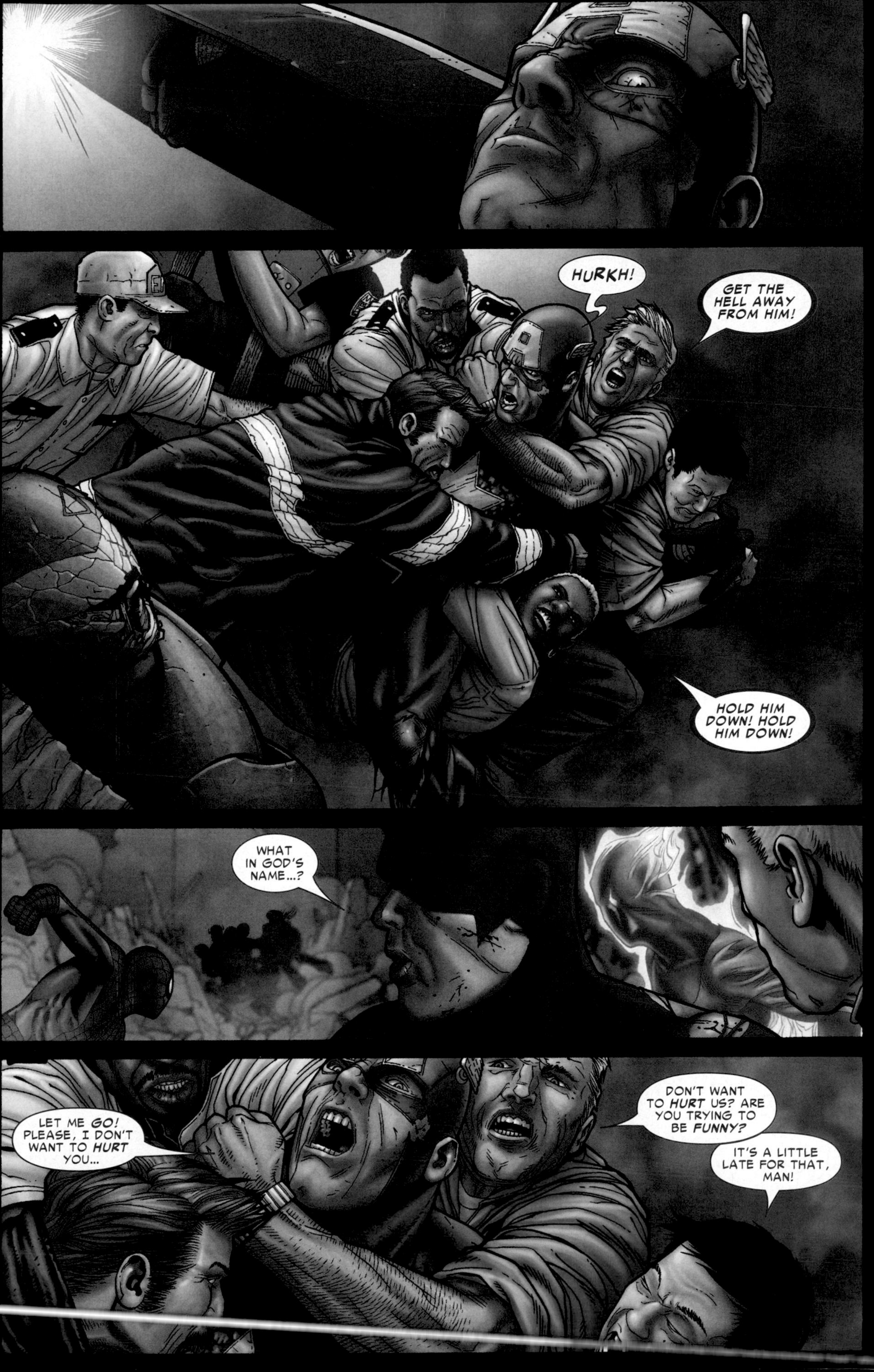
HURKH!
GET THE HELL AWAY FROM HIM!
HOLD HIM DOWN! HOLD HIM DOWN!
WHAT IN GOD'S NAME...?
LET ME GO! PLEASE, I DON'T WANT TO HURT YOU...
DON'T WANT TO HURT US? ARE YOU TRYING TO BE FUNNY?
IT'S A LITTLE LATE FOR THAT, MAN!

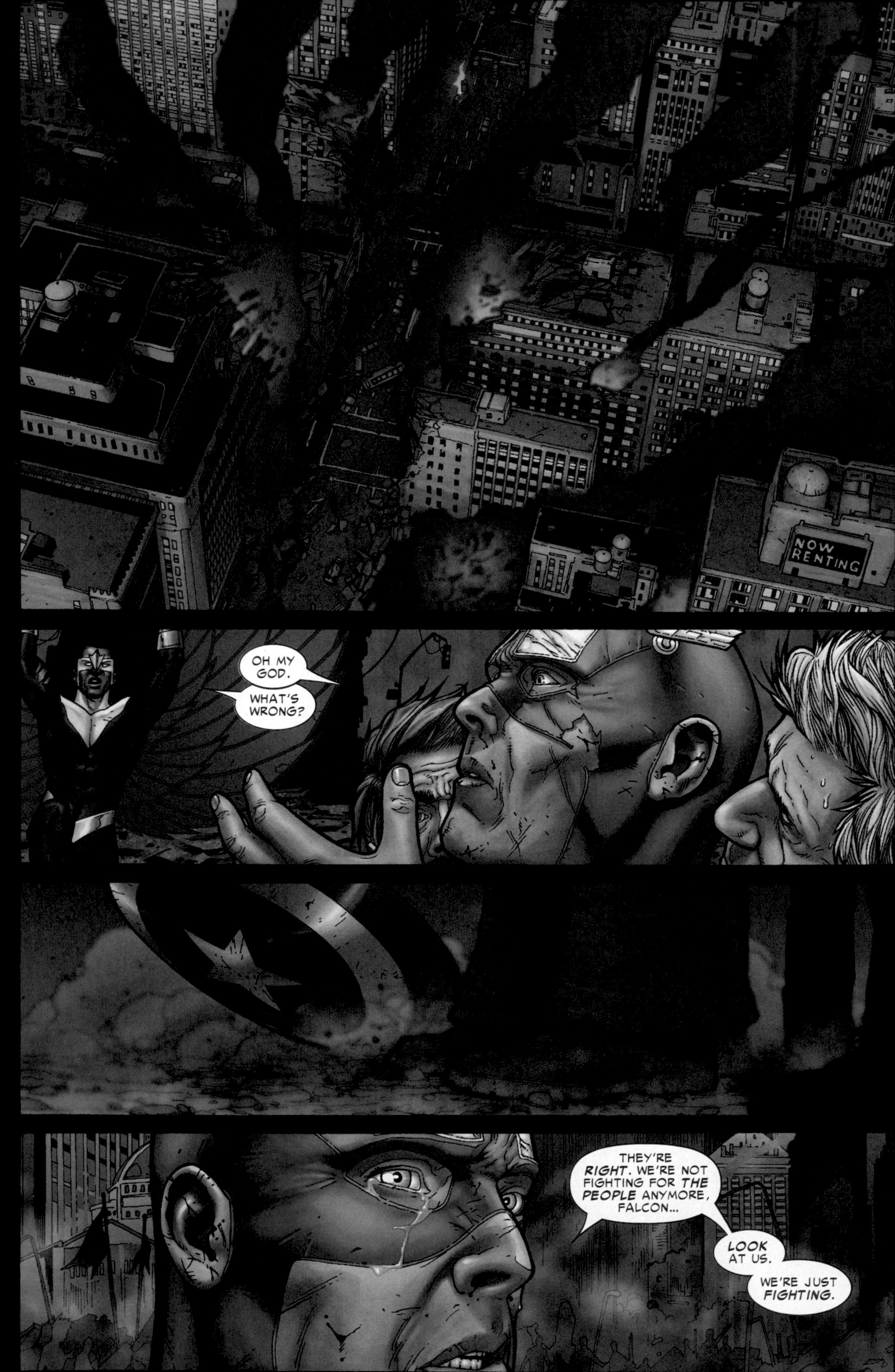
NOW RENTING
OH MY GOD.
WHAT'S WRONG?
THEY'RE RIGHT. WE'RE NOT FIGHTING FOR THE PEOPLE ANYMORE, FALCON...
LOOK AT US.
WE'RE JUST FIGHTING.

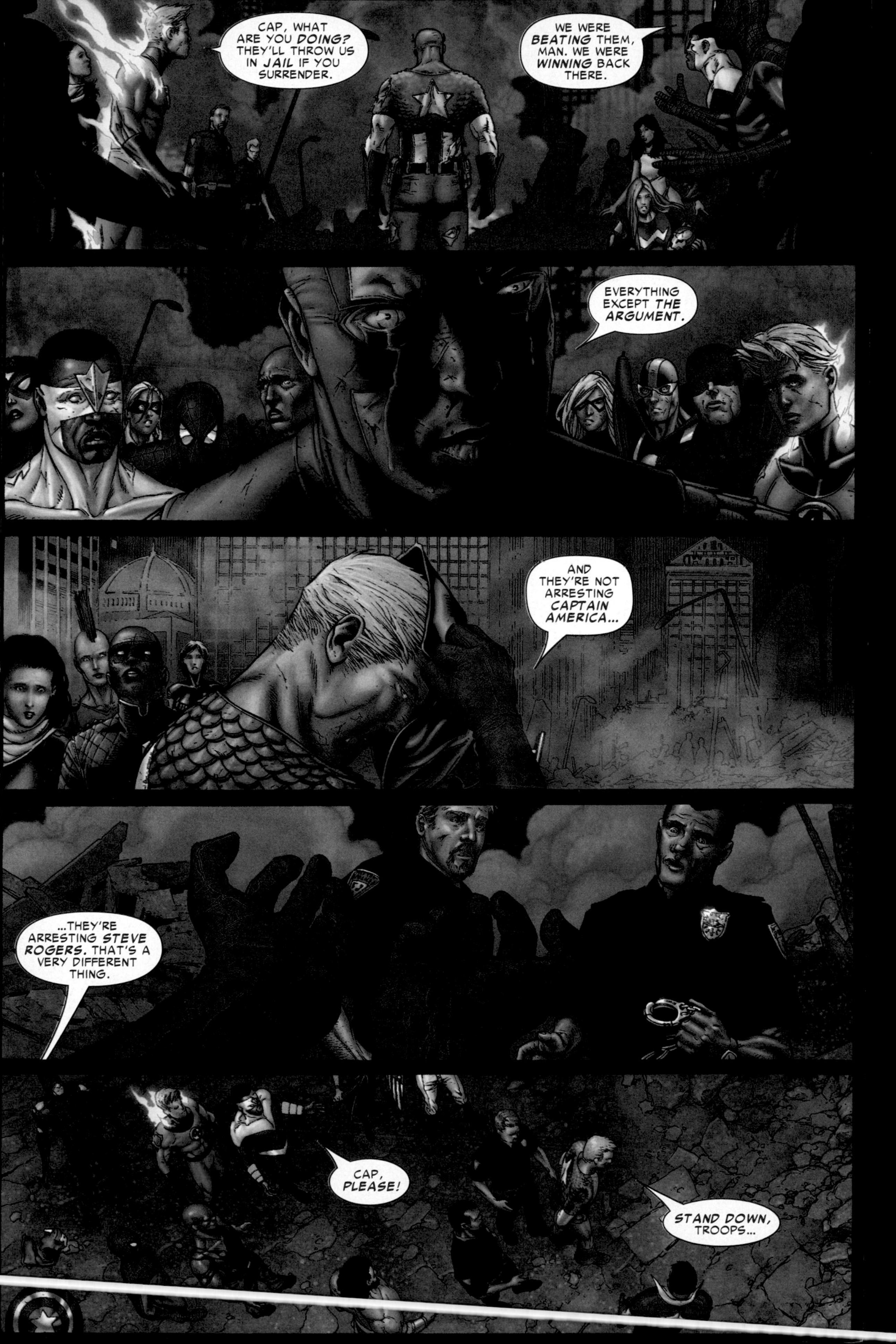
CAP, WHAT ARE YOU DOING? THEY'LL THROW US IN JAIL IF YOU SURRENDER.
WE WERE BEATING THEM, MAN. WE WERE WINNING BACK THERE.
EVERYTHING EXCEPT THE ARGUMENT.
AND THEY'RE NOT ARRESTING CAPTAIN AMERICA...
...THEY'RE ARRESTING STEVE ROGERS. THAT'S A VERY DIFFERENT THING.
CAP, PLEASE!
STAND DOWN, TROOPS...

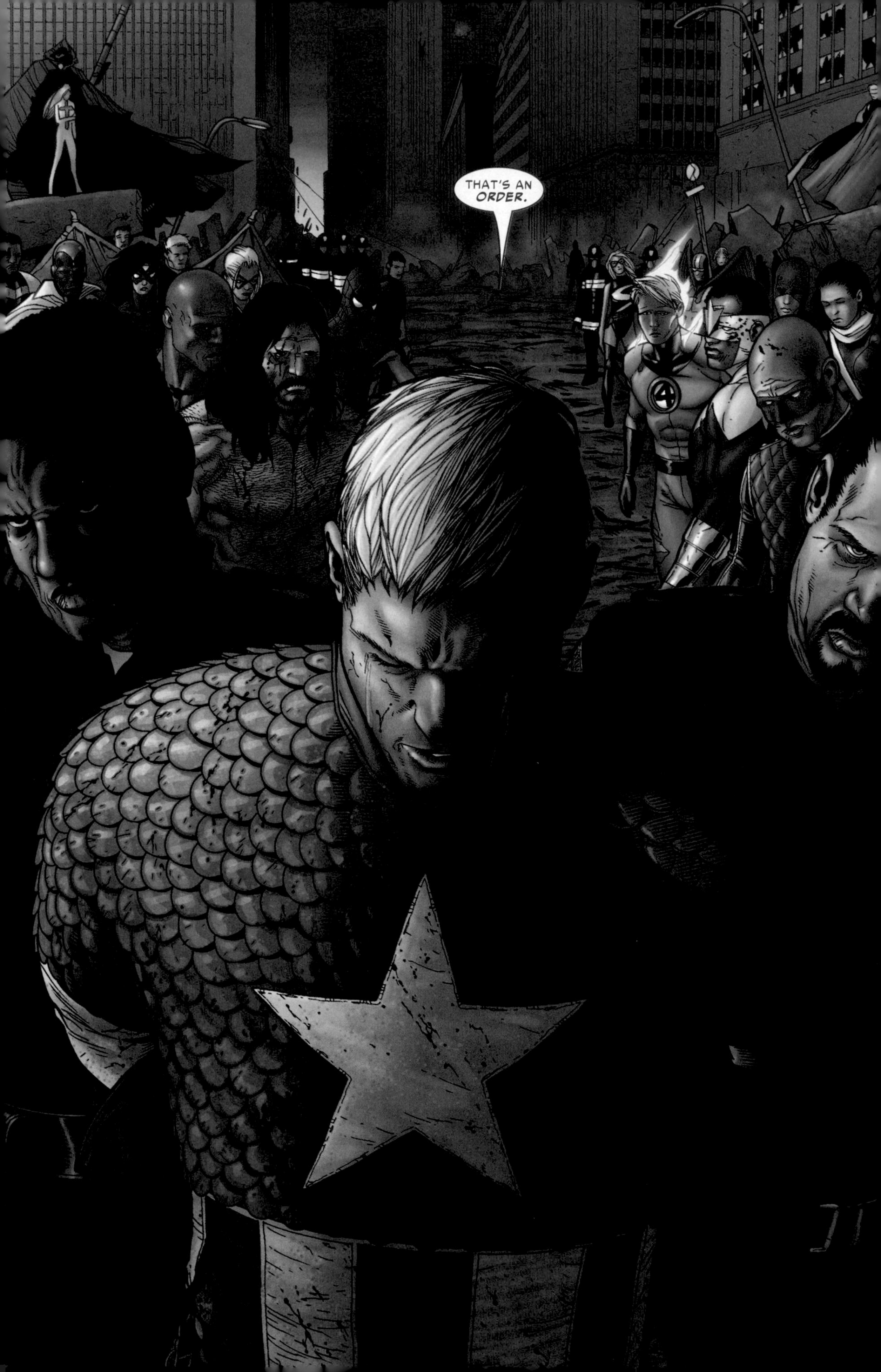
THAT'S AN ORDER.

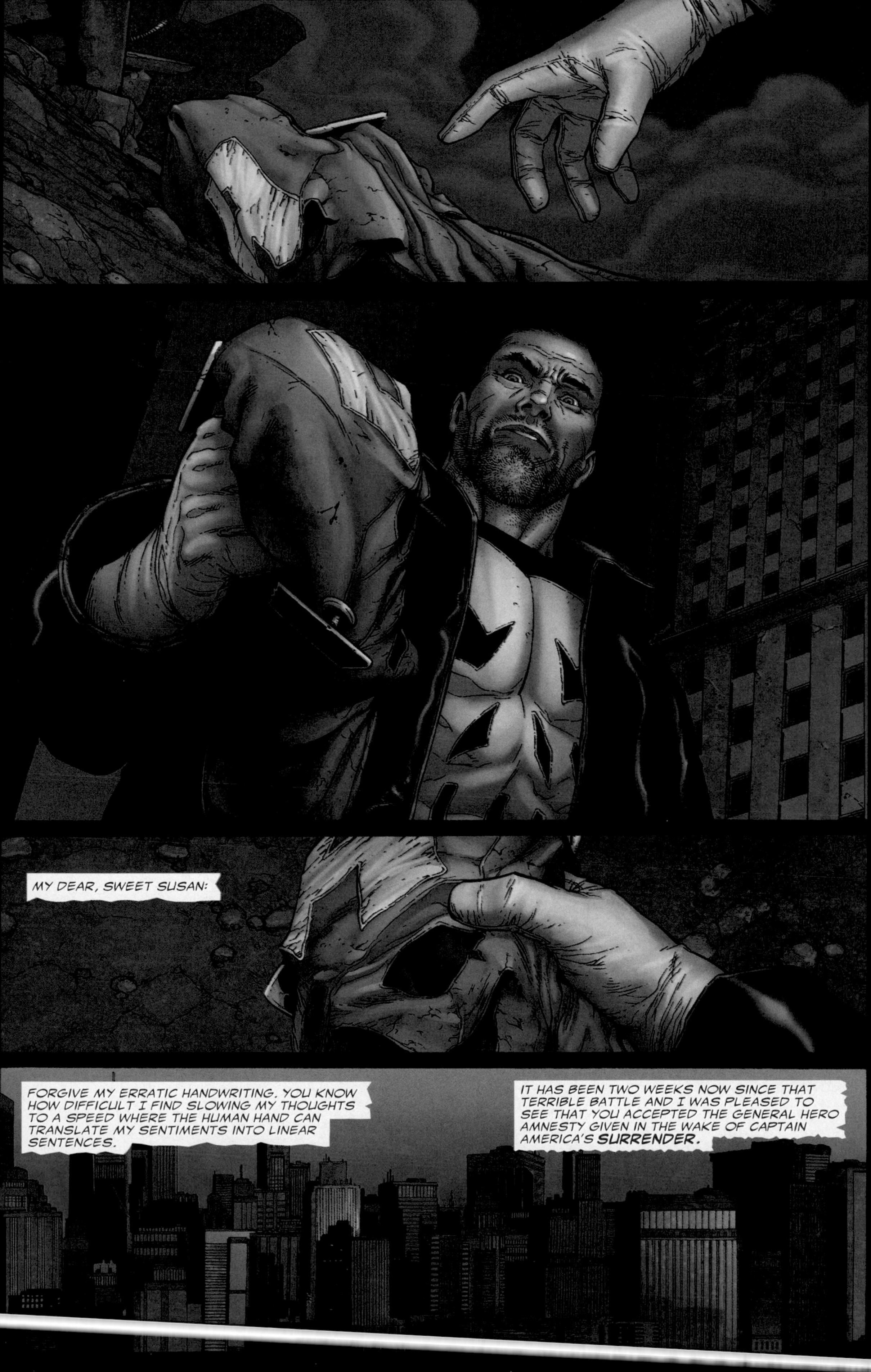
MY DEAR, SWEET SUSAN:
FORGIVE MY ERRATIC HANDWRITING. YOU KNOW HOW DIFFICULT I FIND SLOWING MY THOUGHTS TO A SPEED WHERE THE HUMAN HAND CAN TRANSLATE MY SENTIMENTS INTO LINEAR SENTENCES.
IT HAS BEEN TWO WEEKS NOW SINCE THAT TERRIBLE BATTLE AND I WAS PLEASED TO SEE THAT YOU ACCEPTED THE GENERAL HERO AMNESTY GIVEN IN THE WAKE OF CAPTAIN AMERICA'S SURRENDER.

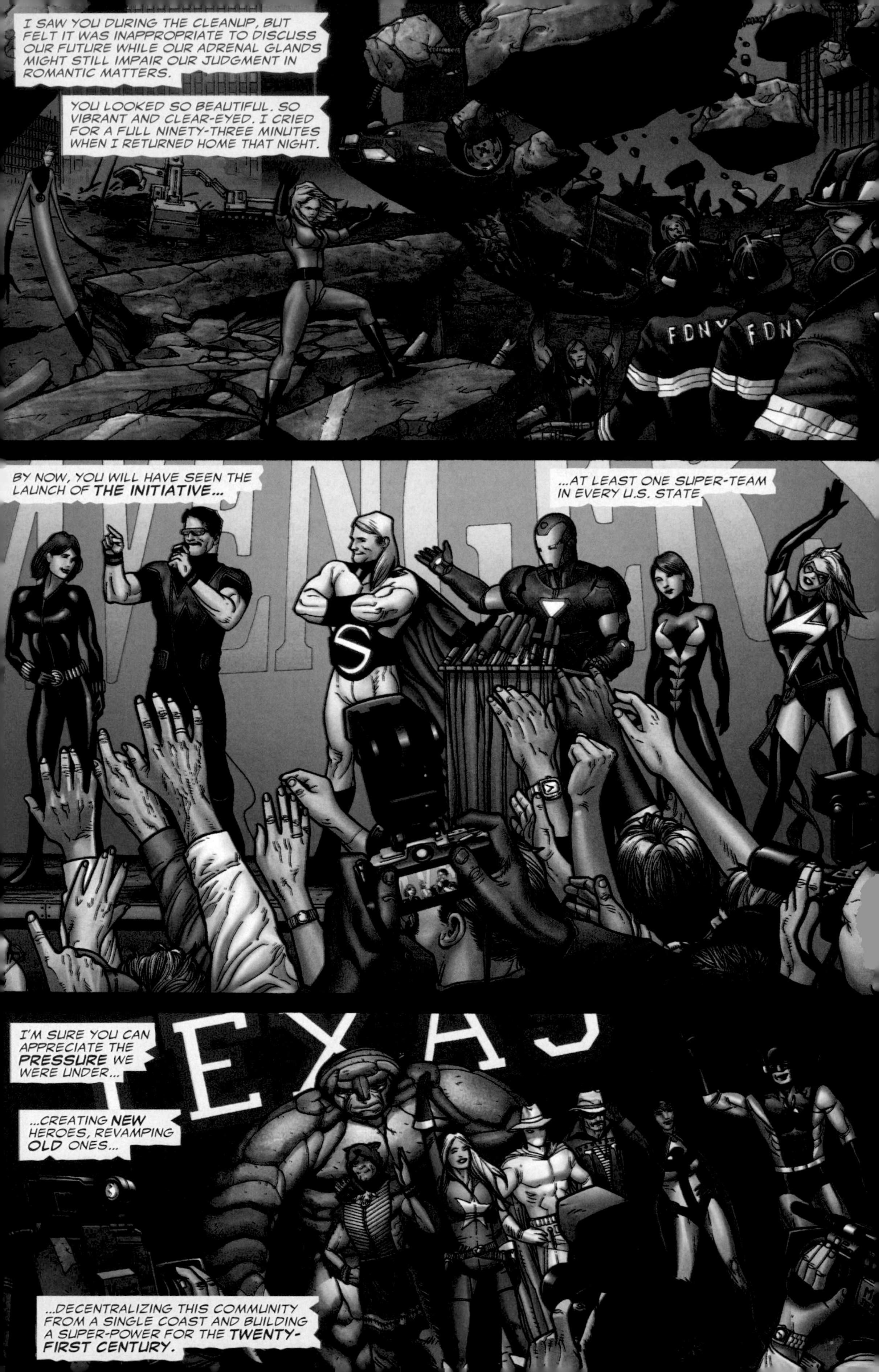

I SAW YOU DURING THE CLEANUP, BUT FELT IT WAS INAPPROPRIATE TO DISCUSS OUR FUTURE WHILE OUR ADRENAL GLANDS MIGHT STILL IMPAIR OUR JUDGMENT IN ROMANTIC MATTERS.
YOU LOOKED SO BEAUTIFUL. SO VIBRANT AND CLEAR-EYED. I CRIED FOR A FULL NINETY-THREE MINUTES WHEN I RETURNED HOME THAT NIGHT.
FDNY
FDNY
BY NOW, YOU WILL HAVE SEEN THE LAUNCH OF **THE INITIATIVE...**
...AT LEAST ONE SUPER-TEAM IN EVERY U.S. STATE.
I'M SURE YOU CAN APPRECIATE THE **PRESSURE** WE WERE UNDER...
...CREATING **NEW** HEROES, REVAMPING **OLD** ONES...
...DECENTRALIZING THIS COMMUNITY FROM A SINGLE COAST AND BUILDING A SUPER-POWER FOR THE **TWENTY-FIRST CENTURY.**

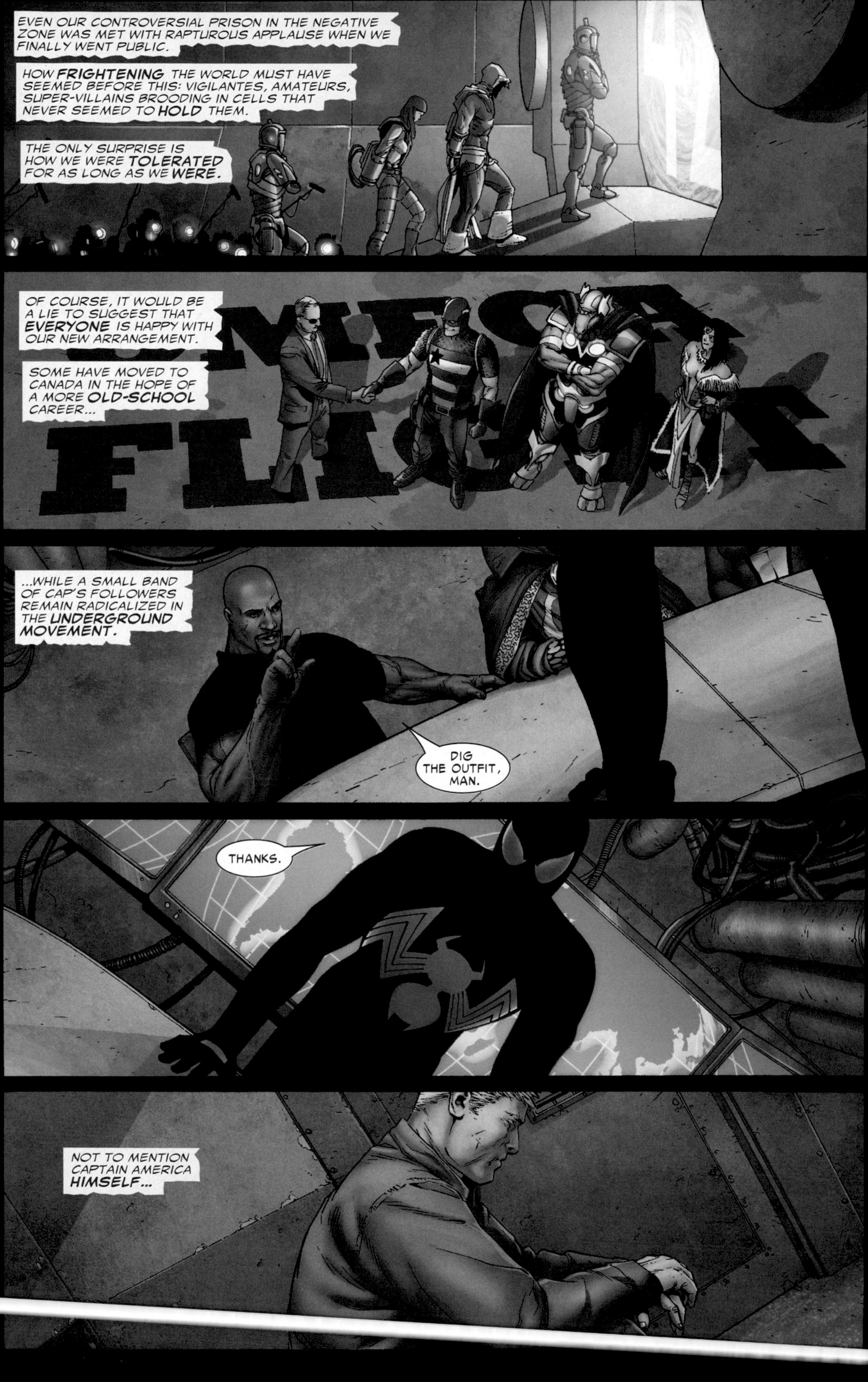
EVEN OUR CONTROVERSIAL PRISON IN THE NEGATIVE ZONE WAS MET WITH RAPTUROUS APPLAUSE WHEN WE FINALLY WENT PUBLIC.
HOW FRIGHTENING THE WORLD MUST HAVE SEEMED BEFORE THIS: VIGILANTES, AMATEURS, SUPER-VILLAINS BROODING IN CELLS THAT NEVER SEEMED TO HOLD THEM.
THE ONLY SURPRISE IS HOW WE WERE TOLERATED FOR AS LONG AS WE WERE.
OF COURSE, IT WOULD BE A LIE TO SUGGEST THAT EVERYONE IS HAPPY WITH OUR NEW ARRANGEMENT.
SOME HAVE MOVED TO CANADA IN THE HOPE OF A MORE OLD-SCHOOL CAREER...
...WHILE A SMALL BAND OF CAP'S FOLLOWERS REMAIN RADICALIZED IN THE UNDERGROUND MOVEMENT.
DIG THE OUTFIT, MAN.
THANKS.
NOT TO MENTION CAPTAIN AMERICA HIMSELF...

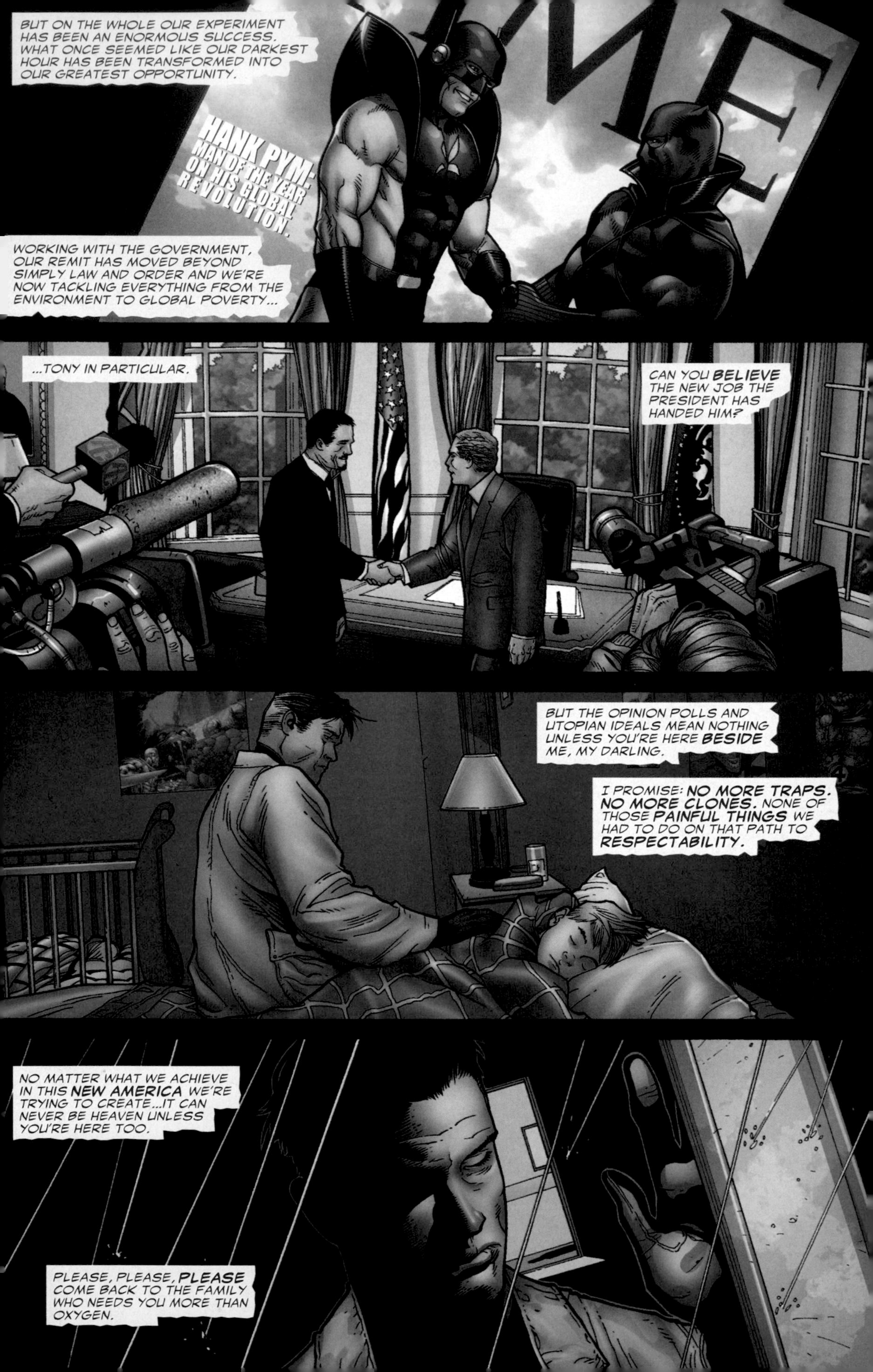

BUT ON THE WHOLE OUR EXPERIMENT HAS BEEN AN ENORMOUS SUCCESS. WHAT ONCE SEEMED LIKE OUR DARKEST HOUR HAS BEEN TRANSFORMED INTO OUR GREATEST OPPORTUNITY.
HANK PYM: MAN OF THE YEAR ON HIS GLOBAL REVOLUTION.
WORKING WITH THE GOVERNMENT, OUR REMIT HAS MOVED BEYOND SIMPLY LAW AND ORDER AND WE'RE NOW TACKLING EVERYTHING FROM THE ENVIRONMENT TO GLOBAL POVERTY...
...TONY IN PARTICULAR.
CAN YOU BELIEVE THE NEW JOB THE PRESIDENT HAS HANDED HIM?
BUT THE OPINION POLLS AND UTOPIAN IDEALS MEAN NOTHING UNLESS YOU'RE HERE BESIDE ME, MY DARLING.
I PROMISE: NO MORE TRAPS. NO MORE CLONES. NONE OF THOSE PAINFUL THINGS WE HAD TO DO ON THAT PATH TO RESPECTABILITY.
NO MATTER WHAT WE ACHIEVE IN THIS NEW AMERICA WE'RE TRYING TO CREATE...IT CAN NEVER BE HEAVEN UNLESS YOU'RE HERE TOO.
PLEASE, PLEASE, PLEASE COME BACK TO THE FAMILY WHO NEEDS YOU MORE THAN OXYGEN.

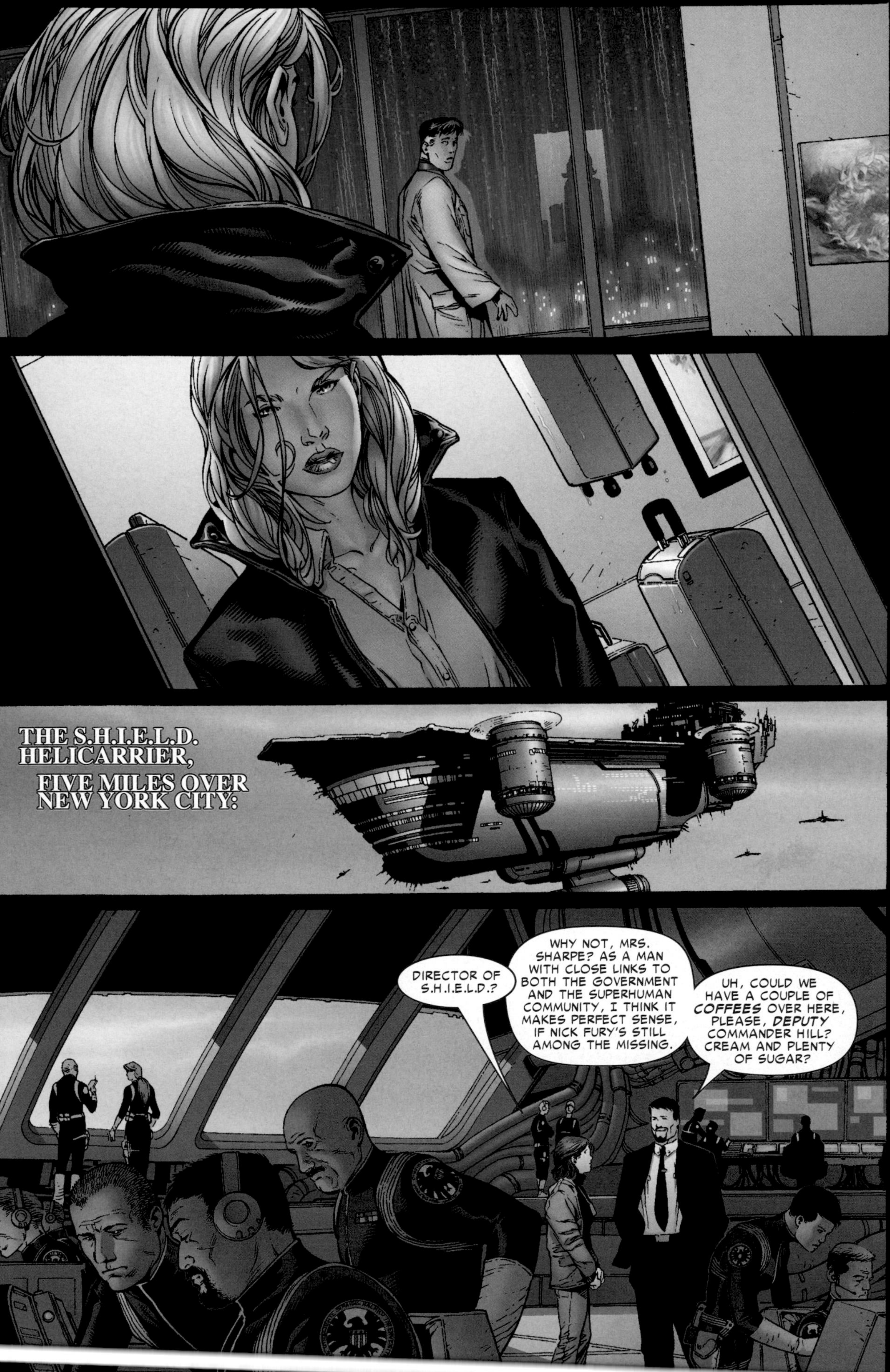
THE S.H.I.E.L.D. HELICARRIER, FIVE MILES OVER NEW YORK CITY:
DIRECTOR OF S.H.I.E.L.D.?
WHY NOT, MRS. SHARPE? AS A MAN WITH CLOSE LINKS TO BOTH THE GOVERNMENT AND THE SUPERHUMAN COMMUNITY, I THINK IT MAKES PERFECT SENSE, IF NICK FURY'S STILL AMONG THE MISSING.
UH, COULD WE HAVE A COUPLE OF COFFEES OVER HERE, PLEASE, DEPUTY COMMANDER HILL? CREAM AND PLENTY OF SUGAR?

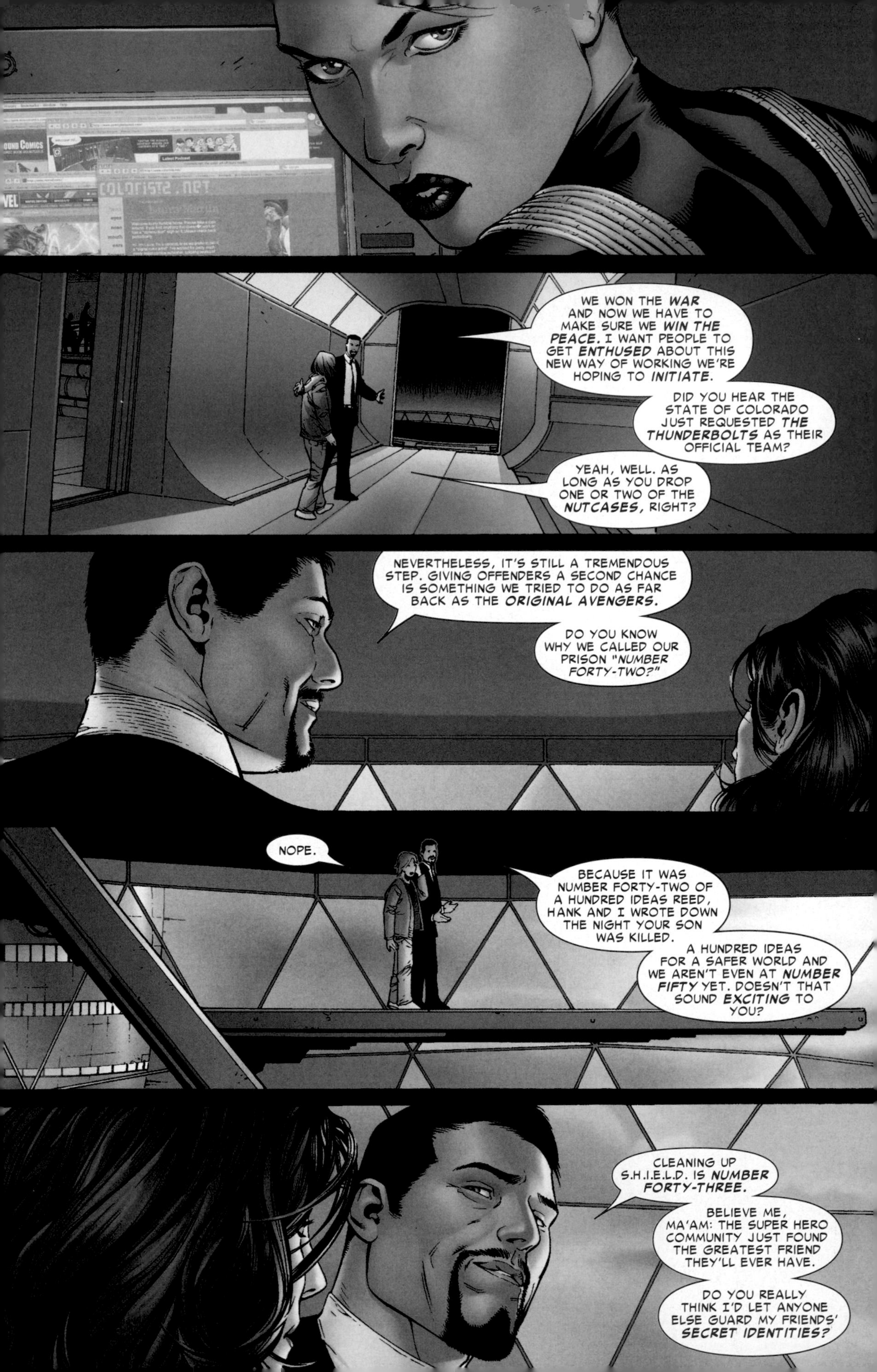
WE WON THE WAR AND NOW WE HAVE TO MAKE SURE WE WIN THE PEACE. I WANT PEOPLE TO GET ENTHUSED ABOUT THIS NEW WAY OF WORKING WE'RE HOPING TO INITIATE.
DID YOU HEAR THE STATE OF COLORADO JUST REQUESTED THE THUNDERBOLTS AS THEIR OFFICIAL TEAM?
YEAH, WELL. AS LONG AS YOU DROP ONE OR TWO OF THE NUTCASES, RIGHT?
NEVERTHELESS, IT'S STILL A TREMENDOUS STEP. GIVING OFFENDERS A SECOND CHANCE IS SOMETHING WE TRIED TO DO AS FAR BACK AS THE ORIGINAL AVENGERS.
DO YOU KNOW WHY WE CALLED OUR PRISON "NUMBER FORTY-TWO?"
NOPE.
BECAUSE IT WAS NUMBER FORTY-TWO OF A HUNDRED IDEAS REED, HANK AND I WROTE DOWN THE NIGHT YOUR SON WAS KILLED.
A HUNDRED IDEAS FOR A SAFER WORLD AND WE AREN'T EVEN AT NUMBER FIFTY YET. DOESN'T THAT SOUND EXCITING TO YOU?
CLEANING UP S.H.I.E.L.D. IS NUMBER FORTY-THREE.
BELIEVE ME, MA'AM: THE SUPER HERO COMMUNITY JUST FOUND THE GREATEST FRIEND THEY'LL EVER HAVE.
DO YOU REALLY THINK I'D LET ANYONE ELSE GUARD MY FRIENDS' SECRET IDENTITIES?

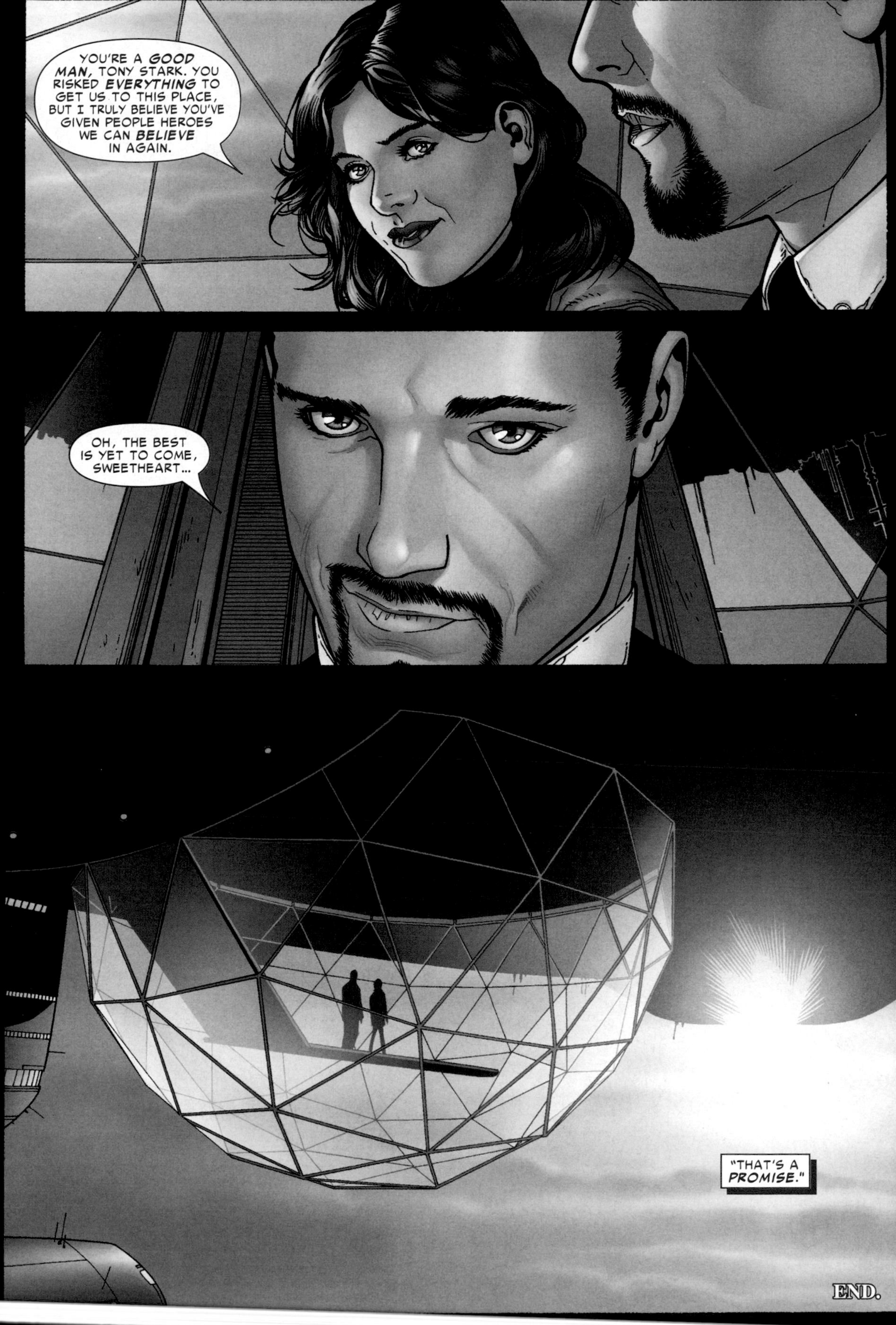

YOU'RE A GOOD MAN, TONY STARK. YOU RISKED EVERYTHING TO GET US TO THIS PLACE, BUT I TRULY BELIEVE YOU'VE GIVEN PEOPLE HEROES WE CAN BELIEVE IN AGAIN.
OH, THE BEST IS YET TO COME, SWEETHEART...
"THAT'S A PROMISE."
END.

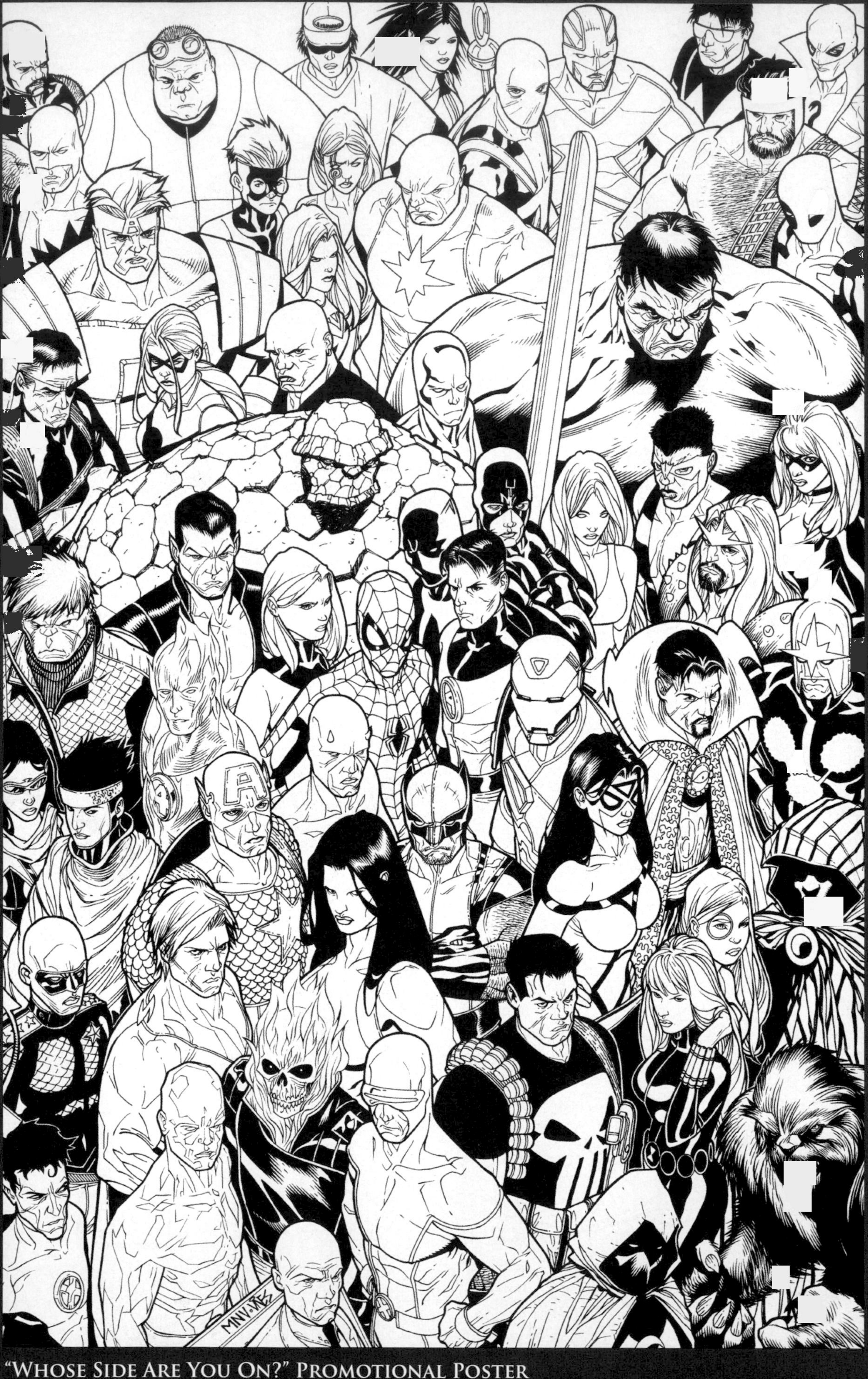

"Whose Side Are You On?" Promotional Poster

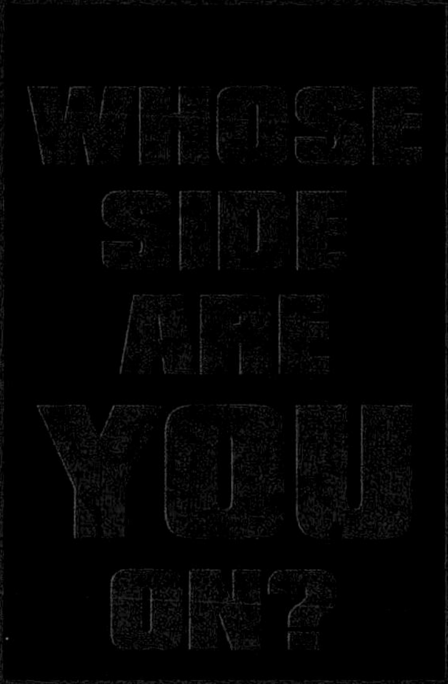
WHOSE
SIDE
ARE
YOU
ON?
CONCEPT

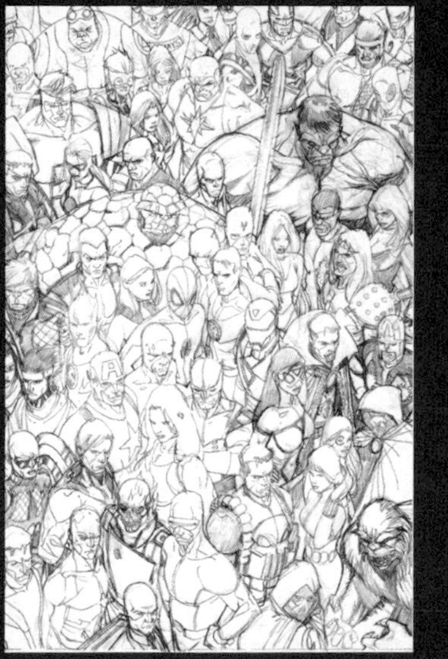
PENCILS

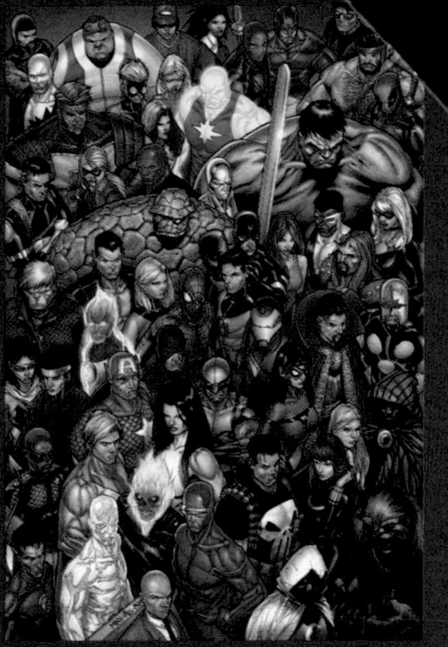
COLORS

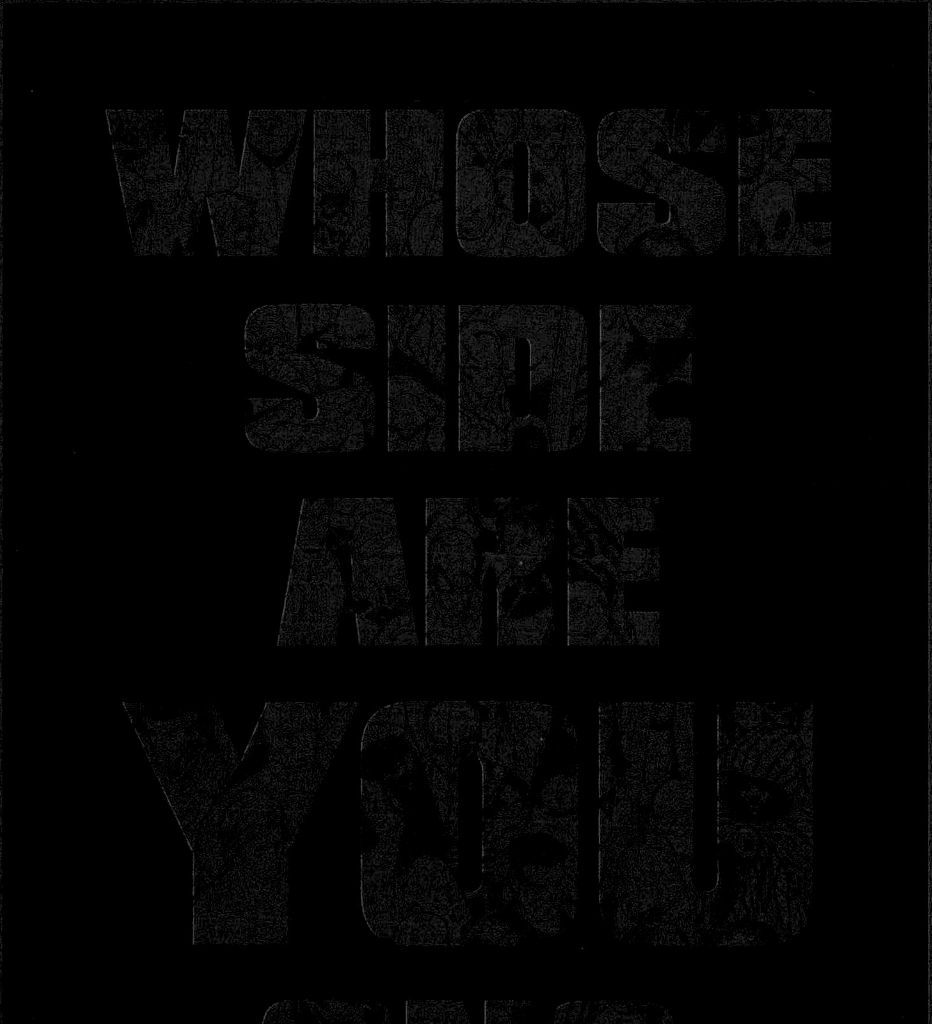
WHOSE
SIDE
ARE
YOU
ON?

"Whose Side Are You On?" Promotional Poster

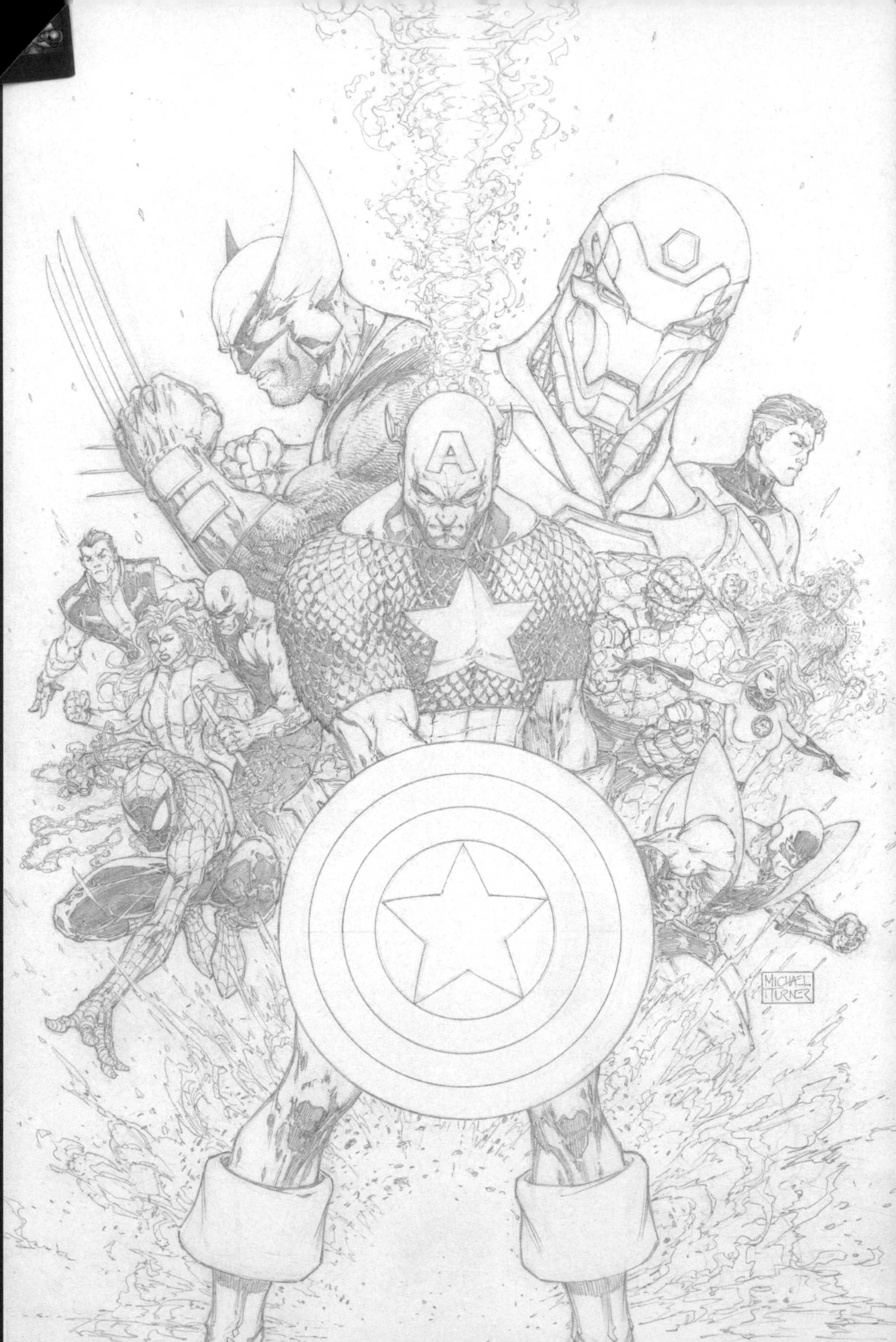
MICHAEL
TURNER

CIVIL WAR #1 SKETCH VARIANT BY MICHAEL TURNER

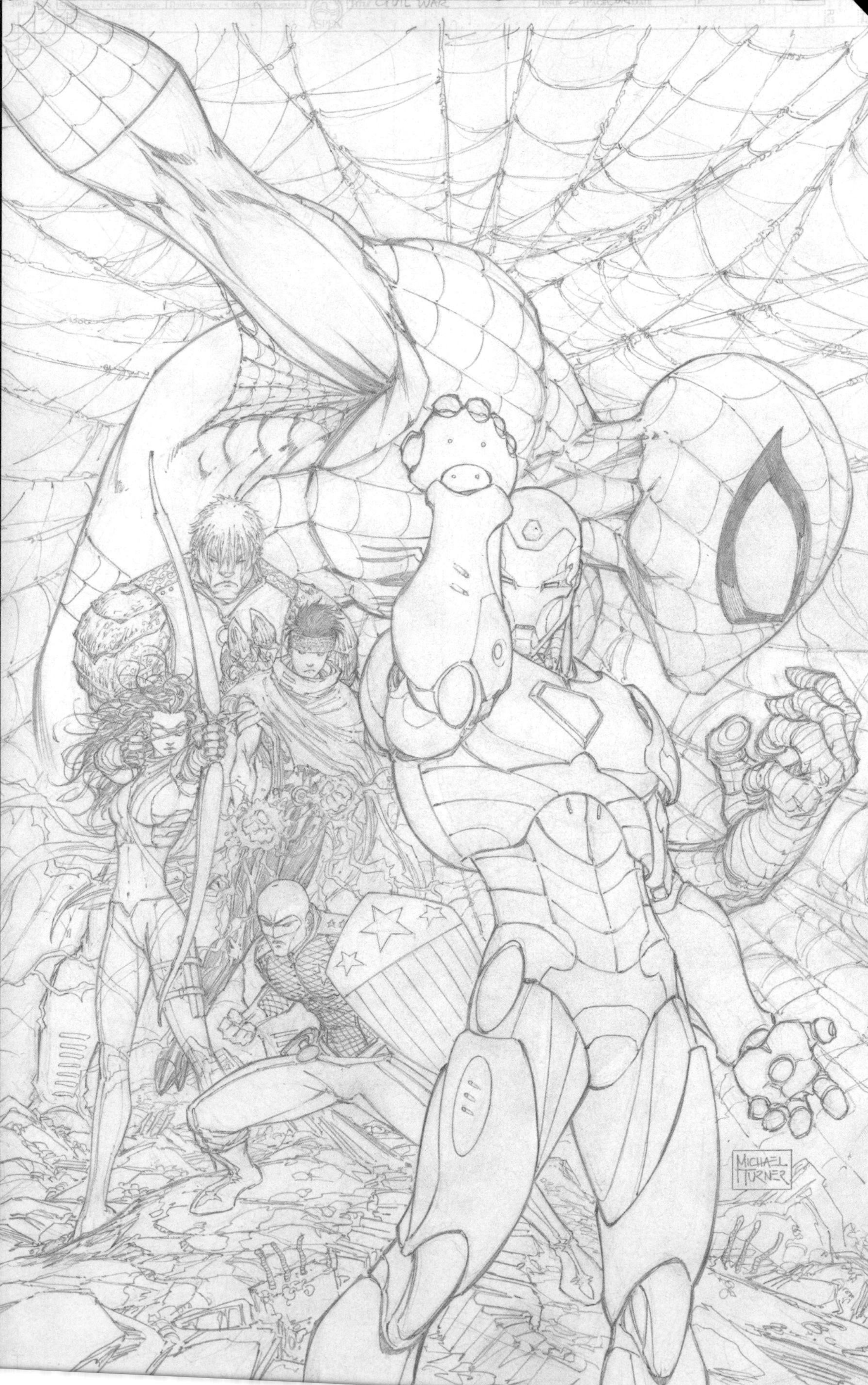
MICHAEL TURNER

CIVIL WAR #2 SKETCH VARIANT BY MICH

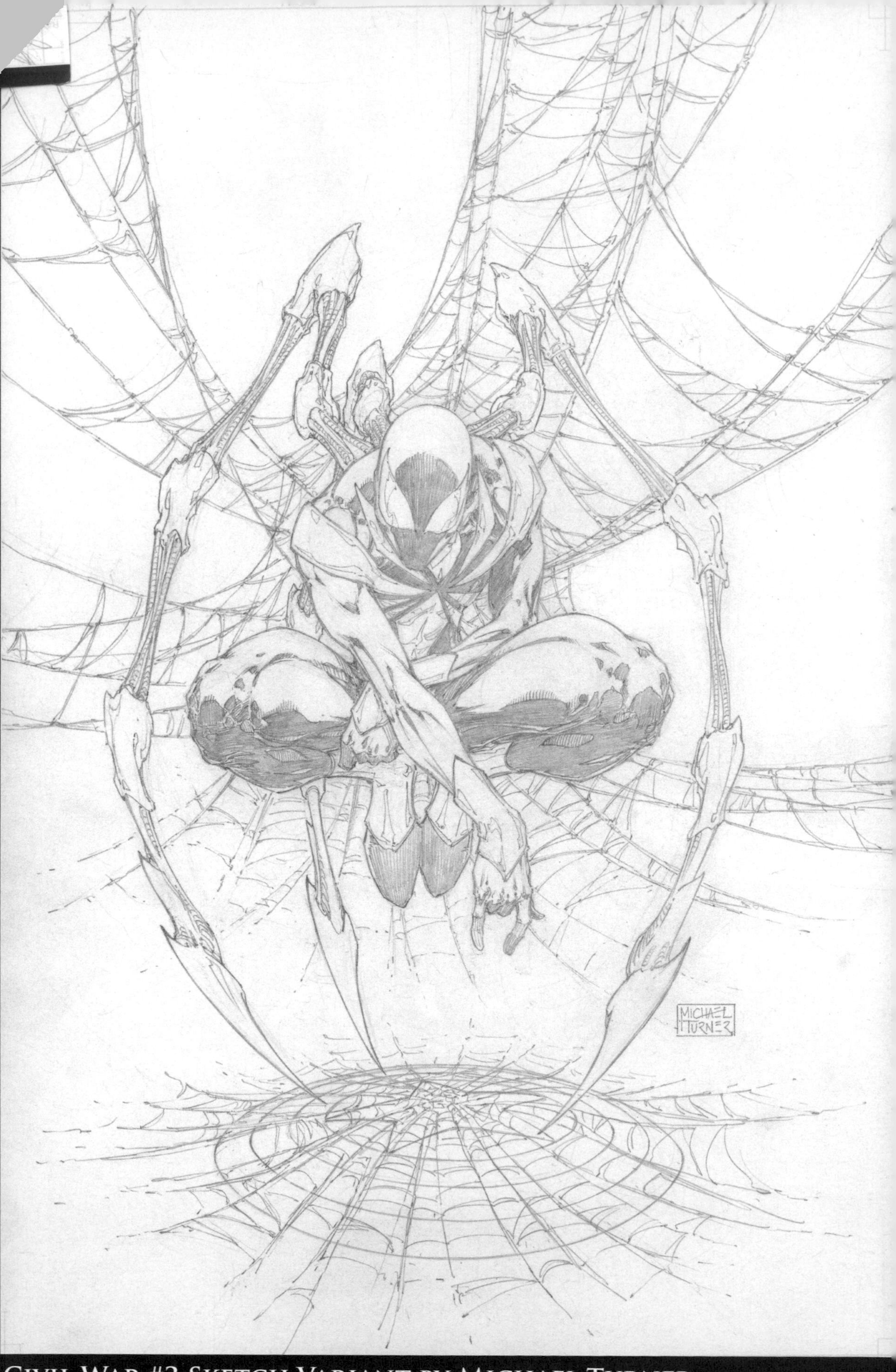
MICHAEL TURNER

Civil War #3 Sketch Variant by Michael Turner

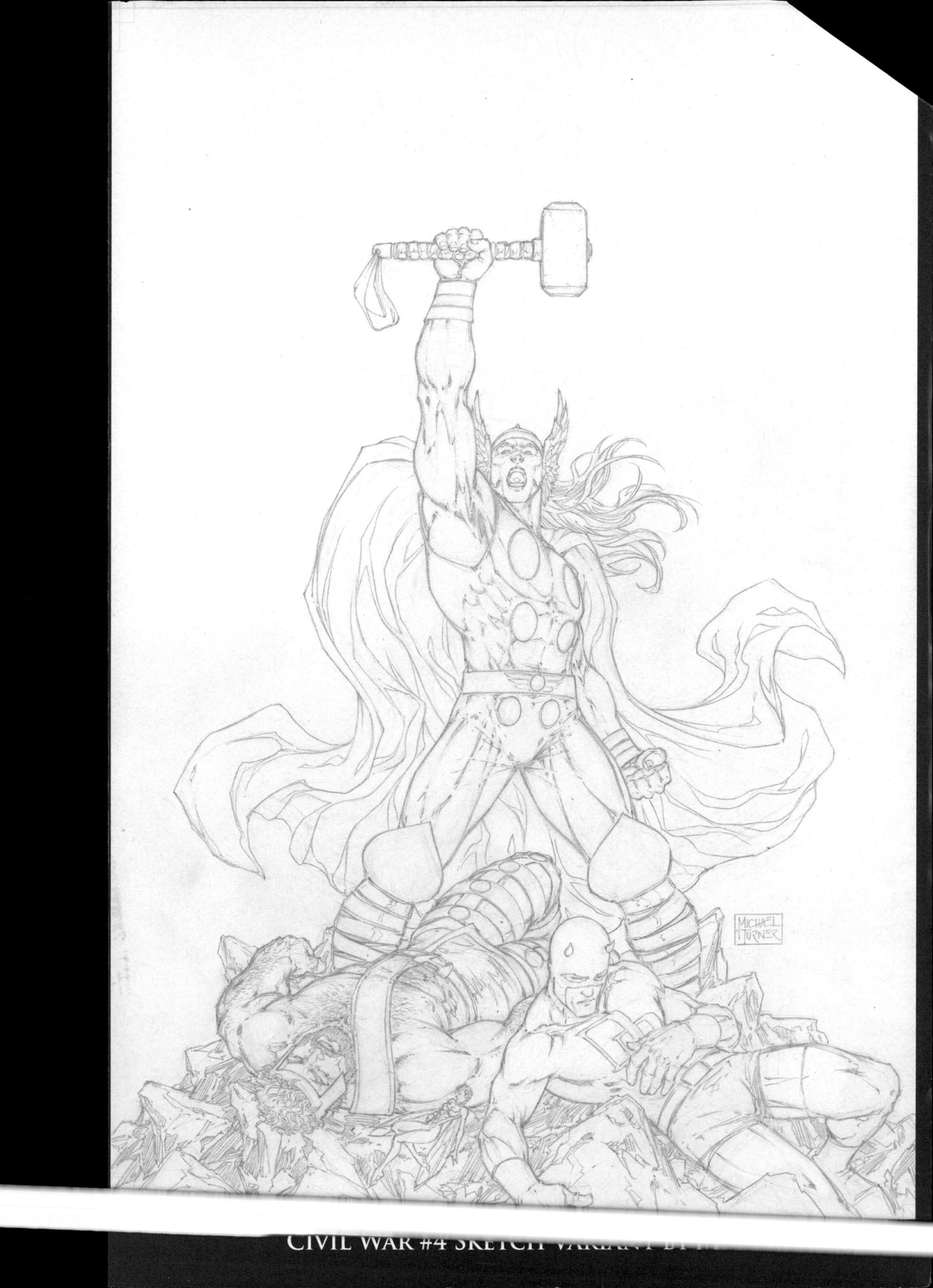
MICHAEL TURNER

CIVIL WAR #4 SKETCH VARIANT BY

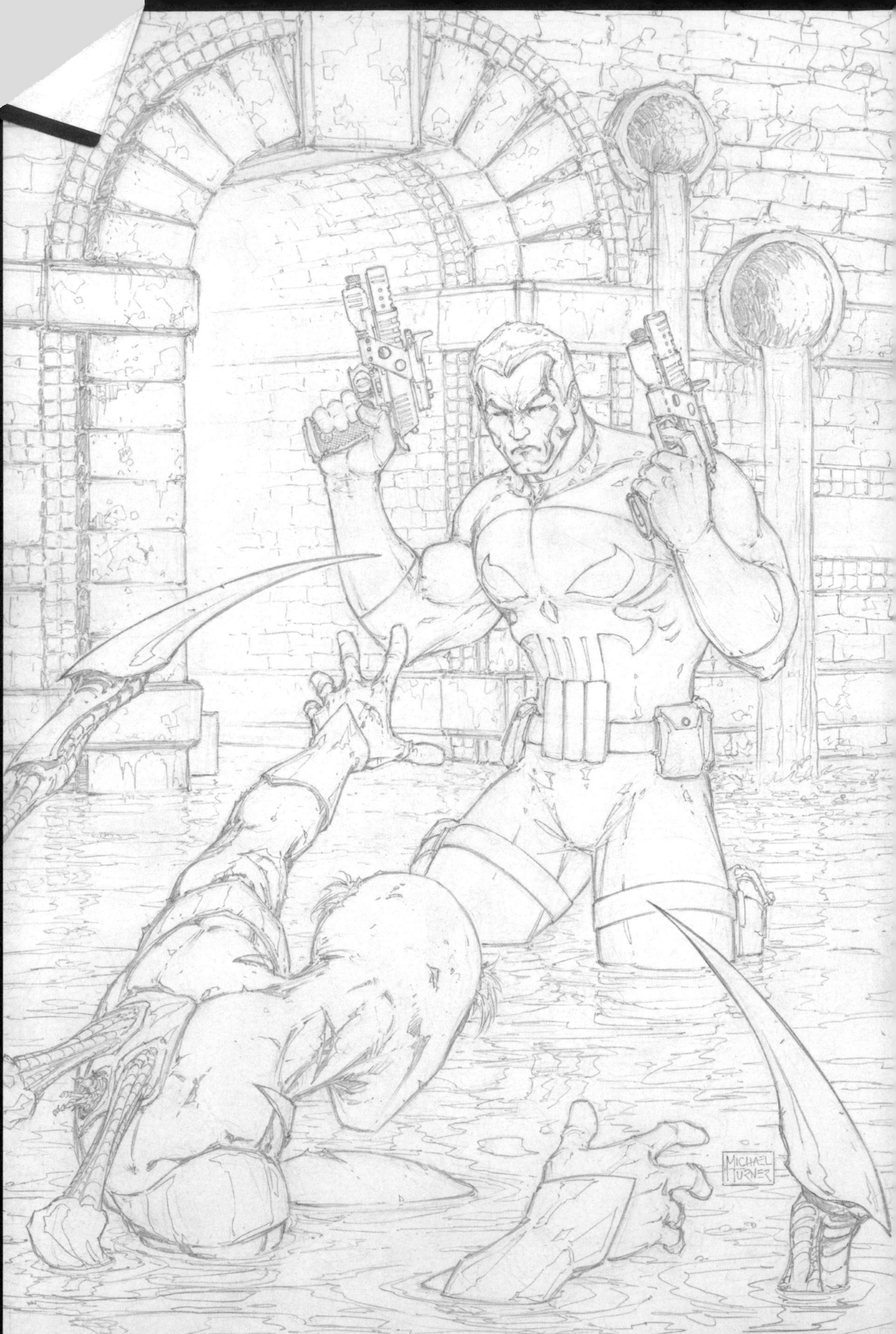
MICHAEL TURNER

Civil War #5 Sketch Variant by Michael Turner

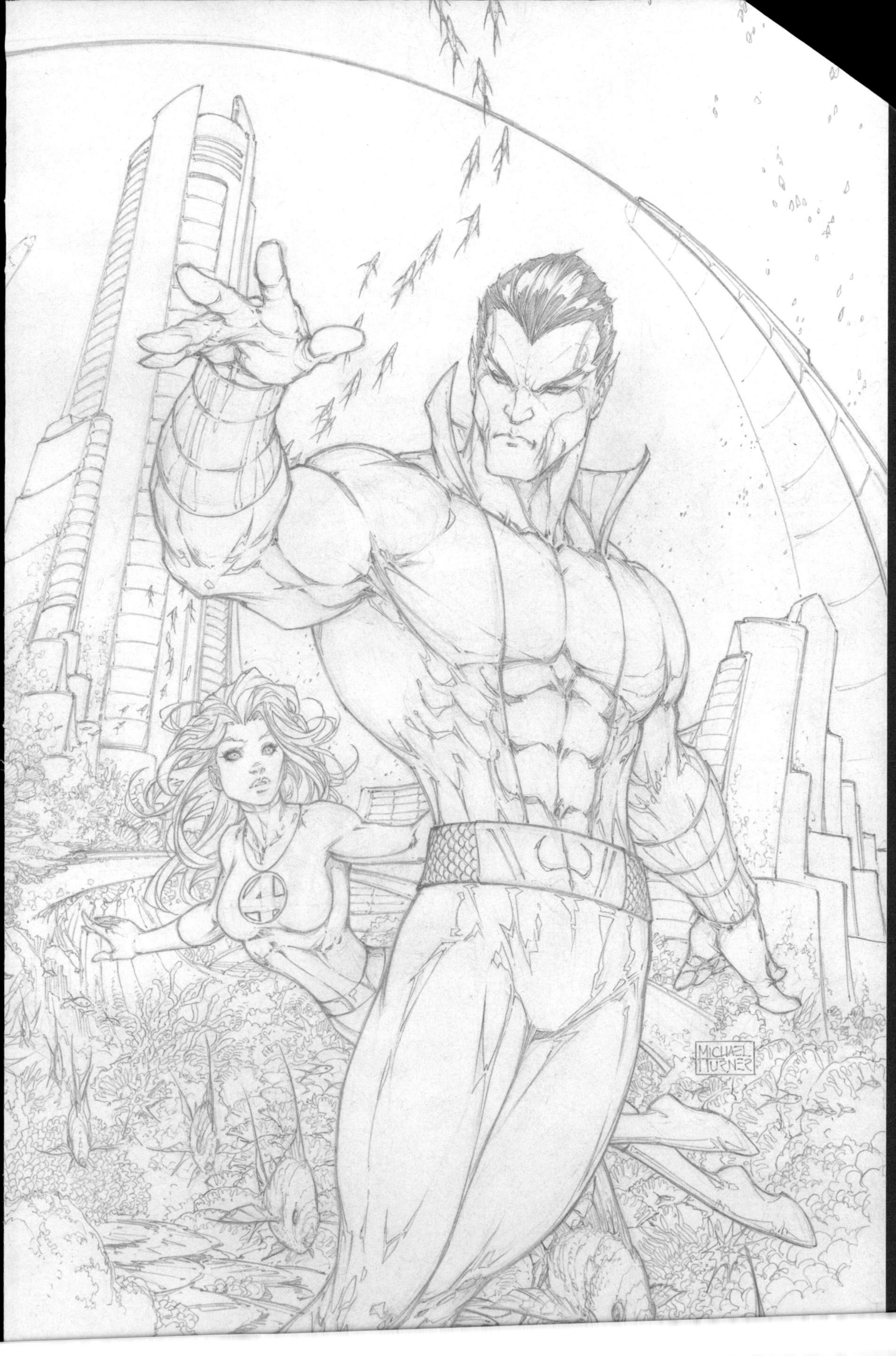
MICHAEL TURNER

WAR #6 SKETCH VARIANT BY MICHAEL TURNER

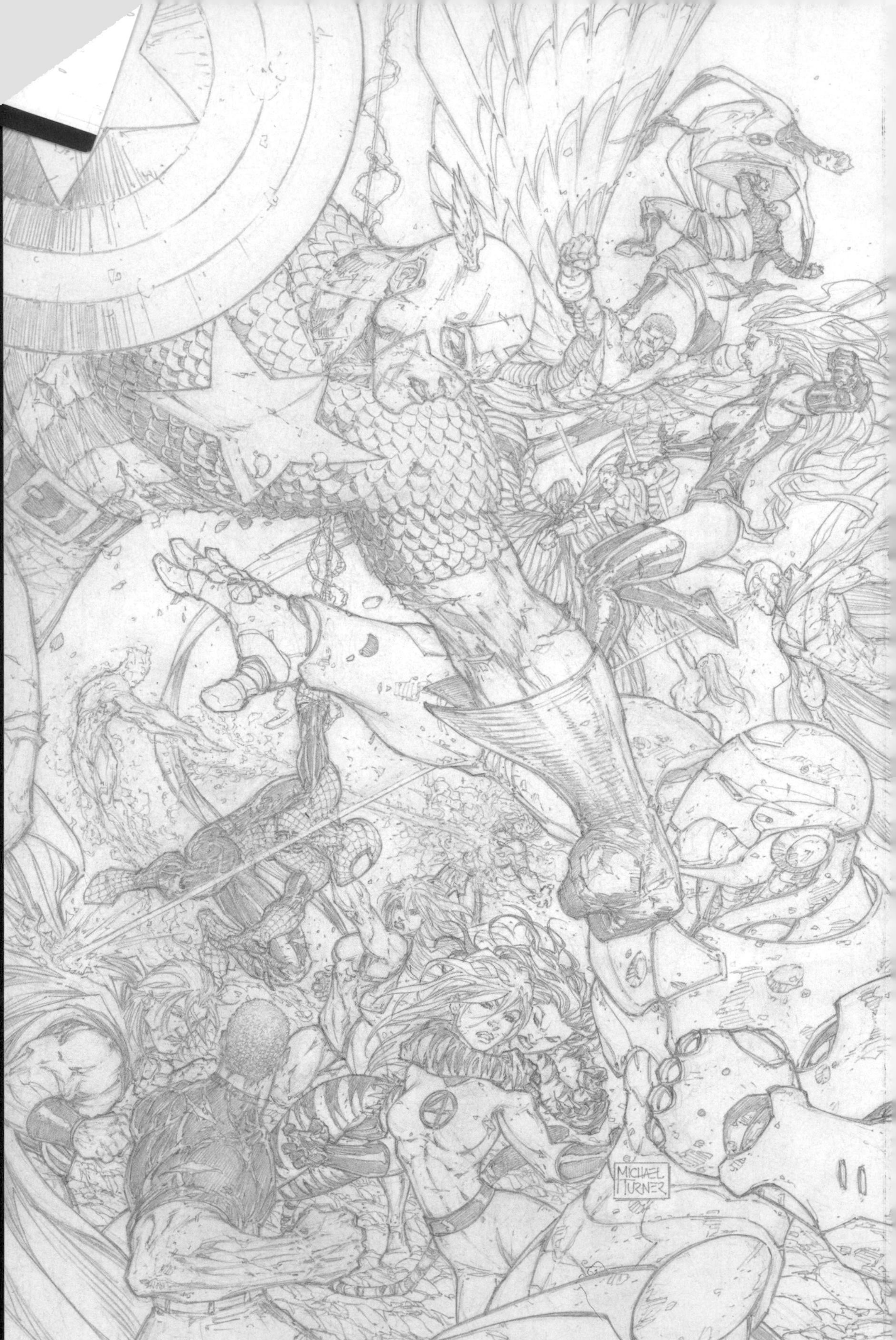
MICHAEL
TURNER

CIVIL WAR #7 SKETCH VARIANT BY MICHAEL TURNER